I0622738

# EMANCIPATION

# EMANCIPATION

## FREEDOM FOR THE INCARCERATED SOUL

# JOHNESHA ROBINSON

of the
Broken

Copyright © 2023 by Johnesha Robinson

All rights reserved. No portion of this book may be reproduced, stored in a retrieval system, or transmitted in any form or by any means–electronic, mechanical photocopy, recording, or other–except for brief quotations in critical reviews or articles without the prior written permission of the author.

The scanning, uploading, and distribution of this book without permission is a theft of the author's intellectual property. If you would like permission to use material from the book (other than for review purposes), please contact info@eyesofthebroken.com. Thank you for your support of the author's rights.

The author is not responsible for any internet addresses (websites, blogs, etc.) or content that the author does not own.

**Publisher's Cataloging-in-Publication**
**(Provided by Cassidy Cataloguing Services, Inc.)**

Names: Robinson, Johnesha, author.

Title: Emancipation : freedom for the incarcerated soul / Johnesha Robinson.

Description: [Oakland, California] : Eyes of the Broken, [2023] |
    Includes bibliographical references.

Identifiers: ISBN: 979-8-9869778-3-6 (paperback) | 979-8-9869778-2-9 (hardback) |
    979-8-9869778-1-2 (ebook) | LCCN: 2023900756

Subjects: LCSH: Liberty. | Liberty--Religious aspects. | Imprisonment--Psychological
    aspects. | Prisoners--Psychological aspects. | Soul--Emancipation. | Spirituality. |
    Spiritual life. | Spiritual formation. | Self-actualization (Psychology) | Social justice. |
    BISAC: RELIGION / Spirituality. | RELIGION / Christian Living / Personal Growth.
    | RELIGION / Christian Living / Inspirational. | RELIGION / Christian Living /
    Spiritual Growth. | RELIGION / Christian Living / Social Issues. | RELIGION / Faith.

Classification: LCC: B105.S64 R63 2023 | DDC: 128--dc23

**THIS BOOK IS DEDICATED TO YOU,**

To all the men and women struggling to break free from society's broken systems, you are why Emancipation Freedom for the Incarcerated Soul was written. This is for you!

*"The Lord said, "I have indeed seen the misery of my people in Egypt. I have heard them crying out because of their slave drivers, and I am concerned about their suffering. So I have come down to rescue them from the hand of the Egyptians and to bring them up out of that land into a good and spacious land, a land flowing with milk and honey—the home of the Canaanites, Hittites, Amorites, Perizzites, Hivites and Jebusites. And now the cry of the Israelites has reached me, and I have seen the way the Egyptians are oppressing them. So now, go. I am sending you to Pharaoh to bring my people the Israelites out of Egypt."*

**EXODUS 3:7-10 NIV**

*"Then the LORD said to Moses, "Go to Pharaoh and tell him, 'Thus says the LORD, the God of the Hebrews: "Let My people go, so that they may serve Me."*

**EXODUS 9:1 AMP**

# CONTENTS

# PART THREE **THE PLAN**

# PART FOUR **THE PURGE**

# PART FIVE **THE PREPARATION**

# PART SIX **THE PROCESS**

# PART SEVEN **THE PURPOSE**

# PART EIGHT **THE SOULUTION**

# PREFACE

*Emancipation Freedom for the Incarcerated Soul* is a faith-based book that includes collections of newsletters I wrote following the incarceration of a close loved one. This book's purpose is to emancipate—set free individuals incarcerated Spiritually, Mentally, Financially, and Physically as well as bring awareness to the social and economic injustices minorities face because of the broken—oppressive systems in society.

*Emancipation Freedom for the Incarcerated Soul* touches on topics such as:

- The social and economic injustices minorities face in society.

- The pain and problems that are the result of said injustices.

- The hope that is needed to keep pushing forward in life.

- The solution to the pain and problems.

- Redemption, Healing, & Restoration.

*Although you may not have suffered in the same manner as I have, I hope the powerful words written within this book blesses and changes your life just as it has mine.*

# INTRODUCTION

In 2016 I was faced with one of the most challenging battles in my life—the incarceration of a close loved one. It was at that moment a mixture of feelings came over me: fear, anger, and sadness. It was at that moment my back was pushed up against a wall, and despite the pressure that was placed on me, I had to make a tough decision; either become a victim of the broken systems in society or turn the tables and become the victor through the power of God.

Looking at my loved one's face through a clear plastic window during visiting pained me. What hurt even more was seeing the negative toll the situation had taken on him. Trauma and pain were trying to kill his hopes and dreams, therefore killing my hopes and dreams. My conclusion: I had to do something; I had to fight. So, I started writing, and through weekly newsletters that included Bible Scriptures and prayers, I would provide my loved one with hope, peace, and love. The newsletters later developed into a concept for a book, this book, *Emancipation Freedom for the Incarcerated Soul.*

*"The words written within this book were built on pain, but from them, you can reap a harvest of bountiful gain (an abundant increase in wealth or resources)."*

Upon starting my journey writing this book, I did not fully understand its meaning. The sole purpose of writing for me was to provide my loved one with hope, peace, and love. I was unaware that God was working to perfect love within me so that He could use what I have been through and what He has allowed me to write about to do the same for others. This meant that God had to change me before I could help others; let me paint a picture.

When my loved one was first incarcerated, anger fuelled me. I wanted everyone to answer for their wrongs and would fight anyone who told me I was not right. I mean, I wanted to go to war with anyone who'd throw the slightest insult his way. But God showed me that war is not the answer; love is. That loving thy neighbor as thyself would solve wars, not anger and hatred.

In the end, God taught me how to turn the anger I held within my heart into love. Through this newfound love, I began to channel my energy into something more positive, these writings. Why is this important?

## LOVE IS POWERFUL; IT'S A WEAPON.

To further clarify, the words I wrote were written to provide my loved one with love, but because I wrote them with love in my heart, what's jam-packed within these messages has the power to heal others by wrapping its arms around them and letting them know they are loved too.

See, the purpose of pain was not to hurt me. It was only used to humble me. To make love more perfect within me so that I could show love to people who need love just as I do. *Emancipation*

*Freedom for the Incarcerated Soul* is a book that enables other people to transform, making it possible for them to do just that. Love thy neighbor as thyself, furthermore, changing the world we live in one heart at a time.

**INSTEAD OF SEEING YOUR PROBLEMS AS PAINFUL, LOOK DEEPER AND THINK, HOW COULD YOU USE THE PAIN OF YOUR PAST TO TRANSFORM SOMEONE ELSE'S FUTURE?**

# PART ONE **THE PROBLEM**

# CHAPTER 1

# THE SYSTEM THROUGH THE EYES OF THE BROKEN

*The systems (Government, Banking, Healthcare, Education, etc.) in society were designed broken. Therefore, they are damaging people. Just as hurting people hurt people. The broken systems in society are breaking people.*

**Ezekiel 22:23-29** GNT "The Lord spoke to me again. "Mortal man," he said, "tell the Israelites that their land is unholy, and so I am punishing it in my anger. The leaders are like lions roaring over the animals they have killed. They kill the people, take all the money and property they can get, and by their murders leave many widows. The priests break my law and have no respect for what is holy. They make no distinction between what is holy and what is not. They do not teach the difference between clean and unclean things, and they ignore the Sabbath. As a result, the people of Israel do not respect me. The government officials are like wolves tearing apart the animals they have killed. They commit murder in order to get rich. The prophets have hidden these sins like workers covering a wall with whitewash. They see false visions and make false predictions. They claim to speak the word of the Sovereign Lord, but I, the Lord, have not spoken to them. The wealthy cheat and rob. They mistreat (oppress) the poor and take advantage of foreigners."

**The Root Problem:**

- Incarceration and oppression, which lead to enslavement.

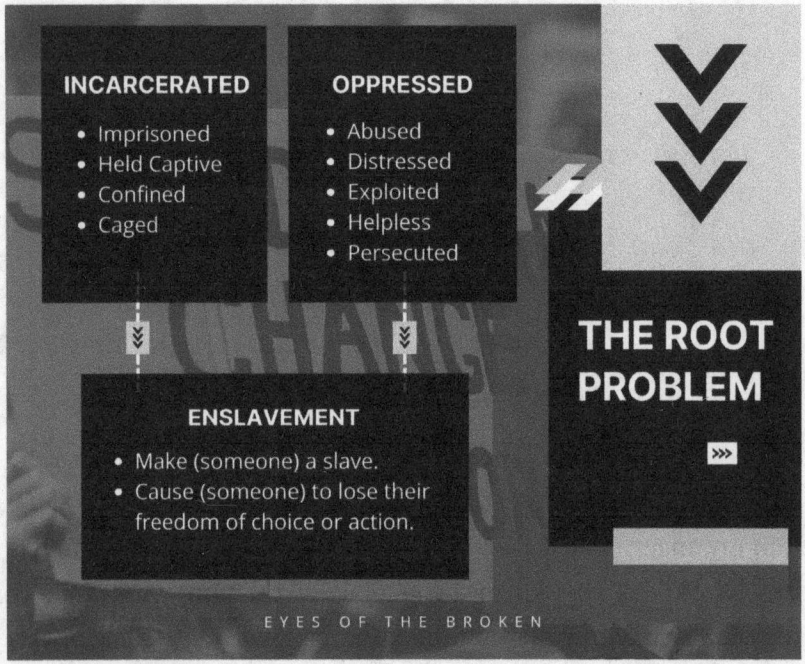

**INCARCERATED**
- Imprisoned
- Held Captive
- Confined
- Caged

**OPPRESSED**
- Abused
- Distressed
- Exploited
- Helpless
- Persecuted

**ENSLAVEMENT**
- Make (someone) a slave.
- Cause (someone) to lose their freedom of choice or action.

**THE ROOT PROBLEM**

EYES OF THE BROKEN

**Incarceration:**

- To imprison, confine, take captive.

- The act of incarcerating or putting in prison or another enclosure.

- Opposite; freedom.

**The New York Times:** "It took only a few decades after the arrival of enslaved Africans in Virginia before white settlers demanded a new world defined by racial caste. The 1664 General Assembly of Maryland decreed that all Negroes within the province "shall serve durante vita," hard labor for life. This enslavement would be sustained by the threat of brutal punishment. By 1729, Maryland law authorized punishments of enslaved people including "to have the right hand cut off... the head severed from the body, the body divided into four quarters, and head and quarters set up in the most public places of the county."

Soon American slavery matured into a perverse regime that denied the humanity of black people while still criminalizing their actions. As the Supreme Court of Alabama explained in 1861, enslaved black people were "capable of committing crimes" and in that capacity were "regarded as persons"—but in almost every other sense they were "incapable of performing civil acts" and considered "things, not persons."

The 13th Amendment is credited with ending slavery, but it stopped short of that: It made an exception for those convicted of crimes. After emancipation, black people, once seen as less than fully human "slaves," were seen as less than fully human "criminals." The provisional governor of South Carolina declared in 1865 that they had to be "restrained from theft, idleness, vagrancy and crime." Laws governing slavery were replaced with Black Codes governing free black people—making the criminal-justice system central to new strategies of racial control.

These strategies intensified whenever black people asserted their independence or achieved any measure of success. During Reconstruction, the emergence of black elected officials and entrepreneurs was countered by convict leasing, a scheme in which white policymakers invented offenses used to target black people: vagrancy, loitering, being a group of black people out after dark, seeking employment without a note from a former enslaver. The imprisoned were then "leased" to businesses and farms, where they labored under brutal conditions." (Stevenson, 2019)

**Oppression:**

- To enslave, abuse, persecute.

- Prolonged cruel or unjust treatment or control.

- Keep (someone) in subservience and hardship, especially by the unjust exercise of authority.

- The feeling of being heavily burdened, mentally or physically, by troubles, adverse conditions, anxiety, etc.

- Opposite; freedom, democracy.

**Overview Bible:** "My power at your expense. Oppression is the unjust use of power at other people's expense. It involves protecting one's power, comfort, security, and privilege at the expense of those with less of these than you. It's a tricky concept to address, because if you've ever experienced oppression, you probably don't need it defined to you. If you need oppression defined, you've probably participated in it.

It's easy to recognize oppression at the individual level. It's the evil stepmother forcing a girl to do the housework. It's the slithery manager harassing his assistant. It's the schoolyard bully taking your lunch money. But oppression isn't just a few thorns—oppression is a worldwide, overgrown briar patch that entangles us at the civilization level.

We observe oppression all around us, and on some level, we all know oppression is wrong. (At least, we know it's wrong when we're the ones being oppressed.) But undoing it is easier said than done.

This is not a new problem. Powerful people have oppressed the weak for millennia." (Kranz, 2020)

> **Side Note:** *First, the systems (Government, Banking, Healthcare, Education, etc.) in society are used to incarcerate (imprison you). Then, they are used to break you down (oppress you). The result of incarceration and oppression is your freedom being taken away (enslavement).*

The broken—oppressive systems in society have been imprisoning, breaking down, and enslaving individuals in nearly the same manner for centuries. To further explain how, I have put together some resources to help paint a picture of the suffering that has been occurring throughout time, past and present.

## THE PAST:

**Final Call – Willie Lynch Letter:** "Let's Make a Slave" "The Original and Development of a Social Being Called 'The Negro.'"

Let us make a slave. What do we need? First of all, we need a black nigger man, a pregnant nigger woman and her baby nigger boy. Second, we will use the same basic principle that we use in breaking a horse, combined with some more sustaining factors. What we do with horses is that we break them from one form of life to another;

that is, we reduce them from their natural state in nature. Whereas nature provides them with the natural capacity to take care of their offspring, we break that natural string of independence from them and thereby create a dependency status, so that we may be able to get from them useful production for our business and pleasure.

"Cardinal Principles for Making a Negro" For fear that our future generations may not understand the principles of breaking both of the beast together, the nigger and the horse. We understand that short range planning economics results in periodic economic chaos; so that to avoid turmoil in the economy, it requires us to have breadth and depth in long range comprehensive planning, articulating both skill sharp perceptions. We lay down the following principles for long range comprehensive economic planning. Both horse and niggers are no good to the economy in the wild or natural state. Both must be broken and tied together for orderly production. For an orderly future, special and particular attention must be paid to the female and the youngest offspring. Both must be crossbred to produce a variety and division of labor. Both must be taught to respond to a peculiar new language. Psychological and physical instruction of containment must be created for both. We hold the six cardinal principles as truth to be self-evident, based upon following the discourse concerning the economics of breaking and tying the horse and the nigger together, all inclusive of the six principles laid down above. NOTE: Neither principle alone will suffice for good economics. All principles must be employed for the orderly good of the nation. Accordingly, both a wild horse and a wild or natural nigger is dangerous even if captured, for they will have the tendency to seek their customary freedom and, in doing so, might kill you in your sleep. You cannot rest. They sleep while you are awake and are awake while you are asleep. They are dangerous near the family house, and it requires too much labor to watch them away from the house. Above all, you cannot get them to work in this natural state. Hence, both the horse and the nigger must be broken; that is breaking them from one form of mental life to another." (Willie Lynch Letter: The Making of a Slave)

If you read the Willie Lynch Letter in its fullness, you'll see some alarming similarities between tactics used to imprison, break down, and enslave men and women in the past to tactics utilized today. The term "let's make a slave" is used to describe the process, and that is precisely what the oppressors in control of the broken systems in society intend to do, make slaves out of you and me.

> **Side Note:** *Some historians, professors, and writers believe Willie Lynch himself, as well as the Willie Lynch Letter, to be a myth. "There are many problems with this document - not the least of which is the fact that it is absolutely fake.*
>
> *I long ago stopped listening to sentences that begin with "The problem with black people is," or end with "and that's why black people can't get ahead now," which partly explains my initial indifference to the now-famous William Lynch Speech." (Cobb, 2003)*

My take on the Willie Lynch Letter: although Willie Lynch may not have truthfully written this letter, one cannot deny the validity of the words written when comparing them to the slavery we suffer through today. I have personally lived through some of the things mentioned in this letter growing up, but I will leave it up to you, the reader, to decide if this letter speaks truth to your life today.

## THE PRESENT:

**Mass Incarceration:**

- Statistics – Prison Policy Initiative: 2.3 Million "The American criminal justice system holds almost 2.3 million people in 1,833 state prisons, 110 federal prisons, 1,772 juvenile correctional facilities, 3,134 local jails, 218 immigration detention facilities, and 80 Indian Country jails as well as in military prisons, civil commitment centers, state psychiatric hospitals, and prisons in the U.S. territories." (Sawyer, 2020)

- Effects – Reducing Mass Incarceration: "Our criminal justice system's policies and laws have created an epidemic of over-criminalization and over-incarceration. Government must reevaluate the policies of the last thirty years that have increased the rate of incarceration by 110 percent.

  Michelle Alexander, the author of The New Jim Crow, describes mass incarceration in America as a massive system of racial and social control. It is the process by which people are swept into the criminal justice system, branded criminals and felons, and locked up for longer periods of time than in most other countries in the world. Former prisoners are then released into a permanent second-class status in which they are stripped of such basic civil and human rights, as the right to vote, the right to serve on juries and the right to be free of legal discrimination in employment, housing and access to public benefits. It is a system that operates to control people, often at early ages, and virtually all aspects of their lives after they have been viewed as suspects in some kind of crime." (Schumake, 2019)

## Unemployment:

- Statistics – Bureau of Labor Statistics (BLS): 5.8 Million "In December 2019, the unemployment rate held at 3.5 percent, and the number of unemployed persons was unchanged at 5.8 million. A year earlier, the jobless rate was 3.9 percent, and the number of unemployed persons was 6.3 million." (The Employment Situation, 2020)

- Effects – Indeed: "Individuals who are unemployed are often more susceptible to several challenges, including difficulty in finding future employment and decreased income. Unemployment also impacts society and the economy as a whole. The longer a person is unemployed, the more likely they are to experience potential negative effects and contribute to the multiplier effect that unemployment has on the community." (Effects of Unemployment on Individuals, Society and the Economy, 2021)

## Homelessness:

- Statistics – National Alliance to End Homelessness: 580,446K "In January 2020, there were 580,466 people experiencing homelessness in America. Most were individuals (70 percent), and the rest were people living in families with children. They lived in every state and territory, and they reflected the diversity of our country." (State of Homelessness: 2021 Edition, 2021)

- Effects – Our Father's House Soup Kitchen: "You may not realize it but homelessness affects not just the individual experiencing homelessness, it leaves an impact on society too. Some of the most significant impacts of homelessness are:

  - Health

- Mental Health
- Increased Propensity to Substance Abuse
- Worsened Violent Tendencies
- Increased Risk of Incarceration
- Sexual Assault" (Ponio, 2021)

**Broken Homes:**

- Statistics – Finances Online: "18.5 Million "Almost one-fourth (23%) of children in the US under the age of 18 live with one parent and no other adult, which is the highest in the world. US figures of children in single parent households are more than three times the number of children around the world under similar living arrangements." (Andre, 2022)

- Effects – How Stuff Works: "Ultimately, the answer to whether single parenting affects any particular child is this: It depends. A single parent with adequate resources may provide a stable, nurturing home in which children thrive just as well as those who have two parents. On the other hand, a single parent who's just scraping by and has little time, energy or skill for parental duties might have children who are at risk for a variety of problems. Including psychological and developmental problems." (Kelly, 2021)

**THE BROKEN SYSTEMS IN SOCIETY HAVE CREATED AN ORBITING CYCLE THAT LEADS TO IMPRISONMENT AND BROKENNESS WITHIN FAMILIES AND COMMUNITIES OR, SHOULD I SAY, ENSLAVEMENT.**

**MASS INCARCERATION:**
2.3 MILLION
More than 2.3 million people are incarcerated throughout the U.S.

**UNEMPLOYMENT:**
5.8 MILLION
In 2019 more than 5.8 million people were unemployed.

**HOMELESSNESS:**
580,466K
In 2020, more than 580,466 people were experiencing homelessness in America.

**BROKEN HOMES:**
18.5 MILLION
In 2020, more than 18.5 million children in the U.S. lived with a single mother or father.

Looking at the brokenness created by society's corrupt and oppressive systems might lead one to begin to despise them. All that one can think is, "I want freedom for my people". Seeing the agony and pain, all that is wanted is to tear down the walls that make up these systems, to build something anew—a free world.

I contemplated what could be done to create a new system, a new world. As crazy as it sounds, I'm serious! I knew what needed to be done was a hefty task, impossible almost because the systems in society are so powerful (from what it looks like), and I am just little me.

There were (I say were because I believe it'll be past tense soon due to the power of you and me) so many variables to the systems in society, and I continuously thought, "well, how do I make it to a place of power so that I can fix what's broken?" Become President, Senator, Pastor, or join a non-profit.

I say this because sometimes, to change something, a person has to go undercover and become one from among them. Meaning becoming intimately connected to the very pain one wishes to heal or problems one wishes to solve.

But what I failed to realize while contemplating was that I was already one from among them. I was one from among the very people I wanted to help. One from among you! I was looking for organizations and positions in power that would allow me to change the world, not realizing that we together are the change.

**Our Problem:**

- Disunity, which leads to division.

**Disunity:**

- Disagreement and conflict within a group.

**Division:**

- The action of separating something into parts or the process of being separated.

## UNITED WE STAND, DIVIDED WE FALL.

We are divided in so many ways, not just in the United States but throughout the world. We say black lives matter, yet we hurt and harm one another. We say black lives matter, yet when someone's view of Black Lives Matter doesn't look like our own, we curse them.

Oh wait, and it doesn't stop there. We say the Church is made up of one body, but we allow denominations or the fact that people choose to worship differently to come in between and disunite us.

**Denomination:**

- A group or branch of any religion.

- A class or kind of persons or things distinguished by a specific name.

## THE CHURCH (THE BODY OF CHRIST) HAS BEEN DISMEMBERED.

**Side Note:** *The very place (Church) which is supposed to symbolize unity, and be an example that people can follow, has become the opposite of what God intended for it to be.*

We have learned from the people who oppress us to use our strengths to tear down and exploit our own people's weaknesses. And as we do so, we contradict the very words we speak. Therefore, as people, we are not taken seriously. None of our matters stand up nor hold any value to other people because our concerns don't even truly matter to us. We don't respect one another, so how can we expect anyone else to do so? And yes, the people who control the oppressive systems in society are the ones creating chaos, but what you don't see is they only do so because they know they can use said chaos to their advantage.

> **Side Note:** *The people who control the oppressive systems in society do not have to take us out because when we are supposed to be united, we easily lose focus and become divided.*

Have you ever been in a situation where you've felt like nothing is going right, but instead of everyone coming together, people start to divide and fall apart? If not, pay close attention because "division" is the gap the devil uses to get you alone, to infiltrate your mind.

**Infiltrate:**

- Enter or gain access to (an organization, place, etc.) surreptitiously and gradually, especially in order to acquire secret information.

**WHEN YOU ARE ALONE, YOU NOT ONLY OPEN YOURSELF UP TO BE ATTACKED, BUT YOU ALSO LOSE THE POWER ONLY A UNION CAN GIVE YOU.**

The devil plays on your nature, as a human, to always want to be in control of everything. Your nature of selfishness leads to fighting and division, causing a rift. Think about it: if so many people are vying for control or are selfish, only seeing their view, no one's worried about coming together for the common goal. This leads everyone to depart and do their own thing, their way; furthermore, opening the door for each person on the outside to one by one be attacked.

Do you not know how much you could accomplish if you stopped fighting if you allowed someone to be a part of your team? To accomplish things together as opposed to going at it alone.

## HOW CAN WE WORK TOGETHER UNLESS WE AGREE?

"Then they brought to Him a man who had a demon. He was blind and could not speak. Jesus healed him and he could talk and see. All the people were surprised and said, "Can this Man be the Son of David?" But when the proud religious law-keepers heard it, they said, "This Man puts out demons only by Satan, the leader of demons." Jesus knew their thoughts and said to them, "Every nation divided into groups that fight each other is going to be destroyed. Every city or family divided into groups that fight each other will not stand. If the devil puts out the devil, he is divided against himself. How will his nation stand?" (Matthew 12:22-26)

The battle starts at home. For us to stand for each other, we have to start within. Within ourselves, within our people, within our communities. Because...

## THE THINGS WE FIGHT OVER ARE WHAT ALLOW THE PEOPLE WHO CONTROL THE OPPRESSIVE SYSTEMS IN SOCIETY TO CONQUER US; AS WE DIVIDE, THEY SLAY US, AND WE FALL.

This is not saying that everyone who works for these oppressive systems, such as law enforcement or a government agency, wants to cause division, is evil, or incorrect. For the most part, some of them can't even see that they are not in control and are only doing what they've been told, failing to realize the actual damage that's being caused. Nevertheless, the systems in society are broken, and they are breaking people.

As people, we are not being judged by the content of our character but by the color of our skin. Our stature and the area we grew up in. To further add fuel to the fire, most are being made to feel like no one cares.

> **Side Note:** *As a person, if you feel like you will never be accepted no matter what you do, you tend to stop caring. Why keep trying, why keep caring if nothing you do will ever be good enough. And yes, some critics may say, "Well, if you don't care for yourself, then why would anyone else care for you?"*

But it's like a relationship between a child and a parent. If a child does all they can but feel like they will never live up to their parent's expectations, or nothing they do can make their parents see that they are at least trying to succeed, they start to feel invisible. Eventually, that child begins to let go of all the cares they have in the world because they are made to feel like none of it matters anymore. That child simply wants to be loved but is placed in an environment where it seems love doesn't exist.

This is what people in poverty-stricken low-income environments feel. Nothing done when trying to progress in life seems good enough.

We are constantly being judged by where we came from, and it feels as if no one notices where we're going.

However, do you not know that these systems wouldn't make money or function without you? Do you know if people worked together, those CEOs in charge of those billion-dollar corporations that are fronts used to hide and clean their dirty money wouldn't be able to live the lifestyle they're accustomed to? If you didn't have a need.

Side Note: *The rich and powerful prey on poor people's needs to get their wants. If only you'd break free; if only you could open your eyes and see that these people are running legal Ponzi schemes that keep people imprisoned in poverty. Yet, if a so-called criminal sets up shop and does the very thing that the rich and powerful do, they'd get years in Federal prison—the irony of it all.*

Overview Bible: "This affects the poor in obvious ways. They're subject to fraud, abuse, slavery, rape, homelessness, and death—and that's if they stay on the "right" side of the law. If an oppressed person should find themselves on the "wrong" side of the law, they're helpless against the system. A poor person has to choose between survival and breaking the law, or their own moral conscience—a struggle the oppressors never have to face.

For example, in the book of Proverbs, a sage says he doesn't want to become rich—as this would lead to him denying the Lord. But he also doesn't want to become poor and have to choose between starvation and stealing (Proverbs 30:8–9). To some readers, this might seem like an obvious "do the right thing" scenario. If you're poor, you can still choose to do what's right and not steal—and if you steal, you face the consequences.

But this is key to understanding how the authors of the Bible viewed this problem: in an oppressive system, the powerful people are already stealing from the weak; they're just not prosecuted. The prophet Ezekiel says this about the wealthy families, the government authorities, and the religious leaders in Jerusalem during his day:

The people of the land practice extortion and commit robbery; they oppress the poor and needy and mistreat the foreigner, denying them justice. (Ezekiel 22:29)

Oppressive systems create a double standard, allowing the powerful to get away with things the weak would never be able to do. This isn't just an issue with primitive civilizations. People are still protesting systemic injustice today. For example, in the USA, a black man accused of paying with a counterfeit $20 bill can lose his life, while a white man accused of ethnic cleansing and war crimes can get his face on the $20 bill." (Kranz, 2020)

For example, you need food for your children, so you steal and wind up in jail. You need a home, so you get on Section 8.

**Side Note:** *Depending on the circumstances (needs) of the individual, being on government assistance can lead to chronic poverty, causing one to develop a poverty mentality (oppressed).*

**Chronic Poverty:**

- "A phenomenon whereby an individual or group is in a state of poverty over an extended period of time." (Wikipedia)

**Poverty Mentality:**

- "Poverty mentality is a mindset that people develop over time based on a strong belief that they will never have enough money. This mindset is driven by fear and can cause poor financial decision-making." (Do You Have a Poverty Mentality?)

Do you see how the healthcare system stays running? For the most part, they don't cure illnesses. They treat the symptoms of the illness with medication. Have you ever heard of Big Pharma (oppressor)?

Or, they'll say be healthy, but the majority of the healthy things are unaffordable. The food most people can afford is the food that's unhealthy—the food that drives people to the hospital in the first place. Why do you think diabetes, high cholesterol, and high blood pressure are highest among the poor? It's because people can't afford the food that keeps them healthy. This then leads to the development of anxiety, depression, and bipolar disorder because people are so stressed just trying to get by.

How does this help the system? It creates a cycle (a need that requires you to keep coming back).

**THE STRUGGLES THAT ARE BEING FOUGHT EVERY DAY ARE WHAT'S CAUSING PEOPLE TO BECOME SICK; IT'S WHAT CREATES A NEED. THE NEED (YOUR NEEDS) IS HOW THE OPPRESSOR KEEPS OPPRESSION ALIVE.**

The people in control of these oppressive systems make the crimes they commit look legit; they make you believe these programs they set up are for your good; they make you think that you can't live life on your own. Training you to be slaves to them, slaves to your needs—slowly but surely taking your freedom and choices away; taking your mind away.

> Side Note: *If your mind is gone, then so are you, and eventually, all that's left is a body to profit from and not a mind that prospers. "The one who gets wisdom loves life. The one who cherishes understanding will soon prosper." (Proverbs 19:8) Yet, how can you prosper if you don't have a mind to understand?*

Now, let's dig deeper! The same societal issues hindering us from progressing in life today occurred in the Bible centuries ago, starting with the Israelites.

## HOW OPPRESSION WORKS:

**Overview Bible:** "Oppression works in the Bible the same way it works today: the powerful take more for themselves at the expense of the weak. This is done in several ways:

- **Violence:** Being physically strong on an individual level or militarily strong on a larger scale allows some people to simply take what they want. It's the crudest form of oppression, and the earliest that we see in the story of Scripture. (Examples include Cain, Joseph's brothers, and Pharaoh.)

- **Coercion:** Sometimes violence isn't necessary—the threat of violence, or the threat of negative consequences for not appeasing the powerful is enough to keep the weak in line. Pharaoh does this when keeping the children of Israel enslaved by upping their work quotas.

- **Corruption:** If you're powerful enough, you can influence or create systems to keep you in power automatically. A common way this was expressed in ancient times was through bribes. Judges had the power to pronounce rulings in courts. But rich, powerful, high-status families could bribe judges to rule in their favor.

- **Veneration:** And if you're really powerful, you can get people to treat you like a god. By positioning yourself as the source of everyone else's power, security, and status, you get to define what's right and wrong in the domain under your control. This means your followers will do the work of oppressing those who oppose you, and even the people you're oppressing might love you." (Kranz, 2020)

The Israelites were slaves to the rich man (Pharaoh/Egyptians), and because the rich man had money, he had all the control. Although the Israelites outnumbered the Egyptians, the years of enslavement and the impression left on their mind made the Israelites believe that they could be nothing on their own. Over time, we have become controlled by the same lies due to our belief systems.

For instance, when Moses went to set the Lord's people free from slavery, they didn't even want to go. Why? Because they believed that the programs the rich man had set up were for their good, and as long as they were getting by, they needed not cause a fuss. "If only the LORD had killed us back in Egypt," they moaned. "There we sat around pots filled with meat and ate all the bread we wanted. But now you have brought us into this wilderness to starve us all to death." (Exodus 16:3)

## NOT MANY FIGHT THE PEOPLE THEY "THINK" ARE HELPING.

Because the Israelites thought the Egyptians were helping them by providing them with food, the moment they had to do for themselves or were hit with opposition, they wanted to retreat and run back to where they came from. "As Pharaoh approached, the Israelites looked up, and there were the Egyptians, marching after them. They were terrified and cried out to the Lord. They said to Moses, "Was it because there were no graves in Egypt that you brought us to the desert to die? What have you done to us by bringing us out of Egypt? Didn't we say to you in Egypt, 'Leave us alone; let us serve the Egyptians'? It would have been better for us to serve the Egyptians than to die in the desert!" (Exodus 14:10-12)

The Israelites wanted to return to the same programs that continued to hurt them, to hurt their minds. After all, these programs help feed a lot of people's families.

But no, what's going on is that these programs are making you believe you can't feed your family without the assistance of the government (oppressor). That you can't get a home without the government; that without the government, you are nothing.

The programs being housing (Section 8), free medical, free dental, and free food (food stamps)—all the things that lead you to believe that the government is helping, that the rich do care about the less fortunate. But really, what these programs have been doing is enslaving your minds, causing you to believe that you need to become dependent upon these people and things to live. Or should I say that mediocrity is all life has to offer you?

## WE LIVE IN A WORLD WHERE THE RICH AND POWERFUL SEEM TO GET RICHER WHILE THE POOR LIVE A LIFE OF MEDIOCRITY.

Realizing the pain and agony the people who control these oppressive systems were causing by trying to control the people's minds led me to look for organizations set up to fight the system. But it dawned on me that even with the assistance of an organization, this could take forever. Until one day, God blessed my mind. He said, "To break the system, you must start with the people it has control of—the people suffering from the problems it creates. To break the system, you have to break the power it has to enslave the people and their minds."

## THE ONLY WAY TO BREAK THE SYSTEM IS TO START BY FREEING THE PEOPLE ENCHAINED BY IT.

In the back of my head, I could hear God saying, "start from within because it's not just the physical fighting that occurs. It's the mental roadblocks within the mind that people continue to battle with due to the problems they have gone through in life. It's about the torment that has been created within the mind."

## GET TO THE HEART OF THE MATTER!

The heart controls the mind, and the mind controls the man. Change the man's heart, and you can change the man's mind, furthermore leading to a change of path of the man.

The heart led you to where you are, "For as he thinks in his heart, so is he." (Proverbs 23:7). The heart hurts when you see your children cry, so you must do whatever it takes to ensure they are taken care of.

Then I thought to myself, start with the people who are incarcerated and enslaved Spiritually, Mentally, Financially, and Physically. Imagine if no people were incarcerated and enslaved; how much money would these systems make? Hit the system where it hurts—its pockets.

If the incarcerated and enslaved are free mentally, they too can be free physically. This meant that the oppressive systems in society that were despised would fall with one simple act—the act from within, the act of love, the act of being there to help and support one another.

**Side Note:** *The simple act of love has the power to remove the rock (pain, pride, and hatred) from a hardened heart, leaving the once flourishing markets (oppressive systems: government, banking, healthcare, education, etc.) with no merchandise (you) to profit from.*

What is seen is a global problem. People profit off of the unfortunate situations of the less fortunate. This is not just jail. It's also banks and government organizations that were set up to "help" the low-income. Jobs because people work like slaves for a CEO to take home the big check.

Look at how much goes into running a jail. How much money is made from people being physically incarcerated, how much money judges make just for "sitting in" on a case, and how much lawyers make just from representing people. Look at how banks profit from the fact that people need loans and have no money to pay in full. Interest rates that cause low-income individuals to pay double for their troubles.

But where there are no cases, there is no revenue. Where there are no loans needed, there is no bank. Where we have our own companies and jobs, there is no CEO to take our money.

## THE ONLY THING STANDING IN YOUR WAY IS YOU.

Some of you may believe that you are free because you're no longer physically slaves or because you're not in an actual jail. "We're not slaves you may say." "To the Jews who had believed him Jesus said, "If you hold to my teaching, you are really my disciples. Then you will know the truth, and the truth will set you free." They answered him, "We are Abraham's descendants and have never been slaves of anyone. How can you say that we shall be set free?" Jesus replied, "Very truly I tell you; everyone who sins is a slave to sin. Now a slave has no permanent place in the family, but a son belongs to it forever. So if the Son sets you free, you will be free indeed." (John 8:31-36)

**Inmate:**

- A person confined to an institution.

**Institution:**

- A society or organization founded for a religious, educational, social, or similar purpose. An established law, practice, or custom.

- An established official organization having an important role in the life of a country, such as a bank, church, or legislature.

- A well-established and structured pattern of behavior or of relationships that is accepted as a fundamental part of a culture.

You see, Moses freed the enslaved people from the hands of the Egyptians, but even though they were free physically, their behavior due to their mindset painted a very different picture.

To put it simply, you can be free physically and still enslaved mentally. And just because you have money doesn't mean you are free. You are still a product of the environment that conditioned you to think the way you think in the first place. This is because it's not about a position; it's about a state of mind. It's where your mind stands, not your body. And as long as your mind stands behind the very thing that corrupts it, you can never truly be free.

To conclude, if your heart and mind are not in the right state, your body cannot move to its true destination. Meaning you can get money or a job, but if you don't develop a positive mindset, you will not be able to obtain true freedom. Therefore, it's essential to start working with God so that He can change your heart and mind because when they are free, you can do anything; you can be anything.

## FINAL CALL: ARE YOU GOING TO BE FREE AT LAST, OR WILL YOU CONTINUE TO ALLOW YOUR ENVIRONMENT TO MAKE YOU ITS PRODUCT?

||||||||||||||||||||||||||||||||||||||||||||||||||||||||||||||||||||||||||||||||||||||||||||||||||||||

"Any system that does not allow one to question it, has its roots digging into manipulation and control. And manipulation and control are devised by people in power. Not by gods and angels. If you fear questioning what you have been taught and if you fear to think freely and make decisions based upon what you feel, see and know; because a system has taught you to have that fear, you should know that you are under that manipulation, you are under that control. You have this one life and you are planning to live it based upon a path dictated to you as the truth, instead of questioning and seeking what the truth might actually be. Truth does not need to tell you not to look left and not to look right, because the validity of its character does not depend upon whether you open your eyes or not! Truth remains true in all times and it will encourage you to think freely, to ask questions, and to seek! Truth is not a fragile thing easily broken if you fail to tiptoe around it. Truth is not a fragile thing easily broken if you fail to wrap your hands around it. Truth is never failing and does not need the human race, or any other race living or dead, to validate it."

— *C. JoyBell C.*

|||||||||||||||||||||||||||||||||||||||||||||||||||||||||||||||||||||||||||||||||||||||||||||||||||||

*Heavenly Father,* I want to thank you for the freedom you have granted me through the blood of Jesus. Though my sins were red as scarlet, you have washed them white as snow. I pray and ask the Holy Spirit to help me through this transition in life. To help me learn what it means to live and how to live so that my mind may be made free from the entrapment of the systems around me. I pray for those who are hurting, and if I may be used to grant them grace and peace, I ask that you enable and allow me to do so. I would also like to pray for the minds of the people who have been down for so long that they no longer know which way is up. May peace and grace be to all who are struggling, seen and unseen, in public and private. May our minds be at peace with you and free at last as your grace reigns over us. Thank you, Lord, for all that you are.

In Jesus' name, Amen!

# PART TWO THE PAIN

# CHAPTER 2

# IMPRESSION OF THE MIND

*Growing up in an environment where poverty and pain are abundant can cause you to self-destruct before you have a chance to think you can make it out. I grew up in Oakland, Ca. And no different from any low-income city with beauty and culture, there is also an abundance of poverty and pain. Unfortunately for me, the impression of my mind was tainted by the pain at the age of four when I lost my dad to gun violence. All I saw was pain, so a walking billboard of pain is what I became.*

**Romans 12:2** NLT "Don't copy the behavior and customs of this world, but let God transform you into a new person by changing the way you think. Then you will learn to know God's will for you, which is good and pleasing and perfect."

When placed in a visionless environment, it is hard to succeed because you risk becoming what you consume. In other words, if you are in an environment where all you can see is violence, hate, hurt, and pain, then you run the risk of becoming violent, hateful, hurtful, and in pain. For this reason, minorities are often faced with obstacles designed to keep people in poverty, in ghettos, and in hoods. It's because when you can't see better, it makes it harder for you to be better. My friend...

## THE BATTLE IS OVER YOUR MIND, NOT YOUR MONEY.

Anything in this world can leave a lasting impression on your mind, whether good or bad. I frequently say things others have said simply because I listen to them speak a lot. What I hear sticks to my mind, and eventually, I repeat their words.

This happens because what you listen to or see influences how you think. Which furthermore influences your actions. For this reason, it's essential to be careful to pay attention to what you listen to and or watch. It's also imperative to keep putting good into your mind because what gets in sooner or later is sure to get out.

> **Side Note:** *Your mind is like the phrase on the Minute Made Orange Juice bottle, which says, "Put Good In. Get Good Out". What you allow into your mind is what you will reciprocate and put out.*

Why do you think a child who has been abused often becomes an abuser? It's simple; that child only imitates what's modeled before them.

As another example, look at individuals who are physically incarcerated. Depending on the facility they are confined to, all they may be able to see is negativity or abuse daily.

For instance, "four deputies were arrested who worked at Santa Rita Jail in Dublin, California back in 2017 for facilitating fights, not feeding inmates, intimidating witnesses, and allowing inmates to throw feces on one another." (Ruggiero & Debolt)

**Side Note:** *Most of the incarcerated individuals targeted by these deputies suffered from mental illnesses.*

Now ask yourself; how can society expect physically incarcerated people to become model citizens if, while incarcerated, the actions displayed by the people who run these programs are harmful and destructive?

## CRIMINALS ARE NOT BORN; THEY ARE MADE. JUST AS A CHILD'S MIND IS NOT AUTOMATICALLY GEARED TOWARDS HATRED, IT IS SHAPED BY THE VISUALS ONE SEES AT HOME AND IN SOCIETY.

People don't just commit crimes; their actions are products of what is seen and consumed daily. Furthermore, if incarcerated individuals don't have someone helping flush out the visions of negativity they consume, they run the risk of their minds corrupting. When that individual returns home, they become destructive, or better yet, they self-destruct simply because they see the people who are supposed to uphold the law not do so, thus giving them the impression (key word) that crime is okay.

**Side Note:** *The harsh reality of life is that there's so much negativity in the world, which means you can't entirely escape it. However, I'm not saying it's okay to sit at home because you want to avoid how the world can negatively affect your mind.*

To illustrate, I lived in a house on a hill. And even though I was separated from the problems that were going on in society for a moment, when I left home, I still had to deal with the issues in the surrounding areas. With that being said, no one is exempt from going through life's troubles. You can be set apart, but you still have to go out and deal with the world's terror while you are in it. The best thing you can do is learn how to triumph while amid that terror.

## THE ONLY WAY OVER IS THROUGH.

If you read your Bible or learned anything from the journey of Jesus, you know the only way to get over your problems is through them. "Even though I walk through the valley of the shadow of death, I will fear no evil for you are with me; your rod and your staff, they comfort me." (Psalm 23:4)

Let me explain how you can move through life without getting caught up in the miseries of this world.

As you keep putting good into your mind, there will always be something or someone trying to cancel it out. Images of positivity, positive role models, prayer, learning the wisdom of the Lord, healthy relationships, and most importantly, your relationship with God is the only way to combat this. "It is true. We live in a body of flesh.

But we do not fight like people of the world. We do not use those things to fight with that the world uses. We use the things God gives to fight with, and they have power. Those things God gives to fight with destroy the strong-places of the devil. We break down every thought and proud thing that puts itself up against the wisdom of God. We take hold of every thought and make it obey Christ." (2 Corinthians 10:3-5)

> **Side Note:** *When you utilize God's tools, it enables you to draw closer to peace; thus, leading to the formation of a safe haven and a sound mind.*

Your home is your safe haven, a temple you can retreat to. Similar to your mind, which is a temple for your thoughts. It is imperative to keep your home, mind, and thoughts safeguarded. Because if your secret safe place is destroyed, you'll have nowhere to flush out the negativity you endured throughout the day, causing your battlefield to become one-sided.

## DON'T UNDERESTIMATE YOUR OPPONENT. THE DEVIL WILL USE WHAT YOU HAVE (YOUR MIND) TO TAKE WHAT HE WANTS (YOUR BODY).

To conclude, there are many things in this world fighting to make an impression on your mind, good and bad. If you are not careful to pay attention to what you consume, you will start being led by the media, thus, causing you to see yourself through the eyes of someone else's image, personality, and maybe even career—eventually leading to you manifesting negative behaviors. For this reason, you must continuously immerse yourself in positivity, feeding and nourishing what you want to grow in your mind and pushing out what you want to be removed.

"And now, dear brothers and sisters, one final thing. Fix your thoughts on what is true, and honorable, and right, and pure, and lovely, and admirable. Think about things that are excellent and worthy of praise." (Philippians 4:8)

There are some things in this world that you have no control over, but there are many things in your life that you do.

- You control what goes on in your home.

- You control what you watch on television.

- You control how your home is decorated.

- You control what behavior your children see modeled by their parents.

- You control the impression that society has on your mind.

**DON'T LET THE IMPRESSION OF THIS WORLD CONTROL YOUR MIND; ALLOW YOUR MIND TO LEAVE A POSITIVE IMPRESSION ON THIS WORLD!**

||||||||||||||||||||||||||||||||||||||||||||||||||||||||||||||||||||||||||||||||||||||||||||||||

"A man's strongest defense against his environment is his mind, the way he thinks."

— *Bishop TD Jakes*

||||||||||||||||||||||||||||||||||||||||||||||||||||||||||||||||||||||||||||||||||||||||||||||||

*Father,* You know all of my thoughts and the attitude of my heart. May my spoken words and unspoken thoughts be pleasing in Your sight, O Lord—my Rock and my Redeemer. You gave me Your Word as a weapon to fight impure and unholy thoughts. Your Word is alive and more powerful than any weapon known to man; it can pull down all evil strongholds. I will concentrate on truth, goodness, and righteousness. I will think about pure and lovely things and dwell on the good attributes in others. I will think about all that I can praise You for and be glad about. Thank you for giving me the helmet of salvation to guard my mind. As I commit to staying in Your Word daily, I will begin to think more and more like You. I will diligently protect my mind and heart by not allowing unhealthy thoughts to control me. Thank You for giving me the mind of Christ. Help me to make all my thoughts obedient to Jesus and your Word.

In Jesus' name, I pray. Amen.

# CHAPTER 3

# I'M ONLY HUMAN

*We all hit rough patches in life that causes us to forget who we are and to whom we belong (God). Furthermore leading to our inability to recognize the "man" in all humans. As stress sets in, in our minds, God steps out. This causes us to become blind to another's pain and battles while only being consumed with our own. The devil uses this to his advantage to break apart unions, knowing most of us, when facing adversity, forget that we are all only human.*

**Ephesians 5:33 NLT** "So again I say, each man must love his wife as he loves himself, and the wife must respect her husband."

For me, the pain and problems started when the criminal justice system took my loved one, a strong man destined for greatness, and persistently tried to break him right before my eyes.

Seeing my loved one, day by day, hurting, knowing there was nothing I could do to help caused me more stress and frustration than I could bear. After a while, the visuals of the pain began to torment me, pushing me into a pit of depression, causing me to become broken, weak, and sick.

When my loved one was taken to jail, I faced many battles. One of which was stress. At times the stress caused me to become angry. At times the stress made me sad. At times I felt like the stress and pressure would kill me, literally. My life was wacky and out of control. Some days I didn't know whether I was going left or right. As time passed, I developed a love-hate relationship with the situation.

When things were going right, the situation pushed me to produce great fruit. My attitude had changed for the better. I had been writing this book. But when things were going left, the situation made me bitter. The bitter days made me feel like I was too weak to keep pushing. Those days made me want to give up; those days made me feel like the load I was carrying was too heavy.

The bitter days broke me down and made my spirit weak.
The bitter days pushed me to take my eyes off God.

**Final Call – Willie Lynch Letter:** "The breaking process of the African woman" "Take the female and run a series of tests on her to see if she will submit to your desires willingly. Test her in every way, because she is the most important factor for good economics. If she shows any sign of resistance in submitting completely to your will, do not hesitate to use the bullwhip on her to extract that last bit of [b****] out of her. Take care not to kill her, for in doing so, you spoil good economics. When in complete submission, she will train her offspring's in the early years to submit to labor when they become of age. Understanding is the best thing. Therefore, we shall go deeper into this area of the subject matter concerning what we have produced here in this breaking process of the female nigger. We have reversed the relationship; in her natural uncivilized state, she would have a strong dependency on the uncivilized nigger male, and she would have a limited protective tendency toward her independent male offspring and would raise male offspring's to be dependent like her. Nature had provided for this type of balance. We reversed nature by burning and pulling a civilized nigger apart and bullwhipping the other to the point of death, all in her presence. By her being left alone, unprotected, with the male image destroyed, the ordeal caused her to move from her psychologically dependent state to a frozen, independent state. In this frozen, psychological state of independence, she will raise her male and female offspring in reversed roles. For fear of the young male's life, she will psychologically train him to be mentally weak and dependent, but physically strong. Because she has become psychologically independent, she will train her female offspring to be psychologically independent. What have you got? You've got the nigger woman out front and the nigger man behind and scared. This is a perfect situation of sound sleep and economics. Before the breaking process, we had to be alertly on guard at all times.

Now, we can sleep soundly, for out of frozen fear his woman stands guard for us. He cannot get past her early slave molding process. He is a good tool, now ready to be tied to the horse at a tender age. By the time a nigger boy reaches the age of sixteen, he is soundly broken in and ready for a long life of sound and efficient work and the reproduction of a unit of good labor force. Continually through the breaking of uncivilized savage niggers, by throwing the nigger female savage into a frozen psychological state of independence, by killing the protective male image, and by creating a submissive dependent mind of the nigger male slave, we have created an orbiting cycle that turns on its own axis forever, unless a phenomenon occurs and re-shifts the position of the male and female slaves." (Willie Lynch Letter: The Making of a Slave)

**THE DEVIL DESTROYS THE MALE IMAGE IN FRONT OF THE WOMAN TO MAKE THE WOMAN BELIEVE THE MAN IS WEAK AND USELESS. AS TIME PASSES, THE WOMAN'S VIEW OF THE MAN LEADS HER TO BECOME DISRESPECTFUL AND UNLOVING. THESE EVENTS LEAD TO BICKERING AND ARGUING, FURTHERMORE CAUSING DIVISION.**

The devil uses the unfortunate situations in life to divide the man and the woman because division leads to undue stress on the woman. For example, if the man is gone and incarcerated, the woman is left to worry about things that could easily be taken care of as a union. This, in turn, leads to frustration and anger.

The woman becomes frustrated because there are needs to be met within the household; the man becomes angry because he can't meet those needs. All of this leads to stress on both parties. After a while, the couple begins to fight and argue, only seeing their battles. This severs their relationship and causes division between the two.

> **Side Note:** *When the woman believes she can no longer rely on the man to protect the family, she begins to take action, rising as the household leader. Which is precisely what the devil wants her to do.*

Remember, as I mentioned in chapter one, *"The System Through the Eyes of the Broken,"* when division occurs, each person on the outside is easily picked off or attacked. This means that when the woman is unable to handle the stress of the home on her own, she finds herself in a trap, where she starts to depend upon the government and other sources to help her provide for the family's needs.

After depending on these sources for some time, the woman becomes fearful, believing that if she tried to branch off and do things without the assistance of the government, she'd be unable to.

## FEAR LEAVES THE WOMAN IN A FROZEN STATE. AND THAT LEADS HER AND HER FAMILY TO LIVE A LIFE OF MEDIOCRITY.

> **Side Note:** *When you begin to believe mediocrity is all life has to offer, it makes you fearful of doing better. It makes you fearful of breaking free from the invisible chains of poverty. This causes you to continuously depend upon the government (oppressor) and other sources to get by. When in reality, you should rely on God (the one who sets you free from oppression).*

"It is better to take refuge in the Lord than to trust in man." (Psalm 118:8) Why? "Cursed are those who put their trust in mere humans, who rely on human strength and turn their hearts away from the Lord. They are like stunted shrubs in the desert, with no hope for the future. They will live in the barren wilderness, in an uninhabited salty land." (Jeremiah 17:5-6)

## THE BEST WAY TO KEEP SOMEONE IN A SALTY LAND (POVERTY) IS TO USE THEIR SITUATION AND CIRCUMSTANCES AGAINST THEM.

The broken systems (government, banking, healthcare, education, etc.) in society are the devil's way of controlling people, the belly of the beast. The system is where chaos reigns, and the most havoc is caused. As people, we, who live in poverty, are the prime targets of these systems simply because of our circumstances.

How often have you been in a predicament or known someone who has become entrapped and oppressed by the broken systems in society and the problems they create?

My loved one being incarcerated left me to take care of all my usual expenses and some additional expenses. This meant not just purchasing food for myself to eat and paying bills such as rent and utility bills. But I now had to make sure there was money on the phone to talk, money for video visits, food for my loved one, and on top of all of that, I was trying to save for a down payment to purchase a home. These circumstances led to me working overtime at my job, and when that became too much stress, I started taking out loans.

The interest rates on the loans I'd taken out were sky-high. This meant I'd not only have a hefty monthly payment I couldn't afford, but I'd also be paying back in interest almost three times the amount I had initially borrowed. This stressed me out even more, eventually causing me to develop anxiety, depression, and high blood pressure—I was unknowingly killing myself. Or should I say the broken systems in society were killing me.

**WHEN A WOMAN BECOMES SO BURNED OUT FROM TAKING CARE OF EVERYTHING ON HER OWN, SHE BECOMES A SLAVE TO BILLS, LOAN COMPANIES, AND VARIOUS GOVERNMENT PROGRAMS.**

"Eventually, a new king came to power in Egypt who knew nothing about Joseph or what he had done. He said to his people, "Look, the people of Israel now outnumber us and are stronger than we are. We must make a plan to keep them from growing even more. If we don't, and if war breaks out, they will join our enemies and fight against us. Then they will escape from the country."

So, the Egyptians made the Israelites their slaves. They appointed brutal slave drivers over them, hoping to wear them down with crushing labor. They forced them to build the cities of Pithom and Rameses as supply centers for the king. But the more the Egyptians oppressed them, the more the Israelites multiplied and spread, and the more alarmed the Egyptians became. So the Egyptians worked the people of Israel without mercy. They made their lives bitter, forcing them to mix mortar and make bricks and do all the work in the fields. They were ruthless in all their demands.

Then Pharaoh, the king of Egypt, gave this order to the Hebrew midwives, Shiphrah and Puah: "When you help the Hebrew women as they give birth, watch as they deliver. If the baby is a boy, kill him; if it is a girl, let her live." (Exodus 1:8-16)

## DESPITE THE APPARENT IMPORTANCE OF MEN BEING PRESENT IN HOMES AND COMMUNITIES, THEY ARE THE MOST INCARCERATED AND OPPRESSED OF ALL PEOPLE.

PRB: "Men make up 90 percent of the prison and local jail population, and they have an imprisonment rate 14 times higher than the rate for women. And these men are overwhelmingly young: Incarceration rates are highest for those in their 20s and early 30s." (Scommeegna, 2012)

## THE OBJECTIVE:

The man is the head of the family, the leader. "But there is one thing I want you to know: The head of every man is Christ, the head of woman is man, and the head of Christ is God." (1 Corinthians 11:3)

This means that when the man (the head) is cut off or taken away from the family (the body), the family is left to wander without direction, making it easier for them to be controlled by society (darkness).

It's similar to Christ, who is the head of the Church. If He is cut off, the Church (the Body of Christ), which is us, would be lost.

**Final Call – Willie Lynch Letter:** "Keep the body, take the mind! In other words, break the will to resist. Now the breaking process is the same for both the horse and the nigger, only slightly varying in degrees. But, as we said before, there is an art in long range economic planning. You must keep your eye and thoughts on the female and the offspring of the horse and the nigger. A brief discourse in offspring development will shed light on the key to sound economic principles. Pay little attention to the generation of original breaking but concentrate on future generations.

Therefore, if you break the female mother, she will break the offspring in its early years of development; and when the offspring is old enough to work, she will deliver it up to you, for her normal female protective tendencies will have been lost in the original breaking process.

For example, take the case of the wild stud horse, a female horse and an already infant horse and compare the breaking process with two captured nigger males in their natural state, a pregnant nigger woman with her infant offspring. Take the stud horse, break him for limited containment.

Completely break the female horse until she becomes very gentle, whereas you or anybody can ride her in her comfort. Breed the mare and the stud until you have the desired offspring. Then, you can turn the stud to freedom until you need him again. Train the female horse whereby she will eat out of your hand, and she will in turn train the infant horse to eat out of your hand, also. When it comes to breaking the uncivilized nigger, use the same process, but vary the degree and step up the pressure, so as to do a complete reversal of the mind. Take the meanest and most restless nigger, strip him of his clothes in front of the remaining male niggers, the female, and the nigger infant, tar and feather him, tie each leg to a different horse faced in opposite directions, set him afire and beat both horses to pull him apart in front of the remaining niggers. The next step is to take a bullwhip and beat the remaining nigger males to the point of death, in front of the female and the infant. Don't kill him, but put the fear of God in him, for he can be useful for future breeding." (Willie Lynch Letter: The Making of a Slave)

**IF ONE CAN USE THE OPPRESSIVE SYSTEMS IN SOCIETY TO BREAK DOWN AND KILL THE WAY A MAN SEES HIMSELF, ONE CAN DESTROY HOW HE THINKS OF HIMSELF. FURTHERMORE, KILLING THAT MAN'S ABILITY TO BE THE LEADER GOD CALLED HIM TO BE.**

A man being incarcerated and oppressed is degrading; it takes away his sense of self-worth. For this reason, the devil uses the oppressive systems in society, such as prisons and jails, to entrap men because doing so helps enslave women and their children.

Remember the rule of thumb: "keep the body, take the mind". In other words, "keep the family (body), take the man (head–mind)".

**Side Note:** *The devil uses prisons and jails to physically and spiritually sever households and families by cutting off the man who is the head (leader) of the body (family), thus leading the remainder into darkness.*

**Sever:**

- To separate (a part) from the whole, as by cutting or the like.

- To divide into parts, especially forcibly; cleave.

- Disunite.

- To become separated from each other.

The woman will often blindly kill herself to make sure the family's needs are met when the male figure is no longer present. This leaves the children open to being attacked.

If the children have no one there to lead and guide them, they become lost. Or puppets that wind up incarcerated or overworked and stressed just like their parents. This happens because the head (man) contains the eyes, and without the eyes, no light is let in the body, making it hard for the family to see. My people perish from a Lack of Vision.

**THE WOMAN, IN NO CIRCUMSTANCE, NO MATTER HOW YOU CUT IT OR SLICE IT, IS MEANT TO PLAY THE ROLE OF A MAN. BUT, BECAUSE OF THE PAIN SHE'S ENDURED, SHE'S BLINDED AND LACKS VISION; THEREFORE, SHE CANNOT SEE THE TRUTH HIDDEN WITHIN THE LIES.**

From the time I spent alone reading my Bible, I learned a lot about the importance of being broken down, or should I say being gracefully broken to be built up by God. "The Lord is near to the broken-hearted and saves those who are crushed in spirit." (Psalm 34:18) "In Him the whole building is fitted together and grows into a holy temple in the Lord. And in Him you too are being built together into a dwelling place for God in His Spirit." (Ephesians 2:21-22)

> **Side Note:** *God often uses the circumstances a person goes through in life to open their eyes to the brokenness that lies within their heart. To push them to lose their lives and what they used to be (prideful and hurtful) for a life of righteousness (love and unity). "Whoever finds their life will lose it, and whoever loses their life for my sake will find it." (Matthew 10:37)*

After a person is allowed to see their mistakes, they are then given a choice to change and be built up by God in His image.

**The Problem:**

- As a woman, being in a situation that's taken a turn for the worse, that truth, God's truth, is not necessarily what is seen.

**What a woman sees when she's been blinded by pain:**

- Someone who left her to raise the children alone.

- Someone who could never love her as she needed.

- Someone who has abandoned her.

*Or should I say that woman sees what the devil has conditioned her to see.*

## WHEN YOU START TO BELIEVE THE MADE-UP FIGMENTS OF SOCIETY, YOU BEGIN TO CON- FORM TO WHAT THEY SAY.

After a while, the woman begins to think the dreams she once had with the man she loves could never come true. Or no man will ever be good enough because, according to society, they're all the same.

I even started to fall into a place of hypnotism. I started believing the lies—the lies that culture and society tell you.

I had a hard time believing that I could stay strong and be there for my loved one when he was weak and in need because our relationship had not always been stable. He betrayed my trust in the past, causing me a type of pain that words cannot explain. Yet still, there I was on the other end of a jail call, having to make a tough decision.

Do I believe God could help my loved one become a better person, not for me but for himself? Or do I believe the lies of society and use the power I had been given to turn away from him, making him feel the pain I'd felt when he'd hurt me.

## THE DEVIL USES A MAN'S PRIDE AGAINST HIM AND THE HURT OF A WOMAN TO DEVOUR HIM.

Men and women, every day, are killing one another by spewing words that are degrading and displaying hurtful actions.

### The Issue:

- When doing so, we become so distracted by the other person's actions that we cannot see the truth...

## WE NEED EACH OTHER MORE THAN WE THINK.

Men and women are meant to be a force that stands back-to-back to support one another. When that union is strongest, the power of the two is magnified—making them unstoppable. "Two people are better off than one, for they can help each other succeed. If one person falls, the other can reach out and help. But someone who falls alone is in real trouble. Likewise, two people lying close together can keep each other warm. But how can one be warm alone? A person standing alone can be attacked and defeated, but two can stand back-to-back and conquer." (Ecclesiastes 4:9-12)

**Side Note:** *The devil knows the power of unity, so he pits men and women against one another.*

People who unite together in love have the power to change the world. Disunity, on the other hand, creates a hostile and hateful environment that destroys the world and the people in it.

This means if the devil can cause separation and dysfunction between you and your spouse, he can use those negative images to corrupt the world.

To go more in-depth, your children will eventually begin to become what they see. They will start to replicate the dysfunctional behavior you let take hold of you—creating a generational curse. Meaning their children and their children's children will be prideful, hateful, hurtful, and dysfunctional, just like you! Need I say it again "we need each other more than we think".

## IT ONLY TAKES ONE FAMILY TO DUPLICATE AND MASS-PRODUCE A GENERATIONAL CURSE.

The problems that currently occur within homes that are broken started with the pride of Adam and the hurt of Eve. "Then the man and his wife heard the sound of the Lord God as he was walking in the garden in the cool of the day, and they hid from the Lord God among the trees of the garden. But the Lord God called to the man, "Where are you?" He answered, "I heard you in the garden, and I was afraid because I was naked; so I hid." And he said, "Who told you that you were naked? Have you eaten from the tree that I commanded you not to eat from?" The man said, "The woman you put here with me—she gave me some fruit from the tree, and I ate it." Then the Lord God said to the woman, "What is this you have done?" The woman said, "The serpent deceived me, and I ate." (Genesis 3:8-13)

Adam was naked (vulnerable), which led to him being ashamed and afraid. His shame led to pride which led to his inability to admit his wrongs.

Eve, on the other hand, was hurt not only because Adam did not stand up for her but also because of the pressure, expectations, and blame that was placed on her. Eve was left alone to tend to the garden (household) and make the decisions for the family because Adam (the head of the household) was not present. Both their dysfunction and fighting led their children to do the same.

When it was all said and done, the chain of events that started with the pride of Adam and the hurt of Eve led to one child killing the other. "Now Cain said to his brother Abel, "Let's go out to the field." While they were in the field, Cain attacked his brother Abel and killed him." (Genesis 4:8)

In turn, this created a nation of dysfunctional people—a generational curse. "The Lord said, "What have you done? Listen! Your brother's blood cries out to me from the ground. Now you are under a curse and driven from the ground, which opened its mouth to receive your brother's blood from your hand. When you work the ground, it will no longer yield its crops for you. You will be a restless wanderer on the earth." (Genesis 4:10-12)

**THIS VICIOUS GENERATIONAL CURSE IS BEING RAPIDLY REPRODUCED BY THE YOUNGER GENERATION, MY GENERATION—THE YOUNG AND THE RESTLESS.**

The curse starts with the young man. The young man was broken down in front of the young woman. This caused the young woman to degrade him. Eventually, the young man became prideful; he decided he needed to prove himself and not let anyone see the "real" him.

**SOCIETY AND CULTURE HAVE MADE MEN FEEL LIKE THEY CAN'T EXPRESS THEIR FEELINGS, MAKING IT HARD FOR ANYONE TO ADDRESS THEIR FEELINGS.**

We are raised in a society that teaches men to mask what they really feel by using filters to make life look good when really, he's dying inside for some attention and likes. That man may post pictures that say everything's okay, but deep down inside, he's screaming, "please save me".

**The Issue:**

- He refuses to move his lips, afraid of how someone may see him.

- A person can't address a man's feelings if he pretends to have none.

59

- A person can't fix what someone leads them to believe isn't broken.

In society, it is said that a man should not cry, a man should not hurt, and a man should not have feelings. But what is failed to see is the "huMAN" in every man. Men are still human, and with that comes those feelings.

## ON THE OTHER HAND, NOT MANY YOUNG WOMEN KNOW THEMSELVES, BELIEVE IN THEMSELVES, AND LOVE AND RESPECT THEMSELVES.

The pressure and expectations placed on women by society lead them to believe they must please men first, be loved last, and find ways to use their sexuality to be accepted.

**The Issue:**

- Life starts with the young woman because children are birthed through her. And when that young woman doesn't believe in or love herself, she instills that same mentality in her children; it's a circle of life.

## BROKEN PEOPLE ARE IN BROKEN RELATIONSHIPS THAT PRODUCE BROKEN CHILDREN AND CREATE A BROKEN SOCIETY.

Let's look at things from the perspective of a young man being left to be raised by a single mother.

When a single mother is left alone to raise the children, she often feels as if she must constantly put on her best warrior face. Showing no hurt or pain to make her children believe all is well.

> **Side Note:** *The tune of life called "All is Well" starts to play its melody in the household when a mother is left alone to raise the kids. This leads to a false façade of what a happy home looks like. It also teaches the child to mask their feelings, as previously mentioned.*

All is well, so my child can be happy. All is well, so my child does not have to worry. All is well because I want my child to have a chance to live a normal life like everyone else.

The thought a mother has is, "my child deserves a normal life, given they didn't ask to be born".

All the while, that woman, that mother, is dying inside. Not knowing to give her child the tools they need to succeed in life, the child needs to have both role models in front of them: mother and father.

So, all is not well because she does hurt. She does feel pain but puts on a mask that makes her child think tears don't exist.

**The Issue:**

- The young man can never learn nor understand the concept of being able to show his feelings without fear.

**The Result:**

- A young man with broken values and no sense of humility

or humanity (cold-hearted). Why? Because what that young man sees when he looks at his mother is power without pain. Therefore, when he grows up, he believes he should be the same. He doesn't think he should cry. He doesn't think he should be vulnerable. And doesn't think he should have feelings because that's what he's used to seeing when he looks at his mother.

### The Bigger Issue:

- The young man doesn't know the danger of power without pain.

For this reason, it is dangerous for children to be brought up by a single parent. A man cannot be a woman, and a woman cannot be a man. This confuses the child.

## IF A CHILD DOES NOT HAVE BOTH PARENTS, THEY ONLY SEE ONE SIDE OF A STORY AND THE ABSENCE OF THE OTHER.

People are sending their children out in the world only half-filled because that's all they have to offer—the piece of them they were created to be, which is either a man or a woman, the disunity.

You can never be both man and woman no matter how hard you try. But being young and restless, children are created from meaningless relationships that one or the other person never intended to stay in.

For example, a young woman, young and restless, creates a child with a man because he has money, and all she wants is a way out.

Or a young man, young and restless, crying out to be accepted, yet no woman can fully give him what he's looking for. Therefore, he jumps from one woman to the next, birthing children with each of them yet committing to none of them.

**LISTEN, YOU'RE YOUNG, AND YOU'RE RESTLESS. WALKING AROUND LIKE YOU HAVE NO HOPE AND A DEATH WISH. BUT JUST BECAUSE YOUR RELATIONSHIP DIDN'T WORK OUT DOESN'T MEAN YOUR CHILDREN SHOULD HAVE TO SUFFER IN THE LONG RUN.**

With that being said, do not break a family if you make a family because you're causing more harm than you could ever know. The child should not have to pay for the sins of his or her father or mother.

Men don't tear down your women, and women, don't tear down your men. Look into the eyes of the children; it can have a significant effect on them.

To recap, the devil starts by breaking you down because your children become what they see, creating a ripple effect. For this reason, husbands, wives, fathers, and mothers need to create images of love.

Even without having your own children to see, your union represents God's love for us. If we hate one another, we show that to the world. And not only to the people of the world but also to the children who live in this world. They start to believe hatred and dysfunction is the only thing a relationship has to offer.

Also, think about it this way. How can we create better lives or even build successful businesses if there is always constant bickering and arguing? To build better lives, we have to learn to build better relationships.

**ARE YOUR ENDEAVORS SUFFERING BECAUSE THE AIR YOU BREATHE HAS BECOME POISONOUS DUE TO SOMEONE ELSE'S WORDS? OR ARE YOU BEING SOMEONE'S BREATH OF FRESH AIR?**

"A wise woman builds her home, but a foolish woman tears it down with her own hands." (Proverbs 14:1) "By wisdom a house is built, and through understanding it is established." (Proverbs 24:3)

God wants you to be a representation of Him so that the children and generations to come that you create or the children that see and look up to you will be made in His image as well.

**WE'RE BETTER TOGETHER, AND I HOPE THAT LETTER DIDN'T BREAK US FOREVER.**

"For wives, this means submit to your husbands as to the Lord. For a husband is the head of his wife as Christ is the head of the church.

He is the Saviour of his body, the church. As the church submits to Christ, so you wives should submit to your husbands in everything. For husbands, this means love your wives, just as Christ loved the church. He gave up his life for her to make her holy and clean, washed by the cleansing of God's word. He did this to present her to himself as a glorious church without a spot or wrinkle or any other blemish. Instead, she will be holy and without fault. In the same way, husbands ought to love their wives as they love their own bodies. For a man who loves his wife actually shows love for himself. No one hates his own body but feeds and cares for it, just as Christ cares for the church. And we are members of his body. As the Scriptures say, "A man leaves his father and mother and is joined to his wife, and the two are united into one." This is a great mystery, but it is an illustration of the way Christ and the church are one. So again, I say, each man must love his wife as he loves himself, and the wife must respect her husband." (Ephesians 5:22-30)

The man has to go out every day and be broken down by society telling him what he's not or can't be. But the damage really occurs when he comes home, and his woman tells him the same.

He has to go into the world and be broken; he shouldn't have to come home to it too. If he's hurting enough out in the world, his home, his safe haven, should be where he can go and be put back together again.

If Humpty Dumpty sat on the wall and Humpty Dumpty had a great fall, and all the devil's hoes and all the devil's tricks couldn't put him back together again, his woman should be able to.

In reality, all a man wants is a woman who loves him. A woman who puts him back together when society breaks him down.

## IF A MAN HAS NO ONE TO PUT HIM BACK TOGETHER OR HOLD HIM UP, HE EVENTUALLY BREAKS OR FALLS, AND VICE VERSA.

A man can't be strong, or should I say, Superman, all the time. Like anyone else, a man needs someplace to rest and regenerate; he needs someplace to be put back together. That's where the nurturing of the woman, the rib of the man, and the body's support system come into play. "It is not good for the man to be alone. "Then the LORD God said, "I will make a helper who is just right for him." (Genesis 2:18) "Then the LORD God made a woman from the rib he had taken out of the man, and he brought her to the man." (Genesis 2:22)

> **Side Note:** *When a man goes out into the world, he may come home broken due to stress and pressure. His woman being a nurturer, is meant to be his shoulder to cry on, his nurse who patches up his wounds and puts him back together.*

## THE WOMAN IS THE MAN'S SAFE HAVEN.

**Safe Haven:**

- A place of refuge or security.

- Temporary refuge given to a persecuted person or group.

**Woman-Haven:**

- A place where the man can run to without fear of being judged.

- A place where the man is not afraid to be himself.

- A place where the man can take off his armor, be naked, and not ashamed.

- A place where the man can be vulnerable.

- A place where the man can be down because he knows his woman will eventually pick him up.

> **Side Note:** *Stop looking for someone that holds you down; they are only useful for that—to keep you down. Read Judges 16 in the Bible if you need a visual. This will help you learn how to acknowledge someone who picks you up and dust you off if you fall.*

In the beginning, when my loved one was first incarcerated, he was down, hurting, and broken. But as time passed, I began to see the broken pieces of him become the best parts of him as God molded him in His image. He started to change in ways my nagging words could never tell him how.

**The Key:**

- Love and unity.

My loved one being broken is what allowed me to see his vulnerable side. His vulnerable side allowed me to see the huMAN and the love that lies within the man. It touched my heart and changed my mind about all the pain from the past.

His vulnerable side opened my heart, making it possible for me to love him despite his weaknesses.

Me loving him despite his weaknesses allowed him to experience love in a way he'd never known was possible. This, in turn, opened his heart, making it possible for God to mold him and chip away at his tough (prideful) exterior. He was naked and no longer ashamed; he was not afraid to cry; he could be his true self. He could be vulnerable and love me the same way I loved him through sickness and health.

**WE REALLY DON'T KNOW HOW MUCH POWER UNITY HAS, DO WE? I THINK IF WE DID, WE WOULD SEE PAST THE HATE AND THE HURT AND RECOGNIZE THAT WE'RE ALL ONLY HUMAN.**

"Mistakes, I know I've made a few. But I'm only human, you've made mistakes, too."

— *Smokey Robinson*

**Heavenly Father,** You know our coming in and going out. I could never escape your magnificence. As you give us the gift of your presence, I want to thank you for sending your son Jesus to die on the cross for our sins. We could never truly show how grateful and appreciative we are of it.

I pray that as your children, we walk and lead a life as examples of your righteousness. Understanding that love is patient and love is kind, we submit ourselves to you, asking that you search our hearts. Shape us, make us, and mold us as you see fit.

Heavenly Father, I pray that you give us the ability to see that we are not perfect people, but even in those events and moments where we may feel as though we have failed, we still have the victory because you are victory. And as your children, you reside within us, giving us all you are.

I pray that you give us faith enough to know that no weapon formed against us shall prosper, and even when it seems like we are down, you grant us the grace to recognize and learn from our mistakes, which continuously make us stronger. Because what the enemy meant for evil, the Lord means for good. As we grow, I pray that we may grow in unity together, not condemning one another but understanding that we are all human, and none of us are perfect. Instead of only seeing faults, grant that we may see things as you do, recognizing the good while pushing each other to become great. As we develop a deeper relationship with you, may there be joy and peace on earth as it is in heaven.

In Jesus' name, Amen!

# CHAPTER 4

# THE GREAT PROSTITUTE

*Revelation:*

- *A surprising and previously unknown fact, especially one that is made known in a dramatic way.*

- *The divine or supernatural disclosure to humans of something relating to human existence or the world.*

- *Truth Revealed.*

**Deuteronomy 31:16-21** NIV "And the Lord said to Moses: "You are going to rest with your ancestors, and these people will soon prostitute themselves to the foreign Gods of the land they are entering. They will forsake me and break the covenant I made with them. And in that day I will become angry with them and forsake them; I will hide my face from them, and they will be destroyed. Many disasters and calamities will come on them, and in that day they will ask, 'Have not these disasters come on us because our God is not with us?' And I will certainly hide my face in that day because of all their wickedness in turning to other Gods.

Now write down this song and teach it to the Israelites and have them sing it, so that it may be a witness for me against them. When

I have brought them into the land flowing with milk and honey, the land I promised on oath to their ancestors, and when they eat their fill and thrive, they will turn to other Gods and worship them, rejecting me and breaking my covenant. And when many disasters and calamities come on them, this song will testify against them, because it will not be forgotten by their descendants. I know what they are disposed to do, even before I bring them into the land I promised them on oath."

## THE GREAT PROSTITUTE (POEM)

### The Frailty of Humanity and our Mentality

We're young, and we're restless.

Walking around like we have no hope and a death wish.

We're weak, but we can't admit it.

Because pride says, I have to go put on these Louis Vuitton's and go get fitted.

You are tempted to tell people, "I'm better than you". But the better in you has on a mask at a ball 24/7 my dude.

Patsies are what you are; they use your face to commit genocide amongst your own and leave real deep scars.

Lacerations to the face cuts to the spirit and soul. They are using your image to line 'em up and sell off your own.

And we knee-deep in this, but we can't get out. Because the more we try to, the more people scream it's a drought.

Yet, when the rain comes, you pray to God, please take me back. Laid up in a shed, drowned out in a shack.

You see, nobody cares about you like the way God does, but you're out here trying to be gangstas, hoes, and thugs.

All to get that money they throw. You're chasing the things that people have made you believe will add depth to your life and help you grow.

But contrary to their actions, they are not selling their souls to the devil. They're selling yours. Because you follow these people like their life is a tour.

Yet the only tour you're going on is to Iraq. That trip that you take and might not come back.

A war zone of hell, hate, fear, and pain. Led by the wrong people and bought by the wrong game.

They're selling your soul while they're feeding their fame.

## BUT YOU MUST HAVE FORGOT; THE GREAT PROSTITUTE IS THE NAME OF THE GAME.

The great prostitute has risen, throwing people in jail, killing people in prisons (the mind).

And she's not who you think. She's not that girl on Instagram bending over at the sink.

She's filling people with spirits of anger and hate because we're not supposed to covet, yet we find ourselves on social media desiring what's on somebody else's plate.

They say the mind is a terrible thing to waste, yet you'd give it away freely for a bag and a date.

Sell yourself off to the highest bidder. Put her on a dress that's too tight to fit her.

Show her to the world so they can see her shame because the great prostitute is the name of the game.

A higher society (Illuminati), some would say people are selling their souls in exchange for money and fame, yet the only one being bought is you. God doesn't owe you anything, so you need to start acting as if you owe Him everything.

## TO BE A PROSTITUTE IS TO BE SOLD; IT'S NOT JUST A WOMAN SELLING HER BODY. IT'S YOU, SELLING YOUR SOUL.

**The Doom of Babylon:** "Then one of the seven angels who had the seven bowls came and spoke with me, saying, "Come here, I will show you the judgment and doom of the great prostitute who is seated on many waters [influencing nations]. She with whom the kings of the earth have committed acts of immorality, and the inhabitants of the earth have become intoxicated with the wine of her immorality." And the angel carried me away in the Spirit into a wilderness; and I saw a woman sitting on a scarlet beast that was entirely covered with blasphemous names, having seven heads and ten horns. The woman was dressed in purple and scarlet, and adorned with gold, precious stones and pearls, [and she was] holding in her hand a gold cup full of the abominations and the filth of her [sexual] immorality. And on her forehead a name was written, a mystery: "BABYLON THE GREAT, THE MOTHER OF PROSTITUTES (false religions, heresies) AND OF THE ABOMINATIONS OF THE EARTH." I saw that the woman was drunk with the blood of the saints (God's people) and with the blood of the witnesses of Jesus [who were martyred]. When I saw her, I wondered in amazement. But the angel said to me, "Why do you wonder? I will explain to you the mystery of the woman and of the beast that carries her, which has the seven heads and ten horns.

"The beast that you saw was [once], but [now] is not, and he is about to come up out of the abyss (the bottomless pit, the dwelling place of demons) and go to destruction (perdition). And the inhabitants of the earth, whose names have not been written in the Book of Life from the foundation of the world, will be astonished when they see the beast, because he was and is not and is yet to come [to earth]. Here is the mind, which has wisdom [and this is what it knows about the vision]. The seven heads are seven hills on which the woman sits; and they are seven kings: five of whom have fallen, one exists and is reigning; the other [the seventh] has not yet come, and when he does come, he must remain a little while. And the beast that [once] was but is not, is himself also an eighth king and is one of the seven, and he goes to destruction (perdition). The ten horns that you saw are ten kings who have not yet received a kingdom, but [together] they receive authority as kings for a single hour [for a common purpose] along with the beast. These [kings] have one purpose [one mind, one common goal], and they give their power and authority to the beast.

## VICTORY FOR THE LAMB

They will wage war against the Lamb (Christ), and the Lamb will triumph and conquer them, because He is Lord of Lords and King of kings, and those who are with him and on His side are the called and chosen (elect) and faithful.

Then the angel said to me, "The waters which you saw, where the prostitute is seated, are peoples and multitudes and nations and languages. And the ten horns which you saw, and the beast, these will hate the prostitute and will make her desolate and naked [stripped of her power and influence] and will eat her flesh and completely consume her with fire. For God has put it in their hearts to carry out His purpose by agreeing together to surrender their kingdom to the beast, until the [prophetic] words of God will be fulfilled. The woman whom you saw is the great city, which reigns over and dominates and controls the kings and the political leaders of the earth." (Revelation 17:1-18)

Babylon is Fallen: "After these things I saw another angel coming down from heaven, possessing great authority, and the earth was illuminated with his splendor and radiance. And he shouted with a mighty voice, saying, "Fallen, fallen [certainly to be destroyed] is Babylon the great! She has become a dwelling place for demons, a dungeon haunted by every unclean spirit, and a prison for every unclean and loathsome bird. For all the nations have drunk from the wine of the passion of her [sexual] immorality, and the kings and political leaders of the earth have committed immorality with her, and the merchants of the earth have become rich by the wealth and economic power of her sensuous luxury."

And I heard another voice from heaven, saying, "Come out of her, my people, so that you will not be a partner in her sins and receive her plagues; for her sins (crimes, transgressions) have piled up as high as heaven, and God has remembered her wickedness and crimes [for judgment]. Repay to her even as she has repaid others, and pay back [to her] double [her torment] in accordance with what she has done; in the cup [of sin and suffering] which she mixed, mix a double portion [of perfect justice] for her. To the degree that she glorified herself and reveled and gloated in her sensuality [living deliciously and luxuriously], to that same degree impose on her torment and anguish, and mourning and grief; for in her heart she boasts, 'I sit as a queen [on a throne] and I am not a widow, and will never, ever see mourning or experience grief.' For this reason in a single day her plagues (afflictions, calamities) will come, pestilence and mourning and famine, and she will be burned up with fire and completely consumed; for strong and powerful is the Lord God who judges her.

**Laments for Babylon:** "And the kings and political leaders of the earth, who committed immorality and lived luxuriously with her, will weep and beat their chests [in mourning] over her when they see the smoke of her burning, standing a long way off, in fear of her torment, saying, 'Woe, woe, the great city, the strong city, Babylon! In a single hour your judgment has come.'

"And merchants of the earth will weep and grieve over her, because no one buys their cargo (goods, merchandise) anymore— cargoes of gold and silver and precious stones and pearls and fine linen and purple and silk and scarlet; all kinds of citron (scented) wood and every article of ivory and every article of very costly and lavish wood and bronze and iron and marble; and cinnamon and spices and incense and perfume and frankincense and wine and olive oil and fine flour and wheat; of cattle and sheep, and cargoes of horses and chariots and carriages; and of slaves and human lives. The ripe fruits and delicacies of your soul's desire have gone from you, and all things that were luxurious and extravagant are lost to you, never again to be found. The merchants who handled these articles, who grew wealthy from [their business with] her, will stand a long way off in fear of her torment, weeping and mourning aloud, saying, 'Woe, woe, for the great city that was robed in fine linen, in purple and scarlet, gilded and adorned with gold, with precious stones, and with pearls; because in one hour all the vast wealth has been laid waste.' And every ship captain or navigator, and every passenger and sailor, and all who make their living by the sea, stood a long way off, and exclaimed as they watched the smoke of her burning, saying, 'What could be compared to the great city?' And they threw dust on their heads and were crying out, weeping and mourning, saying, 'Woe, woe, for the great city, where all who had ships at sea grew rich from her great wealth, because in one hour she has been laid waste!' Rejoice over her, O heaven, and you saints (God's people) and apostles and prophets [who were martyred], because God has executed vengeance for you [through righteous judgment] upon her."

**The Divine Sentence upon Babylon:** Then a single powerful angel picked up a boulder like a great millstone and flung it into the sea, saying, "With such violence will Babylon the great city be hurled down [by the sudden, spectacular judgment of God], and will never again be found. And the sound of harpists and musicians and flutists and trumpeters will never again be heard in you, and no skilled artisan of any craft will ever again be found in you, and the sound of the millstone [grinding grain] will never again be heard in you [for commerce will no longer flourish, and normal life will cease]. And never again will the light of a lamp shine in you, and never again will the voice of the bridegroom and bride be heard in you; for your merchants were the great and prominent men of the earth, because all the nations were deceived and misled by your sorcery [your magic spells and poisonous charm]. And in Babylon was found the blood of prophets and of saints (God's people) and of all those who have been slaughtered on the earth." (Revelation 18:1-24)

## ARE YOU GOING TO WAKE UP AND SEE THE REVELATION (TRUTH) OR DIE BEFORE YOU GET THE CHANCE TO EXPERIENCE IT?

||||||||||||||||||||||||||||||||||||||||||||||||||||||||||||||||||||||||||||||||||||||||||||||||||||||||||||||

"We often need to lose sight of our priorities in order to see them."

— *John Irving*

||||||||||||||||||||||||||||||||||||||||||||||||||||||||||||||||||||||||||||||||||||||||||||||||||||||||||||||

# CHAPTER 5

# HEART OF THE HURRICANE

*There are always moments in life when things get so hard, and we are incapable of recognizing what matters. Or maybe it gets so good that we forget how it got so good in the first place. Perhaps you forgot the sickness you overcame, the death that almost knocked down your door as if it didn't recognize the blood that said PASSOVER. You see, God wants you to turn away from your pride, your sin, and yourself. Your days of thinking you can do bad all by yourself or nobody will be able to say anything when you get to where you are going because you did it all on your own. You see, your first mistake is believing you can do it all on your own—your second mistake is thinking you've gotten to where you are by your power alone.*

Jeremiah 2:1-37 NLT The Lord's Case against His People: "The Lord gave me another message. He said, "Go and shout this message to Jerusalem. This is what the Lord says: "I remember how eager you were to please me as a young bride long ago, how you loved me and followed me even through the barren wilderness. In those days Israel was holy to the Lord, the first of his children. All who harmed his people were declared guilty, and disaster fell on them. I, the Lord, have spoken!" Listen to the word of the Lord, people of Jacob—all you families of Israel! This is what the Lord says: "What did your ancestors find wrong with me that led them to stray so far from me? They worshiped worthless idols, only to become worthless themselves. They did not ask, 'Where is the Lord who brought us safely out of Egypt and led us through the barren wilderness—a land of deserts and pits, a land of drought and death, where no one lives or even travels? "And when I brought you into a fruitful land to enjoy its bounty and goodness, you defiled my land and corrupted the possession I had promised you. The priests did not ask, 'Where is the Lord?' Those who taught my word ignored me, the rulers turned against me, and the prophets spoke in the name of Baal, wasting their time on worthless idols. Therefore, I will bring my case against you," says the Lord. "I will even bring charges against your children's children in the years to come.

"Go west and look in the land of Cyprus; go east and search through the land of Kedar.

Has anyone ever heard of anything as strange as this? Has any nation ever traded its gods for new ones, even though they are not gods at all? Yet my people have exchanged their glorious God for worthless idols! The heavens are shocked at such a thing and shrink back in horror and dismay," says the Lord. "For my people have done two evil things: They have abandoned me—the fountain of living water. And they have dug for themselves cracked cisterns that can hold no water at all!

**The Results of Israel's Sin:** "Why has Israel become a slave? Why has he been carried away as plunder? Strong lions have roared against him, and the land has been destroyed. The towns are now in ruins, and no one lives in them anymore. Egyptians, marching from their cities of Memphis and Tahpanhes, have destroyed Israel's glory and power. And you have brought this upon yourselves by rebelling against the Lord your God, even though he was leading you on the way! "What have you gained by your alliances with Egypt and your covenants with Assyria? What good to you are the streams of the Nile or the waters of the Euphrates River? Your wickedness will bring its own punishment. Your turning from me will shame you. You will see what an evil, bitter thing it is to abandon the Lord your God and not to fear him. I, the Lord, the Lord of Heaven's Armies, have spoken!

"Long ago I broke the yoke that oppressed you and tore away the chains of your slavery, but still you said, 'I will not serve you.' On every hill and under every green tree, you have prostituted yourselves by bowing down to idols. But I was the one who planted you, choosing a vine of the purest stock—the very best. How did you grow into this corrupt wild vine? No amount of soap or lye can make you clean. I still see the stain of your guilt. I, the Sovereign Lord, have spoken!

**Israel, an Unfaithful Wife:** "You say, 'That's not true! I haven't worshiped the images of Baal!' But how can you say that? Go and look in any valley in the land! Face the awful sins you have done. You are like a restless female camel desperately searching for a mate. You are like a wild donkey, sniffing the wind at mating time. Who can restrain her lust? Those who desire her don't need to search, for she goes running to them! When will you stop running? When will you stop panting after other gods? But you say, 'Save your breath. I'm in love with these foreign gods, and I can't stop loving them now!'

"Israel is like a thief who feels shame only when he gets caught. They, their kings, officials, priests, and prophets—all are alike in this. To an image carved from a piece of wood they say, 'You are my father.' To an idol chiseled from a block of stone they say, 'You are my mother. They turn their backs on me, but in times of trouble they cry out to me, 'Come and save us!' But why not call on these gods you have made? When trouble comes, let them save you if they can! For you have as many gods as there are towns in Judah.

Why do you accuse me of doing wrong? You are the ones who have rebelled," says the Lord. "I have punished your children, but they did not respond to my discipline. You yourselves have killed your prophets as a lion kills its prey "O my people, listen to the words of the Lord! Have I been like a desert to Israel? Have I been to them a land of darkness? Why then do my people say, 'At last we are free from God! We don't need him anymore!' Does a young woman forget her jewelry, or a bride her wedding dress? Yet for years on end my people have forgotten me. "How you plot and scheme to win your lovers. Even an experienced prostitute could learn from you! Your clothing is stained with the blood of the innocent and the poor, though you didn't catch them breaking into your houses! And yet you say, 'I have done nothing wrong. Surely God isn't angry with me!' But now I will punish you severely because you claim you have not sinned. First here, then there—you flit from one ally to another asking for help. But your new friends in Egypt will let you down, just as Assyria did before. In despair, you will be led into exile with your hands on your heads, for the Lord has rejected the nations you trust. They will not help you at all."

## I HAVE A "WOULD YOU RATHER CHALLENGE".

Would you rather have the calm before the storm, the rain before the hail, the lightning before the crash of thunder? Or, the protection of prayer, the belt of truth, the breastplate of righteousness, the shield of faith, the helmet of salvation, the sword of the Spirit, and the shoes of peace? By the time you're done reading this chapter, I hope you've come to a clear decision, chosen, and made up your mind.

According to research, tropical storms form in the Atlantic Ocean every year. And every year, the weather is tracked for hurricanes in hopes of notifying people so that they may be able to prepare in advance for the destruction that is to be expected.

## WHEN DO HURRICANES OCCUR?

**Ducksters Education Site:** "Hurricanes that form in the Caribbean and the Atlantic Ocean occur between June 1st and November 30th each year. This is called hurricane season." (Earth Science for Kids)

## HOW ARE HURRICANES TRACKED?

**NASA Space Place:** "The two GOES satellites keep their eyes on hurricanes from far above Earth's surface—22,300 miles above, to be exact!

These satellites, built by NASA and operated by the National Oceanic and Atmospheric Administration (NOAA), save lives by helping weather forecasters predict and warn people where and when these severe storms will hit land." (How Do Hurricanes Form?, 2019)

## BUT HURRICANES ARE NOT ALWAYS THIS DESTRUCTIVE, ARE THEY?

**VOA News:** (SEPTEMBER 08, 2017) "Three powerful ocean storms threaten the Caribbean, the coast of the Southeastern United States, and Southeastern Mexico.

Hurricane Irma has struck Cuba and now threatens the state of Florida with strong winds and rain. The storm has caused deaths and widespread destruction on several Caribbean islands. Hurricane Katia is in the southern Gulf of Mexico. It is nearing Mexico's eastern coast, and Hurricane Jose is gaining strength in the Atlantic Ocean.

The three hurricanes come as the state of Texas recovers from Hurricane Harvey. The huge storm caused severe flooding and billions of dollars in damage in Houston, the country's fourth largest city." (Ritter, 2017)

> **Side Note:** *Just as the storms that form in the Atlantic give warning signs to people in the event of danger, so does God. He gives us and is still giving us signs and time to prepare so that He can protect us from the storm. Hopefully, you'll seek His protection before it's too late.*

**Jesus Speaks about the Future:** "As Jesus was leaving the Temple grounds, his disciples pointed out to him the various Temple buildings. But he responded, "Do you see all these buildings? I tell you the truth, they will be completely demolished. Not one stone will be left on top of another!"

Later, Jesus sat on the Mount of Olives. His disciples came to him privately and said, "Tell us, when will all this happen? What sign will signal your return and the end of the world?"

Jesus told them, "Don't let anyone mislead you, for many will come in my name, claiming, 'I am the Messiah.' They will deceive many. And you will hear of wars and threats of wars, but don't panic. Yes, these things must take place, but the end won't follow immediately. Nation will go to war against nation, and kingdom against kingdom. There will be famines and earthquakes in many parts of the world. But all this is only the first of the birth pains, with more to come.

"Then you will be arrested, persecuted, and killed. You will be hated all over the world because you are my followers. And many will turn away from me and betray and hate each other. And many false prophets will appear and will deceive many people. Sin will be rampant everywhere, and the love of many will grow cold. But the one who endures to the end will be saved. And the Good News about the Kingdom will be preached throughout the whole world, so that all nations will hear it; and then the end will come.

"The day is coming when you will see what Daniel the prophet spoke about—the sacrilegious object that causes desecration standing in the Holy Place." (Reader, pay attention!) "Then those in Judea must flee to the hills. A person out on the deck of a roof must not go down into the house to pack. A person out in the field must not return even to get a coat. How terrible it will be for pregnant women and for nursing mothers in those days. And pray that your flight will not be in winter or on the Sabbath. For there will be greater anguish than at any time since the world began. And it will never be so great again. In fact, unless that time of calamity is shortened, not a single person will survive. But it will be shortened for the sake of God's chosen ones.

"Then if anyone tells you, 'Look, here is the Messiah,' or 'There he is,' don't believe it. For false messiahs and false prophets will rise up and perform great signs and wonders so as to deceive, if possible, even God's chosen ones. See, I have warned you about this ahead of time.

"So, if someone tells you, 'Look, the Messiah is out in the desert,' don't bother to go and look. Or 'Look, he is hiding here,' don't believe it! For as the lightning flashes in the east and shines to the west, so it will be when the Son of Man comes. Just as the gathering of vultures shows there is a carcass nearby, so these signs indicate that the end is near.

"Immediately after the anguish of those days, the sun will be darkened, the moon will give no light, the stars will fall from the sky, and the powers in the heavens will be shaken.

And then at last, the sign that the Son of Man is coming will appear in the heavens, and there will be deep mourning among all the peoples of the earth. And they will see the Son of Man coming on the clouds of heaven with power and great glory. And he will send out his angels with the mighty blast of a trumpet, and they will gather his chosen ones from all over the world—from the farthest ends of the earth and heaven.

"Now learn a lesson from the fig tree. When its branches bud and its leaves begin to sprout, you know that summer is near. In the same way, when you see all these things, you can know his return is very near, right at the door. I tell you the truth, this generation will not pass from the scene until all these things take place. Heaven and earth will disappear, but my words will never disappear.

"However, no one knows the day or hour when these things will happen, not even the angels in heaven or the Son himself. Only the Father knows.

"When the Son of Man returns, it will be like it was in Noah's day. In those days before the flood, the people were enjoying banquets and parties and weddings right up to the time Noah entered his boat. People didn't realize what was going to happen until the flood came and swept them all away. That is the way it will be when the Son of Man comes.

"Two men will be working together in the field; one will be taken, the other left. Two women will be grinding flour at the mill; one will be taken, the other left.

"So, you, too, must keep watch! For you don't know what day your Lord is coming. Understand this: If a homeowner knew exactly when a burglar was coming, he would keep watch and not permit his house to be broken into. You also must be ready all the time, for the Son of Man will come when least expected.

"A faithful, sensible servant is one to whom the master can give the responsibility of managing his other household servants and feeding them. If the master returns and finds that the servant has done a good job, there will be a reward. I tell you the truth, the master will put that servant in charge of all he owns. But what if the servant is evil and thinks, 'My master won't be back for a while,' and he begins beating the other servants, partying, and getting drunk? The master will return unannounced and unexpected, and he will cut the servant to pieces and assign him a place with the hypocrites. In that place there will be weeping and gnashing of teeth." (Matthew 24:1-51)

As you continue to read along, you will learn about what hurricanes are as well as the

difference between being protected and under God's covering when a storm hits and not being protected.

## WHAT ARE HURRICANES?

**Hurricanes:**

- A weather engine fuelled by warm, moist air.

- Trials and tribulations that are experienced due to sin.

**Ducksters:**

- "What is a hurricane? A hurricane is a large rotating storm with high-speed winds that forms over warm waters in tropical areas. Hurricanes have sustained winds of at least 74 miles per hour and an area of low air pressure in the center called the eye.

- Different Names for Hurricanes: The scientific name for a hurricane is a tropical cyclone. Tropical cyclones go by different names in different places. In North America and the Caribbean, they are called "hurricanes", in the Indian Ocean they are called "cyclones", and in Southeast Asia they are called "typhoons."

- How do hurricanes form? Hurricanes form over the warm ocean water of the tropics. When warm moist air over the water rises, it is replaced by cooler air. The cooler air will then warm and start to rise. This cycle causes huge storm clouds to form. These storm clouds will begin to rotate with the spin of the Earth forming an organized system. If there is enough warm water, the cycle will continue and the storm clouds and wind speeds will grow causing a hurricane to form.

- Parts of a Hurricane:
  - Eye: At the center of the hurricane is the eye. The eye is an area of very low air pressure. There are generally no clouds in the eye and the wind is calm. Don't let this fool you, however, the most dangerous part of the storm is at the edge of the eye called the eyewall.

  - Eyewall: Around the outside of the eye is a wall made up of very heavy clouds. This is the most dangerous part of the hurricane and where the highest speed winds are. The winds at the eyewall can reach speeds of 155 miles per hour.

  - Rainbands: Hurricanes have large spirally bands of rain called rainbands. These bands can drop huge amounts of rainfall causing flooding when the hurricane hits land.

  - Diameter: Hurricanes can become huge storms. The diameter of the hurricane is measured from one side to the other. Hurricanes can span a diameter of over 600 miles.

  - Height: The storm clouds that power hurricanes can become very tall. A powerful hurricane can reach nine miles into the atmosphere.

- Where do tropical cyclones occur? Tropical cyclones occur over the ocean in areas near the equator. This is because there is plenty of warm water in these areas to allow the storms to form. There are seven major areas in the world that tend to produce tropical cyclones.

- Why are hurricanes dangerous? When hurricanes strike land, they can cause huge amounts of damage. Most of the damage is caused by flooding and storm surges. Storm surge is when the ocean level rises at the coastline due to the power of the storm. Hurricanes also cause damage with high-speed winds that can blow down trees and damage homes. Many hurricanes can develop several small tornadoes as well." (Weather - Hurricanes Tropical Cyclones)

# PROTECTED/PROTECTION

**Protected:**

- Preserved from harm, especially by means of formal or legal measures.

**Protection:**

- The action of protecting, or the state of being protected.

- A person or thing that prevents someone or something from suffering harm or injury.

- Similar: barrier, buffer, shield, preventive, preventative, armor, safeguard, refuge.

Protection comes from praising God, acknowledging Him, recognizing He is God and realizing that you can do nothing apart from Him.

"These are your instructions for eating this meal: Be fully dressed, wear your sandals, and carry your walking stick in your hand. Eat the meal with urgency, for this is the LORD's Passover. On that night I will pass through the land of Egypt and strike down every firstborn son and firstborn male animal in the land of Egypt. I will execute judgment against all the gods of Egypt, for I am the LORD! But the blood on your doorposts will serve as a sign, marking the houses where you are staying. When I see the blood, I will pass over you. This plague of death will not touch you when I strike the land of Egypt." (Exodus 12:11-13)

"Keep me safe, LORD, from the hands of the wicked; protect me from the violent, who devise ways to trip my feet." (Psalm 140:4)

"I can do all things through Christ who strengthens me." (Philippians 4:13)

"Yes, I am the vine; you are the branches. Those who remain in me, and I in them, will produce much fruit. For apart from me you can do nothing." (John 15:5)

**Faithlife Sermons:** "Some of my favorite memories of church when I was little occurred after the altar services and after the dismissal prayer. My friends and I would gather together and we would play hide and seek.

As a child it was wonderful. As a pastor, I would prefer it not happen! But he didn't seem to mind and no one else did either. I assume they loved the sound of kids in the church. (How many agree?) It is great to hear the sounds of toddlers, children, and teenagers in our congregation.

Back to my story, our church had a lot of places to hide. Our parents made sure we did not get into any Sunday School classrooms alone. In reality, we hid in plain sight.

The seeker would close his or her eyes and count to thirty. The hiders would disperse and hide. The object of the game was to hide so well that we would not be found.

As long as we were hidden we were safe. Our rules may be a little different from others, but if the seeker found us, we had the option to outrun them to base. If we could get to base, then we were safe.

As I read, my mind went back to my childhood, hiding and running to a safe place. If we could see behind the veil of time and space, we would see the game of life is not that different than the childhood game of Hide and Seek.

We have a real adversary named the Devil who is out to get us. The stakes are similar to the childhood game, EXCEPT, if he gets us and we do not get free, the consequences are much more severe.

It is more than mild embarrassment or being "it" next round. If we do not avoid contact with Satan, if we do not learn to overcome temptation, then our eternity will be sealed, apart from God.

But I have good news, there is a realm in God where we can go. God calls it the "secret place." If we get to the secret place, we will abide in supernatural protection.

When we commit to trust God and depend on Him, then He will protect us DURING the attacks of the enemy. As we read this notice that trust in God does not mean that the enemy will cease all attacks.

Instead, God will PROTECT us in the time of trouble! But it ONLY happens when we get to the secret place. How do we get to the secret place? We learn to praise God in progress.

If we will look at our troubles and trials in the face and declare, I praise God, I thank the Lord, audibly, out loud, with hands raised, something supernatural will occur.

We will be moved into the secret place and be protected by the Lord. In the first two verses we find four names for God: the Most High, the Almighty, the Lord, and My God!

- As Most High, He is greater than any threat we face.

- As the Almighty, He has power to confront and destroy every enemy.

- As the Lord, we have confidence that His presence will always sustain us.

- And as My God, we now display confidence that we know God personally. He is not A God, but MY God!

When we call on Him in praise and worship, declaring Him the Most High, the Almighty, the Lord, and My God, we will enter in the secret place and begin to abide under Him!

When we praise God, every member of the Godhead is at work in building protection. Jesus gives us access to our Father, and we are comforted by the Holy Spirit!

The enemy shouts throughout this world, ready or not, here I come. When he comes to destroy us, which is his ultimate goal, we must be hidden in the secret place." (Tidmore)

Side Note: *God never said your journey in life would be easy. God is, however, saying you will go through storms (trials and tribulations), but the problems are not going to break you. They are not going to destroy you because I'm protecting you. Yet only when I'm protecting you and you acknowledge me; will this be so.*

"We have sinned against the LORD," you replied. "We will go up and fight, as the LORD our God has commanded us." Then each of you put on his weapons of war, thinking it easy to go up into the hill country. But the LORD said to me, "Tell them not to go up and fight, for I am not with you to keep you from defeat by your enemies." So, I spoke to you, but you would not listen. You rebelled against the command of the LORD and presumptuously went up into the hill country. Then the Amorites who lived in the hills came out against you and chased you like a swarm of bees. They routed you from Seir all the way to Hormah. And you returned and wept before the LORD, but He would not listen to your voice or give ear to you. For this reason, you stayed in Kadesh for a long time—a very long time." (Deuteronomy 1:41-46)

As you can see, sometimes, no amount of preparation can help you if God is not with you, if you don't have the wisdom that comes from His word. The tools (discernment, faith, patience, altruism) that only He can provide.

Conclusion: *Worshiping God does not mean your life will always be great. But recognize that just as the Atlantic has storms that form every year, so do our lives. Our work in the Kingdom and praise of the Lord determines how we'll be hit, how we'll stumble, how we'll fall, and how we will get back up after the fall.*

## UNPROTECTED

Unprotected:

- Not protected or kept safe from harm or injury.

On the other hand, being unprotected happens when you stop praising God, abandon, and ignore His instructions.

"The Israelites sinned against the LORD their God, who brought them out of Egypt [and rescued them] from the power of Pharaoh (the king of Egypt). They worshiped other gods and lived by the customs of the nations that the LORD had forced out of the Israelites' way. They also did what their kings wanted them to do. The Israelites secretly did things against the LORD their God that weren't right: They built for themselves illegal places of worship in all of their cities, from the [smallest] watchtower to the [largest] fortified city. They set up sacred stones and poles dedicated to the goddess Asherah on every high hill and under every large tree. At all the illegal places of worship, they sacrificed in the same way as the nations that the LORD had removed from the land ahead of them. They did evil things and made the LORD furious. They served idols, although the LORD had said, "Never do this." The LORD had warned Israel and Judah through every kind of prophet and seer, "Turn from your evil ways, and obey my commands and decrees as I commanded your ancestors in all my teachings, the commands I sent to you through my servants the prophets." But they refused to listen. They became as impossible to deal with as their ancestors who refused to trust the LORD their God. They rejected his decrees, the promise he made to their ancestors, and the warnings he had given them. They went after worthless idols and became as worthless as the idols. They behaved like the nations around them, although the LORD had commanded them not to do that. They abandoned all the commands of the LORD their God: They made two calves out of cast metal. They made a pole dedicated to the goddess Asherah. They prayed to the entire army of heaven. They worshiped Baal. They sacrificed their sons and daughters by burning them alive. They practiced black magic and cast evil spells. They sold themselves by doing what the LORD considered evil, and they made him furious. The LORD became so angry with Israel that he removed them from his sight. Only the tribe of Judah was left. Even judah didn't obey the commands of the LORD their God but lived according to Israel's customs. So, the LORD rejected all of Israel's descendants, made them suffer, handed them over to those who looted their property, and finally turned away from Israel.

When he tore Israel away from the family of David, the people of Israel made Jeroboam (Nebat's son) king. Jeroboam forced Israel away from the LORD and led them to commit a serious sin. The Israelites followed all the sins Jeroboam committed and never turned away from them. Finally, the LORD turned away from Israel as he had said he would through all his servants, the prophets. So, the people of Israel were taken from their land to Assyria as captives, and they are still there today." (2 Kings 17:7-23)

A hurricane hit, and people prayed for revival. But guess what, after revival, people stopped praying. When the twin towers were hit on 9/11, thousands died. People basically tore their clothes and wept. "Then David took hold of his clothes and tore them, and so also did all the men who were with him. They mourned and wept and fasted until evening for Saul and his son Jonathan and for the people of the LORD and the house of Israel, because they had fallen by the sword." (2 Samuel 1:11-12). But when the smoke cleared, so did the prayers.

**Side Note:** *When we forget that God brought us out of the struggle, He steps back and allows us to go through life's troubles, bringing us to repentance. Again, one small gesture (prayer) can change the world. But once again, when the water clears, they wash up and take away the prayer right along with it. Just like the Israelites, just like the city of Nineveh and countless Kings mentioned in the Bible, and just like us.*

The Israelites went on with their lives after God had brought them to a place of undeserving blessings. Yet they forgot where they came from every time.

Not the same type of "forgetting where you came from" that people in your old neighborhood may speak of. No, the Israelites forgot exodus: a mass departure of people, especially emigrants.

**Side Note:** *Sometimes, when we've progressed or come a long way, we often forget the God who saved us, only to find ourselves back where we began in the first place. Broke, busted, and disgusted.*

## YOUR LIFE, EXISTENCE, AND ABILITY TO SURVIVE ARE CENTERED AROUND YOU ACKNOWLEDGING YOUR NEED FOR GOD AND HIS PROTECTION.

In other words, the more you pray, the bigger your protection bubble. However, the moment you stop praying so does the protection. Lack of protection leads you to become vulnerable to disaster.

> **Side Note:** *The more you pray, the more you tell God, "I need you". But the less you pray, the more your silence tells Him, "I don't need you".*

It's very similar to having private security. You pay the security company to do a job to protect you. But the moment you stop giving them money is when they will stop being there to protect you. And depending on why you require protection could determine the fine line between life and death for you.

> **Side Note:** *Many people think God does terrible things to them, but it's the total opposite. You do bad things to yourself. The worst thing you could ever do is stop praising God; that's all the bad you need to do to yourself.*

**In Touch:** "As Christ's followers, we have the Holy Spirit within us to guide us into all truth. But if we neglect His divine leadership and insist on going our own way, the Lord will let us face the consequences until we finally repent and turn back to Him.

When we refuse to consult the Lord and are determined to go our own way, we can expect the following results:

1. Confusion. We'll start to question our decision and wonder if we made a wrong choice. God's actions at the Tower of Babel demonstrate how He brings confusion when we make decisions apart from Him. Not only were their plans frustrated, but God

accomplished His will despite them, as they scattered over the surface of the earth.

2. Conflict. We'll experience internal conflict when the Holy Spirit gives us a sense of uneasiness, inadequacy, and doubt over our course of action.

3. Cost. Disobedience is always costly when we don't do the right thing, in the right time, and in the right way.

4. Loss. We will experience loss at some point in our lives, whether emotionally or physically.

5. Regret. God chooses the best direction, time, and way. Therefore, if we go in an opposite direction, don't wait for His timing, or do it our way, we will miss His best and suffer deep regret.

6. Pain. We may experience physical pain as the result of our disobedience, but the worst pain is that which is emotional. As we look back at our choices, we'll be filled with thoughts of "If only I'd done this or not done that."

7. Disaster. It could come to us financially, emotionally, or in countless other ways, but the result of disobedience is always disastrous because we didn't follow the Lord.

8. Discipline. If we will not listen and obey God, He'll discipline us. His goal is that we learn to trust in Him with all our heart instead of leaning on our own understanding (Prov. 3:5-6). Only then will He make our paths straight." (Stanley C. , 2018)

> **Conclusion:** *The fine line between life and death depends on your ability to recognize that no one comes to the Father except through the Son. The fine line between whether you live or die means you have to keep paying God praise. You have to keep paying attention to His word because if you stop paying, death can easily creep in and consume you, just like a hurricane.*

## IT'S NOT THE ANGER OF THE LORD YOU SHOULD BE AFRAID OF, BUT THE HURT THAT HE FEELS WHEN YOU ACT AS IF YOU DON'T CARE. LIKE IN ANY REAL RELATIONSHIP.

The same hurt from feeling I've been there for you all these years, yet you still can't love me the way I deserve to be loved. Or how much I care for you, and you still can't acknowledge all the work I've put into this relationship. How everyone else turned their back on and left you, yet you still worship them. How when you didn't have money, I gave it to you. But you don't care.

We, as people, like to have our cake and eat it too. While God is sitting back saying all you care about is you. But what about me—the one who's been there for you through your ups and downs. The one who formed you in your mother's womb? Because you know, some people like to say I helped make you. Funny, right? But the truth is that God did make you. He also captain saved you.

**GOD IS CALLING FOR REPENTANCE. HE'S CALL-
ING FOR YOU TO TURN AROUND AND AWAY
FROM YOUR WICKED WAYS. HE'S CALLING FOR
YOU TO RECOGNIZE HIM AS THE GOD WHO
SAVED ME. THE GOD WHO SAVES ME.**

**A Call to Repentance:** "The Lord says, "People of Israel, if you want to turn, then turn back to me. If you are faithful to me and remove the idols I hate, it will be right for you to swear by my name. Then all the nations will ask me to bless them, and they will praise me."

The Lord says to the people of Judah and Jerusalem, "Plow up your unplowed fields; do not plant your seeds among thorns. Keep your covenant with me, your Lord, and dedicate yourselves to me, you people of Judah and Jerusalem." (Jeremiah 4:1-4)

All God wants is for you to need Him, for you to rely on Him for all of your needs, and not make decisions without Him.

All God wants is for you to stop rejecting Him as He has always been there protecting you.

All God wants is You! He doesn't want your money, cars, or clothes like some people. All He wants is you, just as it is in any real relationship. If someone really loves you, all they'd want is you, not what you can give them, not what you can do for them. Because a whole person can do for themselves, and God is indeed whole. But He still wants you. He still chose you. How great of a love is that? To know someone needs nothing but still wants you.

**Side Note:** *God loves you, and it pains Him to see you so destructive, so He had to let you go off on your own, to make mistakes. However, He's waiting for you to return home so that you can receive healing, become whole, be under His protection, and be back in His arms.*

**The Prodigal Son:** "Then He said, "A certain man had two sons. The younger of them [inappropriately] said to his father, 'Father, give me the share of the property that falls to me.' So he divided the estate between them. A few days later, the younger son gathered together everything [that he had] and traveled to a distant country, and there he wasted his fortune in reckless and immoral living. Now when he had spent everything, a severe famine occurred in that country, and he began to do without and be in need. So he went and forced himself on one of the citizens of that country, who sent him into his fields to feed pigs. He would have gladly eaten the [carob] pods that the pigs were eating [but they could not satisfy his hunger], and no one was giving anything to him. But when he [finally] came to his senses, he said, 'How many of my father's hired men have more than enough food, while I am dying here of hunger! I will get up and go to my father, and I will say to him, "Father, I have sinned against heaven and in your sight. I am no longer worthy to be called your son; [just] treat me like one of your hired men."' So he got up and came to his father. But while he was still a long way off, his father saw him and was moved with compassion for him, and ran and embraced him and kissed him. And the son said to him, 'Father, I have sinned against heaven and in your sight; I am no longer worthy to be called your son.' But the father said to his servants, 'Quickly bring out the best robe [for the guest of honor] and put it on him; and give him a ring for his hand, and sandals for his feet. And bring the fattened calf and slaughter it, and let us [invite everyone and] feast and celebrate; for this son of mine was [as good as] dead and is alive again; he was lost and has been found.' So they began to celebrate.

"Now his older son was in the field; and when he returned and approached the house, he heard music and dancing. So he summoned one of the servants and began asking what this [celebration] meant. And he said to him, 'Your brother has come, and your father has killed the fattened calf because he has received him back safe and sound.' But the elder brother became angry and deeply resentful and was not willing to go in; and his father came out and began pleading with him. But he said to his father, 'Look! These many years I have served you, and I have never neglected or disobeyed your command. Yet you have never given me [so much as] a young goat, so that I might celebrate with my friends; but when this [other] son of yours arrived, who has devoured your estate with immoral women, you slaughtered that fattened calf for him!' The father said to him, 'Son, you are always with me, and all that is mine is yours. But it was fitting to celebrate and rejoice, for this brother of yours was [as good as] dead and has begun to live. He was lost and has been found.'" (Luke 15:11-32)

To conclude, God was hurt by your actions and He's trying to send you a message. "After I rescued you from Hurricane Katrina, you stopped believing in me. After I put you back together following the attacks on 9/11, you stopped thanking me."

And no, the hurricanes nor the viruses wreaking havoc around the world are something God is doing to you. It's because of your insolence that He had to step back and let you do what you wanted. To allow you to grow up.

Insolence:

- Rude and disrespectful behavior.

> **Side Note:** *Only a child who has grown can recognize as well as be grateful for why they had to make certain mistakes—to learn to be better. Only a wise person, a mature person, can say to the mistakes they've made, thank you, you made me stronger. As opposed to saying, "you left me in my time of need". They'd instead take accountability for their faults and become stronger.*

## IF YOU LOVE SOMEONE AND KNOW THAT THEY LOVE YOU, YOU'LL TAKE THEIR CORRECTION AS PROOF OF THAT LOVE.

A person that loves you will be honest with you. They will tell you what's real even if it hurts you. Nonetheless, they'll be there to console you through it all. Because a genuinely loving person doesn't want to see you fall, they'd instead warn you about things that could potentially hurt you so that you don't have to fall. But even if you do fall, they'll stand by you and pick you up when it's all said and done. They won't tell you what you've done is right if it is indeed wrong, but they also won't condemn you. That's genuine love and real compassion. That's God's Love.

Disclaimer: This chapter is in no way saying that the people who have been hit by certain disasters (hurricanes, diseases such as COVID-19, fires, etc.) have in particular, done something wrong.

What I'm trying to say is that the problems we currently face through-out the world are "worldwide, me plus you" issues.

These disasters don't just affect the people whose homes or fam-ilies it takes away. It affects the world as a whole. And without prayer and repentance, no one heals.

**GOD IS CALLING YOU BACK TO HIM. THE HUR-RICANE (STORMS, TRIALS, AND TRIBULATIONS) IN YOUR LIFE WILL SUBSIDE, BUT ONLY WHEN YOU DECIDE!**

"The pattern of the prodigal is: rebellion, ruin, repentance, reconciliation, restoration."

— *Edwin Louis Cole*

*Heavenly Father,* I want to thank you for the gift of today, the gift of repentance and acceptance. Thank you for helping me recognize my need for you. Knowing apart from you, I can do nothing. My behavior may have caused me to make some mistakes, but I'm so grateful for I know there is no condemnation in Jesus Christ. I want to ask for your forgiveness for my time of not appreciating the things that you granted me. I now see the love you have for me in a greater magnitude. I pray that I can keep my eyes focused on you as I know how important it is now to seek you first above all else. I pray that you shine your face upon me and let your love rain down, making me whole again within you. Sincerely, your child who was grafted in. And no matter what storm we are in, I know we will win. May the glory be yours as peace is still. I give you my life Jesus; take the WILL.

In Jesus' name, AMEN!

# PART THREE THE PLAN

# CHAPTER 6

# THE GREAT ESCAPE

*God was hurt by what you did, so He stepped back and allowed the storms of life to flood in. But remember where there was a flood later brings about repentance, rescue (exodus), reconciliation, rejuvenation, and restoration!*

Isaiah **57:14-21** NLT God Forgives the Repentant: "God says, "Rebuild the road! Clear away the rocks and stones so my people can return from captivity." The high and lofty one who lives in eternity, the Holy One, says this: "I live in the high and holy place with those whose spirits are contrite and humble. I restore the crushed spirit of the humble and revive the courage of those with repentant hearts. For I will not fight against you forever; I will not always be angry. If I were, all people would pass away—all the souls I have made. I was angry, so I punished these greedy people. I withdrew from them, but they kept going on their own stubborn way. I have seen what they do, but I will heal them anyway! I will lead them. I will comfort those who mourn, bringing words of praise to their lips. May they have abundant peace, both near and far," says the LORD, who heals them. "But those who still reject me are like the restless sea, which is never still but continually churns up mud and dirt. There is no peace for the wicked," says my God."

God can be harsh if He wants to, but He chooses to be gentle and patient. "But do not forget this one thing, dear friends: With the Lord a day is like a thousand years, and a thousand years are like a day. The Lord is not slow in keeping his promise, as some understand slowness. Instead, he is patient with you, not wanting anyone to perish, but everyone to come to repentance. But the day of the Lord will come like a thief. The heavens will disappear with a roar; the elements will be destroyed by fire, and the earth and everything done in it will be laid bare. Since everything will be destroyed in this way, what kind of people ought you to be? You ought to live holy and Godly lives as you look forward to the day of God and speed its coming. That day will bring about the destruction of the heavens by fire, and the elements will melt in the heat. But in keeping with his promise we are looking forward to a new heaven and a new earth, where righteousness dwells. So then, dear friends, since you are looking forward to this, make every effort to be found spotless, blameless and at peace with him. Bear in mind that our Lord's patience means salvation. Just as our dear brother Paul also wrote you with the wisdom that God gave him." (2 Peter 3:8-15)

God continues to forgive us when we can't even forgive each other. God is not mean; God is not harsh; God is a parent who loves you. "For the Lord corrects those he loves, as a father the son he delights in." (Proverbs 3:12)

But you can't always expect to take if you continuously come to the table with nothing or no intention to give.

**Side Note:** *God gives you your daily bread; you sit at the table and eat it, yet you don't even take two seconds to bless it. That's a problem. That's where the clean-up has to start; with the crumbs you left at the table—the crumbs you didn't even take time to bless.*

This is the reconciliation process where you will briefly learn about how all of the negative within your heart will be brought to the surface, burned, and later washed away.

### YOU ARE ABOUT TO BE BAPTIZED WITH FIRE AND WASHED IN THE BLOOD OF THE HOLY ONE! IT'S TIME TO SINK OR SWIM.

"I baptize with water those who repent of their sins and turn to God. But someone is coming soon who is greater than I am—so much greater that I'm not worthy even to be his slave and carry his sandals. He will baptize you with the Holy Spirit and with fire." (Matthew 3:11)

In this chapter, you will explore what happens after the *Hurt of the Hurricane—the Aftermath*. This part includes learning about God's plans for your life and the first steps that lead to reconciliation: repentance and rescue (exodus).

1.  Repent of and renounce sin.

## Repentance:

- Feel or express sincere regret or remorse about one's wrong-doing or sin.

## Renounce:

- Formally declare one's abandonment of (a claim, right, or possession).

- Reject and stop using or consuming.

"Now repent of your sins and turn to God, so that your sins may be wiped away. Then times of refreshment will come from the presence of the Lord, and he will again send you Jesus, your appointed Messiah." (Acts 3:19-20)

"Peter replied, "Repent and be baptized, every one of you, in the name of Jesus Christ for the forgiveness of your sins. And you will receive the gift of the Holy Spirit." (Acts 2:38)

"You will never succeed in life if you try to hide your sins. Confess them and give them up; then God will show mercy to you." (Proverbs 28:13)

**Bible Study Tools:** "The most common translation of "repent" is "turn" or "return". Two requisites of repentance are to turn from evil, and to turn to the good—the idea of returning to God or turning away from evil. If one turns away from God, danger is a step away. When a person is guilty of sin, he must confess in order to be cleansed and forgiven of them. In the New Testament, the key term for repentance is metanoia—change in one's way of life resulting from penitence:

the action of feeling or showing sorrow and regret for having done wrong or spiritual conversion. It has two usual senses: a change of mind and regret or remorse. True repentance leads a person to say, "I have sinned" and prove it with a 180-degree change of direction. Repentance requires true brokenness. Repentance is NOT asking the Lord for forgiveness with the intent to sin again. Repentance is an honest, regretful acknowledgement of sin with commitment to change. Repentance leads us to cultivate Godliness while eradicating habits that lead into sin." (Repentance Bible Verses)

God has plans for your life. And those plans include a way through the pain and problems (storms). But you can only make it through to exodus when you repent and allow God to enter your heart—to cleanse you of your sins, and help you change your ways.

**Bible Tools:** "Before there can be at-one-ment, or unity, there must first be reconciliation. Before reconciliation, there must be repentance. And before repentance, there must be something else—belief! Our belief must be strong enough and with sufficient understanding that it does not just drive us to our knees to save our skin, but also compels us to make the sacrifices necessary to change our conduct.

Luke quotes Jesus as saying, "Unless you repent you will all likewise perish" (Luke 13:3, 5). Repent means "to think differently after." It signifies a change of mind strong enough to produce both regret and change of conduct. Marvin R. Vincent defines it as, "Such a virtuous alteration of the mind and purpose as begets alike virtuous change of life and practice" (Word Studies of the New Testament, vol. 1, p. 23). The only way that we will change our minds is when we allow ourselves to believe something different from what we formerly believed." (Ritenbaugh J. )

**Conclusion:** *When you decide to open your mouth and repent, it activates God's power and allows Him to cleanse you of your sins. But remember, just as a closed mouth doesn't get fed, it's the same with a mouth without prayer and repentance. It doesn't get blessed.*

||||||||||||||||||||||||||||||||||||||||||||||||||||||||||||||||||||||||||||||||||||||||||||||||||||||||||||||||||||||

"Four marks of true repentance are: acknowledgement of wrong, willingness to confess it, willingness to abandon it, and willingness to make restitution."

— *Corrie Ten Boom*

||||||||||||||||||||||||||||||||||||||||||||||||||||||||||||||||||||||||||||||||||||||||||||||||||||||||||||||||||||||

2.  God rescues and leads you out of bondage.

**Rescue:**

- Save (someone) from a dangerous or distressing situation.

- An act of saving or being saved from danger or distress.

**Exodus:**

- A going out; a departure or emigration, usually of a large number of people.

"Moses answered the people, "Do not be afraid. Stand firm and you will see the deliverance the Lord will bring you today. The Egyptians you see today you will never see again. The Lord will fight for you; you need only to be still." Then the Lord said to Moses, "Why are you crying out to me? Tell the Israelites to move on. Raise your staff and stretch out your hand over the sea to divide the water so that the Israelites can go through the sea on dry ground. I will harden the hearts of the Egyptians so that they will go in after them. And I will gain glory through Pharaoh and all his army, through his chariots and his horsemen. The Egyptians will know that I am the Lord when I gain glory through Pharaoh, his chariots and his horsemen."

Then the angel of God, who had been traveling in front of Israel's army, withdrew and went behind them. The pillar of cloud also moved from in front and stood behind them, coming between the armies of Egypt and Israel. Throughout the night the cloud brought darkness to the one side and light to the other side; so neither went near the other all night long.

Then Moses stretched out his hand over the sea, and all that night the Lord drove the sea back with a strong east wind and turned it into dry land. The waters were divided, and the Israelites went through the sea on dry ground, with a wall of water on their right and on their left." (Exodus 14:13-22)

**Got Questions:** "The word "exodus" means departure. In God's timing, the exodus of the Israelites from Egypt marked the end of a period of oppression for Abraham's descendants (Genesis 15:13), and the beginning of the fulfilment of the covenant promise to Abraham that his descendants would not only live in the Promised Land but would also multiply and become a great nation (Genesis 12:1-3, 7)." (Summary of the Book of Exodus, 2008)

**BEFORE YOU MOVE FORWARD ON THIS JOUR-
NEY, YOU HAVE TO ASK YOURSELF, WILL YOU
KEEP LOOKING TO THE STORM, OR WILL YOU
TAKE TIME TO LOOK UP AND SEE THE EXIT?**

We've all gone through or are going through storms and battles. The keyword is always through, which means something is on the other side of that storm or battle. But you have to choose whether to sink in the sorrow the storm caused or look up so that you may be able to look out and see the exit—the light at the end of the tunnel (God).

Conclusion: *Even if you repent to escape, you will still need to decide whether you'll remain in whatever has held you captive or be reconciled to what sets you free.*

"From the tiny birds of the air and from the fragile lilies of the field, we learn the same truth, which is so important for those who desire to live a life of simple faith: God takes care of His own. He knows our needs. He anticipates our crises. He is moved by our weaknesses. He stands ready to come to our rescue. And at just the right moment, He steps in and proves Himself as our faithful heavenly Father."

*— Charles R. Swindoll*

**YOUR STORM IS NOT THE END OF YOU, BUT YOUR ESCAPE IS ALSO NOT THE END OF YOUR JOURNEY. IT'S JUST YOUR TICKET TO GET ON THE TRAIN THAT TAKES YOU TO THE PROMISED LAND. EXODUS IS ONLY THE BEGINNING.**

"But watch yourselves, or your hearts will be weighed down by dissipation, drunkenness, and the worries of life—and that day will spring upon you suddenly like a snare. For it will come upon all who dwell on the face of all the earth. So keep watch at all times, and pray that you may have the strength to escape all that is about to happen and to stand before the Son of Man." (Luke 21:34-38)

To conclude, life can bring about many storms, but God holds the key to every door of escape. If you take a step back for a second, read your Bible, and connect with Him, you'll see what He's been trying to tell you all along.

**REPENT, BE RECONCILED, AND REMAIN STRONG.**

||||||||||||||||||||||||||||||||||||||||||||||||||||||||||||||||||||||||||||||||||||||||||||||||||||

"Anxiously you ask, 'Is there a way to safety? Can someone guide me? Is there an escape from threatened destruction?' The answer is a resounding yes! I counsel you: Look to the lighthouse of the Lord. There is no fog so dense, no night so dark, no gale so strong, no mariner so lost but what its beacon light can rescue. It beckons through the storms of life. It calls, 'This way to safety; this way to home.'"

— *Thomas S. Monson*

||||||||||||||||||||||||||||||||||||||||||||||||||||||||||||||||||||||||||||||||||||||||||||||||||||

"**Lord Jesus,** I'm tired of the sin struggle in my life. I feel distant from You. My choices have not led me into the right places. I've listened to the whispers of my enemy instead of Your words in Scripture, and the result has been disastrous.

I once walked with you, my heart tender to Your leading. Yet little by little, I exchanged Your truths for temptations and deceit that led me away from You. Instead of taking thoughts captive and confessing them immediately, I allowed them to grow totally out of control. Repentance was not in my vocabulary. Blame, cover-ups, or trying to reason and rationalize sin never work. They only give birth to deeper sin entanglements.

You created me in Your image, Lord. You know my thoughts before I speak them. You x-ray my heart and see through my excuses and intentions. Your Spirit warned me, but I ignored You. Disappointment and discouragement have taken their toll on me.

So today, I'm confessing my desperate need for You. You have promised that if we confess our sin, You will forgive us and make us clean again. Lord, I truly need Your forgiveness. Repentance is on my heart and lips. I want to turn around and head in another direction—back to You, Lord. But I need Your help.

Just as You created the world out of nothing, Lord, create a clean heart out of my "nothingness." You paid for my sin with your death. Restore my life and the fellowship we once shared. You don't condemn me, and You won't disown me; I am Your child forever. But I take all the blame—I own my sin. I am the one who broke fellowship with You and am crushed over the way I treated You and Your name.

Lord, root out the darkness and light up my life with Your holy presence. Help me understand what went wrong. Show me how my destructive patterns first began. What did I allow to become more important than loving and honoring You? Why did I seek satisfaction in others or other things than You? You are the only One Who provides all my needs. You fill up the soul with deep-down joy and peace beyond all understanding.

Lord, may your restoration include new boundaries around my life. I can't flirt with sin and not be hurt. In restoring me, teach me how to say no again to things that could harm myself or my testimony. If my actions have wounded others, show me where and to whom I need to ask forgiveness or how to make amends. Help me to surround myself with positive encouragers who will hold me accountable and who will speak the truth in love. Truly, shame melts away and we are healed when we confess to others and ask for their help.

I understand that my repentance won't eliminate the consequences of my sin. Knowing that You don't hold our sins to our account—You remember them no more--and that You place them as far as the east is from the west both humbles me and fills me with amazement and gratitude. No consequence could ever be as painful as knowing how my sin hurt You or how You suffered for me out of love.

Your crucifying death gave me eternal life with You. Lord, You place grace next to my regrets and give me hope for a new future.

Thank You, Lord, that sin does not disqualify us. Instead, like a runner who has fallen but who gets up again, I, too, am willing to start again and finish the race You have set for me.

In Jesus' name, Amen." (Jordan, 2018)

# CHAPTER 7

# UNFINISHED BUSINESS

*Everything was good about a week ago. And had it stayed that way. You probably would have never even thought to stop and thank God for something as simple as your day.*

**2 Corinthians 7:8-11** AMP "For even though I did grieve you with my letter, I do not regret it [now]; though I did regret it—for I see that the letter hurt you, though only for a little while—yet I am glad now, not because you were hurt and made sorry, but because your sorrow led to repentance [and you turned back to God]; for you felt a grief such as God meant you to feel, so that you might not suffer loss in anything on our account. For [Godly] sorrow that is in accord with the will of God produces a repentance without regret, leading to salvation; but worldly sorrow [the hopeless sorrow of those who do not believe] produces death. For [you can look back and] see what an earnestness and authentic concern this Godly sorrow has produced in you: what vindication of yourselves [against charges that you tolerate sin], what indignation [at sin], what fear [of offending God], what longing [for righteousness and justice], what passion [to do what is right]."

In this chapter, you will continue to study what happens during the *Aftermath of the Hurt*. But this time around, you are going to focus on learning more about reconciling with God, as well as being rejuvenated and restored by Him.

1.  Reconcile with God.

Reconciliation:

- The restoration of friendly relations.

- The action of making one view or belief compatible with another.

**Peace with God Through Faith:** "Therefore, since we have been justified by faith, we have peace with God through our Lord Jesus Christ. Through him we have also obtained access by faith into this grace in which we stand, and we rejoice in hope of the glory of God. Not only that, but we rejoice in our sufferings, knowing that suffering produces endurance, and endurance produces character, and character produces hope, and hope does not put us to shame, because God's love has been poured into our hearts through the Holy Spirit who has been given to us. For while we were still weak, at the right time Christ died for the ungodly. For one will scarcely die for a righteous person—though perhaps for a good person one would dare even to die—but God shows his love for us in that while we were still sinners, Christ died for us. Since, therefore, we have now been justified by his blood, much more shall we be saved by him from the wrath of God. For if while we were enemies we were reconciled to God by the death of his Son, much more, now that we are reconciled, shall we be saved by his life. More than that, we also rejoice in God through our Lord Jesus Christ, through whom we have now received reconciliation." (Romans 5:1-11)

**Got Questions:** "The Bible says that Christ reconciled us to God. (Romans 5:10; 2 Corinthians 5:18; Colossians 1:20-21) The fact that we needed reconciliation means that our relationship with God was broken. Since God is holy, we were the ones to blame. Our sin alienated us from him. Romans 5:10 says that we were enemies of God: "For if, when we were God's enemies, we were reconciled to him through the death of his Son, how much more, having been reconciled, shall we be saved through his life!"

When Christ died on the cross, He satisfied God's judgment and made it possible for God's enemies, us, to find peace with him. Our "reconciliation" to God, then, involves the exercise of His grace and the forgiveness of our sin. The result of Jesus' sacrifice is that our relationship has changed from enmity to friendship. "I no longer call you servants... Instead, I have called you friends" (John 15:15). Christian reconciliation is a glorious truth! We were God's enemies but are now His friends. We were in a state of condemnation because of our sins, but we are now forgiven. We were at war with God, but now have the peace that transcends all understanding. (Philippians 4:7)" (What is Christian reconciliation?, 2004)

So, God had to show you what was at stake to be lost by stepping away and allowing you to navigate life on your own. To make you appreciative. Appreciative of the things you may have lost. The things He blessed you with. Appreciative of the people you've lost, could potentially lose, or still have with you. Appreciative of Him.

Think of it like this: if a person is not faithful or trustworthy and their bad behavior continues without any effort being made on their part in terms of them changing. As you continue to allow that person to be in your life, you only hurt yourself. Their bad behavior continues, and that person doesn't learn from their mistakes. Sometimes the only way for them to learn is for you to step back, allowing them to see what's at stake to be lost. This also allows you to see the true nature of that person.

## THE STORMS IN LIFE WILL TEST YOU; THE STORMS IN LIFE WILL DETERMINE YOU.

"Everyone then who hears these words of mine and does them will be like a wise man who built his house on the rock. And the rain fell, and the floods came, and the winds blew and beat on that house, but it did not fall, because it had been founded on the rock. And everyone who hears these words of mine and does not do them will be like a foolish man who built his house on the sand. And the rain fell, and the floods came, and the winds blew and beat against that house, and it fell, and great was the fall of it." (Matthew 7:24-27).

||||||||||||||||||||||||||||||||||||||||||||||||||||||||||||||||||||||||||||||||||||||||||

"The rain came to reveal what your house was really built on."

— *Steven Furtick*

||||||||||||||||||||||||||||||||||||||||||||||||||||||||||||||||||||||||||||||||||||||||||

The storm will let the Lord know whether you genuinely want to reconcile as well as if you truly belong to Him. The storm will show

God whether you'll grasp at anything simply because it looks good, allowing temptation to take hold of you. Or whether you'll do things right, the righteous way, God's way. "Then Jesus was led by the Spirit into the wilderness to be tempted there by the devil. For forty days and forty nights he fasted and became very hungry. During that time the devil came and said to him, "If you are the Son of God, tell these stones to become loaves of bread." But Jesus told him, "No! The Scriptures say, 'People do not live by bread alone, but by every word that comes from the mouth of God." (Matthew 4:1-4)

**Conclusion:** *If a person does not want to learn from their mistakes or do right by you, in generally speaking. Then maybe that person doesn't love you wholeheartedly. It's the same with your relationship with God, if you truly love Him, you'd learn from what you did that hurt Him, and you'd come back to Him and not only reconcile but also come back as a better person. True reconciliation brings about an unbreakable bond and unconditional love.*

"There is no reconciliation until you recognize the dignity of the other, until you see their view - you have to enter into the pain of the people. You've got to feel their need."

— John M. Perkins

2. Be rejuvenated by God.

## Rejuvenation:

- Give new energy or vigor to; revitalize.

- The action or process of making someone or something look or feel better, younger, or more vital.

**The Lord Will Rejuvenate His People:** "The spirit of the sovereign Lord is upon me because the Lord has chosen me. He has commissioned me to encourage the poor, to help the broken-hearted, to decree the release of captives, and the freeing of prisoners to announce the year when the Lord will show his favor, the day when our God will seek vengeance, to console all who mourn, to strengthen those who mourn in Zion, by giving them a turban, instead of ashes, oil symbolizing joy, instead of mourning, a garment symbolizing praise, instead of discouragement. They will be called oaks of righteousness, trees planted by the Lord to reveal his splendor. They will rebuild the perpetual ruins and restore the places that were desolate. They will re-establish the ruined cities, the places that have been desolate since ancient times. Foreigners will take care of your sheep; foreigners will work in your fields and vineyards. You will be called, the Lord's priests, servants of our God. You will enjoy the wealth of nations and boast about the riches you receive from them. Instead of shame, you will get a double portion; instead of humiliation, they will rejoice over the land they receive. Yes, they will possess a double portion in their land and experience lasting joy." (Isaiah 61:1-7)

**WHAT IS AFTER YOUR DEVASTATION? HAS THE HURT THAT HAS RESULTED FROM THE HURRICANE MADE YOU CHANGE YOUR WAYS? HAS IT GIVEN YOU A RENEWED STRENGTH AND SPIRIT? OR ARE YOU STILL UPSET AND BLAMING GOD FOR THE MISFORTUNES IN LIFE?**

A hurricane can swallow you whole if you let it. The aftermath, the clean-up, depends on who's doing the cleaning. Who's doing the mending. Who's making things new and whole. Who has given you new life and strength? Is it God or man? Because clean-up (rejuvenation) by man will get dirty shortly after, wholeness by man will soon break.

> **Side Note:** *When you're broken, you don't want cheap glue putting you back together. You want something waterproof, foolproof, someone that is wise in all His ways. Because sooner or later, your brokenness will come together. But true wholeness can only be achieved when your foundation is built on solid ground, on rock.*

**GOD IS URGING YOU TO ALLOW HIM TO BUILD YOUR HOUSE ON ROCK AND NOT SAND. TO BE REJUVENATED BY HIM AND NOT MAN.**

The rock is God; the sand is man. God is bringing you back to Him to be built up on His foundation. He wants the aftermath of your trials and tribulations to be sweet, not bitter. But that's up to you. It's up to you to choose whether the water from the flood will wash out your prayers or wash out the negativity of your past and assist in rejuvenating (preparing) you for the blessings that have yet to come.

> **Side Note:** *When walking with God, the journey may be challenging. It may be long. But the aftermath brings about a type of joy that is endless. How is this so? Because God builds you up on a foundation that cannot be broken. This means the blessings are lifelong. And the joy that comes from the blessings cannot be taken away. The only one that can take what God has given to you is God.*

## IF GOD BLESSES YOU, NO ONE CAN CURSE YOU. IF GOD CURSES YOU, NO ONE CAN BLESS YOU.

"Behold, I have received His command to bless [Israel]. He has blessed, and I cannot reverse it." (Number 23:20)

"Write this letter to the angel of the church in Philadelphia. This is the message from the one who is holy and true, the one who has the key of David. What he opens, no one can close; and what he closes, no one can open: "I know all the things you do, and I have opened a door for you that no one can close." (Revelation 3:7-8)

"For God's gifts and his call can never be withdrawn." (Romans:11-29)

**Eric Dunbar:** "Only God's Words Will Stand: People try to assassinate your character by saying negative things about you. But just because people speak negatively about you doesn't mean you are cursed. Their words will not affect you. When God says you are blessed, no one can curse you.

Balaam could not curse Israel because God had already blessed them. Not even Satan can curse you, and he knows it. Remember that you are blessed because God says you are blessed. It doesn't matter what people say about you. If God says you are blessed, then you are blessed.

So the next time you feel like you need a blessing, remember that God has already blessed you and no one can reverse your blessing." (No One Can Curse Your Blessing, 2016)

**Conclusion:** *Stop wallowing in the tears the storm (trials and tribulations) has caused and start allowing God to rejuvenate (prepare) you for your future. That's the only way you're going to get through this storm.*

"Health is not simply the absence of illness. Real health is the will to overcome every form of adversity and use even the worst of circumstances as a springboard for new growth and development. Simply put, the essence of health is the constant renewal and rejuvenation of life."

— *Daisaku Ikeda*

3. Be Restored by God.

Restoration:

- The action of returning something to a former owner, place, or condition.

- The return of a hereditary monarch to a throne, a head of state to government, or a regime to power.

"You have allowed me to suffer much hardship, but you will restore me to life again, and lift me up from the depths of the earth. You will restore me to even greater honor, and comfort me once again." (Psalm 71:20-21)

"Then the Lord became jealous for his land and had pity on his people. The Lord answered and said to his people, "Behold, I am sending to you grain, wine, and oil, and you will be satisfied; and I will no more make you a reproach among the nations. "I will remove the northerner far from you, and drive him into a parched and desolate land, his vanguard into the eastern sea, and his rear guard into the western sea; the stench and foul smell of him will rise, for he has done great things. "Fear not, O land; be glad and rejoice, for the Lord has done great things! Fear not, you beasts of the field, for the pastures of the wilderness are green; the tree bears its fruit; the fig tree and vine give their full yield. "Be glad, O children of Zion, and rejoice in the Lord your God, for he has given the early rain for your vindication; he has poured down for you abundant rain, the early and the latter rain, as before. "The threshing floors shall be full of grain; the vats shall overflow with wine and oil. I will restore to you the years that the swarming locust has eaten, the hopper, the destroyer, and the cutter, my great army, which I sent among you. "You shall eat in plenty and be satisfied, and praise the name of the

Lord your God, who has dealt wondrously with you. And my people shall never again be put to shame. You shall know that I am in the midst of Israel, and that I am the Lord your God and there is none else. And my people shall never again be put to shame. **The Lord Will Pour Out His Spirit:** "And it shall come to pass afterward, that I will pour out my Spirit on all flesh; your sons and your daughters shall prophesy, your old men shall dream dreams, and your young men shall see visions. Even on the male and female servants in those days I will pour out my Spirit. "And I will show wonders in the heavens and on the earth, blood and fire and columns of smoke. The sun shall be turned to darkness, and the moon to blood, before the great and awesome day of the Lord comes. And it shall come to pass that everyone who calls on the name of the Lord shall be saved. For in Mount Zion and in Jerusalem there shall be those who escape, as the Lord has said, and among the survivors shall be those whom the Lord calls." (Joel 2:25-32)

**Got Questions:** "The statement of Joel 2:25—"I will restore to you the years that the swarming locust has eaten"—is a reference to the produce of food from the years the locusts destroyed the harvest. A closer look at the context and details of this verse offers additional insight into the goodness of God.

Israel's crops had been destroyed by a locust invasion (Joel 1:4), and the impact lasted more than one year. This could indicate that locusts invaded in consecutive years. However, it is more likely that the damage of one invasion had a multi-year impact. When locusts destroyed a crop, they wiped out the seed saved from the previous year, the harvest of the current year, and the seed that would be used the next year. Locust devastation of grapevines and fruit trees would take years to redevelop (Joel 1:12).

Joel 2:25 complements the preceding verse, which says, "The threshing floors shall be full of grain; the vats shall overflow with wine and oil." The restoring of the years the locust had eaten would include an abundant harvest of grain, grapes, and olives.

Joel had used the locust invasion as an illustration of God's judgment. In His promise to "restore" the years lost to the locust, God is pledging to restore His repentant people to a place of blessing after judgment. The context describes many other positive things that would take place during this restoration:

- Green pasture for livestock: "the pastures of the wilderness are green" (Joel 2:22).

- Trees and vines that bear fruit: "the tree bears its fruit; the fig tree and vine give their full yield" (Joel 2:22).

- The spring and summer rains would come as needed for a good crop: "he has given the early rain" (Joel 2:23).

The results of this restoration would be both physical and spiritual. Physically, "You shall eat in plenty and be satisfied." Spiritually, they would "praise the name of the LORD your God, who has dealt wondrously with you" (Joel 2:26).

The conclusion of this section of Joel summarizes God's intention for the restoration: "And my people shall never again be put to shame. You shall know that I am in the midst of Israel, and that I am the LORD your God and there is none else. And my people shall never again be put to shame" (Joel 2:26-27). God must deal with sin, but when His people repent, they find abundant blessing that more than compensates for what was lost in the judgment. His grace abounds." (How does God restore the years that the locusts have eaten (Joel 2:25)?, 2012)

# GOD HAS TO DO SOME GROOMING SO THERE CAN BE JOY WHEN THE TIME COMES FOR YOU TO BEGIN BLOOMING.

Don't be upset with yourself if it took you a long time to come back to God. Don't be upset if it took a sharp turn for you to see the signs God was sending you. Why? Because it's not about the fall but how you get back up after the fall.

||||||||||||||||||||||||||||||||||||||||||||||||||||||||||||||||||||||||||||||||||||||||||||||||||||||||||||||||||||

"There comes a time in your life when you walk away from all the drama and people who create it. You surround yourself with people who make you laugh. Forget the bad and focus on the good. Love the people who treat you right, pray for the ones who do not. Life is too short to be anything but happy. Falling down is a part of life, getting back up is living."

— *Jose N. Harris*

||||||||||||||||||||||||||||||||||||||||||||||||||||||||||||||||||||||||||||||||||||||||||||||||||||||||||||||||||||

The only thing that matters is that you recognize what you have done wrong. Acknowledge your need for God, and believe that he whom the Son sets free is free indeed.

You are free from those chains the devil tried to place on you. "He led them from the darkness and deepest gloom; he snapped their chains." (Psalm 107:14) This means you are free to be who God called you to be.

**YOU ARE KINGS AND QUEENS BECAUSE OF CHRIST. "BUT YOU ARE A CHOSEN RACE, A ROYAL PRIESTHOOD, A HOLY NATION, A PEOPLE FOR HIS OWN POSSESSION, THAT YOU MAY PROCLAIM THE EXCELLENCIES OF HIM WHO CALLED YOU OUT OF DARKNESS INTO HIS MARVELOUS LIGHT." (1 PETER 2:9). BUT YOU DO HAVE TO CONTINUE WALKING SIDE-BY-SIDE WITH GOD ON THIS JOURNEY TO ACHIEVE SUCH GREATNESS (DON'T GROW WEARY). "BUT THE ONE WHO ENDURES TO THE END WILL BE SAVED." (MATTHEW 24:13)**

You're constantly changing, always learning. Just don't grow weary in doing so. Never stop believing that you need God and never stop seeking His face because the restoration process is only successful when His transformational power is at work and you are restored by Him.

**Conclusion:** *God wants to restore you to your rightful place on the throne. He's grooming you to be a King or Queen, which requires you to be patient, loving, and kind—not comfortable, but patient. Patience, love, and kindness are God, and you are to become like Him in order to live in the fullness of His righteousness, the fullness of His restoration.*

||||||||||||||||||||||||||||||||||||||||||||||||||||||||||||||||||||||||||||||||||||||||||||||||||||||||||||||||

"But resurrection is not just consolation—it is restoration. We get it all back—the love, the loved ones, the goods, the beauties of this life—but in new, unimaginable degrees of glory and joy and strength."

— *Timothy Keller*

||||||||||||||||||||||||||||||||||||||||||||||||||||||||||||||||||||||||||||||||||||||||||||||||||||||||||||||||

To conclude, your boat (life) was shaking, and so was your past. Your boat (life) was not built properly, and neither was your past. So, the storm hit, breaking apart what you thought was all you had. The storm hit and washed away all that you cherished. But to be reconciled with the Lord, you must let those things go knowing whatever has been washed away must not have been meant to stay.

> **Side Note:** *Don't get washed away by the flood. Let the flood wash away your sin. But remember never to forget the one who dried you off and put you back together (God). Because the flood is the blood of Jesus, and it's the only thing that can make you whole and wash you clean.*

Now, the chapter is not over just yet. You still have a choice to make. Either let the hurt of all your mistakes lead you to reconciliation (with God) or die with negative thoughts lingering in your head because of poor representation.

## WHO WILL YOU ALLOW TO REPRESENT YOU— THE SIN OF YOUR PAST (THE DEVIL) OR THE LIGHT OF YOUR FUTURE (JESUS)? IT'S YOUR CHOICE: DEATH ROW OR AFTERMATH?

IIIIIIIIIIIIIIIIIIIIIIIIIIIIIIIIIIIIIIIIIIIIIIIIIIIIIIIIIIIIIIIIIIIIIIIIIIIIIIIIIIIIIIIIIIIIIIIIIIIII

"Better the discomfort that leads to repentance and restoration than temporal comfort and eternal damnation."

— *Francine Rivers*

IIIIIIIIIIIIIIIIIIIIIIIIIIIIIIIIIIIIIIIIIIIIIIIIIIIIIIIIIIIIIIIIIIIIIIIIIIIIIIIIIIIIIIIIIIIIIIIIIIIII

***Dear Lord,*** thank you for your forgiveness. Thank you for not abandoning me when I made mistakes but for reaching out instead to bring me home. I pray that you help me to continue to recognize your ways and see them for what they are so that I may be able to change. I know that the process to promise may be long, but I just pray that you give me the strength to buckle down and hold on. The flood has washed away what was not meant to stay, but you spared me because you love me. And although you allowed me to go through some things to lead me to repent and be reconciled with you, I am forever grateful. You've given me a new life, cleansed and free—another day to live and another day to love. Another day to draw closer to you and live out your plans for my life. I believe that you are working things out for my good, so I can still be grateful in times of sorrow. I pray that you help me restore relationships in my life so that they may be made in your image and represent your love for me. Please give me the strength to live but also let go. The strength that enables me to walk away from sin so that I can become a better me for the future.

Thank you for the love you have poured out on me. Help me live out of that love today. I know tomorrow has its own problems, so I need not worry. After all, you have already painted a picture that I know will later be revealed as a beautiful masterpiece.

In Jesus' Name, Amen.

# CHAPTER 8

# BEFORE BLESSINGS COMES BLOOD

*You have accepted God into your life, but before continuing on this journey, you must first know what it means to be a true follower of Christ! "Stay alert! Watch out for your great enemy, the' devil. He prowls around like a roaring lion, looking for someone to devour. Stand firm against him and be strong in your faith. Remember that your Christian brothers and sisters all over the world are going through the same kind of suffering you are. In his kindness God called you to share in his eternal glory by means of Christ Jesus. So, after you have suffered a little while, he will restore, support, and strengthen you, and he will place you on a firm foundation. All power to him forever!" Amen." (1 Peter 5:8-11)*

**2 Timothy 2:12** NLT "If we endure hardship, we will reign with him. If we deny him, he will deny us."

Often when people speak about the Kingdom of Heaven and God, they do not teach about the pain that believers endure when calling on God or walking with Christ (the blood before the blessings). No one tells you that being or becoming Christlike is a tough battle. Often people only preach about the aftermath of the storm. Therefore, that is all anyone on the outside can visualize.

Maybe that person is afraid they will lose followers if they teach people more about the blood. Or maybe that person just doesn't fully understand the importance of teaching the principles of pain.

> **Side Note:** *Almost everyone talks about the aftermath, what it looks like to be built up by God. But almost no one tells you how important it is for you to be gracefully broken. Or should I say emptied so that you can later become full of all the right things. The right character so that you can have a right heart.*

In this chapter, you will learn about the principles of blood before blessings and decide whether you would like to continue on this journey.

God has given you the escape plan (exodus), the key to life (Jesus), and the tools needed to succeed (Jesus's journey/the map/Bible). But before you continue on this journey to freedom, you need to be sure that you are ready to receive the blessings God has in store for you and are also prepared for the blood that comes before.

## BEFORE DRINKING THE BLOOD OF CHRIST, YOU NEED TO BE SURE YOU ARE READY TO BLEED!

Often people think accepting God into their lives and receiving the blood of Jesus means they will always have good times, but this is not true. Often people believe that when calling on the Lord, their suffering will immediately fade away. The truth is, in most cases, trouble, struggles, and pain will be magnified.

**Side Note:** *Trouble, struggles, and pain are magnified because you are being put under a magnifying glass to be examined by the Lord. When this is done, the negative characteristics within your heart is brought to the surface, weeded out, burned, and washed away. Through pain and suffering, there is cleansing.*

## THE LORD IS THE LIGHT, AND YOU ARE THE OBJECT THAT, THROUGHOUT THIS JOURNEY, WILL BE INSPECTED AND MAYBE EVEN BURNED.

The moment I entered the wilderness it seemed like my life was turned upside down. I was taken by my feet and beaten like a pinata (literally and physically). My loved one was incarcerated. A couple of weeks later I received a letter stating to pay a ticket, or my license would be suspended. Right after that, my family had to move in with my grandmother.

But that was not the end of it; there's more. A loved one who I am very close to was battling with mental health issues. My grandmother got very sick. My car broke down, and so on. All of this happened in less than a couple of weeks. Trouble seemed to be a part of my life.

Now, I'm not telling you this to scare you. I'm telling you this so you can be more aware of what is yet to come. So you can have the opportunity to face the fire head-on and be courageous when doing so.

> **Side Note:** *Notice Mark 1:12-13 states that Jesus was led into the wilderness by the Holy Spirit. This means every problem you face in life is not simply a trial from the devil. Trials are also another word for test, which comes from God. The key thing to remember though is because these trials (tests) are from God, you know the victory is yours. You just have to make it through the wilderness to claim it.*

## GOD WILL PROMISE YOU BLESSINGS, BUT BLOOD WILL BE SOWED BEFORE YOU REAP THEM.

When you are going through tough times or trouble hits your life like a whirlwind, remember it's not always because you have done something wrong or because God does not love you. God is always with you, but you will have to go through the wilderness and possibly bleed before reaching the promised land (your dreams, purpose, and destiny in a state where they are fully revealed). "Beloved, do not be surprised at the fiery trial when it comes upon you to test you, as though something strange were happening to you. But rejoice insofar as you share Christ's sufferings, that you may also rejoice and be glad when his glory is revealed. If you are insulted for the name of

Christ, you are blessed, because the Spirit of glory and of God rests upon you." (1 Peter 4:12-14)

## REMEMBER, EXODUS IS YOUR TICKET ON THE TRAIN. IT'S NOT THE TRIP.

Look at it this way; when you first call on God, that's exodus. He plans your way of escape.

"Therefore, say to the Israelites: 'I am the Lord, and I will bring you out from under the yoke of the Egyptians. I will free you from being slaves to them, and I will redeem you with an outstretched arm and with mighty acts of judgment. I will take you as my own people, and I will be your God. Then you will know that I am the Lord your God, who brought you out from under the yoke of the Egyptians. And I will bring you to the land I swore with uplifted hand to give to Abraham, to Isaac and to Jacob. I will give it to you as a possession. I am the Lord.'" (Exodus 6:6-8) <--- **THE PLAN**

But things are not peachy and cream right afterward because after exodus comes the wilderness.

"When Pharaoh let the people go, God did not lead them on the road through the Philistine country, though that was shorter. For God said, "If they face war, they might change their minds [that is, that there will be war] and return to Egypt." So God led the people around by the desert road toward the Red Sea. The Israelites went up out of Egypt ready for battle." (Exodus 13:17-18) <--- **THE WILDERNESS**

## THIS MEANS YOU WILL HAVE TO FIGHT; YOU WILL HAVE TO BLEED.

For this reason, it is vital to learn about Jesus and His journey. Because if you are to receive His Blood which cleanses your sins and sets you free, you are also called to receive His Journey and His Cross. "For the life of the body is in its blood. I have given you the blood on the altar to purify you, making you right with the LORD. It is the blood, given in exchange for a life, that makes purification possible." (Leviticus 17:11)

The journey and life of Jesus did not simply consist of Him performing miracles and having joy. Jesus was crucified on the cross. He had blood all over Him as pain coursed through His body before being seated at the right hand of God.

"They came to a place called Golgotha. This name means the place of a skull. They gave Him wine with something in it to take away the pain. After tasting it, He took no more. When they had nailed Him to the cross, they divided His clothes by drawing names. It happened as the early preacher said it would happen. He said, "They divided My clothes among them by drawing names to see who would get My coat." Then they sat down and watched Him. Over His head they put in writing what they had against Him, THIS IS JESUS THE KING OF THE JEWS. They nailed two robbers to crosses beside Him. One was on His right side. The other was on His left side. Those who walked by shook their heads and laughed at Him. They said, "You are the One Who could destroy the house of God and build it up again in three days. Now save Yourself. If You are the Son of God, come down from the cross." The head religious leaders and the teachers of the Law and the other leaders made fun of Him also. They said, "He saved others but He cannot save Himself. If He is the King of the Jews, let Him come down from the cross. Then we will believe in Him. He trusts God. Let God save Him now, if God cares for Him. He has said, 'I am the Son of God.'" And the robbers who were nailed to crosses beside Him made fun of Him the same way also." (Matthew 27:33-44)

## THE COURTROOM OF CRUCIFIXION

Similar to the crucifixion of Jesus is the crucifixion that happens in the court of law (society) daily: the modern-day crucifixion.

In today's courtroom (society), people are crucified by being put on a stand (cross) while being put to shame in front of a crowd. The accuser sits across from the accused, throwing accusations, slander, and hate as the loved ones of that individual must sit and watch their family member be sentenced to death by the hands of a society filled with individuals who lack humility and harbor hatred in their hearts. Some of which are the same individuals who swore to protect and serve. "Near the cross of Jesus stood his mother, his mother's sister, Mary the wife of Clopas, and Mary Magdalene." (John 19:25) **The Death of Jesus**: "After this, Jesus, knowing that all was now finished, said in fulfillment of the Scripture, "I am thirsty." A jar full of sour wine was placed there; so they put a sponge soaked in the sour wine on [a branch of] hyssop and held it to His mouth. When Jesus had received the sour wine, He said, "It is finished!" And He bowed His head and [voluntarily] gave up His spirit." (John 19:28-30)

The imagery of Jesus on the cross alone makes this chapter very important. It prepares you visually for what is yet to come instead of you walking into something that can make you think that God has forsaken you. Furthermore, scaring you away from your blessings altogether.

> **Side Note:** *God did not call you to have a spirit of fear but a spirit of great courage. Yet, courage takes time and preparation. "Dear woman, that's not our problem," Jesus replied. "My time has not yet come." (John 2:40)*

You do not simply wake up in the middle of the night and no longer have fears. You do not just walk up to a lion and are ready to fight. Jesus did not immediately go to the cross after being born. Therefore, you cannot go to God and say, "Lord, I am ready to be healed and whole," thinking the results will be immediate. I imagine the response of God being, "ok great, you're ready to be healed and whole, but what type of pressure are you willing to be put under to be healed and whole".

The Israelites were saved from the hands of Pharaoh but what they didn't expect was the long road they had to take to get to the land the Lord had promised them. They didn't expect to be put "under pressure".

## UNDER PRESSURE

The wilderness (struggles that you go through in life) is similar to the refining process of gold. Before gold can become a desired shape or form (molded), one must use heat to refine it. This process can be done more than one way, but for this discussion, the chemical process will be used to explain how gold is refined.

**Gold-Traders:** "Refining gold involves the use of chemicals. Strong acids are used to dissolve the impurities in the gold ore and afterwards, are neutralized and washed away, taking the impurities with them. The resulting product is a muddy substance that is almost pure gold (99.999% or 24K). This muddy substance is dried until it is a powdered residue and then heated with a torch or other source of heat to melt the gold powder into useable gold. The acids used for this process are Nitric acid and Hydrochloric acid." (How to refine gold)

The trials (heat) in your life are no different from the refining process of gold. "The Angel of the Lord appeared to him in a blazing flame of fire, yet it was not consumed. So Moses said, "I must turn away [from the flock] and see this great sight—why the bush is not burned up."

When the Lord saw that he turned away [from the flock] to look, God called to him from the midst of the bush and said, "Moses, Moses!" And he said, "Here I am."

Then God said, "Do not come near; take your sandals off your feet [out of respect], because the place on which you are standing is holy ground." (Exodus 3:2-5)

Yet gold is simply an object. You, on the other hand, are God's Holy ground, a child of the one and only faithful God. Therefore, God will not allow the trials (heat) to kill you. He will use them to mold you, develop your character, stretch your faith, and strengthen it.

"We are hard-pressed on every side, but not crushed; perplexed but not in despair; persecuted, but not abandoned; struck down, but not destroyed." (2 Corinthians 4:8-9)

When you are tempted, God will provide you with hope so that you can endure. When His work is complete, He then kicks the devil (fire/trials) out of the way—only using him for the divine purpose He has in store for your future.

## THE DEVIL MAY THINK HE HAS YOU, BUT HE'S BEING USED.

"Then the Lord said to Moses, "Tell the Israelites to turn back and encamp near Pi Hahiroth, between Migdol and the sea. They are to encamp by the sea, directly opposite Baal Zephon. Pharaoh will think, 'The Israelites are wandering around the land in confusion, hemmed in by the desert.' And I will harden Pharaoh's heart, and he will pursue them. But I will gain glory for myself through Pharaoh and all his army, and the Egyptians will know that I am the Lord." So the Israelites did this." (Exodus 14:1-5)

## THE LORD DOES NOT WANT TO HANG YOUR PAST PROBLEMS OVER YOUR HEAD. HE WANTS TO HELP YOU PUT THEM IN THEIR RIGHTFUL PLACE.

In your situation, the problems or enemies you face may not be physical things or people. They may be insecurities, fears, or anger that need to be put away. "Then Moses stretched out his hand over the sea, and all that night the Lord drove the sea back with a strong east wind and turned it into dry land. The waters were divided, and the Israelites went through the sea on dry ground, with a wall of water on their right and on their left. The Egyptians pursued them, and all Pharaoh's horses and chariots and horsemen followed them into the sea. During the last watch of the night the Lord looked down from the pillar of fire and cloud at the Egyptian army and threw it into confusion. He jammed the wheels of their chariots so that they had difficulty driving. And the Egyptians said, "Let's get away from the Israelites! The Lord is fighting for them against Egypt." Then the Lord said to Moses, "Stretch out your hand over the sea so that the waters may flow back over the Egyptians and their chariots and horsemen." Moses stretched out his hand over the sea, and at daybreak the sea went back to its place. The Egyptians were fleeing toward it, and the Lord swept them into the sea. The water flowed back and covered the chariots and horsemen—the entire army of Pharaoh that had followed the Israelites into the sea. Not one of them survived." (Exodus 14:21-28)

To sum things up, when you go through the heat or face trials in life, it's not for God to crush you. It's first off to strengthen you. Secondly, weed out your enemies, allowing them to be burned and washed away. Lastly, trials will enable you to become moldable.

When you become moldable, not only can God bless you. But He can also use you to bless other people. The reason being is that once the refining process is complete, the result of what that gold (you) emulates is Jesus.

Emulate:

• To match or imitate.

God molds you making you more Christlike, which leads you to exhibit behavior that emulates the behavior of Jesus, thus allowing God to bless you as He would his son. "After all, God chose you to suffer as you follow in the footsteps of Christ, who set an example by suffering for you." (1 Peter 2:21)

## LIKE GOLD AND DIAMONDS, PEOPLE ARE CONSIDERED HOT COMMODITIES (VALUABLE), YET ONE RARELY SEES THE PRESSURE THEY MUST ENDURE BEFORE BEING REVEALED.

When I was presented with the purpose and plans God had in store for me, no one told me I would have to go through battles, that God would use my circumstances and the pressures of life to shape me, to mold me, to reveal destiny to me. My lack of understanding led to confusion, which almost led to me aborting the mission that God had presented me with. The mission of *Emancipation Freedom for the Incarcerated Soul.* The mission of freeing the people held captive by the broken systems in society. For the reasons stated above, I am here to tell you what nobody told me. There is a blessing on the other side of your problems, which you have the opportunity if you make it through the blood to become the solution to.

Some of you may have run away from your problems after being saved thinking that pain is not a part of God's plan. Yet, pain is a part of the plan, the wilderness is a part of the plan, and blood is a part of the plan. There's always blood before blessings. Read Matthew 14 in the Bible. God was not calling Peter out of the storm. He was calling Him into it. "Yes, come, Jesus said. So Peter went over the side of the boat and walked on the water toward Jesus. But when he saw the strong wind and the waves, he was terrified and began to sink. "Save me, Lord!" he shouted." (Matthew 14:29-30)

So, don't be surprised when you must get dirty. When you must get bloody.

**THE BLOOD OF JESUS IS THE STORM, AND IT'S WHAT WASHES AWAY YOUR SIN ALONG WITH YOUR ENEMIES. BUT THAT CAN ONLY HAPPEN WHEN YOU DECIDE TO BECOME IMMERSED IN IT.**

**Side Note:** *Blood cleanses and heals; it removes pride, replacing it with humility, which allows you to be a blessing, not just simply receive a blessing.*

With that being said, don't become discouraged when you go through the bloody fires of life, nor when you see others getting blessed quickly. Grit your teeth and focus on the people being sanctified (made holy; consecrated; free from sin)—the people who are becoming whole and staying whole.

As you continue to focus on the important aspects of life, God will grant you His peace and give you the strength to rise out of the bloody bath of fire one thousand times better than before. "And may the LORD, the God of your ancestors, multiply you a thousand times more and bless you as he promised!" (Deuteronomy 1:11)

## TO ACCEPT THE BLOOD AND SALVATION OF JESUS IS TO ACCEPT THE JOURNEY AND LIFE OF JESUS.

To conclude, often, people think because God saved them, He will give them everything they want on a silver platter. That's what the Israelites believed. They thought their suffering in Egypt meant they would never be put in a predicament where they would have to struggle, feel the pressures of life, or see pain anymore. Yet, had the Lord given the Israelites the promised land the moment they prayed or taken them through the shortest route, they wouldn't have built up the courage to fight the biggest battle, the battle which led to the promised land being revealed.

That's what this book will do. Give you the courage to fight the biggest battle, the war within.

Side Note: *You must conquer the war within because it's not only about getting out of the ghetto or the struggle. It's also about the tools needed to fight to stay out; spiritual warfare.*

Spiritual warfare is necessary when going through trials because you don't become sanctified by simply wanting to. It does start with a confession, but sanctification is all about progression. Jesus sacrificed His life for everyone's sins but what's in his blood is more than just the power to cleanse. You must be willing to take the good with the bad. Pray and maybe not feel heard. "At noon, darkness fell across the whole land until three o'clock. At about three o'clock, Jesus called out with a loud voice, "Eli, Eli, lema sabachthani?" which means "My God, my God, why have you abandoned me?" (Matthew 27:45-46)

**THE FIGHT IS NOT ALWAYS IN WHETHER YOU FEEL GOD HEARS YOU. THE BATTLE IS WHETHER YOU WILL KEEP PRAYING AND PUSHING FORWARD EVEN WHEN YOU THINK HE DOESN'T HEAR YOU.**

Whether in the courtroom or the boardroom, you will go through trials in life that will test you, but if you continue to pray and believe God as Jesus did the enemies you see today, you will see no more. "Moses answered the people, "Do not be afraid. Stand firm and you will see the deliverance the Lord will bring you today. The Egyptians you see today you will never see again." (Exodus 14:13)

The end of this chapter is near. Now is your chance to take a moment and ponder on the principles of blood before blessings. Think about whether you would like to take up your cross  and walk with the Lord. It will not be easy, and it is not like becoming a pop star. You are not going to be an overnight sensation. This takes work. Therefore I encourage you to take your time before deciding.

**BLOOD IS A PROCESS THAT PREPARES YOU FOR BLESSINGS. THEREFORE, THE BLOOD OF JESUS IS WHAT YOU HAVE TO GO THROUGH TO REACH THE PROMISED LAND. THE CHOICE IS YOURS—BLOOD BEFORE BLESSINGS OR THE WAGES OF SIN, WHICH IS DEATH.**

"Morality may keep you out of jail, but it takes the blood of Jesus Christ to keep you out of hell."

*— Charles Spurgeon*

*Lord,* thank you for sending me through the blood and the fire. Although the pain has been more than I could bear, I recognize it has helped me change for the better. Through your power, I have been allowed to be as great as you have planned for me to be. I am stronger because of you and wiser because of your Word. I have decided to continue this journey knowing there is hope because of Christ and his act of selflessness. Thank you for guiding me on this journey and holding my hand as I move through these valleys. As I make my way towards the promises you've stored away for me, allow me to become every dream you have placed in me.

In Jesus' name, Amen!

# PART FOUR THE PURGE

# CHAPTER 9

# NEW INFECTIONS ROOTED IN OLD WOUNDS

*The first time you encounter God, He comes to live in you "Don't you yourselves know that you are God's temple and that the Spirit of God lives in you?" (1 Corinthians 3:16) But God does not want to just live in you. He wants you to know Him on a deeper level. The Problem: God is in your heart. This means you need to get to the root of your problems so that you can get to the root of your God. He is underneath all the things (hurt, unforgiveness, pride, and people) you've placed over him.*

**Psalm 38:4-8 BSB** "For my iniquities have overwhelmed me; they are a burden too heavy to bear. My wounds are foul and festering because of my sinful folly. I am bent and brought low; all day long I go about mourning. For my loins are full of burning pain, and no soundness remains in my body. I am numb and badly crushed; I groan in anguish of heart."

In this chapter, you will be going deep and examining the *Matters of the Heart;* this includes learning about the pain trauma causes and how it can leave lasting effects on your mind, body, and spirit (heart).

## WOUNDS, INFECTIONS, AND SCARS EXPLAINED.

### Wound:

- An injury to living tissue caused by a cut, blow, or other impact, typically one in which the skin is cut or broken.

- An injury (injustice, hurt, pain, or traumatic event).

### Infection:

- The process of infecting or the state of being infected.

- "An infection is the invasion of an organism's body tissues by disease-causing agents, their multiplication, and the reaction of host tissues to the infectious agents and the toxins they produce. An infectious disease, also known as a transmissible disease or communicable disease, is an illness resulting from an infection." (Wikipedia)

- A poorly healed wound that has caused problems (PTSD, anxiety, anger, fear, hatred, depression, etc.) and now poses the risk of infecting (ruining) your entire life.

- A poorly healed wound that negatively impacts the rate at which new wounds that were only supposed to be superficial (surface level) becomes severely infected.

Scar:

- A mark left on the skin or within body tissue where a wound, burn, or sore has not healed completely, and fibrous connective tissue has developed.

- A lasting effect of grief, fear, or other emotion left on a person's character by an unpleasant experience.

- Emotional and or psychological trauma left behind after an injury has occurred.

**Side Note:** *A wound is the result of a traumatic event. An infection is the result of a poorly healed or infected wound. A scar is the lasting effect of a traumatic event or an infected wound.*

## WHAT IS THE CAUSE OF INFECTED WOUNDS?

**Summit Medical Group:** "Most skin infections follow breaks in the skin (for example, from cuts, puncture wounds, animal bites, splinters, thorns, or burns). Bacteria (especially staphylococcus or streptococcus) then invade the wound and cause the infection. Some infections start with a closed rash (that is, the skin is not broken). Examples are insect bites, chickenpox, scabies, or acne. If a child picks at these rashes, the skin can become broken and then infected.

Deeper wounds (for example, puncture wounds) are much more likely to become infected than superficial wounds (for example, scrapes). The hands are at increased risk for infection from puncture wounds. The penetrating claws or teeth of cats pose a major risk for infection.

Cellulitis (skin infection) can sometimes start without any recent wound infection. This type of cellulitis is spread from the bloodstream and can be serious if it is not treated." (Wound Skin Infection)

Before you learn about the different steps you can take to heal your broken heart, you will go back to school and receive a crash course on trauma. This will help you understand the type of trauma you may have experienced, identify the problems the trauma has created, and prepare for healing.

To help you better understand trauma and its effects, I have created a list of references sourced from different websites explaining the various types of trauma.

## DIFFERENT TYPES OF TRAUMA (WOUNDS, INFECTIONS, AND SCARS):

**Your Experiences Matter:**

- "Acute trauma: Results from exposure to a single overwhelming event/experiences (car accident, natural disaster, single event of abuse or assault, sudden loss or witnessing violence).

- Repetitive trauma: Results from exposure to multiple, chronic and/or prolonged overwhelming traumatic events (i.e., receiving regular treatment for an illness).

- **Complex trauma:** Results from multiple, chronic and prolonged overwhelming traumatic events/experiences which are compromising and most often within the context of an interpersonal relationship (i.e., family violence).

- **Developmental trauma:** Results from early onset exposure to ongoing or repetitive trauma (as infant, children or youth) includes neglect, abandonment, physical abuse or assault, sexual abuse or assault, emotional abuse witnessing violence or death, and/or coercion or betrayal. This often occurs within the child's care giving system and interferes with healthy attachment and development.

- **Vicarious trauma:** Creates a change in the service provider resulting from empathetic engagement with a client's/patient's traumatic background. It occurs when an individual who was not an immediate witness to the trauma absorbs and integrates disturbing aspects of the traumatic experience into his or her own functioning.

- **Historical trauma:** A cumulative emotional and psychological wounding over the lifespan and across generations emanating from massive group trauma. Examples of historical trauma include genocide, colonialism (i.e., residential schools), slavery and war.

- **Intergenerational trauma:** Describes the psychological or emotional effects that can be experienced by people who live with people who have experienced trauma. Coping and adaptation patterns developed in response to trauma can be passed from one generation to the next." (Types of Trauma)

**The National Traumatic Stress Network:**

- "**Early Childhood Trauma:** Early childhood trauma generally refers to the traumatic experiences that occur to children aged 0-6. Because infants' and young children's reactions may be different from older children's, and because they may not be able to verbalize their reactions to threatening or dangerous events, many people assume that young age protects children from the impact of traumatic experiences. A growing body of research has established that young children may be affected by events that threaten their safety or the safety of their parents/caregivers, and their symptoms have been well documented. These traumas can be the result of intentional violence—such as child physical or sexual abuse, or domestic violence—or the result of natural disaster, accidents, or war. Young children also may experience traumatic stress in response to painful medical procedures or the sudden loss of a parent/caregiver.

  - ◆ **Effects of childhood trauma ages 0-2:**

    - » Demonstrate poor verbal skills

    - » Exhibit memory problems

    - » Scream or cry excessively

    - » Have poor appetite, low weight, or digestive problems

  - ◆ **Effects of childhood trauma ages 3-6:**

    - » Have difficulties focusing or learning in school

    - » Develop learning disabilities

» Show poor skill development

» Act out in social situations

» Imitate the abusive/traumatic event

» Be verbally abusive

» Be unable to trust others or make friends

» Believe they are to blame for the traumatic event

» Lack self-confidence

» Experience stomach aches or headaches

- **Traumatic Grief:** Childhood Traumatic Grief is a condition in which children develop significant trauma symptoms related to the death of an attachment figure. (e.g., parent or sibling) or another important person (e.g., grandparent, other relative, friend or peer).

  ◆ **Effects of traumatic grief:**

  » Intrusive memories about the death. These can appear through nightmares, guilt, or self-blame about how the person died, or recurrent or intrusive thoughts about the horrifying manner of death.

  » Avoidance and numbing. These can be expressed by withdrawal, the child acting as if not upset, or the child avoiding reminders of the person, the way she or he died, or the event that led to the death.

» Physical or emotional symptoms of increased arousal. These can include irritability, anger, trouble sleeping, decreased concentration, drop in grades, stomach-aches, headaches, increased vigilance, and fears about safety for oneself or others." (Trauma Types, 2018)

**Help Guide:**

- **"Emotional and Psychological Trauma:** Emotional and psychological trauma is the result of extraordinarily stressful events that shatter your sense of security, making you feel helpless in a dangerous world. Psychological trauma can leave you struggling with upsetting emotions, memories, and anxiety that won't go away. It can also leave you feeling numb, disconnected, and unable to trust other people.

  Traumatic experiences often involve a threat to life or safety, but any situation that leaves you feeling overwhelmed and isolated can result in trauma, even if it doesn't involve physical harm. It's not the objective circumstances that determine whether an event is traumatic, but your subjective emotional experience of the event. The more frightened and helpless you feel, the more likely you are to be traumatized.

  ♦ **Emotional and psychological trauma can be caused by:**

  » One-time events, such as an accident, injury, or a violent attack, especially if it was unexpected or happened in childhood.

  » Ongoing, relentless stress, such as living in a crime-ridden neighborhood, battling a life-threatening illness or experiencing traumatic events that occur repeatedly, such as bullying, domestic violence, or childhood neglect.

» Commonly overlooked causes, such as surgery (especially in the first 3 years of life), the sudden death of someone close, the breakup of a significant relationship, or a humiliating or deeply disappointing experience, especially if someone was deliberately cruel.

◆ **Symptoms of psychological trauma:**

» We all react to trauma in different ways, experiencing a wide range of physical and emotional reactions. There is no "right" or "wrong" way to think, feel, or respond, so don't judge your own reactions or those of other people. Your responses are NORMAL reactions to ABNORMAL events.

◆ **Emotional & psychological symptoms:**

» Shock, denial, or disbelief

» Confusion, difficulty concentrating

» Anger, irritability, mood swings

» Anxiety and fear

» Guilt, shame, self-blame

» Withdrawing from others

» Feeling sad or hopeless

» Feeling disconnected or numb

- **Physical symptoms:**

  » Insomnia or nightmares

  » Fatigue

  » Being startled easily

  » Difficulty concentrating

  » Racing heartbeat

  » Edginess and agitation

  » Aches and pains

  » Muscle tension" (Emotional and Psychological Trauma)

## DIFFERENT TYPES OF TRAUMATIC EVENTS AND THEIR EFFECTS:

### The National Traumatic Stress Network:

- "Bullying: Bullying is a deliberate and unsolicited action that occurs with the intent of inflicting social, emotional, physical, and/or psychological harm to someone who often is perceived as being less powerful.

  - **Effects of bullying:**

    » Stress, anxiety, and depression

    » Anger or frustration

» Loneliness and isolation

» Feelings of rejection, or poor self-esteem

» Changes in sleep and eating patterns

» Health complaints

» Poor relational skills

» School avoidance, missing or dropping out of school

» Poor academic performance

» Separation anxiety

» Self-injury

» Eating disorders

» Suicidal or homicidal ideas or actions

- **Community Violence:** Community violence is exposure to intentional acts of interpersonal violence committed in public areas by individuals who are not intimately related to the victim. Common types of community violence that affect youth include individual and group conflicts (e.g., bullying, fights among gangs and other groups, shootings in public areas such as schools and communities, civil wars in foreign countries or "war-like" conditions in US cities, spontaneous or terrorist attacks). Although people can anticipate some types of traumatic events, community violence can happen suddenly and without warning. Consequently, youth and families who live with community violence often have heightened fears that harm could come at any time and experience the world as unsafe and terrifying. In addition, although some types of trauma are accidental, community violence is an intentional attempt to hurt one or more people and includes homicides, sexual assaults, robberies, and weapons attacks (e.g., bats, knives, guns).

- ◆ **Effects of community violence:**

  - » I don't know who to trust anymore.

  - » I'm on edge all the time, like something's going to happen to me, and I can't be caught off guard.

  - » I'll do anything to stay safe. That's why I carry a gun or knife, like my friends do.

  - » I don't expect to graduate from school. I'll probably die young anyway.

  - » I worry most about my little brother and sister getting shot.

  - » My friends say I'm different since the shooting.

  - » Sometimes thoughts pop up in my head, and I'm right back to the night my world changed.

  - » I'm more tempted to get drunk or high to numb it all.

  - » I feel angry even when nobody is messing with me.

  - » I get jumpy or nervous at the smallest things or little sounds.

  - » I just can't stop thinking about all the violence, how it's never going to end.

- • **Intimate Partner Violence:** Intimate Partner Violence (IPV), also referred to as domestic violence, occurs when an individual purposely causes harm or threatens the risk of harm to any past or current partner or spouse. While abuse often occurs as a pattern of controlling and coercive behavior, an initial episode of abuse may also be cause for concern. Tactics used in IPV can be physical, sexual, financial, verbal, or emotional in nature against the partner. Individuals may also experience stalking, terrorizing, blame, hurt, humiliation, manipulation, and intentional isolation from social supports and family. IPV can vary in frequency and severity. Children are often the hidden or silent victims of IPV, and some are directly injured, while others are frightened witnesses. Children with IPV exposure are more likely to have also experienced emotional abuse, neglect, physical abuse, and community violence.

- **Effects of intimate partner violence (Immediate):**

  » Generalized anxiety

  » Sleeplessness

  » Nightmares

  » Difficulty concentrating

  » High activity levels

  » Increased aggression

  » Increased anxiety about being separated from a parent

  » Intense worry about their safety or the safety of a parent

- **Effects of intimate partner violence (Long Term):**

  » Physical health problems

» Behavior problems in adolescence (e.g., delinquency, alcohol or substance abuse)

» Emotional difficulties in adulthood (e.g., depression, anxiety, PTSD)" (Trauma Types, 2018)

### Early Childhood Mental Health Consultation:

- **"Physical Abuse:** Actual or attempted infliction of physical pain with or without use of an object or weapon and including use of severe corporal punishment." (Types of Traumatic Experiences)

  ◆ **Effects of physical abuse:**

  » "People who've been physically abused may struggle with developing and maintaining friendships

  » They don't trust authority figures

  » They don't feel good about themselves or see themselves as worthy

  » They may blame themselves for the abuse and feel that they must keep what goes on in their families a secret

  » Become aggressive themselves or have other behavioral problem

  » They don't seem to care anymore if they are hit; they've lost the normal fight or flight reactions built-in to protect us from danger

  » They may stop trying to make friends or succeed at school or plan for the future

» May become anxious and fearful rather than numb and withdrawn" (Trauma Types, 2018)

**Early Childhood Mental Health Consultation:**

- **"Sexual Abuse:** Actual or attempted sexual contact, exposure
to age-inappropriate sexual material or environments, sexual
exploitation, unwanted or coercive sexual contact." (Types of
Traumatic Experiences)

  ♦ **Effects of sexual abuse:**

  » "An increase in nightmares and/or other sleeping difficulties

  » Withdrawn behavior

  » Angry outbursts

  » Anxiety

  » Depression

  » Not wanting to be left alone with a particular individual(s)

  » Sexual knowledge, language, and/or behaviors that are inap-
  propriate for the child's age" (Trauma Types, 2018)

# IF YOU WOULD LIKE TO LEARN MORE ABOUT TRAUMA AND ITS EFFECTS, I SUGGEST YOU VISIT THESE WEBSITES:

**Medical News Today**

- https://www.medicalnewstoday.com/articles/trauma#treatment

**The National Child Traumatic Stress Network:**

- https://www.nctsn.org/what-is-child-trauma/trauma-types

**Your Experience Matter:**

- https://yourexperiencesmatter.com/learning/trauma-stress/types-of-trauma/

**Early Childhood Mental Health Consultation:**

- https://www.ecmhc.org/tutorials/trauma/mod1_3.html

**Help Guide**

- https://www.helpguide.org/articles/ptsd-trauma/coping-with-emotional-and-psychological-trauma.htm

If any of the traumatic events or symptoms mentioned in this chapter describe the pain or problems you've experienced in the past or are currently experiencing, you should one please seek support. Support could be in the form of a support group, family member, friend, the Bible (God), or even in the form of medication prescribed by your doctor. Two, know that it's okay to not be okay. And three, keep reading along so that you can receive the healing you desire and deserve.

> **Side Note:** *Although traumatic events, as well as the healing process that needs to take place after said trauma, is a topic that no one really wants to talk about. It's hard to ignore the fact that almost everyone in this world is suffering or has suffered spiritually, mentally, or physically from problems brought about by an injustice or traumatic event.*

**Sidran Institute:** "An estimated 70 percent of adults in the United States have experienced a traumatic event at least once in their lives and up to 20 percent of these people go on to develop posttraumatic stress disorder, or PTSD.

- An estimated 5 percent of Americans—more than 13 million people—have PTSD at any given time.

- Approximately 8.7 percent of all adults—1 of 13 people in this country—will develop PTSD during their lifetime.

- About 3.6% of adults in the United States suffer from PTSD during the course of a year.

- An estimated 1 out of 9 women will get PTSD at some time in their lives. Women are about twice as likely as men to develop PTSD." (Traumatic Stress Disorder Fact Sheet)

What does this mean? Everyone's battling (has an infected wound needing to be unpeeled, unpacked, and cleansed). But most are not, simply because they either don't want to or don't know how to.

**Joyce Meyer Ministries:** "Today, people everywhere are struggling through life with damaged emotions. They've endured a lot of negative things, causing untold damage that needs to be dealt with. But all too often, these hurts are simply swept under the rug in an attempt to make them go away." (Meyer, Three Steps to Emotional Healing That Lasts)

**Ladies Loving God by Tonika Breeden:** "Emotional healing is a topic that no one really wants to talk about, yet we all have at one time or the other suffered from emotional or spiritual wounds. We live in treacherous and crazy times. We cannot escape the senseless violence and the painful, horrific images we see daily on TV. There is no way any human being can escape being touched by some form of physical, emotional, spiritual or psychological pain as long as they are living on this earth. The question is not whether or not we will be wounded, but rather how do we handle the wounds when they come? How can we deal with the wounds that puncture our souls?" (Breeden, Unpacking & Unpeeling: The Process of Healing Emotional Wounds – Part I, 2013)

To close, trauma and the events that lead to trauma can damage your mind, body, and spirit. It does not discriminate—whether older or younger, rich or poor, trauma and pain are experienced by all. For this reason, all, meaning the world and everyone who occupies it needs healing.

**YOU CAN'T CHANGE THE PAINFUL EVENTS THAT MAY HAVE OCCURRED IN THE PAST, BUT YOU CAN ALLOW GOD TO HEAL THE WOUNDS AND PROBLEMS IT MAY HAVE CREATED.**

"In every community, there is work to be done. In every nation, there are wounds to heal. In every heart, there is the power to do it."

— *Marianne Williamson*

*Heavenly Father,* at this moment, I ask that you breathe life into my spirit. Breathe life into the areas where my brokenness has lied to me—telling me that I would be nothing because of my old wounds. I proclaim that the devil is a liar and my place in Your Heart and Your Kingdom still stands. I am who you always said I would be, regardless of what the wounds that have been placed on me look like. These wounds do not determine who I am. You do. And for that, I am forever grateful.

In Jesus' name, Amen!

# CHAPTER 10

# UNPEELING, UNPACKING, AND CLEANSING WOUNDS

*We all have infected wounds within our hearts resulting from past traumatic events that need to be unpeeled, unpacked, and cleansed. Wounds that tell a story most of us would rather not have told. Wounds that if not dealt with and cleansed properly, can infect and ruin your soul (life).*

**Proverbs 18:14 KJV** "The spirit of a man will sustain his infirmity; but a wounded spirit who can bear?"

For many years I struggled spiritually, mentally, and physically (brokenness) but never truly knew it. It was not until my loved one's incarceration (when I got really close to God) that He was able to help me unpack as well as identify the problems that have led to my current struggles. For example, I currently struggle with different types of anxiety (generalized and social). As well as have trust issues—issues that are rooted in the fact that I buried my dad a month before my fifth birthday. February 15, 1997, was the date to be exact.

Because of Valentine's Day, the month of February was supposed to symbolize love and be filled with candy, cards, and balloons—but it wasn't. It was filled with blood and pain because of my dad's death. That moment in time led me to feel as though love did not exist in this world. That moment in time led to me building barriers to block the visuals of the pain I'd experienced. That moment is where my real problems and need for cleansing and healing began.

In this chapter you will continue to learn about the *Matters of the Heart.* But this time around you will be focusing on how to overcome your struggles, battles, problems, and pain, so that you can take those matters and turn them into solutions that will not only heal and bless you but will also heal and bless anyone you encounter. Let's get to it.

**Side Note:** *The problems you've gone through, are going through, or will go through in life can be very damaging to your heart. For this reason, the heart is where your journey and struggles begin. It's where the work that leads to cleansing and healing begins.*

iBelieve: "Has betrayal, rejection, sin, loss, or abuse cut you to your core? And are the wounds still open? I understand, friend. I've had my share of spiritual wounds, some lasting for decades because I wasn't willing to commit to treatment. Good news, though...

The Great Physician can completely heal our broken heart and bind up our wounds, healing and making us whole. But, just as with any physical wound, we have a role to play in our healing. There are steps The Healer would have us take to partner with Him in our recovery and restoration. Yes, sometimes God chooses to work a miracle in our lives, healing us immediately of the pain and completely shutting up our wounds for good. It can happen!

However, for many of us, spiritual healing will be a process." (Davis, 2016)

Get ready and strap yourself in. This journey that leads to your heart being cleansed and prepared for healing will not be a walk in the park. There will be pain and tears, but there will also be joy and happiness.

## WHAT DOES IT MEAN TO UNPEEL, UNPACK, AND CLEANSE INFECTED WOUNDS?

Unpeel:

- To remove an outer covering.

- To peel; especially to strip away (an outer layer).

- Unpeeled: to strip (something) of its skin, rind, bark, etc.

Unpack:

- Open up and reveal the contents of something.

- To undo or remove the contents of something.

- To analyze and explain in detail: to unpack a complex idea.

- Similar, analyze: to examine the nature or structure of something, especially by separating it into its parts, in order to understand or explain it.

Cleanse:

- Make (something, especially the skin) thoroughly clean.

- A process or period during which a person attempts to rid the body of substances regarded as toxic or unhealthy, typically by consuming only water or other liquids.

## REASONS WHY YOU MAY NOT WANT TO UNPEEL, UNPACK, AND CLEANSE YOUR INFECTED WOUNDS.

There are several reasons why you may not want to address the pain brought about by past traumatic experiences. I've listed a few reasons to help you dig deep and figure out your reason why.

- The pain is too much for you to deal with.

- You didn't know the scars the trauma left behind had not healed properly.

- You've covered up the pain with pride.

- You're afraid of what people will think of you if they find out what's hurting you.

- You're afraid of feeling rejected, misunderstood, or unloved by the people you care about.

- You don't know how to deal with the pain or who to give it to (God).

## WHY IS IT IMPORTANT TO UNPEEL, UNPACK, AND CLEANSE INFECTED WOUNDS?

1. It's important to unpeel, unpack, and cleanse infected wounds because what's in your heart, whether it be love or hatred. Will determine the course of your life.

"Guard your heart above all else, for it determines the course of your life." (Proverbs 4:23)

**Bible Study Tools:** "God reveals that the condition of our hearts will determine the course of our lives. What is inside your heart is taking you somewhere! Sick heart = sick life. Healthy heart = healthy life." (Thomas)

**Experiencing God | First15 Daily Devotional:** "All of us have experienced trial and pain. All of us are living life wounded and scarred. We learn to deal with our wounds and press forward, but whether we acknowledge it or not, wounds and scars change us. There are no perfect parents. There are no perfect friends. There are no perfect siblings or spouses. We live in an imperfect world with imperfect humans. We lash out and hurt others because we are broken and in need of healing.

One of the most critical spiritual exercises we can undergo is allowing God to heal our past wounds and guide us to a lifestyle of forgiving present scars. Without healing and forgiveness, other people's mistakes will affect our future. Without the inner working of the Holy Spirit, we will live in continual suffering from the sins of others." (Healing Past Wounds and Forgiving Present Scars, 2020)

> **Conclusion:** *Because the condition of your heart determines the course of your life, some work needs to be done on your heart before you can move forward on this journey and in life.*

||||||||||||||||||||||||||||||||||||||||||||||||||||||||||||||||||||||||||||||||||||||||||||||||||||||||||

"The secret of joy is the mastery of pain"

**— *Anais Nin***

||||||||||||||||||||||||||||||||||||||||||||||||||||||||||||||||||||||||||||||||||||||||||||||||||||||||||

2.  It's important to unpeel, unpack, and cleanse your wounds because one, you cannot fix what you don't know is broken. And two, the problems you don't fix will eventually lead to more problems.

"Pride goes before destruction, a haughty spirit before a fall." (Psalm 16:18)

When not dealt with promptly or properly, infected wounds can lead to further infection throughout other parts of the body. For example, as the previous scripture mentions. Pride (infection) goes before or leads to destruction (more problems).

**#1 You cannot fix what you don't know is broken:**

- **Ligonier Ministries:** "Zig Ziglar, the famous salesman and motivational speaker, once said, "The first step in solving a problem is to recognize that it does exist." Various versions of this sentiment have been expressed by other people. The thought makes a good deal of sense. If a problem goes unrecognized, how can it even begin to be addressed?" (Jesus, the Great Physician)

*Side Note: You need the Holy Spirit to help you unpack (reveal) the problems and trauma left lingering in your heart because you can't fix a problem you never even realized existed.*

**#2 The problems you don't fix will eventually lead to more problems:**

- **Medical News Today:** "Wound infections can also lead to other symptoms, such as:

  - Warm skin around the wound
  - Yellow or green discharge coming from the wound
  - The wound giving off an unpleasant odor
  - Red streaks on the skin around the wound
  - Fever and chills
  - Aches and pains
  - Nausea
  - Vomiting" (Leonard, 2019)

My father being taken away from me left me feeling abandoned, helpless, and alone (infections that can pollute your mind and heart). Those feelings led to me starting a I need to be in control rampage.

- I needed to be in control of my life because I couldn't control the fact that my dad was gone. I couldn't control losing him.

- I needed to be in control of my life because the people who were supposed to protect me and be there for me didn't, couldn't, or weren't. And that made me afraid.

As time passed on, I not only grew older, but I also started to act tough when really I was hurting. I became angry when really, I was suffering. I told everyone all was well when really, I was sick. I unconsciously learned and began to build up walls called defense mechanisms.

Defense Mechanism:

- A mental process (e.g., repression or projection) initiated, typically unconsciously, to avoid conscious conflict or anxiety.

I didn't know how to process the pain that came from me losing my dad, but I did understand the pain. I understood that my dad was gone, and I would never get the chance to see him again. But when I saw his face in the casket and put two and two together, I simply couldn't process it properly. So, I internalized the pain. I buried it behind a wall for more than eighteen years, and that led to me becoming numb.

Although I didn't get into much trouble growing up as I became an excellent student, receiving many awards, not having my dad with me became tough. I started to do poorly in school because I was missing something that I did not know I desperately needed as a child. I pushed myself into a corner to deal with my feelings alone. Pride kicked in, and I later felt like I didn't need anybody. In my eyes, I had lost what I needed. Even though my mom did all she could do for me while growing up, I still desperately needed and missed my dad.

## ISN'T IT FUNNY HOW THINGS CAN HAPPEN IN LIFE, AND WE DON'T REALIZE HOW IT KICKS OFF OTHER BEHAVIORS?

Losing my dad to gun violence broke me and made me numb. It also set the tone for the rest of my life as I began to process every injustice, hurt, or painful event in the same way I had processed my dad's death. I understood what was going on. I put two and two together. But when it came time to cry—to properly deal with the pain or problems, I simply buried them and kept going (that was how I dealt with it).

At the age of five, I had to learn how to swallow my tears and keep pushing, so that's what I continued to do even after losing my dad. I never processed pain; I never knew how.

Until—I was cheated on. That moment is when I started to feel pain again because the situation not only broke my heart it also assisted in tearing down the walls and tough exterior I had built up over the years to protect myself from pain.

> The cheating that assisted in tearing down the walls I
> had built up was just the tip of the iceberg. The trauma,
> the pain, and the result of said trauma and pain on the
> other hand had been building up within my heart since
> I was a child. And that is dangerous.

Because I had never really dealt with my feelings, the pain and problems I'd experienced due to the cheating drove me over the edge, to the point where I began to experience anxiety attacks and other physical illnesses. This was because I had been numb for so long. It was like a shock to my system to experience pain again. And everything that I had not dealt with as in pain that I'd experienced in the past—it was as if it flowed and hit me all at that moment. That is the dangerous effect of experiencing trauma and not knowing how to process it or express yourself (be cleansed).

**Ladies Loving God by Tonika Breeden:** "When a person has a physical wound it is very painful to clean out dead tissue, but it is extremely necessary in order to prevent infection. If this is the case naturally, then it is true spiritually. Our spiritual wounds are cleansed by activating our faith and applying the Word of God through consistent prayer and study. In John 15:3, Jesus states that we are clean because of His spoken Words to us. The power in the blood of Jesus cleanses us from sin (1 John 1:7). When we fail to clean out the dead mess, we provide an opening for the adversary, Satan to come in with his minions and bring further infection on top of the original wound.

From the physical perspective, a deep wound can quickly develop a surface level scar, but the remaining tissue still healing underneath is very fragile and bleeds easily because it is not yet mature. Spiritually speaking, a person can function like this for years and may think they are healed but underneath the surface, they are very fragile and immature emotionally and spiritually. It would take very little pressure to cause the wound to open all over again. This helps to explain why people who have survived tremendous trauma lash out, become overly sensitive, hard to forgive, very irritable, very angry towards God, engage in escapism (addictions), etc. when pressure, trials and tribulations come.

The big, deep wound is still sitting there unhealed on their hearts and covered with a little band-aid." (Breeden, Unpacking & Unpeeling: The Process of Healing Emotional Wounds – Part I, 2013)

**Conclusion:** *The injury (injustice, hurt, pain, or traumatic event) you should have dealt with a long time ago. Those things that haunt you in your dreams and steal away your peaceful nights. Those are the infections (problems) that will lead to more problems if not dealt with.*

||||||||||||||||||||||||||||||||||||||||||||||||||||||||||||||||||||||||||||||||||||||||||||||||||||||||||

"There are wounds that never show on the body that are deeper and more hurtful than anything that bleeds."

**— Laurell K. Hamilton**

||||||||||||||||||||||||||||||||||||||||||||||||||||||||||||||||||||||||||||||||||||||||||||||||||||||||||

3. It's important to unpeel, unpack, and cleanse infected wounds because doing so allows God to take your ashes (problems and pain) and exchange them for beauty (blessings).

"The Spirit of the Sovereign Lord is upon me, for the Lord has anointed me to bring good news to the poor. He has sent me to comfort the brokenhearted and to proclaim that captives will be released and prisoners will be freed. He has sent me to tell those who mourn that the time of the Lord's favor has come, and with it, the day of God's anger against their enemies. To all who mourn in Israel, he will give a crown of beauty for ashes, a joyous blessing instead of mourning, festive praise instead of despair. In their righteousness, they will be like great oaks that the Lord has planted for his own glory." (Isaiah 61:1-3)

When you call on God, you call on Him to shine a light (Jesus—the Holy Spirit) into your heart. You invite His light into your heart where you have problems or pain, so that beauty can be given in exchange for the ashes that the light turns the problems or pain into.

For example, I've always been very smart, stayed in books, and did my best to be a good student. But what I lacked due to the loss of my dad was social skills. Nevertheless, when I called on God, He entered my life and transformed my deficits.

My heightened intellectual and writing abilities were further developed because of my lack of social skills. To explain further, I was able to tune into books and write over all else because I spent most of my time alone. In turn, what seemed like a deficit to me (mainly because people tried to make me believe this was so), God was able to help me take that thing and transform it into a blessing that just so happens to be this book you are reading right now.

## GOD GAVE ME "BEAUTY FOR MY ASHES".

Long story short, I am who I am because I was able to recognize my problems, give them to God, and accept who I am not. I am an introvert; I am not an extrovert, nor an ambivert. And guess what, I am still fearfully and wonderfully made despite how the people in this world may see me or feel about me. "For You formed my inmost being; You knit me together in my mother's womb. I praise You, for I am fearfully and wonderfully made. Marvelous are Your works, and I know this very well. My frame was not hidden from You when I was made in secret, when I was woven together in the depths of the earth. Your eyes saw my unformed body; all my days were written in Your book and ordained for me before one of them came to be." (Psalm 139:13-19)

Introvert:

- A person who prefers calm environments, limits social engagement, or embraces a greater than average preference for solitude.

- Having a disposition that is taxed by social engagement and energized by calm environments, resulting in the preference for quiet solitude.

- Psychology: to direct (the mind, one's interest, etc.) partly to things within the self.

Define Introvert: "Introverts prefer solitude and quiet, but are neither shy nor timid, nor withdrawn. A confident introvert will have what Susan Cain calls Quiet Power. Introverts gain energy from solitary activities, and find social interaction exhausting and draining.

They tend to have several very close connections with others who are more brothers and sisters than friends." (Porter, 2016)

Inspirational Introverts include:

- **Rosa Parks:** "The Civil Rights legend who refused to give up her bus seat for a white man in 1955 was also considered an introvert. Susan Cain wrote in the introduction of her book Quiet: The Power Of Introverts In A World That Can't Stop Talking: "I had always imagined Rosa Parks as a stately woman with a bold temperament, someone who could easily stand up to a busload of glowering passengers. But when she died in 2005 at the age of 92, the flood of obituaries recalled her as soft-spoken, sweet, and small in stature. They said she was 'timid and shy' but had 'the courage of a lion.' They were full of phrases like 'radical humility' and 'quiet fortitude.'

- **Albert Einstein:** The world-renowned physicist who developed the theory of relativity was often thought to be an introvert. Like many introverts, he did his best thinking alone: "The monotony and solitude of a quiet life stimulates the creative mind," he's widely quoted as saying.

- **J.K. Rowling:** The Harry Potter creator, who was recently revealed as the author of The Cuckoo's Calling under the pseudonym Robert Galbraith, is frequently cited as an introvert. People who identify as introverts often report feeling most creative when they're alone with their own thoughts, rather than in groups. Indeed, Rowling recalls on her website that she first had the idea for Harry Potter in 1990 when she was traveling alone on a delayed train from Manchester to London.

- **Mahatma Gandhi:** Gandhi's work is proof positive that you don't have to be an extrovert to be an effective leader. He once said, "In a gentle way, you can shake the world." (Schocker, 2013)

- **Barack Obama:** "The current president of the United States made history in 2008 by becoming the first African-American elected into the office. He's also a known introvert. In fact, columnist David Brooks stated in The New York Times, "Being led by Barack Obama is like being trumpeted into battle by Miles Davis. He makes you want to sit down and discern." (Rampton, 2015)

**Extrovert:**

- An outgoing, gregarious person who thrives in dynamic environments and seeks to maximize social engagement.

- Having a disposition that is energized through social engagement and languishes or chafes in solitude, resulting in a personality that is gregarious, outgoing, and sociable.

- Psychology: to direct (the mind, one's interest, etc.) outward or to things outside the self.

**Define Introvert:** "Extraverts prefer intense sensory stimulation-noise and lights, and crowds. They are confident and outgoing, loud and boisterous, and gain energy from social interaction. They find solitude and quiet boring and dull. They seem to know everyone, have many friends, and can make new friends easily." (Porter, 2016)

**Inspirational Extroverts Include:**

- **Martin Luther King Jr:** "Rosa Parks stated Martin Luther King, Jr. was "the type of person that people really gravitated towards and they seemed to like him personally, as well as his leadership." King had an enormous impact on civil rights in the 1950s and 1960s; his efforts earned him a Nobel Peace Prize in 1964.

King attracted followers in part because he was a reported extrovert who used his charisma to challenge racism. On August 28, 1963, King made his famous "I Have a Dream" speech to hundreds of thousands in the historic March on Washington.

- **Muhammad Ali, Boxer:** I'm not the greatest, I'm the double greatest," declared Muhammad Ali, a gold medal-winning Olympian and the most celebrated boxer of all time. He was an energetic and performative athlete, but Ali's energy wasn't just confined to the ring: he was also an outspoken opponent of the Vietnam War.

  After refusing to serve in the military in 1967, Ali was arrested and sentenced to five years in prison—a decision the US Supreme Court overturned in 1971.

- **Steve Jobs:** "From 2007 through its first real decade on the market, Apple sold over a billion iPhones. A fair share of the credit goes to Steve Jobs, the co-founder of Apple, who combined revolutionary inventions with a born ability to sell.

  Time magazine listed Jobs as one of the greatest extroverts of our time, describing him as "an exacting boss" who was "comfortable with demanding the world's attention."" (Carlton, 2018)

Ambivert:

- A person whose personality has a balance of extrovert and introvert features.

**Define Introvert:** "The ambivert embraces qualities of both the introvert and the extrovert. Ambiverts are comfortable with others, but also value solitude. They are equally at home in a dance club or a library. Ambiverts are described as flexible, emotionally stable, intuitive, and influential (Kim, 2014). In one study, ambiverts performed better on a sensorimotor performance test than either introverts or extroverts (Yordanov, Christina, Christov, and Philipova, 2014)." (Porter, 2016)

> **Side Note:** *There is not enough research available to compile a list of inspirational ambiverts. Maybe if you are reading this and you are an ambivert, you can be one of the first to be listed in history.*

**Word of advice:** Stop beating yourself up because you are not like everyone else. God has made each one of us different for a reason. Your abilities or personal attributes are not like the next person simply because there are so many different problems to be solved in this world, and one solution does not fit all. Be yourself, appreciate who you are, and continue to push forward despite what or how people may think you should or shouldn't be. And if ever you need encouragement, remember this one thing: you are who you are because of who you are not, and that is what makes you unique.

> **Conclusion:** *When you give your problems to God, He can use said problems that have resulted from your pain to help further develop the areas in your life that you may already be proficient in (the thing that makes you great, the blessing that blesses others).*

||||||||||||||||||||||||||||||||||||||||||||||||||||||||||||||||||||||||||||||||||||||||||||||

"My scars remind me that I did indeed survive my deepest wounds. That in itself is an accomplishment. And they bring to mind something else, too. They remind me that the damage life has inflicted on me has, in many places, left me stronger and more resilient. What hurt me in the past has actually made me better equipped to face the present."

— *Steve Goodier*

||||||||||||||||||||||||||||||||||||||||||||||||||||||||||||||||||||||||||||||||||||||||||||||

## HOW DOES ONE DEAL WITH THE MATTERS OF THE HEART (UNPEEL, UNPACK, AND CLEANSE INFECTED WOUNDS)?

Step 1. Unpeel and unpack the wound.

Unpeeling and unpacking the wound involves you asking God to search you to help you identify what areas of your heart need to be cleansed and healed.

"Search me [thoroughly], O God, and know my heart; Test me and know my anxious thoughts." (Psalm 139:23)

**Experiencing God | First15 Daily Devotional:** "What past experience, trial, hurtful word, or person is still harmfully affecting your life today? Where do you need the Holy Spirit to come and speak healing over you? Where do you need to cry out to God in anger or frustration over a wound? Opening the wounded places of our hearts is an emotional and difficult process, but until we allow God into the harmful events of our pasts we will never experience true freedom and restoration from them. Until we allow ourselves space to deal with what for some have been harmful and defining moments, we will never experience the entirety of the abundant life available to us." (Healing Past Wounds and Forgiving Present Scars, 2020)

> **Conclusion:** *You could have been cut (hurt) by family, friends, a lover, or, like me, a situation you had no control over (me losing my dad). But no matter what it is that cut you, you, and everyone else living and breathing on this earth must come to the same conclusion. That conclusion is to pray and ask the Holy Spirit to shine His light on your heart—to reveal what is hurting you.*

"Awareness is the first step in healing."

— *Dean Ornish*

Step 2. Face (deal with) the pain.

Of course, unpeeling and unpacking your wounds is not enough to fully be cleansed of your pain. For this reason, you must take another step forward and face the pain of your past.

"Be strong and courageous; do not be frightened or dismayed, for the Lord your God is with you wherever you go." (Joshua 1:9)

> **Side Note:** *Because the battle starts within your heart and leads to your mind, which needs to be continuously renewed and cleansed. You need to face your problems head-on with God! He is the only one that will be able to help you fully see your way through the darkness and deal with the demons that lurk within.*

**Psychology Today:** "Start by facing what cannot be denied. Allow yourself to be aware of your thoughts, feelings, and inner experiences. There's no need to dig into what is going on... just let yourself be open to what comes to you." (Becker-Phelps, 2018)

**Joyce Meyer Ministries:** "Through my own life experiences and from many years of helping others through this process, I've discovered that although God wants to help those who really want emotional healing, there are some very important steps these individuals must take for themselves. If you want to receive emotional healing, one of the first steps you must take is to face the truth. You can't be set free while living in denial. You can't pretend that certain negative things didn't happen to you. I've come to realize that we're experts at building walls and stuffing things into dark corners, pretending they never happened.

I spent the first eighteen years of my life in an abusive environment, but as soon as I got away from that situation, I acted as though nothing was wrong. I never told anyone what had gone on in my private life." (Meyer, Three Steps to Emotional Healing That Lasts)

## TO PREPARE FOR HEALING, YOU MUST DIG DEEP AND FACE YOUR PROBLEMS SO THAT YOU DON'T ALLOW YOUR PROBLEMS TO TAKE CONTROL OF YOU.

I'm now twenty-eight, and I can finally say that I have been able to work on getting to the root of my hurt, pain, and problems (facing the truth). The reason for me being so uptight was that I never truly let go of the pain and anger that resulted from my dad's death. My hands were clenched; my heart was closed. Therefore, I couldn't fully receive what God wanted to give me (healing and peace).

> **Side Note:** *Until the pain of your past becomes the basis of your current reality. Until you are smacked in the face with pain, you never really know how bad the hurt from your past damaged your heart. When you come face-to-face with your demons and realize that you have to stop blaming people and start looking to God for healing, it's not always easy, but it is possible.*

**Joyce Meyer Ministries:** "Even though our problems may have been brought upon us because of something done against our will, we have no excuse for allowing the problem to persist, grow and even take control over our entire life. Our past experiences may have made us the way we are, but we don't have to stay that way. We can take the initiative by taking positive steps to change things—and we can ask for God's help. Whatever your problem may be, face it, consider confessing it to a trusted friend, and then admit it to yourself.

## FACE THE TRUTH—IT CAN BE THE BEGINNING OF A HAPPIER LIFE!" (MEYER, THREE STEPS TO EMOTIONAL HEALING THAT LASTS)

**Psychology Today:** "Simply put, to heal pain from the past, you must first acknowledge it. Get to know it. Then hold it with acceptance and compassion. As you develop this compassionate self-awareness, you will also increase your tolerance for it. Along the way, you must learn to recognize when you are approaching your threshold for what you can tolerate and learn to calm yourself at those times. But by continuing to return to your struggles from the perspective of compassionate self-awareness, you will gain greater insights. Your way of relating to yourself and your pain won't change the past, but it will transform your experience, releasing you to move forward more positively in your life." (Becker-Phelps, 2018)

> **Conclusion:** *You need to face your pain/problems so that you can move forward in life and stop reliving the traumatic events that have had you enchained and held captive.*

||||||||||||||||||||||||||||||||||||||||||||||||||||||||||||||||||||||||||||||||||||||||||||||||||

"You can accept or reject the way you are treated by other people, but until you heal the wounds of your past, you will continue to bleed. You can bandage the bleeding with food, with alcohol, with drugs, with work, with cigarettes, with sex, but eventually, it will all ooze through and stain your life. You must find the strength to open the wounds, stick your hands inside, pull out the core of the pain that is holding you in your past, the memories, and make peace with them."

— *Iyanla Vanzant, Yesterday, I Cried*

||||||||||||||||||||||||||||||||||||||||||||||||||||||||||||||||||||||||||||||||||||||||||||||||||

Step 3. Cleanse the wound.

One of the best ways to free yourself of the pain and cleanse your wounds is to take some time alone to not just pray to God but simply talk to Him about what has or is hurting you. Ask Him to help cleanse and heal your heart.

"Create in me a clean heart, O God, and renew a right spirit within me. Cast me not away from your presence, and take not your Holy Spirit from me. Restore to me the joy of your salvation, and uphold me with a willing spirit." (Psalm 51:10-12)

**Side Note:** *To be cleansed of the pain, you must go to God in prayer and purge (let out/rid yourself of) the pain and problems that's been hurting you.*

**iBelieve:** "As with any physical wound, spiritual wounds must be thoroughly cleansed in order to prepare for complete healing. And that can really be a painful process.

Our cleansing starts with prayer. We must come to Him, earnestly asking in faith that He heal us and make us whole. And we must be willing to receive our healing." (Davis, 2016)

This next part will be a challenge, and I know it will be hard. But you must go back to the first thing that hurt you and give it to God (pray about it). To learn how to forgive, which is what the next chapter talks about.

> **Side Note:** *The first thing that cut (hurt) you is what led you to the road you're on now. So, for you to become a better person, you have to attack (cleanse) the pain at the root, at the source, the place where the devil first tried to kill you and poison your mind.*

## THE BEST WAY TO SOLVE A PROBLEM IS TO ELIMINATE, OR RESOLVE, ITS ROOT CAUSE.

**Daring to Live Fully:** "There's a huge difference between hacking away at the branches of a problem and striking at the root. When most people have a problem, they limit themselves to addressing the immediate and obvious causes of the problem, which leads to the implementation of superficial solutions. Taking this approach won't provide you with a long-term solution to whatever problem you may be facing.

When you don't eliminate the root cause of a problem, the problem will keep recurring. Fortunately, there are several different tools you can use for identifying the root cause of any problem. One of the best of these is called the 5 Whys. It's a simple, but powerful tool.

Below you'll find an explanation of the 5 Whys, and you'll discover how you can start applying this approach to begin identifying the root cause of any problem you may be having.

Although the 5 Whys is a technique from lean manufacturing, it can be applied to almost any problem you may be having at work or in your daily life. The technique consists of the following:

- Start by identifying a problem that you're having.

- Ask "why" that problem is occurring. Make sure that your answer is grounded in fact. You should be able to state the proof or evidence that you're relying on for your assertion of the reason why the problem is occurring.

- Once you have an answer, ask "why" again.

- Continue the process until you reach the root cause of the problem. Usually, you'll be able to identify the root cause of a problem after asking "why" five times.

- Once you've identified the root cause of the problem, come up with a counter-measure that prevents it from recurring.

Here's an example:

- *Problem:* You got caught speeding.

- *First "Why?":* You were late for work.

- *Second "Why?":* You got up late.

- *Third "Why?"*: When the alarm rang you were too tired to get up and you hit the snooze button.

- *Fourth "Why?"*: You went to sleep late.

- *Fifth "Why?"*: You were watching TV past midnight. (This is the root cause of the problem.)

- *Solution:* Fix the root cause of the problem by setting a rule stating that you will turn the TV off at 10:30 p.m. every night." (Fabrega, 2015)

## WHEN DID THE DEVIL FIRST TRY TO TAKE YOU DOWN? START THERE AND PRAY ABOUT IT.

For me, it was losing my dad that broke me and opened me up to the need for someone else to love me in a way that only God could. And, because I wasn't whole when I moved forward in life when I got cheated on, it led to the devastation of my first hurt being relived again (re-infection).

Reinfection:

- Infection following recovery from or superimposed on infection of the same type.

**Side Note:** *The worst wounds are the ones that continue to be reopened because they're more prone to infection. Better yet, the worst wounds are the ones you don't cleanse properly. Therefore they keep getting re-infected.*

I never really knew until now how much I allowed the pain of my past infections that were not cleansed to steal the joy of my yesterdays (infect my entire life).

While writing this chapter, I realized that I had never really had much of a childhood. Or I never truly had the opportunity to be a child because of the pain that occurred in my past.

I wanted to be a child, but I had to grow up so fast because of fear. It was like life was stripped right from my hands, and there was nothing I could do. What I shouldn't have understood as a child, I did; my dad was gone, and there was nothing I could do to bring him back. All I wanted was for him to be there, to love me, but he didn't have a choice. So, for everyone who did have the option to be there for me but didn't, I would walk away from them and act as if I didn't care. That was the result of my record (heart) not being properly cleansed.

## I'VE SEEN HURT, AGONY, PAIN, AND BLOOD DRIPPING ON CONCRETE FROM INFECTIONS CALLED FEAR.

When you hold on too tight to your past, the scars are constantly being reopened, causing you to bleed and experience repeated trauma. It's like playing a song on repeat, but it's not one that you like. The record keeps playing, and as you keep rewinding it, you keep reminding yourself of all the scratches, skips, and bumps. But guess what? God knew you would have problems—problems create a need. "I have told you these things, so that in me you may have peace. In this world, you will have trouble. But take heart! I have overcome the world." (John 16:33)

## DO YOU THINK YOU WOULD CALL GOD IF YOU FELT LIKE YOU DIDN'T NEED HIM?

**Ladies Loving God by Tonika Breeden:** "Deep physical wounds that are filled with large amounts of dead cells, blood clots and other debris must be cleansed in order for healing to take place. This can be painful because there is more inflammation, soreness and tenderness with deep wounds. Foreign bodies add to the discomfort and can also delay the healing process. For healing of emotional and spiritual wounds to take place, the foreign bodies of guilt, shame, thinking God is mad at you, anger towards God, self and others must be cleaned away. All of these things will delay the process." (Breeden, Unpacking & Unpeeling: The Process of Healing Emotional Wounds – Part I, 2013)

**Conclusion:** *Any record played long enough will come across some scratches, skips, and bumps. In other words, any life lived long enough will experience some sort of hurt, pain, or problems. But the problem is not always with the scratches, skips, and bumps. The problem is that you're not dealing with the problem. It's that you're not opening yourself up to God. And you're not allowing your record (heart) to be cleansed of the scratches, skips, and bumps so that it may be able to play smoothly. So that you may be able to go on to the next record. This is the one you like. The life you've dreamed of living—a life filled with happiness and joy.*

"For a wound to heal, you have to clean it out. Again, and again, and again. And this cleaning process stings. The cleaning of a wound hurts. Yes. Healing takes so much work. So much persistence. And so much patience. But every process has an end and an appointed term. Your healing will come, God willing. And like all created things, your worldly pain will die."

**— *Yasmin Mogahed***

Step 4. Replace the old garment of pain & suffering with a new garment of blessings, joy, and happiness.

To replace the pain of your past, you need to allow God to help you transform your pain and suffering into blessings and joy. This happens when you entirely release to God your problems, meaning stop trying to seek vengeance for yourself and allow God to take care of you. To lead you and guide you.

"The young women will dance for joy, and the men—old and young—will join in the celebration. I will turn their mourning into joy. I will comfort them and exchange their sorrow for rejoicing." (Jeremiah 31:13)

"Hear, O Lord, and be merciful to me! O Lord, be my helper!" You have turned for me my mourning into dancing; you have loosed my sackcloth and clothed me with gladness, that my glory may sing your praise and not be silent." (Psalm 30:10–12)

Life can get you down. Trauma can take you out, but you still have a decision to make. Wallow in the pain of your past or push through the pain with God and allow Him to help you use the pain for good.

**Ladies Loving God by Tonika Breeden:** "According to The FreeDictionary.com, wound healing is defined as the "restoration of integrity to injured tissues by replacement of dead tissue with viable tissue…" We can look at emotional healing as a process in which a person is restored to integrity (wholeness) by first removing the dead stuff (sins—hatred, bitterness, resentment, unforgiveness, blaming others, unresolved/prolonged grief, sadness, unruly passions and other deadly heart issues) with viable tissue–love, joy, peace, patience, and other Fruits of the Spirit." (Breeden, Unpacking & Unpeeling: The Process of Healing Emotional Wounds – Part I, 2013)

**YOU CAN EITHER USE YOUR HURT AND PAIN TO BUILD YOU AND BLESS YOU. OR ALLOW YOUR HURT AND PAIN TO BE AN EXCUSE FOR WHY YOU DON'T PUSH FORWARD, ULTIMATELY LEADING TO THOSE HURTS KILLING YOU AND CURSING YOU.**

I didn't let the fact that I lost my dad break me completely. I kept on pushing; I am still pushing. But I had to decide to take the higher road, the road less traveled.

> I had the choice to allow the loss of my dad to stop me from moving forward in life. Or allow God to transform my grief and pain into a powerful source that motivates me to continue moving forward—towards a better future. I chose the latter, the road less traveled.

For example, according to judgment and statistics, I wasn't supposed to graduate high school. During my senior year, the principal told my mom I wouldn't make it. I needed one hundred or more credits she said. At that time, I was battling and sick. But no one even thought to ask if something was wrong, so I laughed. Not to mock the principal that told every child's parent they weren't going to graduate, but because I had a different kind of ammo—the kind of motivation that was unseen.

What didn't kill me (my dad being gone) was transformed into a force that motivated me as well as gave me the strength to get back on track and finish getting my credits in my senior year. And drumroll, with less than six months until graduation, I finished getting all of my credits before the rest of my senior class. The Superintendent of my school district walked up to me on the day of graduation, called me by my name, and started talking to me. He said we've been talking about you and reading your essays. You've done such an amazing job.

The twist was I didn't even know who this man was. I had never seen him a day in my life. Nonetheless, the girl who wasn't supposed to make it because the hurt of her past tried to move into and rob her of her future was being talked about in the boardroom of her school by people she didn't even know.

You see, the devil meant for the hurt of my dad to be used for evil, but because God is present in my life, He used it for good and is still using it for good. I didn't recognize that then, but as I'm dealing with my hurt and pain, I can see that today.

> **Side Note:** *Do recognize you may continue to still go through problems and pain because cleansing and healing don't take place overnight. But also remember that as long as you continue to use your pain as a solution instead of it being a problem, you will become bolder when it comes time to conquer anything in life.*

**Possibility Change:** "Healing from the pain of the past doesn't mean your memories are erased or that you'll never have those difficult feelings again.

It does mean that when these experiences visit you, they don't get to be in charge. They stop defining you. They no longer direct your actions.

When a memory or emotion appears – and it will, don't touch it. Don't feed it with your attention, and it will float on through like a cloud in the sky.

This is real, effortless freedom. Any experience can arise, but you remain stable, undisturbed, free of its influence." (Brenner, 2016)

**Conclusion:** *Often, it's not recognizable how many times the past has been used to try to hurt you (keyword try), yet the Lord granted you victory. And, even though you may not have seen what God had done for you then (when the blessings were taking place), now is the time to recognize it. So you can continue to use what the devil tried to hurt you with as a source that motivates you to keep pushing forward toward a better future.*

||||||||||||||||||||||||||||||||||||||||||||||||||||||||||||||||||||||||||||||||||||||||||||||||||||

"Most people carry that pain around inside them their whole lives, until they kill the pain by other means, or until it kills them. But you, my friends, you found another way: a way to use the pain. To burn it as fuel, for light and warmth. You have learned to break the world that has tried to break you."

— *Lev Grossman*

||||||||||||||||||||||||||||||||||||||||||||||||||||||||||||||||||||||||||||||||||||||||||||||||||||

In the end, when it's all said and done, I can honestly say I can't fully be upset about the pain that I've gone through in life because it's what helped shape me into the woman I am today. It might have broken me for a moment, but it didn't take me out. There was still just enough fight left in me to walk with God, talk with God, and be transformed by God into the woman who wrote this book. The woman who has a dream and is walking said dream out.

The pain gave me a testimony (story), but I am the one who controls the narrative. Because I (with the help of God) am the one who writes the book. I am in control because I have dealt with my problems. I've reconciled that yes, I was hurt, but the pain does not define me.

> A lot of the things that I proclaim throughout this book, like having a successful business or healing and motivating people throughout the world, were written while I was going through problems, pain, and struggling. I had not yet fully possessed those things. They are prophecies that I have written about my own life. I'm saying this to say that if a broken little girl from Oakland, Ca, can write her own story and walk it out, you can change the narrative of your story too. You just have to believe it is possible and walk with God through whatever you are going through. Trust me, blessings, healing, and joy await.

To conclude, unpeeling and unpacking the pain of your past is one of the most important steps you can take on your journey toward healing, as it helps you become more aware of what's currently hurting you. Furthermore, providing you with the opportunity to recognize and conquer your pain.

# DEAL WITH THE MATTERS OF YOUR HEART SO THAT YOU CAN OPEN UP TO GOD AND ALLOW HIM TO NURTURE YOUR SOUL.

||||||||||||||||||||||||||||||||||||||||||||||||||||||||||||||||||||||||||||||||||||||||||||||||||||||||||||||||||

"You may encounter many defeats, but you must not be defeated. In fact, it may be necessary to encounter the defeats, so you can know who you are, what you can rise from, how you can still come out of it."

— *Maya Angelou*

||||||||||||||||||||||||||||||||||||||||||||||||||||||||||||||||||||||||||||||||||||||||||||||||||||||||||||||||||

*Heavenly Father,* thank you for being a part of my life—for giving me gifts and talents that I may not yet understand. I realize that to move in those talents you have blessed me with and be of service to others, I must first deal with what's burdening me. I know that to save lives, I must be taught how to be saved by you first. To call on you first. To have my heart cleansed by you first. So, I'm starting my journey towards healing today. I'm calling on you to search me, search my heart. To reveal to me the things that I need to let go of, the hurt that I need to deal with from the root, the pain of my yesterdays. And as these things are revealed to me, I humbly pray that I may be able to come to you and give them to you. I want these problems and pains to be cleansed by you. And because I know that change and transformation do not happen overnight, I ask that you give me patience for the process as well as grant patience and understanding to those around me as they may not understand what I am going through.

In Jesus' Name, Amen!

# CHAPTER 11

# THE ART OF FORGIVENESS

*Learning to forgive is one of the biggest obstacles you may ever face. It was one I battled with and battled hard. It's funny though that God will seemingly push you into situations that cause you to forgive even when you do not mean to. For me, it was the agony and pain I saw on my loved one's face while he'd been incarcerated that made me see that to be angry with him about the past, to hold on to grudges, to not forgive, was not only pointless but poisonous.*

**Matthew 6:14-15** AMP "For if you forgive others their trespasses [their reckless and willful sins], your heavenly Father will also forgive you. But if you do not forgive others [nurturing your hurt and anger with the result that it interferes with your relationship with God], then your Father will not forgive your trespasses."

## WHAT IS FORGIVENESS?

Forgiveness:

- The action or process of forgiving or being forgiven.

To help you better understand forgiveness, I have created a list of references sourced from different websites.

**Psychology Today:** "Forgiveness is the release of resentment or anger. Forgiveness doesn't mean reconciliation. One doesn't have to return to the same relationship or accept the same harmful behaviors from an offender." (Forgiveness)

**Sunshyne Gray:** "The word forgive, is actually a verb – an action. It is defined as canceling a debt. Forgiveness is an intentional choice we make to cancel another person's debt. We do this by releasing them from our punishment (Romans 12:17-19). In other words, forgiveness is accomplished through entrusting the situation to God." (Sunshyne, 2019)

**Wikipedia:** "Forgiveness is the intentional and voluntary process by which a victim undergoes a change in feelings and attitude regarding an offense, and overcomes negative emotions such as resentment and vengeance (however justified it might be)." (Wikipedia)

## DIFFERENT TYPES OF FORGIVENESS:

Exoneration:

- The action of officially absolving someone from blame; vindication.

**Full Life Reflections:** "This is what we generally have in mind when we think of the word forgiveness. Exoneration essentially means that the slate is completely wiped clean and the relationship is fully restored to its previous sense of innocence. Basically, exoneration means to "forgive and forget," as the old saying goes. When you exonerate someone, it's as if the harmful action never took place at all." (Roes, 2018)

**Studio 5:** "This type of forgiveness is used after accidents, or when children are involved who don't know any better, or if someone like a partner or family member is truly contrite about their actions or behaviors. This is closest to what we usually think of when we use the word, "forgiveness." Exoneration is wiping the slate entirely clean and restoring the relationship to its original state. Exoneration is "for giving" yourself the gift of a fresh start with others.

**Common circumstances where exoneration fits:**

- Genuine Accident

- Unintentional Hurt

- Responsible, Remorseful & Reparative" (Hale, 2018 )

Forbearance:

- Patient self-control; restraint and tolerance.

**Full Life Reflections:** "This second level of forgiveness applies when an offender either makes a partial apology or lessens their apology by suggesting that you are also partially to blame for their wrongdoing. They may even explicitly state that you did something to cause them to behave badly. While an apology may in fact be offered here, it's usually not what was hoped for and may feel inauthentic (the often heard, "I'm sorry you feel that way" or "If I did anything to upset,

I'm sorry," come to mind). Forbearance comes into play when the relationship at hand is one that matters to you. If the person is someone who is important in your life, you should exercise forbearance even if you bear no responsibility for what happened.

Forbearance means that you should stop dwelling on the offense, release any grudges you hold, and banish all revenge fantasies. However, unlike exoneration, the slate is not wiped completely clean with forbearance. Instead, it's recommended that the person offering forbearance maintain a degree of watchfulness over the other person. This is similar to "forgive but don't forget" or "trust but verify." With forbearance, you're able to continue relationships with people who are important to you but who may not be fully trustworthy, at least at the present time." (Roes, 2018)

Studio 5: "You should always assess your responsibility in a communication breakdown. And, even when you sincerely bare no blame, you will likely want to exercise Forbearance if the relationship matters to you. Forbearance requires tolerance and restraint. Forbearance is used "for giving" yourself the gift of self-restraint.

**Common circumstances where Forbearance fits:**

- Partial Apology

- Inauthentic Apology

- Apology Mingled with Blame" (Hale, 2018 )

**Release:**

- Allow or enable to escape from confinement; set free.

**Full Life Reflections:** "Release is the lowest level of forgiveness and applies to situations in which the person who hurt you has never acknowledged any wrongdoing. He or she has either never apologized or has offered an incomplete or insincere apology. Apology or not, no reparations have been given and the perpetrator has done little or nothing to improve the relationship. Some examples of where release may apply include:

- Survivors of child abuse

- Businesspeople cheated by partners

- Betrayal by friends or relatives" (Roes, 2018)

**Studio 5:** "Release does not exonerate the offender. Nor does it require Forbearance which again is "forgive but not forget" or "trust but verify." That would be unwise in certain circumstances. Release does not even require that you continue the relationship.

Release does something that is critically important: it allows you to let go of the burdens that are weighing you down and eating away at your chance for happiness. If you do not release the pain and anger and move past dwelling on old hurts and betrayals, you will be allowing the one who hurt you to live rent-free in your mind, reliving forever the persecution that the original incident started.

**Common circumstances where Release fits:**

- No Acknowledgement of Hurt

- Obviously Insincere Apology

- No Reparation or Amends Attempted" (Hale, 2018 )

**Christian Counseling Centers:**

- "**Decisional forgiveness:** Involves deciding to forgive a personal offense and letting go of angry and resentful thoughts and feelings toward the person who has wronged you.

- **Emotional forgiveness:** Involves replacing the negative emotions with positive feelings like compassion, sympathy, and empathy. Research shows that emotional forgiveness is where the most health benefits lie." (Burns)

## REASONS WHY YOU MAY NOT WANT TO FORGIVE OTHERS:

- You are afraid to revisit a past problem or pain.

- Forgiving makes you feel vulnerable because it says to you if you forgive, you must try open your heart to love again.

- You are still angry about who or what hurt you.

- You truly don't know how.

## WHY IS IT IMPORTANT FOR YOU TO FORGIVE?

1. You need to forgive because if you don't, you will be unable to go beyond a surface-level relationship with God.

To know God on a deeper level, you have to be willing to peel away all the hurt and pain, all of the unforgiveness. Why? Unforgiveness is a sin, and sin damages your relationship with God.

"Surely the arm of the LORD is not too short to save, nor His ear too dull to hear. But your iniquities have built barriers between you and your God, and your sins have hidden His face from you, so that He does not hear. For your hands are stained with blood, and your fingers with iniquity; your lips have spoken lies, and your tongue mutters injustice." (Isaiah 59:1-3)

"Love prospers when a fault is forgiven, but dwelling on it separates close friends." (Proverbs 17:9)

## Unforgiveness is a sin:

- **Higher Aim:** "Unforgiveness is sin. This truth is hard to hear, and even harder to obey – especially for those who have been deeply wounded by the sins of another. It is for our good, however, that we not only hear it, but also believe it. Why is this true? First, because the Bible says that if we do not forgive those who sin against us, God will not forgive us. Second, because an unforgiving and bitter spirit will destroy a person's heart. God's Word makes it clear that unforgiveness is a serious sin." (The Sin of Unforgiveness, 2018)

## Sin damages your relationship with God:

- **Bible Tools:** "A damaged relationship with God. Isaiah 59:1-2 shows that sin creates division between God and us because of the breach of trust. Sin is a breaking of the terms of the covenant agreed on by both God and us." (Ritenbaugh J. W., 2009)"

- **Ligonier Ministries:** "Sin also puts us at enmity with God. It has broken our relationship with Him and has made us His enemy (Hos. 1:2; Rom. 3:23). We have wronged God by our sin and destroyed the relationship, and the only way to restoration is through Christ the Mediator. Despite our having broken this bond with our Creator, God sent His Son to atone for the sins of His people. In Christ, we are God's children, we have peace with God, and our relationship with Him is restored (John 3:16; Rom. 5:1; 8:1–17; Eph. 1:3–6)." (Sin and Our Relationship to God)

- **Andrew K. Gabriel:** "Therefore, "separation" between God and humanity is metaphorical. We are only separated from God relationally. Most of us understand what this means. I can even be sitting right beside someone with whom my relationship has (in a sense) been cut off! Similarly, Isaiah 59:2 explains how this "separation" from God means that God is not responding positively to the Israelite's prayers; metaphorically speaking, God "does not hear" them (v. 2). It certainly does not, however, mean that God does not love them (John 3:16!), as a human relationship "separation" might imply." (Gabriel, 2013)

As people, when someone hurts us, yet we refuse to forgive them, that unforgiveness develops into anger or pride (a wall) that blocks off any love that is presented to us. It makes us see everyone who would love us as anyone who has hurt us, making it hard for us to build a healthy relationship with God.

For example, that relationship you got out of months or even years ago can still be a burden on your relationship with God if when God tries to come into your life next, the burden is still on your heart. Why? When you choose not to forgive, you're not just blocking the individual who hurt you; you are also blocking God.

Now the individual who hurt you is gone and has moved on, but the burden of heartbreak remains. And as long as said individual is there (in your heart), you make it hard for God to be.

## HAVE YOU BEEN TELLING YOURSELF THAT YOU'RE OVER WHAT'S BURDENING YOU? WHEN REALLY, IT'S BEEN OVER YOU (HOVERING). CONTROLLING YOUR SOUL (MIND, WILL, EMOTIONS). WHICH LATER LEADS TO SAID BURDEN TAINTING YOUR SPIRIT (THE MOST HOLY PLACE).

Side Note: *The most Holy Place is where God and man (you) meet, which is in the spirit or the heart. But if your heart is blocked because of unforgiveness, God can't be let in.*

As Joyce Meyer puts it, "the Holy Spirit is a gentleman; He will not push away what you already have in place". So, He sits back and patiently waits until "you" decide that you are ready for change.

Conclusion: *No matter what you've gone through, no matter who hurt you, never allow yourself to become numb to the feelings that the creator (God) has given you. These feelings allow you access to Him—feelings that a hardened heart cannot feel, access to a doorway that a hardened heart cannot move through.*

||||||||||||||||||||||||||||||||||||||||||||||||||||||||||||||||||||||||||||||||||||||||||||||||||||||

"The self-protective walls we put up around ourselves through anger and resentment can also keep out those who would give us genuine love and support."

— *Jenny Hewett*

||||||||||||||||||||||||||||||||||||||||||||||||||||||||||||||||||||||||||||||||||||||||||||||||||||||

2. You need to forgive because darkness will grow within your heart if you don't.

When you don't forgive others, the possibility for darkness and bitterness to grow within your heart is imminent.

"Look after each other so that none of you fails to receive the grace of God. Watch out that no poisonous root of bitterness grows up to trouble you, corrupting many." (Hebrews 12:14-15)

**Cru.org:** "When you refuse to forgive and hold onto pain, hurt and injustice, it becomes bitterness. That bitterness can take root and becomes poisonous to your spiritual life." (Eng)

## HAS THE UNFORGIVENESS WITHIN YOUR HEART BEEN LEFT TO BUILD UP SO SEVERELY THAT YOUR ONCE POSITIVE WORDS AND SPIRIT HAVE BECOME A DANGER ZONE OF HATE?

When you allow the hurt that has resulted from past painful experiences to turn into anger and friends to turn into strangers, that is a sign that the anger and unforgiveness you are holding on to, that pain is now spilling over into your now, your current relationships.

## THE HARD PART:

You need to allow God to help you deal with the problems that have resulted from your unforgiveness to come to terms with the past so that you can reconcile. Not necessarily reconcile with the person that hurt you but reconcile with yourself. Because maybe the person that hurt you was hurt too. And no, it's not an excuse for people to do bad things. But the reality we face is that there are so many broken people, so many people who are not whole walking around in the world, and they don't even know it; we may not even know it. This is why you need to work on yourself before moving forward in life. So you can be whole—so you don't go around hurting others because you are hurting.

**Jenny Hewett Coaching:** "An initial choice to forgive is a starting place, but then forgiveness has different depths or layers. A superficial expression of forgiveness can be good to begin with, but true forgiveness needs to come from our heart, where most of the pain of the wrong has been stored. This means the pain needs to be faced in order to unlock it. This involves allowing the pain and fear to come to the surface, not to wallow in it (which will NOT help,) but to be able to truly acknowledge what we are forgiving. This may need to be repeated, again and again over time, each time choosing to forgive, until release comes.

Something that can be helpful in this process is being able to see from the other person's perspective. "Hurting people hurt people," so they may well have their own struggles which caused them to behave the way they did. They may even be unaware of how they hurt you. This doesn't make the hurt less, neither does it excuse it, but it can give you an understanding which can help you to forgive. (It does not mean you can necessarily trust them though, unless there is evidence they have changed)." (Hewett, 2020)

> **Side Note:** *If you don't work on yourself and your unfor-giveness, you can potentially hurt someone else with your hurt. Remember, hurt people hurt people.*

**Joyce Meyer Ministries:** "Many people ruin their health and their lives by taking the poison of bitterness, resentment and unforgiveness. Matthew 18:23-35 (AMPC) tells us that if we do not forgive people, we get turned over to the torturers. If you have a problem in this area or have ever had one, I'm sure you bear witness with what I'm saying. It's torture to have hateful thoughts toward another person rolling around inside your head." (Meyer, The Poison of Unforgiveness)

## ARE YOU UNNECESSARILY HOLDING ON TO UNFORGIVENESS, CHUGGING DOWN A GALLON OF DARKNESS? NOT RELEASING IT IS TORTURING YOU.

The build-up from unforgiveness leads to darkness and torment. It starts with the repeated replay of your hurt, leading you to believe that whatever problems you are facing is all your fault. As it continues to build up, you become like a teapot. And once your heart and mind are burdened with so much negativity, it starts to wreak havoc on your spirit, on your soul. You become low, tired, groggy, and angry. You go from the "what ifs" to the "*shoulda, coulda, woulda's.*" "If only my dad were around, I coulda had a better life. If only I didn't get my heart broken at a young age when the time came, I coulda been a better wife."

As time passes and the torment continues, it becomes too much for you to bear. And without the light of God, darkness takes over and consumes you. Is that what you want for yourself?

**Conclusion:** *When you build up barriers and give yourself all of these reasons why forgiveness is impossible, you fill yourself with darkness. The problem: darkness makes it hard for you to see that you're not hurting them (the people who have hurt you) but killing yourself by not forgiving.*

||||||||||||||||||||||||||||||||||||||||||||||||||||||||||||||||||||||||||||||||||||||||||||||||||||

"Unforgiveness is like drinking poison yourself and waiting for the other person to die."

— *Marianne Williamson*

||||||||||||||||||||||||||||||||||||||||||||||||||||||||||||||||||||||||||||||||||||||||||||||||||||

3. You need to forgive because forgiveness is the key to spiritual, mental, and physical freedom.

Forgives is indeed the key to freedom, but to receive said key from God, you must be forgiven by Him. This means you must first forgive others of their trespasses (reckless sins).

"But when you are praying, first forgive anyone you are holding a grudge against, so that your Father in heaven will forgive your sins, too." (Matthew 11:25)

iBelieve: "Though most spiritual wounds are caused by others, we ourselves can be the cause of our spiritual damage. No matter the cause, unforgiveness is at the root. We must ask God to help us forgive those who've hurt us (even if that means asking Him to help us forgive ourselves). Forgiveness is a choice that has to be made to break the cycle of chronic spiritual debilitation and bondage." (Davis, 2016)

Jenny Hewett Coaching: "Although we may feel in control, in truth, holding on to unforgiveness keeps us enslaved to the person who wronged us. It keeps us chained to the past. President Clinton once asked Nelson Mandela how he was able to forgive his jailers and his reply was 'As I walked out of the door towards freedom, I knew that if I didn't leave bitterness behind I would still be in prison.'

Forgiveness frees us to live in the present rather than being chained to the past. It may not change the past, but it will radically change our future. So, I've said a bit about what forgiveness isn't. Let me now suggest what forgiveness actually is, because true forgiveness brings immeasurable freedom.

First of all, forgiveness is a choice, not a feeling. If you wait until you feel like forgiving someone, the chances are you never will. Similarly, if you wait for an apology from a person who wronged you before you forgive them, that apology may never come. You hold the key to your own freedom, no one else does. You cannot always choose what happens to you, but you can choose how to respond." (Hewett, 2020)

## THE MOMENT YOU DECIDE TO FREE YOURSELF FROM THE UNNECESSARY BURDEN OF UNFOR-GIVENESS IS THE MOMENT YOU CHOOSE TO BE FREE.

Freedom is a choice. And the way to receive it is you must come to a place of understanding that the hurt of your past does not define you. The only way it defines you is if you allow it to and continue to harbor unforgiveness in your heart. The longer you hold on to it, the longer you hold up the walls it caused you to build. The longer you remain imprisoned by said walls.

**Compelling Truth:** "We cannot receive a life freed from our deserved fate unless God forgives our sin (Acts 26:18). The word forgiveness comes from the Greek word aphiemi, which means "to let go, to give up, to keep no longer." We can think of forgiveness metaphorically, as an outstanding debt that we owe that is wiped clean by someone who loves us. We no longer carry the burden of that debt. Psalm 103:12 says that because we are forgiven, God will never hold our sins against us." (How are salvation and forgiveness related?)

We all deserve forgiveness, don't we? But being human, we only forgive when we come to the point that we feel it's deserved. But here you are on a daily basis in need of and asking God to forgive you. You're asking Him to forgive you when you can't even forgive the people you feel don't deserve your forgiveness. So, you create a double standard. That when you should be forgiven; God should just let you free. But you hold captive the people you choose not to forgive and set free. The "it's okay for you to cheat" rule. But let the individual you're in a relationship with do the same, and approaching around the corner will be World War III.

## WHAT DOUBLE STANDARDS HAVE YOU BEEN CREATING? "WHY DO YOU LOOK AT THE SPECK OF SAWDUST IN YOUR BROTHER'S EYE AND PAY NO ATTENTION TO THE PLANK IN YOUR OWN EYE?" (MATTHEW 7:3)

**Side Note:** *You cannot play both sides of the field. You cannot expect to receive forgiveness yet refuse to forgive others.*

We all need forgiveness every day, whether we recognize it or not. It's something you've done today or yesterday, whether it be gossip, judging someone else's faults, telling a lie, or otherwise. You need forgiveness; we (humanity) need forgiveness.

## ARE YOU ASKING FOR MORE THAN WHAT YOU SHOULD RECEIVE BUT NOT GIVING MORE THAN WHAT THEY SHOULD?

"They," meaning the people who hurt you. "They," meaning the half of a parent who left you because they were not whole when you were born. "They," meaning the people that fired you from that job.

Can you watch a building go down in flames and not feel anything inside because you still haven't forgiven "they" on that job that let you go last year?

## WORD OF ADVICE: FORGIVENESS ISN'T FOR THEM. IT'S FOR YOU.

**Got Questions:** "Misunderstanding forgiveness often keeps us in bondage to grudges. We think that to forgive is to excuse sin or pretend the offense did not matter. Neither is true. Forgiveness is not about the other person. Forgiveness is God's gift to us to release us from the control of someone who has hurt us." (What does the Bible say about grudges?, 2014)

Lastly, for those of you who have been on the other side of the stick and are the ones who feel the need for forgiveness; meaning maybe you're the one who hurt someone. Possibly you've been hurt and have hurt others all at the same time. I'm sure I've hurt others, whether it be a snarky word or otherwise. Either way, I've learned that even if you may need forgiveness, you have to understand that not everyone will forgive you—no matter how sorry or remorseful you are. Also, other people forgiving you does not determine God's forgiveness of you.

**Side Note:** *There will be some people who will not forgive you. So, if you have asked God for forgiveness and have genuinely decided to change your life, you can't hold the grief of someone else's unforgiveness of you in your heart. You still have to push forward with God—knowing He has forgiven you.*

Ultimately, forgiveness isn't determined by whether people decide to let you free. It's determined by your willingness to open up your mouth and heart to either be the forgiver or the forgiven. Forgiveness is determined by God.

**Conclusion:** *The pain that the people who have hurt you left only controls your freedom when you allow it to. The moment you take charge, take back your life and release them from the debt you've added all this interest, fees, and surcharges on will be the moment you can pack up your U-Haul and move on with your life.*

||||||||||||||||||||||||||||||||||||||||||||||||||||||||||||||||||||||||||||||||||||||||||||||||||

"Forgiveness is unlocking the door to set someone free and realizing you were the prisoner!"

**— Max Lucado**

||||||||||||||||||||||||||||||||||||||||||||||||||||||||||||||||||||||||||||||||||||||||||||||||||

4. You need to forgive because God has instructed us not to hold on to grudges and to forgive continuously.

You must not be a fugitive who harbors the pain of old crimes. Instead, you are instructed to be the righteous light of God—forgiving always.

"Then Peter came to him and asked, "Lord, how many times will my brother sin against me and I forgive him and let it go? Up to seven times?" Jesus answered him, "I say to you, not up to seven times, but seventy times seven." (Matthew 18:21-22)

**Got Questions:** "We all have reasons to hold grudges. People wrong us. Situations hurt us. Even God does not always do what we think He should do, so we get angry. We hold offenses against those who have wronged us, and often against God who we think should have done things differently. A grudge is nothing more than a refusal to forgive. So, since this tendency is inherent in all of us and seemingly unavoidable, what does the Bible say about it?

God has such a strong concern about grudges that He included a specific command about them when He gave the Law to the Israelites. Leviticus 19:18 says, "Do not seek revenge or bear a grudge against anyone among your people, but love your neighbor as yourself. I am the Lord." It is interesting that God concluded this particular command with the words "I am the Lord." In doing so, God reminded us that He is the Lord, not us. To hold a grudge is to set ourselves up as judge and jury—to determine that one person's wrong should not be forgiven. No human being has the right or authority to do that." (What does the Bible say about grudges?, 2014)

God doesn't want you to hold on to grudges. In the Bible, as many times as King Saul tried to kill David for no reason, David remained humble and forgave him. "Then he shouted to Saul, "Why do you listen to the people who say I am trying to harm you? This very day you can see with your own eyes it isn't true. For the Lord placed you at my mercy back there in the cave. Some of my men told me to kill you, but I spared you. For I said, I will never harm the king—he is the Lord's anointed one. Look, my father, at what I have in my hand. It is a piece of the hem of your robe! I cut it off, but I didn't kill you. This proves that I am not trying to harm you and that I have not sinned against you, even though you have been hunting for me to kill me." (1 Samuel 24:9-11)

> **Side Note:** *David had many chances to avenge him-self, but he didn't. He put his situation in God's hands, trusting that He'd take care of him.*

Even when Saul died, David did not rejoice. He even had the indi-vidual who thought they were bringing him good news about Saul's death killed. "David said to the young man who informed him, "Where are you from?" He answered, "I am the son of a foreigner (resident alien, sojourner), an Amalekite." David said to him, "How is it that you were not afraid to put out your hand to destroy the Lord's anointed?" David called one of the young men and said, "Go, exe-cute him." So he struck the Amalekite and he died. David said to the [fallen] man, "Your blood is on your own head, for your own mouth has testified against you, saying, I have killed the Lord's anointed." (2 Samuel 1:13-16)

This person thought that because Saul previously tried to kill David, he would be able to get in good with David, who was King at the time, if he had been the one to tell him the news about Saul's death. This person tried to use David's past problems and pain to become a fake ally. But David saw right through the schemes of the devil.

**Desiring God:** "According to Ephesians 4:27 this is what Satan is watching for—the gap called grudge. If there is any way that Satan can assist you to hold a grudge, he will do it. For there are six goals of Satan which are greatly advanced when professing Christians hold grudges.

1. To Make Us Put Ourselves in the Place of God

2. To Make Us Act as If We Are Judge, Not God

3. To Make the Cross of Christ Look Weak and Foolish

4. To Cultivate Disunity in the Body of Christ

5. To Crush Broken Christians into Depression

6. To Help You Destroy Yourself" (Piper, 1984)

**Side Note:** *The devil will try to use your past problems and the unforgiveness of others to create pride in you, to make you allies with him in hate. But you don't have to take the bait. You can trust God with your hurt and pain—with your tears.*

**EVERY TEAR THAT YOU'VE CRIED REPRESENTS A (THEY). THEY THAT HURT OR LEFT YOU. THEY THAT GOD WILL TAKE CARE OF FOR YOU. YOU JUST HAVE TO FORGIVE (RELEASE THEM TO HIM).**

**Got Questions:** "We often hold on to grudges because we feel we have the responsibility to see that justice is done or that others know how badly we were hurt. But when we release the situation to God, along with the right to dictate the ending, we free the Lord to work as He sees fit without our anger getting in the way (Matthew 18:21–22)." (What does the Bible say about Grudges?, 2014)

The tears you've shed or are currently shedding, God sees them when they drop from your eyes. He collects them and keeps track of every account. "You keep track of all my sorrows. You have collected all my tears in your bottle. You have recorded each one in your book." (Psalm 56:8) Every account (injustice) that you thought went unnoticed. Every account (betrayal) that made you feel your heart was overdrawn. God will take care of every account (painful event) that made your heart go bankrupt. He will be your avenger. You only need to do as He's instructed and release your burden. "Beloved, never avenge yourselves, but leave it to the wrath of God, for it is written, "Vengeance is mine, I will repay, says the Lord." (Romans 12:19)

**Conclusion:** *Forgiveness may be a challenging obstacle to overcome, but it's an act that God has instructed you to exercise regularly. Not simply for the sake of others, but for the sake of yourself.*

||||||||||||||||||||||||||||||||||||||||||||||||||||||||||||||||||||||||||||||||||||||||||||||||||||

"Forgiveness is not an occasional act, it is a permanent life-style."


— *Dr. Martin Luther King Jr.*

||||||||||||||||||||||||||||||||||||||||||||||||||||||||||||||||||||||||||||||||||||||||||||||||||||

**SO, ARE YOU READY TO FORGIVE? OR WILL YOU CONTINUE TO MAKE BRICKS TO BUILD A HOUSE STURDY ENOUGH TO STAY IN THE PAST WITH YOUR PAIN AND RELIVE?**

The pain I am going through right now (my loved one being incarcerated) has helped me see how important it is to forgive the pain of my yesterdays. To forgive the one who took my dad's life.

Constantly looking into the eyes of the men who are incarcerated and in pain has allowed me to see the frailty in humanity—the frailty in me. That alone has encouraged me to change my ways. To be free of grudges and forgive.

Frailty:

- The condition of being weak and delicate.

- Moral weakness; liability to yield to temptation.

**TAKE INVENTORY OF THE INSIDE OF YOURSELF, AND YOU'LL BEGIN TO SEE THE FRAILTY AND BROKENNESS WITHIN YOU TOO!**

After living in torment for nearly twenty years due to my dad's death, God finally showed me how to forgive and let go. Pain is what taught me how to forgive, and through the toughness of God's love, it's what led me to heal.

**TO LEARN HOW TO LOVE AGAIN, TO FORGIVE, SOMETIMES YOU HAVE TO HURT AGAIN.**

As crazy as it sounds, it can be true. When someone who previously brought you to tears brings you to tears over the tears they currently shed—it does something to you. It's the pain that sets you free from unforgiveness. The pain that brings you to your knees making you see things in life differently. And not differently because you avenged yourself, but because the person that previously hurt you is hurting, and all you can see is pain.

**Side Note:** *Even after all you've done to disobey God, He is still compelled to forgive you because the hurt you've inflicted doesn't compare to the agony, pain, and sorrow He sees in your eyes when He looks into them. Your pain hurts Him. "In all their distress he too was distressed, and the angel of his presence saved them. In his love and mercy he redeemed them; he lifted them up and carried them all the days of old." (Isaiah 63:9)*

To conclude, no amount of anger nor hurt is worth your freedom. You can still be more than the dad who wasn't around to teach you. You can still be more than the person that beat you. You can still be more than the emotional and physical scars life has left on you. You just have to trust God, forgive, and be forgiven.

## BECAUSE TO WHOM MUCH IS GIVEN, MUCH IS REQUIRED!

||||||||||||||||||||||||||||||||||||||||||||||||||||||||||||||||||||||||||||||||||||||||||||||||||||||

"Forgive others, not because they deserve forgiveness, but because you deserve peace."

— *Jonathan Huie*

||||||||||||||||||||||||||||||||||||||||||||||||||||||||||||||||||||||||||||||||||||||||||||||||||||||

*The Lord's Prayer:* "Our Father, who is in heaven, Hallowed be Your name. Your kingdom come, Your will be done. On earth as it is in heaven. Give us this day our daily bread. And forgive us our debts, as we have forgiven our debtors [letting go of both the wrong and the resentment]. And do not lead us into temptation but deliver us from evil. For Yours is the kingdom and the power and the glory forever." (Matthew:9-13)

*Heavenly Father,* I ask that you help me forgive the people who hurt me; help me forgive the people who left me; help me forgive myself for the pain that I have caused others; help me to forgive because you have forgiven me.

In Jesus' name, Amen.

# CHAPTER 12

# TELL IT LIKE IT IS

*I'm afraid of being vulnerable because I'm afraid of being hurt. I'm afraid of being susceptible. I'm afraid of being naïve. I'm afraid of being childlike.*

*But...*

*I AM INNOCENT.*

*I AM BLAMELESS.*

*I AM NOT RESPONSIBLE.*

**1 Peter 5:5-7** AMPC "Clothe (apron) yourselves, all of you, with humility [as the garb of a servant, so that its covering cannot possibly be stripped from you, with freedom from pride and arrogance] toward one another. For God sets Himself against the proud (the insolent, the overbearing, the disdainful, the presumptuous, the boastful)—[and He opposes, frustrates, and defeats them], but gives grace (favor, blessing) to the humble. Therefore humble yourselves [demote, lower yourselves in your own estimation] under the mighty hand of God, that in due time He may exalt you, Casting the whole of your care [all your anxieties, all your worries, all your concerns, once and for all] on Him, for He cares for you affectionately and cares about you watchfully)."

**Side Note:** *If you wonder why I started this chapter like this, stay tuned and keep reading along. The rest of the chapter will tell you everything you need to know.*

More often than not, as people, we go through life fronting. Acting like trauma doesn't cause pain, and the scary things in life don't make us fearful. We go through life saying, "I'm fine, I'm good, I'm okay". When the truth is, "I'm afraid, I'm hurting, I'm broken".

## WHY DO WE DO THIS?

Well, it's not simply because it's something we as people just believe in doing. It's because that's what we're taught to do. Not just on the streets but also in the church.

For example, on the streets, you are weak if you are scared. People even say if you are scared, go to church because to express hurt, or pain is unacceptable in the streets, and so is fear. In church, if you are scared, you're also weak because it means you don't have enough faith. If you had faith and knew God, you wouldn't be scared, is what some would say.

## THE STREETS AND THE CHURCH SEEM TO HAVE SOME SIMILARITIES. BOTH ARE TEACHING PEOPLE HOW TO BUILD UP PRIDE AND BLOCK OFF GOD.

Whenever you are hurting or are going through problems in life but cannot express yourself, you are unknowingly using a band-aid (pride) to close or block off the door that would allow anything (including God) to flow in or out of your life. As time passes, your unexpressed fear turns into a spirit of darkness. Eventually, that darkness that lies dormant in your heart leads to you becoming numb or cold-hearted.

Side Note: *Because people are teaching others that expressing pain and or needing love through hard times signifies weakness. Or to be open means you're a silly or foolish person. Most people don't want to say how they really feel. As a result, people bottle up their feelings and harden their hearts—ultimately blocking off their access to God.*

The Problem:

- Unexpressed fear (stressor) turns into pride which turns into other things such as anxiety, depression, frustration, and anger. This is because fight or flight doesn't operate properly when a person never expresses fear or pain. Fight (survival mode, which causes adrenaline to rush) is almost always in motion, no matter the situation, which is very dangerous.

**Stressor:**

- Something that causes a state of strain or tension.

**Child Savers:** "It can be negative when a child has been exposed to stress over a long period of time. For example, starting school is stressful, so is moving to a new neighborhood. Both scenarios are commonly experienced and produce low levels of stress in children. But what happens when a child lives in a dangerous environment? What happens to a child when the stress response is turned on, but is not turned off? Imagine feeling like you've just slammed on your breaks to avoid an accident and the sensation never really leaves you.

A child who grows up in a home where domestic violence is common experiences stress constantly. Same with the child who lives in fear of the bully or the abuser. That jittery sensation of just having avoided a car accident stays active in the child constantly. When in constant survival mode, the nervous system remains activated and continues to pump out extra stress hormones (i.e. adrenaline and cortisol). This is called toxic stress. In adults and children, this can leave a body feeling overwhelmed, depleted, weakened, and worn out. Those experiencing low-level stress long-term can even have a weakened immune system and get sick more often.

How do you know if your child is stressed? You can look for certain signs:

- Moodiness or irritability

- Inability to concentrate

- Hyperactivity

- Tantrums

- Trouble sleeping

- Anxiety

- Panic attacks

- Sadness or depression

- Stomach aches, chest pain, or headaches

- Sudden allergic reactions including asthma or eczema

That child "acting out in school" may be experiencing long-term stress. In extreme circumstances, children who have experienced stress long-term can become traumatized and experience Post-Traumatic Stress Disorder (PTSD). When children have experienced trauma, they may require mental health therapy to help them recover, cope, and heal." (Children and Stress, 2016)

## NOT BEING ABLE TO "TELL IT LIKE IT IS" CAN BECOME A ROADBLOCK THAT EVENTUALLY CAN BECOME A HEART BLOCK THAT CAN ULTI-MATELY MAKE YOUR HEART STOP.

**Side Note:** *Because the flow of life is similar to the way blood flows through your heart, if there is a blockage (pride), the blood (Jesus) cannot flow properly. Eventually, the blockage stopping the blood from flowing leads to a build-up of pressure—making you more prone to health issues or even death.*

And you wonder why you are sick. There's too much pressure built up within you, too much hypertension (high blood pressure) and no release, no medication (Holy Spirit) just band-aids (pride).

**Maria Erving | Transformational Teacher and Energy Healer:** "When living in opposition to the flow of Life there's struggle. Struggle comes from distrust in your oneness with Life, so you exist in survival mode, and doing this for extended periods of time there's a risk of falling into depression and even despair. Because when Truth (flow) is denied the person becomes confused (denial or rejection of your true Self causes confusion) and depending on their beliefs they can even feel abandoned by that which they call "God". There's a disconnect, and this disconnect is what causes struggle and pain. Most people don't trust themselves enough to choose the alignment with the Greater Self within them." (Erving, 2019)

**ARE YOU GUILTY OF UNKNOWINGLY BLOCKING YOUR BLESSINGS? HAS YOUR INABILITY TO ALLOW GOD INTO YOUR LIFE LEFT YOU STAGNANT? DON'T YOU WANT YOUR CUP TO RUN OVER? WELL, FOR YOUR CUP TO RUN OVER, YOU NEED TO FIRST REMOVE THE LID YOU PLACED ON IT.**

Before you move forward in life and become successful or accomplish whatever goals you have set for yourself, you must take the first step towards recovery: do the opposite of being prideful—allow yourself to be vulnerable and humble yourself.

**Mental Help:** "The flip side of pride and opposite end of the polarity is humility, usually defined in dictionaries as the absence of pride or self-assertion and the state of being humble. This definition, in turn, means showing or having a consciousness of one's shortcomings or defects, modest, not proud and not self-assertive." (Will Joel Friedman)

## THE FIRST STEP TOWARDS RECOVERY AND OUT OF PAIN IS ADMITTING THAT YOU, YES, YOU, HAVE A PROBLEM.

If you want to get on the road to recovery, you need to open your heart to God and admit that you have a problem called pride, a problem that the pain you've experienced in life has caused. Or maybe the environment you grew up in caused you to be prideful in general. Either way, completing this step is very important as it will help keep you from slipping back into that place where there is nothing but hurt and pain. Furthermore, allowing you to move on with your life.

*Side Note: If you can get rid of your pride (open your heart to God and humble yourself), you can move forward in life instead of continuously going backward.*

**Relevant Magazine:** "People who get stuck in fear get trapped because they see fear as evidence of a shameful weakness. They don't see fear as crucial information alerting them to danger; they believe fear is a confirmation of weakness that is now being exposed to everyone.

Shame is a self-conscious emotion, and it causes people to be self-focused. Shame directs your attention onto yourself in ways that make it difficult for you to care about what other people are feeling around you. Shame-proneness causes people to mismanage fear. Rather than using fear to direct your attention outward to an approaching problem, shame forces your attention inward toward a bigger problem—painful feelings of inadequacy. Shame-prone people tend to respond to fear by either trying to hide it or to forcefully overcome it. But the best response to fear is neither of these strategies. The best response to fear is to face it, with vulnerability." (Baker, 2018)

## WHAT ARE THE REQUIREMENTS FOR BEING VULNERABLE AND HUMBLING YOURSELF?

Vulnerability requires you to make yourself available to God, which means you must open up and let Him into your heart. "Look! I stand at the door and knock. If you hear my voice and open the door, I will come in, and we will share a meal together as friends." (Revelation 3:20)

**Dechalert:** "To be vulnerable means to put yourself out there and be open to possibilities and opportunities." (Aphinya, 2020)

On the other hand, humbling yourself requires you to be truthful and honest about your feelings. This includes being truthful about your current and past problems or pain.

**God.Net:** "Humility is not true humility unless it lines up with truth. For instance, we work with many poor people in the Philippines mostly children. Sometimes an older child may be hungry and would not have eaten for a day or two, but when you ask him if he is hungry, he will say no. The reason may be that he is too embarrassed to admit his situation. In his mind, he may think that he is being humble by choosing to suffer. However, it is really pride that is keeping him from eating when we offer him food. The truth may require him to humble himself. Truth lines up with humility. In our ministry, we always do things in ways to avoid embarrassing anyone. When we feed the hungry, we feed all of them together. Only when I am talking with a child by himself do I ask him about his needs. We treat everyone with respect and honor because each person is special and created in the image of God." (Grace to the Humble)

**Side Note:** *It's considered humility when you open up and tell the truth about your problems and seek someone other than yourself to help you solve them.*

## WHY IS VULNERABILITY (OPENING YOUR HEART UP TO GOD) AND HUMBLING YOURSELF (TELLING GOD HOW YOU FEEL) AN IMPORTANT PART OF YOUR JOURNEY?

1. Being vulnerable (opening your heart up to God) and humbling yourself (telling God how you feel) allows Him to meet the needs that you express to Him.

When you tell God how you really feel, He can meet your needs. But if you need God and do not express your needs to Him, your needs go unmet. Very similar to if you are married and need your spouse to take your car to get fixed, but you don't speak up. How would they know what you need if you don't tell them?

## GOD IS NOT GOING TO BLESS WHAT YOU ARE NOT WILLING TO EXPRESS.

"A man with leprosy came and knelt in front of Jesus, begging to be healed. "If you are willing, you can heal me and make me clean," he said. Moved with compassion, Jesus reached out and touched him. "I am willing," he said. "Be healed!" Instantly the leprosy disappeared, and the man was healed." (Mark 1:40-42.)

> **Side Note:** *God expects that you begin to learn how to use your words to let Him know what you need as you grow up and mature. And to clarify, it's not that He doesn't already know what you need. He is God. Therefore He knows all things. But what He's teaching you by saying you need to speak up is communication skills, which teaches you how to remove pride and build healthy relationships.*

Another example would be a small child who walks around pouting, expecting that their parent (in this case, your parent is God) will read their minds. Now, the child could be hungry, or they could need to use the restroom. But instead of saying so, they just keep quiet, leaving their parent to make assumptions about what's wrong with them.

The Problem:

- When a person does not speak up and say what they need, their needs are left up to the interpretation of the giver. The receiver is given whatever the giver decides to give them, and, in the end, the receiver's true needs go unmet.

## WHEN YOU DON'T SPEAK UP AND SAY HOW YOU REALLY FEEL, YOUR TRUE NEEDS GO UNMET.

For example, you may say, "I don't care," when the love of your life decides that the problems within your relationship are not getting any better, and they would like to break up. But deep down inside, you do care.

The Problem:

- Because you refuse to move your lips and tell them how much you care, they may walk away and leave—possibly forever. Cat didn't get your tongue though. Pride did. But here's the kicker: pride will move on to its next victim and leave you "alone" to deal with the heartache and pain that it created.

Some people may say women are more often victims of men, but men are victims of pride. Pride simply lives in a man or woman for the moment it wants to take residence. We are all victims. But you have to be the one to stop allowing pride into your home (heart) to couch surf and kick pride out of the door so that God can move into your home and meet your needs.

2. Being vulnerable (opening your heart up to God) and humbling yourself (telling God how you feel) leads to spiritual, mental, and physical freedom.

This is the important part that I wanted you to stay tuned for. Pay close attention. There is a connection between each definition, sentence, and scripture.

## CHECK THIS HERE I'M GOING TO CREATE A RAINBOW OF TRUTH.

**Side Note:** *Each of the definitions referenced below are actual definitions from dictionary.com and thesaurus.com, where each definition/synonym leads directly from one to the other.*

## DEFINITION:

Vulnerable:

- Susceptible (exposed) to the possibility of physical or emotional attack or harm.

- Of a person in need of special care, support, protection because of age, disability, risk of abuse, or neglect.

- Synonyms: helpless, defenseless, powerless, impotent, weak, susceptible. "He was scared and vulnerable."

## Susceptible:

- Exposed and naïve.

## Naïve:

- Childlike, trusting.

## Childlike:

- Innocent.

## Innocent:

- Blameless.

## Blameless:

- Not responsible.

## Not Responsible:

- Faultless, not to blame.

- Not guilty.

- Without fault, flaw, or defect; perfect.

## SENTENCE:

First, you are vulnerable, weak, and helpless (meaning you can't help yourself; you can't get through life alone). This leads to your need for special care, support, or protection.

> **Side Note:** *Your weaknesses and inability to go through life alone make you need God; it's what makes you need a Savior (Jesus).*

## SO, WHAT IS GOD TRYING TO TELL YOU:

**Vulnerable:** Understand that the trials you are going to go through or are going through in life may lead to weapons being formed against you. But, if you open your heart up to Me while you're in a state of weakness, I will be able to protect you, and the weapons will not be able to prosper. ---> **Susceptible:** These trials or threats will work out in your favor, as they are only being used to help expose you to your sins and make you more aware of them. ---> **Naïve:** Once your sins are exposed, you will realize that you are a naïve human being (not God, who is all-knowing) who truthfully does not know what to do with your life, and it will bring you to repentance. ---> **Childlike:** Repenting will open up your eyes, helping you see that to enter the Kingdom (be saved and set free), you must become like a little child who admits that they need guidance from their Father (Me/God). ---> **Innocent:** After receiving guidance from your father (Me), you will come to trust and believe Me when I tell you that you are innocent because of the blood of Christ. ---> **Blameless:**

And because you are innocent when the time comes, you will be presented spotless and blameless before Me. ---> **Not Responsible:** In other words, because you have opened your heart up to Me, the battle (your battle) belongs to Me (God), which means you are free (innocent, blameless, and not responsible).

## WOW! RIGHT?

**Side Note:** *God defends the weak, protects those who call on Him, and no weapon formed against you shall prosper. And yes, it does say weapons will be formed, but it also says they will not prosper. This means that whatever is threatening to harm you will not succeed. It's a terrorist threat, and threats are a warning of danger.*

**Threat:**

- A warning of danger.

## SCRIPTURE:

**VULNERABLE:**

- "Open up before God, keep nothing back; he'll do whatever needs to be done: He'll validate your life in the clear light of day and stamp you with approval at high noon. Quiet down before God, be prayerful before him. Don't bother with those who climb the ladder, who elbow their way to the top. Bridle your anger, trash your wrath, cool your pipes—it only makes things worse. Before long the crooks will be bankrupt; God-investors will soon own the store." (Psalm 37:5-9)

## SUSCEPTIBLE:

- "Well then, am I suggesting that the law of God is sinful? Of course not! In fact, it was the law that showed me my sin. I would never have known that coveting is wrong if the law had not said you must not covet." (Romans 7:7)

## NAIVE:

- "Jesus said, "Father, forgive them, for they don't know what they are doing." And the soldiers gambled for his clothes by throwing dice." (Luke 23:24)

## CHILDLIKE:

- "He called a little child and set him before them, and said, "I assure you and most solemnly say to you, unless you repent [that is, change your inner self—your old way of thinking, live changed lives] and become like children [trusting, humble, and forgiving], you will never enter the kingdom of heaven. Therefore, whoever humbles himself like this child is greatest in the kingdom of heaven." (Matthew 18:2-4)

## INNOCENT:

- "So we have stopped evaluating others from a human point of view. At one time we thought of Christ merely from a human point of view. How differently we know him now! This means that anyone who belongs to Christ has become a new person. The old life is gone; a new life has begun! And all of this is a gift from God, who brought us back to himself through Christ. And God has given us this task of reconciling people to him. For God was in Christ, reconciling the world to himself, no longer counting people's sins against them. And he gave us this wonderful message of reconciliation. So we are Christ's ambassadors; God is making his appeal through us. We speak for Christ when we plead, "Come back to God!" For God made Christ, who never sinned, to be the offering for our sin, so that we could be made right with God through Christ." (2 Corinthians 5:16-21)

## BLAMELESS:

- "Yet now he has reconciled you to himself through the death of Christ in his physical body. As a result, he has brought you into his own presence, and you are holy and blameless as you stand before him without a single fault." (Colossians 1:22)

## NOT RESPONSIBLE:

- "He said, "Listen, all you people of Judah and Jerusalem! Listen, King Jehoshaphat! This is what the LORD says: Do not be afraid! Don't be discouraged by this mighty army, for the battle is not yours, but God's." (2 Chronicles 20:15)

So here we go again. You open yourself up to God, and you are exposed to your sin. Jesus pleads for your sins to be forgiven because He knows you don't know any better. After Jesus pleads for you and you repent, you are given a second chance (a new life) where you will be able to live life as a child of God who God blesses through

His teachings and guidance. "For all who are led by the Spirit of God are children of God." (Romans 8:14) As God leads and guides you through life, He uses the example of a child who is innocent to show you the right way to live. (Jesus is the child who is innocent, so God uses His life as an example to lead you. Jesus' life is the MAP.) And because you have allowed God to take the lead, your walk is blameless in His sight, just as Jesus' was. This means you are no longer responsible for your sins because Jesus died in your place for them once and for all. What does this mean?

**TO ENTER THE KINGDOM OF HEAVEN (BE SAVED AND SET FREE), YOU MUST BECOME VULNERABLE, SUSCEPTIBLE, NAIVE, CHILD-LIKE, INNOCENT, BLAMELESS, AND NOT RESPONSIBLE.**

You are not responsible, and the battle is not yours because a child is not responsible for themselves—their parent or guardian is (God is your Father). But isn't it funny that the layers that lead to blameless, innocent, and not responsible are the things in life nobody wants to be? Is it that nobody wants to be saved and set free, or is it that nobody really knows how?

**Side Note:** *Regardless of if you are a woman or a man, a boy or a girl. If you want to be set free, you will have to, at some point in life, allow yourself to be vulnerable and admit that you don't know everything. You don't always have it all together. Or yes, you may have been hurt by what someone did to you. God wants to hear the confession from your mouth. It's called prayer and supplication.*

**Prayer:**

- A solemn request for help or expression of thanks addressed to God.

**Supplicate:**

- To pray humbly; make humble and earnest entreaty or petition.

You have to pray (open up your mouth and release the fruit from your lips) if you want to see things change in your life. The moment you open up is the moment you can be free.

**GOD WORKS BEST THROUGH YOUR WEAK-NESSES WHICH MEANS IF YOU OPEN YOUR HEART AND HUMBLE YOURSELF, "THEN YOU WILL KNOW THE TRUTH, AND THE TRUTH WILL SET YOU FREE." (JOHN 8:32)**

How I really feel:

- The fact that I'm anxious about and fearful of things in life means I'm not close to God as I should be.

- I'm tired of telling people I'm constantly ill because it seems to me that nobody truly wants to hear **HOW I REALLY FEEL!**

- I'm afraid of losing myself to this world.

- I'm afraid of someone hurting someone I love.

- I'm afraid to get to know people because I have social anxiety.

- I'm afraid to get close to people because I lost my dad when I was younger.

- I'm afraid of getting my heart broken again.

- **I'M AFRAID OF DYING!**

These are some of my fears. Admit to God your fears. Just start to run them down to Him. Trust me. It's freeing.

## How do you really feel?

- _____
  _____
  _____

- _____
  _____
  _____

- _____
  _____
  _____

- _____
  _____
  _____

- _____
  _____
  _____

- _____
  _____
  _____

## EVERYONE NEEDS TO BE ABLE TO SAY HOW THEY REALLY FEEL WITHOUT FEELINGS OF SHAME, GUILT, OR FEAR OF BEING JUDGED.

If I'm afraid of dying, I should be able to express that if it's what I genuinely feel. But, if someone truly feels that way, they don't say it because it's made to believe that anyone who's of God shouldn't be afraid of dying or anything for that matter. But either way, regardless of the fact, shouldn't I be able to express my fears without my faith being judged?

"Stop judging, so that you won't be judged, because the way that you judge others will be the way that you will be judged, and you will be evaluated by the standard with which you evaluate others." (Matthew 7:1-2)

The sad reality is that as long as people keep judging, it'll continue to make it hard for others to stop pretending.

Side Note: *The bullying and the hate going on worldwide make people feel the need to pretend to be who they are not simply because they are too fearful to be who they really are.*

## WE'RE HURTING EACH OTHER AND DON'T EVEN KNOW IT. OR DO WE AND JUST DON'T CARE?

I came to a place in life where I had been going through so much and felt that if I added another "so much" and explained that I was going through another problem, people would look at me crazy. I say this because things were hitting me back-to-back at one time in my life, and some people knew this. I overheard a conversation in which someone said something to the tune of, "she'd better start praying". But it wasn't said lovingly. It was said in a joking way, as if the problems I had been going through were something to laugh about.

I am using this illustration to say that, yes, sometimes it may seem like the better option would be to stay quiet when you are hurting as opposed to speaking up because deep down inside, we all know that we live in a world that's not genuinely full of compassion and love. As bad as we want to believe it is, we know it is not true.

But even though you may not feel comfortable telling people what you're going through, you should still take your problems to the altar and leave them with God. Also, just because someone else did not handle the problems or pain you've expressed the way you wanted them to does not mean God won't.

**WITH GOD, YOU CAN EXPRESS OR CONFESS WHATEVER YOU NEED TO, AND HE WILL LISTEN TO YOU AND HELP YOU THROUGH WHATEVER YOU ARE GOING THROUGH.**

If you can't trust anyone with your secrets or pain, you can trust God. If you can't find hope or believe in anyone when going through your darkest hour, you can find hope and believe in God. And because

God is in you, you can hope and believe in yourself too. He's also promised that even if you are weak, you are strong through Him. "But he said to me, "My grace is sufficient for you, for my power is made perfect in weakness." Therefore I will boast all the more gladly about my weaknesses, so that Christ's power may rest on me. That is why, for Christ's sake, I delight in weaknesses, in insults, in hardships, in persecutions, in difficulties. For when I am weak, then I am strong." (2 Corinthians 12:9-11)

3. Being vulnerable (opening your heart up to God) and humbling yourself (telling God how you feel) helps you remove the blockage from your heart that stops you from having an intimate relationship with God. Which, might I add, prevents you from moving forward and receiving God's best (being exalted).

"God resists the proud, but gives grace to the humble. Therefore, submit to God. Resist the devil, and he will flee from you. Draw near to God and He will draw near to you. "Cleanse your hands, you sinners; and purify your hearts, you double-minded. Lament and mourn and weep! Let your laughter be turned to mourning and your joy to gloom. Humble yourselves in the sight of the Lord, and He will lift you up." (James 4:6-10)

When you build up walls trying to protect yourself from hurt or try to block the pain out without God, you hurt yourself even more. Because pride only weighs you down and prevents you from moving forward in life. But, once you open your heart up to God, you grow closer to and build an intimate relationship with Him. Being close to God then gives Him the ability to reveal to you and help you get rid of your pride—the only thing stopping you from accomplishing your goals and becoming who you were always created to be.

**Relevant Magazine:** "Vulnerability is taking the risk to expose yourself emotionally. It feels uncertain, but there is no other path to the most meaningful experiences you will ever have. We were created for the purpose of connection to God and others, and vulnerability is the requirement for achieving that purpose." (Baker, 2018)

**Side Note:** *Once you open your heart to God, the wall (pride) that was stopping you from building an intimate relationship with Him can be knocked down, and you can move closer to your destiny.*

## THUS, VULNERABILITY ---> INTIMACY WITH GOD ---> TRUTHFULNESS ---> HUMILITY ---> EXALTED (BLESSED).

Intimacy:

- Closeness between people.

Truthfulness:

- The fact of being true; truth.

- The fact of being realistic or true to life; realism.

Humble:

- Not proud or arrogant: modest: to be humble although successful.

- Having or showing a modest estimate of one's own importance.

**Exalted:**

- Promote; to raise in rank, honor, power, character, quality; elevate. To honor.

- Raised or elevated, as in rank or character.

- Held in very high regard; think or speak very highly.

To be intimate with someone, you must be able to be vulnerable with them. To feel as though you can trust that what you express to them will be taken care of. To be intimate requires you to remove all walls within your heart because you can't get close to anyone with a wall up, can you?

> **Side Note:** *A relationship cannot be successful if a person has walls up. And yes, being vulnerable may make you afraid, but when you acquire what's on the other side of that fear, let me tell you, it's beautiful.*

"Your word, your character is everything. Put your ego to the side and do what you said you would do. Be who you said you would be. Is your word only good when your pride is intact?" This is a conversation that I had internally as I prayed to God about an argument between myself and a loved one.

At the time of the incident, I wanted to run away because their actions—past and present, hurt me. But as I sat back and reflected on the situation, the oddest thing happened to me. I heard God telling me (yes, me), "when you stop being prideful when you invite me into your problems and stop making everything about you, you'll be able to see the blessings that are right before your eyes, as well as become the blessing you were created to be".

|||||||||||||||||||||||||||||||||||||||||||||||||||||||||||||||||||||||||||||||||||||||||||||||||||||

"When you stop thinking everything in life is all about you, you'll be free from the anx-I-ety. Get the I out of the center and put God back on the throne of your heart."

— *Steven Furtick*

|||||||||||||||||||||||||||||||||||||||||||||||||||||||||||||||||||||||||||||||||||||||||||||||||||||

At that moment, when God spoke to me, I had an epiphany. Although I was not the one who was initially wrong, I was also not right simply because instead of me opening up my heart to God, I allowed the pain caused by someone else to lead me to believe that it was ok to build up a wall (pride) to protect myself.

**Side Note:** *Don't let pain or fear cause you to become too prideful to tell God or your loved ones how you really feel because if you or your loved ones were to leave this earth today, you'd be stuck with the pain (the result of not expressing yourself) tomorrow.*

So, what did I have to do? I had to put my pride aside, put my ego away, and remove myself from the equation to see that what God wanted to do in this world was bigger than me.

To clarify, because I had been hurt and had not expressed that I was afraid to lose my loved one as I had lost my dad, a wall (pride) was built up. That wall blocked my relationship with God, which prevented me from seeing the blessings right in front of me (how God was using this book).

For me to see the result of what I had written unfold right before my eyes, to hear my loved one say, "it made me think; it made me see things differently," it was a blessing. It reassured me of this book's ability to save lives and gave me the strength to continue writing. The only problem was, at that time, I was unable to see the blessing because I could only see myself and the problems that revolved around the situation—not what the situation was producing.

In the end, I came to see that the suffering of the present time couldn't compare to the blessings that had yet to come (Romans 8:18). Meaning, because God's grace has allowed me to endure and push through my pain and pride, I can now use what I've learned throughout my journey to help others do the same just as Jesus has done for all of humanity. He humbled Himself and put His pride (feelings about Himself and His own pain) to the side so that He could be who God created Him to be (a King whose name is above every name), and we (all of humanity) could be saved.

"And being found in human form, he humbled himself by becoming obedient to the point of death, even death on a cross. Therefore God has highly exalted him and bestowed on him the name that is above every name, so that at the name of Jesus every knee should bow, in heaven and on earth and under the earth, and every tongue confess that Jesus Christ is Lord, to the glory of God the Father." (Philippians 2:8-11)

**MY ADVICE TO YOU: DON'T GIVE IN TO YOUR FEARS THINKING THEY MAKE YOU LOOK WEAK BUT KNOW THAT YOU EXHIBIT HUMILITY AND VULNERABILITY, WHICH IS CONSIDERED REAL STRENGTH WHEN YOU ADMIT THEM.**

Relevant Magazine: "Avoiding physical pain is a good thing; avoiding emotional pain is not. Jesus said, "Whoever does not take up their cross and follow me is not worthy of me" (Matthew 10:38). And He wasn't kidding. This wasn't just a metaphor for Jesus, because He ended up dragging His cross to His own crucifixion. Jesus taught a lot about joy and love, but He never taught His followers to avoid pain. Quite the opposite, it was central to Jesus's teachings that facing suffering well is a crucial element in developing a mature character and that our vulnerability to suffering is not only not a bad thing but is the best path to finding a clear picture of who God really is. To Jesus, vulnerability was certainly not a weakness but was actually a sign of spiritual strength." (Baker, 2018)

To conclude, if you are broken, stop acting like you're whole. If you are hurting, stop acting like you're healed. If you are faking because you are too fearful to be yourself, stop fronting like you're real. Come to Jesus and be cleansed, free, and filled. Your blessing is released when you yield (produce) the words that can save your life.

## COME TO JESUS AND TELL IT LIKE IT IS, OR CONTINUE TO LIVE IN THE PAST WITH PRIDE, DEATH, AND SIN.

DISCLAIMER: I am not telling you to intentionally expose yourself to toxic situations, relationships, or people you know are harmful to you or your well-being. This chapter is about vulnerability, humility, pride, and opening yourself up to God. Not about you knowingly allowing yourself to be continuously hurt by anyone or anything.

||||||||||||||||||||||||||||||||||||||||||||||||||||||||||||||||||||||||||||||||||||||||||||||||||||||||||||

"On the mountains of truth, you can never climb in vain: either you will reach a point higher up today, or you will be training your powers so that you will be able to climb higher tomorrow."

*— Friedrich Nietzsche*

||||||||||||||||||||||||||||||||||||||||||||||||||||||||||||||||||||||||||||||||||||||||||||||||||||||||||||

*Lord,* I have many fears and sometimes too many to explain. But I trust you. I know that pride is not protecting me. You are. I release pride and ask that you help me be awakened by this truth you have sent to set me free. May peace and love spread through this earth one person at a time as hate and fear is removed from our lives. I proclaim that fear no longer has a hold on me because you have taken hold of fear. I thank you and praise you as I live by every word you speak. I pray for your grace as you help me with these fears and teach me how to overcome them. May your love cast out all my fears, and may my journey and victory teach others how to conquer theirs.

In Jesus' name, Amen!

# CHAPTER 13

# COMPLETE WITH YOU VS COMPETE WITH YOU

*You have purged from your heart the hurt and pain of your past. It is now time for you to evaluate and purge from your life the people who are hindering you from reaching your goals.*

**Proverbs 13:20 NLT** "Walk with the wise and become wise; associate with fools and get in trouble."

A relationship, whether with a family member, business partner, spouse, or friend, can lead you into a place of prosperity or despair. For this reason, choosing the right people to build positive, healthy relationships with is a very important part of your life. That one decision alone could be one of the most important decisions you will continuously have to make.

## The Problem:

- It can be hard to allow God to lead you to positive people to build positive relationships with simply because it's often hard to branch out and away from what's familiar to you, as in family and friends you know and have been close to all of your life.

## The Bigger Problem:

- To grow or excel in life, you need a challenge; you need a push that the comfort of the familiar sometimes cannot give you.

||||||||||||||||||||||||||||||||||||||||||||||||||||||||||||||||||||||||||||||||||||||||||||||||||||||||

"If the people in your circle aren't contributing to your growth, then you're not in a circle, you're in a cage."

— *Kianu Starr*

||||||||||||||||||||||||||||||||||||||||||||||||||||||||||||||||||||||||||||||||||||||||||||||||||||||||

**Side Note:** *Because the familiar (people you are accustomed to) comforts you and makes you feel safe, you may not be able to recognize how they are hindering you from reaching your goals. For this reason, there comes a point in time and in life where you must evaluate your surroundings, family and friends included, and make a choice to either minimize contact with certain people or let them go altogether.*

## ARE YOU GUILTY OF STICKING TO WHAT YOU KNOW AND ARE FAMILIAR WITH WITHOUT EVALUATING WHO OR WHAT YOU ARE STICK-ING TO?

As you continue to read the rest of this chapter, you will learn how to do two things. One, recognize and weed out the people you shouldn't be in close relationships with, as in people who are bad for you. And two, learn how to identify and choose the right people to be in close relationships with, as in the people who are good for you. It's evaluation time!!!

## IT'S NOW TIME FOR YOU TO BEGIN TO EVAL-UATE THE PEOPLE YOU ARE IN CLOSE RELA-TIONSHIPS WITH, STARTING WITH THE PEOPLE WHO ARE BAD FOR YOU.

**The Bad #1:** The person that does not want to see you do better.

This person is afraid to see you do better or shine (i.e., do something productive with yourself or succeed) because they fear that you will make it further than them in life. So, instead of collaborating with you, they fight you on everything you do and throw wrenches in all your plans to make sure you don't reach your goals.

**Conclusion:** *This individual is afraid to see you glow up because they fear that your light will outshine theirs. So, they compete with you instead of trying to ensure that you both win by completing things with you.*

**The Bad #2:** The person who is already comfortable in the state they are in.

This person likes where they are at in life, but they would also like to keep you in that place, to keep them company. This is why the age-old song "Misery Loves Company" comes to play its tune whenever they are in your presence.

**Conclusion:** *This individual likes where they are in life, and they don't want to progress. But they also don't want you to progress because they need a friend who is just as miserable as they are to validate their bad behavior and make them feel good about themselves.*

**The Bad #3:** The person that's a dream catcher or stealer, I should say.

This person is not your friend. They only wish to be close to you so that they may hear your dreams which allows them to steal your dreams.

**Conclusion:** *This individual only wants to know you because they want something from you. They never really cared about you. They only cared about the "what you can do for them" aspect of the relationship. Meaning they only want to be in a relationship with you so that they can latch onto you and steal the harvest (blessings) that you've sowed blood, sweat, and tears over.*

**The Bad #4:** The person who takes away from you instead of building you up and adding to you.

This person is a liability, not an asset. And I don't know about you, but I already have a high insurance premium on my car that I have to pay, and I don't need to be walking around paying a high insurance premium for people too. What about you? Are you paying a hefty monthly payment for the relationships that you are in? Do you constantly feel drained because you are continuously trying to change the negative perspective of the person you are in a relationship with into a positive one? Sorry to say, this person is killing you, not adding to or building you!

**Conclusion:** *This individual is like the cookie monster, but their main objective isn't stealing cookies. Their main objective is to steal your energy. They are constantly taking away from you spiritually, mentally, and physically, yet they rarely have anything to give.*

Before moving past this point, you should take some extra time to digest what you've just read and think about the people you need to let go of or minimize contact with and why.

**CONGRATULATIONS! YOU HAVE NOW SUCCESSFULLY EVALUATED AND WEEDED OUT PEOPLE WHO ARE WRONG FOR YOU. NOW IT'S TIME FOR YOU TO LEARN HOW TO IDENTIFY AND CHOOSE THE RIGHT PEOPLE TO BUILD HEALTHY RELATIONSHIPS WITH.**

There are way too many good people in this world for you to be sitting around, allowing any one person to bring you down. You should be seeking to be in relationships with people that speak positive words of encouragement into your life. People that will tell you the truth and then console you if that truth makes you sad. People who will love and support you through the good and the bad. People who are not going to be afraid to help you reach your goals or allow you to have the leg up and boost you when you are down. And to clarify, yes, they may become drained when helping you, but when they do, that's when you reciprocate that act.

> **Side Note:** *Healthy relationships are similar to walking up stairs. You don't simply use one leg to climb the stairs (reach the goal). Both legs must work together and push one another until they get to where they need to go. When one leg gets up, that leg is used for stability, giving the leg that was down the opportunity to make it up. This simple process is called reciprocity or give and take.*

**Reciprocity:**

- A reciprocal state or relation.

- Reciprocation; mutual exchange.

These are the type of people you should be building relationships with. Better yet, it's evaluation time!!!

**The Good #1:** "Greater love has no one than this: to lay down one's life for one's friends." (John 15:13)

- This person is a true friend who is willing to make sacrifices for you.

- They are ready to battle any giant because the genuine love and respect they have for you gives them the courage to take on challenges they would not ordinarily.

- They will do anything to see you prosper in life and spiritually.

**THIS PERSON DOES NOT WANT TO BEAT YOU. THEY ONLY WANT TO SHOW YOU HOW MUCH THEY LOVE YOU BY FIGHTING ANYONE OR ANYTHING THAT TRIES TO COME UP AGAINST OR DEFEAT YOU.**

"Meanwhile, the Philistine, with his shield bearer in front of him, kept coming closer to David. He looked David over and saw that he was little more than a boy, glowing with health and handsome, and he despised him. He said to David, "Am I a dog, that you come at me with sticks?" And the Philistine cursed David by his Gods. "Come here," he said, "and I'll give your flesh to the birds and the wild animals!" David said to the Philistine, "You come against me with sword and spear and javelin, but I come against you in the name of the Lord Almighty, the God of the armies of Israel, whom you have defied. This day the Lord will deliver you into my hands, and I'll strike you down and cut off your head. This very day I will give the carcasses of the Philistine army to the birds and the wild animals, and the whole world will know that there is a God in Israel. All those gathered here will know that it is not by sword or spear that the Lord saves; for the battle is the Lord's, and he will give all of you into our hands." As the Philistine moved closer to attack him, David ran quickly toward the battle line to meet him. Reaching into his bag and taking out a stone, he slung it and struck the Philistine on the forehead. The stone sank into his forehead, and he fell facedown on the ground. So, David triumphed over the Philistine with a sling and a stone; without a sword in his hand he struck down the Philistine and killed him." (1 Samuel 17:41-50)

> **Conclusion:** *This individual has a love for you that is unconditional. A love that gives them the power to stand up and fight for you even if everyone else leaves or loses faith in you.*

## LOVE PERFECTED, UNCONDITIONAL, AND AT ITS BEST, WILL FIGHT WITHOUT THE COMPANY OF THE REST.

David was able to beat Goliath (giant) because of his love for God. Or should I say the insults that Goliath spoke about God and God's people gave David strength. Love gave David the strength to defeat what tried to come up against those he loved.

**The Good #2:** "Be completely humble and gentle; be patient, bearing with one another in love. Make every effort to keep the unity of the Spirit through the bond of peace." (Ephesians 4:2-3)

- This person desires unity and does not want to fight with you. But they would if they saw you going down a road that could potentially lead to destruction.

- They would rather sacrifice everything to tell you what's hurting you because sometimes love hurts.

- They are patient and will stand by you in times of need and not because misery loves company, but because they would rather stand in your misery with you rather than let you go at it alone.

- This person hurts when you hurt but are strong enough through the power of the Lord to help you push through your pain and struggles.

- They are one in the battle with you regardless of the fight. And although God is always over you (protecting you), they are always beside you.

## THIS PERSON BEARS THE BURDEN OF YOUR TROUBLE AND PAIN, BUT IT'S NOT FOR THEIR GAIN.

"David escaped from Prophets Village. Then he ran to see Jonathan and asked, "Why does your father Saul want to kill me? What have I done wrong?" "My father can't be trying to kill you! He never does anything without telling me about it. Why would he hide this from me? It can't be true!" "Jonathan, I swear it's true! But your father knows how much you like me, and he didn't want to break your heart. That's why he didn't tell you. I swear by the living Lord and by your own life that I'm only one step ahead of death." Then Jonathan said, "Tell me what to do, and I'll do it." David answered: Tomorrow is the New Moon Festival, and I'm supposed to eat dinner with your father. But instead, I'll hide in a field until the evening of the next day. If Saul wonders where I am, tell him, "David asked me to let him go to his hometown of Bethlehem, so he could take part in a sacrifice his family makes there every year." If your father says it's all right, then I'm safe. But if he gets angry, you'll know he wants to harm me. Be kind to me. After all, it was your idea to promise the Lord that we would always be loyal friends. If I've done anything wrong, kill me yourself, but don't hand me over to your father. "Don't worry," Jonathan said. "If I find out that my father wants to kill you, I'll certainly let you know." (1 Samuel 20:1-9)

> **Conclusion:** *This individual wants to see you fly, not be held down bound by the miseries of this world and left to die. Be an asset to them as they are to you because the bond of this relationship can help you see your way through your darkest hour.*

## A TRUE FRIEND WILL LEAD YOU AWAY FROM THE DARK, NOT GRAB YOUR HAND AND PULL YOU DEEPER INTO IT.

During his reign as King, Saul disliked and wanted to kill David. And it was not because David had done something wrong, but solely because David had a good heart, and Saul could recognize that the Lord recognized David's good heart. This made Saul jealous, and instead of him uniting with David to fight a common enemy (the Philistines), Saul decided that he wanted to attempt to lead David into the dark by killing him. But what Saul didn't expect was his son Jonathan would develop a relationship with David that would, in the end, help David reach the goals God had set before him.

The Good #3: "The man of too many friends [chosen indiscriminately] will be broken in pieces and come to ruin, but there is a [true, loving] friend who [is reliable and] sticks closer than a brother." (Proverbs 18:24)

- This person is someone you can trust. Someone that if you tell them your dreams, they'll get excited and want to work with you, to help you elevate and make those dreams come true. And no, not for recognition, but because they genuinely care about and believe in you.

- They are someone you can talk to and know that they wouldn't steer you in the wrong direction or use the words that you've spoken to them against you.

- They are a confidant or mentor who may have been through what you are going through, someone who has accomplished what you desire to accomplish, a David who's already beaten Goliath.

Confidant:

- A person with whom one shares a secret or private matter, trusting them not to repeat it to others.

Mentor:

- An experienced and trusted advisor.

**THIS PERSON'S PURPOSE IS NOT TO STEAL YOUR DREAMS. IT'S TO USE THE GIFTS THAT GOD HAS PLACED IN THEM TO HELP YOU MAKE YOUR DREAMS BECOME A REALITY.**

"Come out to the field with me," Jonathan replied. And they went out there together. Then Jonathan told David, "I promise by the Lord, the God of Israel, that by this time tomorrow, or the next day at the latest, I will talk to my father and let you know at once how he feels about you. If he speaks favorably about you, I will let you know. But if he is angry and wants you killed, may the Lord strike me and even kill me if I don't warn you, so you can escape and live. May the Lord be with you as he used to be with my father. And may you treat me with the faithful love of the Lord as long as I live. But if I die, treat my family with this faithful love, even when the Lord destroys all your enemies from the face of the earth." So, Jonathan made a solemn pact with David, saying, "May the Lord destroy all your enemies!" And Jonathan made David reaffirm his vow of friendship again, for Jonathan loved David as he loved himself." (1 Samuel 20:11-17)

> **Conclusion:** *This individual does not wish to shoot down nor steal your dreams for fear of you making it further than them like King Saul wanted to do with David. They are an ideal friend. Someone you would want in your corner with you, whether winning or losing.*

## A FRIEND WHO FIGHTS TO THE END IS A FRIEND WORTHY ENOUGH TO SHARE THE WIN.

Johnathan was more than just a confidant; he was a true friend to David. He believed in him and did whatever was necessary to see David succeed, which is why it was only right for David to share the win with Johnathan's family after he became King.

The Good #4: "And let us consider how we may spur one another on toward love and good deeds, not giving up meeting together, as some are in the habit of doing, but encouraging one another—and all the more as you see the Day approaching." (Hebrews 10:24-25)

- This person wants to do all they can to challenge you to be greater. They may be a family member, business partner, spouse, or friend who's not only pushing you to take risks but willing to take those risks right along with you.

- They are not a liability because they are responsible enough to pay their own insurance bills.

## THIS PERSON WANTS TO HELP YOU BUILD A BETTER FUTURE FOR YOURSELF, NOT TRICK YOU INTO PAYING A HEFTY MENTAL AND SPIRITUAL INSURANCE BILL.

"Jonathan went to find David and encouraged him to stay strong in his faith in God. "Don't be afraid," Jonathan reassured him. "My father will never find you! You are going to be the King of Israel, and I will be next to you, as my father, Saul, is well aware." So the two of them renewed their solemn pact before the Lord. Then Jonathan returned home, while David stayed at Horesh." (1 Samuel 23:16-18)

**Conclusion:** *This individual does not mind using the last bit of strength they have left to push you past the mark they have yet to reach. They don't mind helping you because they not only know who they are, but they are happy with who they are. So they don't become intimidated by your drive. They are, in fact, one of the people behind you pushing the car if ever you should run out of gas while trying to accomplish your goals.*

## NO INSURANCE POLICY IS NEEDED HERE BECAUSE LOVE AND ENCOURAGEMENT ARE POWERFUL ENOUGH TO PAY FOR THEMSELVES.

Jonathan was one of David's closest friends who often risked his own life to stand up for, encourage, and reassure David that everything would work out for his good. He was even willing to take the seat beside David, acknowledging him (David) as soon to be King and not himself, even though it was his birthright (humility at its greatest).

## HOW MANY OF THE ABOVE EXAMPLES SAY SOMETHING ABOUT A PERSON YOU ARE IN A RELATIONSHIP WITH? WHO ARE YOUR FRIENDS, BUT MOST IMPORTANTLY, DO YOU RECOGNIZE YOUR FRENEMIES?

At this point in the chapter, you should take some time and ask yourself. Are the people you think you need to be in a relationship with like Johnathan, completing things with you (helping you progress in life by building you up and encouraging you to become a better person)? Or are they like King Saul, competing with you (trying to show you that they are better than you and fighting against you)?

> **Side Note:** *Although these examples are meant to help you evaluate the people in your life, they are also in place to help you evaluate who you have been to others. Are you being made into and being an example of the Lord's Characteristics: loving, supportive, and kind to others? Or are you treating others in a manner that you would not want to be treated?*

To close, even though you may not be able to choose your family or the people you're surrounded by. You do have a say in how you allow their actions to affect you spiritually, mentally, and physically. Whether you'll have a relationship with them or how deep (intimate) that relationship will be, it's all up to you.

## MY ADVICE: DON'T WAIT UNTIL IT'S TOO LATE TO EVALUATE!

"Evaluate the people in your life; then promote, demote, or terminate. You're the CEO of your life."

— *Tony Gaskins*

**Heavenly Father,** thank you for the people you have allowed into my life and those you have chosen not to be. I trust you Lord. And I believe that the people you place in my path, the people you desire me to connect with, are the right fit for me. Teach me, dear Lord, to be more like you as I learn how to complete things with others instead of fighting and competing with others.

In Jesus' name, Amen!

# PART FIVE THE PREPARATION

# CHAPTER 14

# GROUND LEVEL ZERO

*Now here you are, empty. Back where God intended for you to be in the beginning so that "He" could fully fill and occupy your heart.*

**Genesis 1:1-2** NLT "In the beginning God created the heavens and the earth. The earth was formless and empty, and darkness covered the deep waters. And the Spirit of God was hovering over the surface of the waters."

Before starting I want to inform you that this part of the book *The Preparation* revolves around you learning about how to be and being *Comfortable with Empty*. Below is a list of the four subjects you will be focusing on:

- **Part I:** Ground Level Zero – Chapter Fourteen (the chapter you are reading now)

- **Part II:** The Wait – Chapter Fifteen

- **Part III:** Time Spent – Chapter Sixteen

- **Part IV:** Survival of the Fittest – Chapter Seventeen

In this chapter, you will focus on what it means to be empty and why it's important.

Emptiness:

- The state of containing nothing.

- The product of repentance.

- The result of getting rid of the junk on the inside of you (purification/cleansing).

**GOD HAS PROVIDED YOU WITH THE HOLY SPIRIT, WHO HAS HELPED YOU GET RID OF ALL OF THE JUNK (HURT, UNFORGIVENESS, AND PRIDE) THAT YOU'VE HELD ON TO OVER THE YEARS SO THAT YOU COULD MOVE FORWARD TO ONE OF THE MOST IMPORTANT STAGES IN YOUR JOURNEY. THE EMPTY STAGE OF THE WILDERNESS.**

This particular stage of your journey (the empty stage of the wilderness) is one of the most important stages that you'll have to go through on your journey in life because emptiness is sort of like the beginning of the end. Meaning the beginning of your new life (new relationship) with God (good nature) dwelling within your heart (temple), and the end of your old life (old relationship) with the devil (sinful nature) dwelling within your heart.

**Side Note:** *The empty stage is the result of you divorcing the devil and moving forward with your decision to build a new relationship with and marry God. This includes you starting a whole new life.*

**Faith Ventures:** "Then I saw "a new heaven and a new earth," for the first heaven and the first earth had passed away, and there was no longer any sea. I saw the Holy City, the new Jerusalem, coming down out of heaven from God, prepared as a bride beautifully dressed for her husband. And I heard a loud voice from the throne saying, "Look! God's dwelling place is now among the people, and he will dwell with them. They will be his people, and God himself will be with them and be their God. (Revelation 21:1-3)

Truth: God's ultimate goal of renewal is to become perfectly united with His people, as things were in the Garden of Eden. The truth is you are new. These Bible verses about a new beginning reveal that every moment brings a fresh start. God has made and is making all things new–this includes you.

Do not lie to each other, since you have taken off your old self with its practices and have put on the new self, which is being renewed in knowledge in the image of its Creator. Here there is no Gentile or Jew, circumcised or uncircumcised, barbarian, Scythian, slave or free, but Christ is all, and is in all." (2 Colossians 3:9-11)

Truth: Your old, sinful nature is dead. You learn to grow in your new identity in Christ as you learn more about His character." (Johnson, 2019)

To give you a more in-depth explanation of being made new and starting a new life (a new relationship with God). The stages of a pregnancy journey which includes the relationship that leads to becoming pregnant, will be used as an example to describe the process.

| PREGNANCY TERMS USED IN CHAPTER | TRANSLATION |
|---|---|
| • Courtship | • Intimacy with God |
| • Embryo/Fetus/Baby | • Good Nature/Spirit/Good Character |
| • Your Womb | • Your Heart (Gods Temple) |
| • Pregnancy | • Process where Good Character is developed within you |
| • Preconception Health Care | • Preparation for pregnancy |
| • Pre-Pregnancy Requirements | • Requirements for creating a stable environment for the baby (Good Character) to grow and be developed in |
| • Prenatal Care | • Daily alone time with God |
| • Trimester | • Stages |
| • Physician/Nurse/Mid-Wife | • God/Jesus/The Holy Spirit |

## COURTSHIP

*(Intimacy with God)*

**Institute in Basic Life Principles:** "Courtship is a relationship between a man and a woman in which they seek to determine if it is God's will for them to marry each other. Under the protection, guidance, and blessing of parents or mentors, the couple concentrates on developing a deep friendship that could lead to marriage, as they discern their readiness for marriage and God's timing for their marriage. (See Proverbs 3:5–7.)

Courtship is a choice to avoid temptation and experience the blessings of purity. It is a choice to not emotionally give away your heart, piece by piece, to many others through casual dating relationships and instead to give your whole heart to your life partner.

It is a choice to wait for God's best, for His glory. It is a decision to walk by faith, to trust in God, to honor others above yourself, and to believe that God will deal bountifully with you, because He is love. (See 2 Corinthians 5:7, Psalm 9:10, Romans 12:10, Psalm 13, and I John 4:8.)" (How is courtship different than dating?)

**Wikipedia:** "Courtship is the period of development towards an intimate relationship wherein a couple get to know each other and decide if there will be an engagement, followed by a marriage. A courtship may be an informal and private matter between two people or maybe a public affair, or a formal arrangement with family approval. Traditionally, in the case of a formal engagement, it is the role of a male to actively "court" or "woo" a female, thus encouraging her to understand him and her receptiveness to a marriage proposal." (Wikipedia)

Before embarking on your pregnancy (journey where good character is developed within you), you must first start from ground level zero and learn about what it means to be intimate with God.

## WHAT IS INTIMACY?

Intimacy:

- Close familiarity or friendship; closeness.

- Closely acquainted; familiar.

- Private and personal.

"Come close to God and He will come close to you. Wash your hands, you sinners. Clean up your hearts, you who want to follow the sinful ways of the world and God at the same time." (James 4:8)

GoodTherapy.org: "Intimacy usually denotes mutual vulnerability, openness, and sharing. It is often present in close, loving relationships such as marriages and friendships. The term is also sometimes used to refer to sexual interactions, but intimacy does not have to be sexual.

## THERE ARE FOUR TYPES OF INTIMACY:

Experiential Intimacy:

- When people bond during leisure activities. People may "sync up" their actions in teamwork or find themselves acting in unison.

- Example: A father and son work together to build a model train, developing a rhythm to their teamwork.

Emotional Intimacy:

- When people feel safe sharing their feelings with each other, even uncomfortable ones.

- Example: A woman confides in her sister about her body image issues. She trusts her sibling to offer comfort rather than using her insecurities against her.

Intellectual Intimacy:

- When people feel comfortable sharing ideas and opinions, even when they disagree.

- Example: Two friends debate the meaning of life. They enjoy hearing each other's opinions and don't feel the need to "win" the argument.

Sexual Intimacy:

- When people engage in sensual or sexual activities. When people use the word "intimacy," they are often referring to this type.

- Example: Two lovers engage in foreplay, knowing how each other prefers to be touched." (What is Intimacy?)

## WHAT INTIMACY INVOLVES:

**Psych Central:**

- **"Knowing:** A truly intimate relationship lets both people know on the deepest level who they each truly are. They have looked into each other's souls and found something they value and appreciate so much that it can withstand the inevitable differences that exist between any two individuals.

- **Acceptance:** Neither person feels the need to change the other or to change themselves in fundamental ways. Oh yes, minor changes always occur when people accommodate each other to live together. But neither member of the couple thinks to him or herself, "Well—with time, I'll get him or her to change who they are."

- **Appreciation of differences:** Both understand that they don't need to be entirely the same to be close. In fact, part of the delight of relationships is the discovery of differences and appreciation for each other's uniqueness. Learning about each other's points of view is seen as an opportunity to expand their worlds.

- **Safety:** True intimacy happens when both people feel safe enough to be vulnerable. There is support for each other's weaknesses and celebration of each other's strengths. The couple has agreed on a definition of fidelity and both feel secure that the other will not violate that understanding.

- **Compassionate problem-solving:** Elephants don't come to stay in the middle of the "room" of the relationship. Issues are confronted by both people with love, compassion, and a willingness to engage with whatever problems have come up. The two work to be on the same team, solving a problem, rather than on different teams competing with each other.

- **Emotional connection:** Intimacy grows when people stay emotionally connected, even when there are problems to solve. It doesn't require that either person walk on eggshells or withhold what they really think in order to stay connected." (Marie Hartwell-Walker, 2018)

## WHY IS INTIMACY WITH GOD IMPORTANT?

Transformation:

- A thorough or dramatic change in form or appearance.

In Touch Ministries: "No one can have an intimate relationship with God and remain unchanged. A "Sunday Christian" lifestyle will no longer satisfy. As we begin to understand who He is, our love for Him grows and motivates us to radical obedience. Our experiences with Him teach us that He is faithful and can be trusted. Recognition of the wisdom and goodness of His plans prompts willing submission to His leadership. And before long, time spent with Him becomes the best part of each day. Instead of watching the clock, we'll want to stay longer because His presence satisfies our souls as nothing else can." (Stanley C. F., 2014)

"Moses remained there on the mountain with the Lord forty days and forty nights. In all that time he ate no bread and drank no water. And the Lord wrote the terms of the covenant—the Ten Commandments—on the stone tablets.

When Moses came down Mount Sinai carrying the two stone tablets inscribed with the terms of the covenant, he wasn't aware that his face had become radiant because he had spoken to the Lord. So when Aaron and the people of Israel saw the radiance of Moses' face, they were afraid to come near him.

But Moses called out to them and asked Aaron and all the leaders of the community to come over, and he talked with them. Then all the people of Israel approached him, and Moses gave them all the instructions the Lord had given him on Mount Sinai. When Moses finished speaking with them, he covered his face with a veil. But whenever he went into the Tent of Meeting to speak with the Lord, he would remove the veil until he came out again. Then he would give the people whatever instructions the Lord had given him, and the people of Israel would see the radiant glow of his face. So he would put the veil over his face until he returned to speak with the Lord." (Exodus 34:28-35)

> **Side Note:** *The more time you spend in God's presence getting to know Him intimately, the more He rubs off on and transforms you.*

## Healing:

- The process of making or becoming sound or healthy again.

When you have an intimate relationship with God, you grow closer to Him and begin to trust Him. When you trust Him, you'll open your heart to Him fully, thus allowing Him to heal your heart. Your healed heart (damage-free heart without holes) allows God to begin to develop your character and change your life for the better because you are no longer going to be leaking out whatever it is, He places in your heart.

> **Side Note:** *This stage of your journey (Comfortable with Empty) is why you had to face and rid yourself of the problems from your past in the last section of the book **The Purge**. The role of **The Purge** was to empty and clean you out, thus preparing you for a close and intimate relationship with God which provides healing.*

## HOW CAN ONE COME TO KNOW GOD INTIMATELY (BUILD A CLOSE RELATIONSHIP WITH GOD THAT LEADS TO TRANSFORMATION AND HEALING)?

Most intimate relationships start with a solid foundation and are built from the ground up. This means your new relationship with God is no different.

> **Side Note:** *The key to successfully reaching the penthouse suite in a relationship is to start on ground level zero with a solid foundation.*

Knowing God intimately, which includes building a long-lasting relationship with Him, is an intricate subject matter that I cannot alone begin to break down and explain. For this reason, I have done some research and have compiled a list that includes references from a host of sources to describe how to do so.

**To build an intimate relationship with God one must:**

1. Be an individual God can trust by starting the relationship with truth and honesty.

"Whoever speaks the truth gives honest evidence, but a false witness utters deceit." (Proverbs 12:17)

"Lying lips are an abomination to the Lord, but those who act faithfully are his delight." (Proverbs 12:22)

Honesty is always the best policy, whether in your relationship with God or with people. It is also one of the key components that determines how strong a relationship will be or how long it will last.

> **Side Note:** *Because honesty leads to trust and trust leads to the development of a strong, unbreakable bond (love), it is one of the most crucial building blocks in any relationship.*

**Medium:** "The key in a relationship isn't communication, it isn't trust, and it isn't commitment. It's honesty. Honesty builds the foundation for communication and trust. This in turn builds the foundation for commitment. You cannot have good communication in a relationship if honesty isn't there. Same thing with trust. Trust comes with honesty. It builds on honesty. No doubt, communication, trust, and commitment are important, but they build on a base first.

Building a relationship when one partner isn't honest, is building a house using sand instead of using brick. The house will inevitably collapse, and it can only grow so big before it begins to crumble. Starting a relationship with someone on lies will lead to disaster. Gaps down the road, misunderstandings, lack of trust, deceit, frustration, and pain." (Panait, 2017)

> **Side Note:** *Whether your relationship with God is built on lies or on truth and honesty, it will determine how strong it will be and how long it will last.*

**Hope for Children Foundation:** "Honesty in a relationship provides a strong foundation for a lasting or enjoyable relationship, whether with a family member, friend, or romantic interest. Honesty is a strong sensitive voice for love that builds trust. Without honesty in a relationship, the words 'I love you' become a lie in itself and there's no real security in the relationship.

When the truth is missing, some people may try to guess exactly what is the truth in various situations. Failing to be honest about something causes people to try and figure out what is not being said, or what the truth actually is. These actions can cause many negative results such as gossip, which can then foster more lies and deception that other people may mistake as truth. Finally, this causes many more people to feel hurt and betrayed when the truth is finally revealed, all of which could be avoided if honesty were present in the beginning." (Patricia, 2019)

> **Side Note:** *If one does not trust an individual because they have been dishonest, they will not feel safe enough to express nor be themselves, and that alone can make or break a relationship.*

**Hope for Children Foundation:** "Lies and distorted truth undermines the relationship and it hurts us emotionally and in other manifestations. Undermining a relationship breaks trust and is the opposite of real intimacy found in an honest relationship. The significance in having an honest relationship opposed to a dishonest relationship is the exclusive feeling of security in the fact that you know the other person and are known by them in turn. When lies or distorted truth become part of the relationship, doubts about that person surface, and one no longer feels totally safe in that particular relationship." (Patricia, 2019)

2. Trust and have faith in God.

"And without faith it is impossible to please him, for whoever would draw near to God must believe that he exists and that he rewards those who seek him." (Hebrews 11:6)

"The fear of man lays a snare, but whoever trusts in the LORD is safe." (Proverbs 29:25)

As previously mentioned, relationships without trust cannot grow, be strong, or last. This means it is not only important for God to trust you, but it is also equally as important for you to trust Him and feel safe in His presence.

Side Note: *When you trust someone, you feel comfortable, safe, and secure with them. You are not afraid to be open, let down your walls, and allow yourself to be vulnerable.*

In Touch Ministries: "God becomes our shelter in life's storms when we crawl under His wings of protection and cling to Him in total dependence. "For You have been my help, And in the shadow of Your wings I sing for joy. My soul clings to You; Your right hand upholds me." (Psalm 63:7-8) Those who know intimacy with Him feel the safety that comes with submission to His will. Since they know His heart and trust His goodness and wisdom, they have no cause for fear." (Stanley C. F., 2014)

> **Side Note:** *Openness and vulnerability are key components to a successful relationship because you cannot truly get to know someone who refuses to allow anyone to see who they really are.*

**In Touch Ministries:** "Another important factor is our willingness to be open and honest, exposing every area of our lives to the Lord. No one can be forced into an intimate friendship with God. In fact, the depth of this relationship is limited by the extent of our transparency with Him. Although the natural response is to shrink from such vulnerability, we need to remember that He already knows us inside and out and loves us more than we can comprehend." (Stanley C. F., 2014)

> **Side Note:** *God knows all of your scars and the pain that has caused them. But He is not here to judge you for what you have done or what has happened to you in life. He simply wants you to let your walls down, to know you can trust Him, to know you are safe in His presence, and that He loves you no matter what.*

**Desiring God:** "God wants intimacy with you. Christ has done all the hard work on the cross to make it possible. All he requires is that you believe in him (John 14:1). He wants you to trust him with all your heart (Proverbs 3:5). This means his invitation to you to enjoy intimacy with him is the providences in your life that are testing your faith more than anything else. What you must trust God most for right now is where he means for you to draw closer to him." (Bloom, How to Have Intimacy with God, 2016)

3. Get to know God by spending time alone with Him, seeking Him with all of your heart, listening to sermons, reading the Word (the Bible), and reading books written about Him.

"In the beginning was the Word, and the Word was with God, and the Word was God." (John 1:1)

"You will seek me and find me when you seek me with all your heart. I will be found by you," declares the LORD, "and will bring you back from captivity. I will gather you from all the nations and places where I have banished you," declares the LORD, "and will bring you back to the place from which I carried you into exile." (Jeremiah 29:13-14)

If you want your relationship to last, it is very important to spend time getting to know an individual before deciding to get married or have children. Besides, if you don't know the individual, how can you truly grow with the individual?

> **Side Note:** *Because God is the Word, you can get to know and become intimate with Him by digging deeper into the Bible, "the Word of God," and other books about Him. This gives you a better understanding of who God is.*

**Compelling Truth:** "Though we cannot know God fully in this lifetime (Isaiah 55:8-9; 1 Corinthians 13:12), we can know Him in part.

He has revealed certain things about Himself to us. We find these revelations in God's written Word—the Bible—and the Word incarnate—Jesus." (How can I come to really know God?)

Inspiring Tips: "You cannot truly love God if you don't know Him. Therefore, strengthen your connection with God by knowing Him better. You can know and understand God deeper by reading His words and teachings in the Scriptures, listening about Him from a true preacher, and practicing what you have learned from Him." (Abrugar)

Side Note: *For any couple to grow closer, one must spend time alone together. Whether it be physically, through video, or by telephone, it's important to do so.*

In Touch Ministries: "We will never achieve closeness with the Lord unless we invest time and effort in getting to know Him. A neglected relationship simply won't grow in richness or depth. Are you too busy to spend time each day with Him? If that is the case, the immediate demands of your schedule are robbing you of an awesome eternal treasure—deep, satisfying communion with God." (Stanley C. F., 2014)

4. Communicate with God and listen when He speaks.

"The LORD is close to all who call on him, yes, to all who call on him in truth." (Psalm 145:18)

"Rejoice in hope, be patient in tribulation, be constant in prayer." (Romans 12:12)

"But whoever listens to me will dwell secure and will be at ease, without dread of disaster." (Proverbs 1:33)

I know you've frequently heard people say communication is key in any relationship. Well, your relationship with God is no different. If you are feeling indifferent or even feeling a sense of joy or happiness, you need to communicate such things with God. It's what keeps your relationship strong. It also shows Him that you trust and love Him simply because you took time out of your day to express yourself to Him.

> **Side Note:** *One of the most common ways to communicate with God is through Prayer. It is the key that unlocks blessings, gifts, talents, healing, and so much more. Without it, your relationship with God is dead.*

**Getting To Know Your Bible:** "It is impossible to develop a relationship with God without prayer. Everyone can agree that the key to any good relationship is communication, whether it be between a husband and wife, manager and employee, or just close friends. Your relationship with God will be the same—it will not grow unless you consistently communicate with Him. Jesus demonstrated this well during His earthly ministry. Here are a few examples:

- "So He Himself often withdrew into the wilderness and prayed." (Luke 5:16)

- "Now in the morning, having risen a long while before daylight, He went out and departed to a solitary place; and there He prayed." (Mark 1:35)

- "Coming out, He went to the Mount of Olives, as He was accustomed, and His disciples also followed Him." (Luke 22:39)

Jesus is not the only figure in Scripture who did this. You will be hard-pressed to find someone in Scripture who had a deep relationship with God and did not pray. Old and New Testament alike, from the Prophets to the Apostles, they all prayed devoutly to strengthen their relationship with God." (A Guide on How to Build a Relationship With God)

**Focus on the Family:** "Just as a close relationship with another person requires conversation, your relationship with God is the same. Conversing with Him happens through reading the Bible (His main way of communicating with those who love Him) and prayer (a two-way conversation between you and God).

When you pray, God is not asking for a formula; He doesn't want you to pretend to be something that you are not. He doesn't want you to only praise Him, never ask Him for anything, or to say particular phrases to make yourself sound "religious." Instead, He just wants you to tell Him what is on your heart and mind, just as you would with a trusted friend (1 Peter 5:6-8)." (Schutte, 2009)

> **Side Note:** *Although the most common way to communicate with God is through prayer, there are many other ways. Some involve simply talking to Him throughout the day. The same way you would with your spouse or friend.*

**Heartspoken:** "Being in touch with God doesn't have to be only during times of meditation or prayer. It can be while you're on the run, when you're in the midst of activities, or when you have a moment's break." (Cottrell, 2014)

**Hope For Children Foundation:** "It is important to remember people cannot read your mind. So do not expect someone to read your mind. It is humanly impossible to be accurate with such an undertaking. It is so important to be honest and share your feelings with those in a relationship. Honesty means telling the truth about factual information, and about the way you are feeling. If you were hurt by something someone said or did, they may not even realize they hurt you by what they said or by their actions unless you are honest with them about how it affected you. Hiding one's hurt feelings might make one feel safe. Unfortunately, hiding hurt feelings can also disempower others in a relationship from doing something positive to correct the hurtful problem. Hiding one's feelings does not help a relationship to be nurtured and grow stronger with love. Various things can grow until the relationship is clearly damaged. Being honest about your feelings can bring healing, solve a problem, renew hope and foster good communication." (Patricia, 2019)

> **Side Note:** *In a relationship, communication is not simply a one-way street. This means one must learn to also listen to and hear God's voice when He speaks. Just as you expect God to listen to your concerns, wants, or desires, it's important that you do the same. Another thing to remember is that you cannot learn about someone (grow close to them) if you never listen to them.*

**In Touch Ministries:** "The most obvious way to become better acquainted with the Lord is through two-way communi-cation. But our prayers are often monologues rather than dialogues. We come to Him with our list of concerns, but how often do we take time to listen for His response? Although God delights in hearing our prayers, He also wants us to be still and listen to Him.

Since He speaks to us primarily through His Word, that's where we will most likely hear His voice. Try interacting with the Lord by praying as you read Scripture. Meditate on His words and ask Him questions: "What are You saying to me? How does this apply to my life?" Then be still and listen, giving Him time to speak to your spirit. Just remember that whatever He says will never contradict His written Word. The more you listen, the more you'll hear His voice, and soon your time with Him will become your greatest delight." (Stanley C. F., 2014)

**Heartspoken:** "Remember to make it a two-way conversation and expect to hear from God, just as you would from a trusted friend. God wants you to know how much He loves you. He wants to offer support and guidance to you. If you don't take the time to listen, you won't hear His "still, small voice." For me, this communication from God comes in various forms: thoughts, feelings, music, reading, nature, other people, or circumstances. Sometimes I only recognize God's voice in retrospect." (Cottrell, 2014)

**Readers Digest:** "Making time to really see your partner communicates that you value them and appreciate all that makes them who they are. Miller encourages couples to slow down and truly hear what their partner is saying on a daily basis. She explains in her book, "One of my favorite quotes is by Paul Tillich, the Christian existentialist philosopher, 'The first duty of love is to listen.' How often do we really do this? How often do we actively listen to our partners?" She advises her readers, "Do me a big favor: the next time your partner is speaking to you, no matter what it is, just listen. And when I say just listen, I also mean with your eyes; i.e., look at your partner's face and body. Drop your need to interrupt, or to think about something else, or to steer the conversation in another direction. Just focus on what he is saying, even if you don't agree with him. Especially if you don't agree with him." Are you really listening?" (Babakhan, 2019)

5. Take baby steps and be patient.

"The Lord is good to those who wait for him, to the soul who seeks him. It is good that one should wait quietly for the salvation of the Lord." (Lamentations 3:25-26)

"Better is the end of a thing than its beginning, and the patient in spirit is better than the proud in spirit." (Ecclesiastes 7:8)

As with any relationship, intimacy (closeness) with another individual is not developed nor built overnight. It takes time, which requires the two individuals involved in the relationship to be patient with one another.

> **Side Note:** *Deeply intimate relationships that can stand and or last through the highs and lows in life are built over time and requires much patience.*

**GoodTherapy.org:** "Intimacy in a romantic relationship is usually something that is built over time. New relationships might have moments of intimacy, but building long-term intimacy is a gradual process that requires patience and communication." (What is Intimacy?)

**Side Note:** *To build a deeply intimate relationship with God, you must be patient. His greatness and glory are beyond anything you can comprehend. This means it will take time to get to know Him, grow close to Him, and develop an unbreakable bond and love for Him. "My thoughts are nothing like your thoughts," says the Lord. "And my ways are far beyond anything you could imagine. For just as the heavens are higher than the earth, so my ways are higher than your ways and my thoughts higher than your thoughts. (Isaiah 55:8-9)*

**PsychCentral:** "Intimacy means deeply knowing another person and feeling deeply known. That doesn't happen in a conversation in a bar or during a lovely day at the beach or even at times during sex. It doesn't happen in the first weeks and months of a new and exciting relationship. It doesn't develop when one person nurtures a relationship more than the other. No. Intimacy, like fine wine takes time to deepen and mellow. It takes gentle handling and patience by all involved. It takes the willingness to make mistakes and to forgive them in the name of learning." (Marie Hartwell-Walker, 2018)

**Focus on the Family:** "Lastly, remember that just as developing intimacy with another person takes time, so it is with your relationship with God. As you grow to trust Him and believe what He says in His Word more and more, your love affair with Him will become increasingly fulfilling and the abundance of zoe will grow inside your spirit and soul." (Schutte, 2009)

6. Love, accept, appreciate, and be loyal to Him.

"Teacher, which is the great commandment in the Law?" And he said to him, "You shall love the Lord your God with all your heart and with all your soul and with all your mind. This is the great and first commandment." (Matthew 22:36-38)

Everybody wants to be with someone who loves and accepts them for who they are not simply for who the other individual wants them to be. Someone who appreciates them and not simply what they can do. God is no different.

> **Side Note:** *For a relationship to grow to a certain level or degree of intimacy and love, you must at some point love and accept the other person for who they are instead of constantly trying to make them be who you want them to be.*

**Marriage.com:** "Love is acceptance and loving someone fully and unconditionally for who they are.

The best way of developing acceptance skills in a relationship is to be proud of your partner's milestones achieved, big or small.

Recognize their wins publicly, acknowledge the hardships of their journey, and compliment them on their personality, smile, thoughtfulness, compassion, and several other things that make them special.

By not focusing on your partner's flaws and learning to accept them for who they are in a relationship you will bring genuine happiness in their most insipid days, inspiring them to grow as a better person." (Strelnick, 2019)

**Readers Digest:**

- **"Release your need to fix them:** One of the most common pitfalls in any committed relationship is assuming that the other person is the one who needs to change. Though it's tempting to place all of the blame for your relationship troubles on your partner, Andrea Miller, CEO and founder of yourtango.com and author of Radical Acceptance: The Secret to Happy, Lasting Love, believes that one of the best ways to overcome arguments is to stop trying to change your SO. Miller believes that radically accepting those you are in close relationship with reduces tensions and draws you closer to your partner. By releasing yourself from the burden of making your partner your project, you allow yourself to fully accept your loved one, faults and all. This introduces a new dynamic in the relationship, in which both partners feel mutually loved and respected.

- **Replace judgment with compassion:** Everyone wants to find a relationship that feels completely safe and free of judgment. When partners find themselves clashing repeatedly and judging one another for poor decisions or actions, it only drives a larger wedge between them instead of building intimacy and the ability to be vulnerable. Instead of judging your partner for the way they load the dishwasher, take a moment to remove the judgmental thought and replace it with a sense of gratitude that your partner shares the housework. If you find yourself angry about your partner coming home late from work once again, decide instead to re-frame your thoughts into compassion for him or her, for having such a long day at work. Miller says, "This is the heart of Radical Acceptance. It's a powerful, beautiful, and, ultimately, transformative practice—emphasis on practice! The key is to commit yourself to this intention and to simply be aware of when you're being judgmental, and to call yourself out accordingly." She continues," I use this with my husband and with all of the other important relationships in my life—especially the ones that press my buttons. I know that when I'm judging someone else, that negativity is coming right back to me.

- **Vow to love your partner unconditionally:** Unconditional love is the ultimate goal of most committed relationships. To love and be known for your true self is a gift that keeps giving, providing endless fulfillment and happiness that permeates all corners of life. It gives you the confidence to achieve your fullest potential, and in turn, gives the safety and security you need to encourage your partner to do the same. Miller writes in her book, "There is no such thing as meeting him halfway when it comes to Radical Acceptance. Radical Acceptance means you always have his back—even when he is wrong. Radical Acceptance is unconditional love—even when it feels unbearably difficult, when you feel deeply hurt or disappointed, or when you feel he is at fault." (Babakhan, 2019)

**Side Note:** *With unconditional love comes emotional intimacy, and emotional intimacy sets the stage for loyalty and devotion.*

When you love someone unconditionally, they become a part of you which means you would not want to do anything to hurt them. This type of love develops into loyalty and devotion. Loyalty and devotion bring about a sense of comfort and security which helps to strengthen the intimate bond in a relationship.

**Bustle:** "The active practice of being able to emotionally walk in someone else's shoes, but also to perform acts of service for them, are two key components to the practice of empathy," relationship expert Dr. Gary Brown tells Bustle. "This is one of the most important keys to building love and loyalty." By sharing in shouldering that burden alongside of them, you will not only prove to your partner that their problems are now yours as well, but it will also help to establish trust." (Hariri-Kia, 2018)

> **Side Note:** *Next up on the love list is being appreciative. Nobody wants to be in a relationship with someone who does not appreciate them nor their presence, somebody who only loves them for the material possessions they can provide.*

**Heartspoken:** "If we're going to grow in oneness with God, we must learn to share His interests. He is always attentive to our concerns, but do we really care about His desires and purposes? Are you more interested in the Lord or in what He can give you? Self-focused prayers, neglect of His Word, and overly busy schedules send an unspoken message to Him: "I'm not interested in You!" If your relationship with the Lord seems stagnant, maybe you have drifted into a self-centered focus that is hindering your friendship with Him." (Cottrell, 2014)

You can show God you love Him by praising and complimenting Him. Tell Him how much you appreciate Him and all that He has done for you or how much you simply appreciate who He is.

> **Side Note:** *Finally, another way to show God you love Him is by loving and being intimate (close) with His children.*

If you had a child before going into a new relationship, would you not want your spouse to get acquainted with and love your children?

Because we are all God's children (have his DNA), are created in His image, and are a part of one body, becoming acquainted with one another is the same as being intimate with and loving God. Another thing to note is that it brings God great joy to know that you love Him enough to love who belongs to Him.

**Inspiring Tips:**

- **"Love your neighbors:** God truly loves His people. Hence, if you want to strengthen your relationship with God, make sure that you are also creating a good relationship with your neighbors and other people. You cannot build a healthy relationship with God if you hate and hurt your neighbors. Thus, do good to them, offer to help them, and maintain a harmonious relationship with them.

   "And a second is like it: You shall love your neighbor as yourself." (Matthew 22:39)

- **Love your family:** Your parents, brothers, and sisters are the people whom you have been living with under the same roof for years. If you cannot build a good relationship with these people whom you have always seen, then how can you build a good relationship with God whom you have not seen? Therefore, learn to love, honor and respect your parents and siblings to strengthen your relationship with God.

   "Whoever claims to love God yet hates a brother or sister is a liar. For whoever does not love their brother and sister, whom they have seen, cannot love God, whom they have not seen." (1 John 4:20)

- **Love your spouse:** Your husband or wife is the person whom you want to spend the rest of your life with. God has commanded husbands to love their own wife as themselves and wives to respect their own husband. If you want to fortify your relationship with God, then do not hurt your spouse. Do not cheat on your wife. Do not shame your husband. But cherish your love with one another with your children and let God be the center of your marriage.

"Nevertheless, let each one of you in particular so love his own wife as himself, and let the wife see that she respects her husband." (Ephesians 5:33)" (Abrugar)

Side Note: *For further detail on building an intimate relationship with God, I highly suggest you read Joyce Meyers' book Knowing God Intimately.*

To conclude, intimacy with God (the starting point of your new life) is very important because you can't reach your full potential and become spiritually mature if you have not been healed of your pain and problems simply because of the holes that were left within you when you experienced heartbreak or pain will never allow you to. They will continuously lead to whatever God fills you with to leak out.

**DON'T BECOME A DANGER TO YOUR SUCCESS BECAUSE INTIMACY WITH GOD HAS BECOME AN OBSTACLE AND NOT A GOAL.**

"Be much alone with God and take time to get thoroughly acquainted. Converse over everything with Him. Unburden yourself wholly - every thought, feeling, wish, plan, doubt - to Him... He wants not merely to be on good terms with you, but to be intimate."

— *Horatius Bonar*

"**God,** I want to see You. God, I want to hear You. God, I want to know You. God, I want to follow hard after You. And even before I know what I will face today, I say yes to You.

In Jesus Name, Amen!"

— *Lysa TerKeurst*

# CHAPTER 15

# THE WAIT

*The earth, which is now home to billions of people, was created empty. This means that before being filled by God with all the good things that currently define its character, the earth had to go through a period of waiting. And my friend, you are no different. "Do you not know? Have you not heard? The LORD is the everlasting God, the Creator of the ends of the earth. He never grows faint or weary; His understanding is beyond searching out. He gives power to the faint and increases the strength of the weak. Even youths may faint and grow weary, and young men stumble and fall. But those who wait upon the LORD will renew their strength; they will mount up with wings like eagles; they will run and not grow weary, they will walk and not faint." (Isaiah 40:28-31)*

**Isaiah 45:18** NIV "For this is what the LORD says--he who created the heavens, he is God; he who fashioned and made the earth, he founded it; he did not create it to be empty, but formed it to be inhabited--he says: "I am the LORD, and there is no other."

In this chapter, you will learn more about the healing process. This includes the requirements necessary to be healed. Why it's important to wait on God to be healed, and what happens when you don't. Let's get to it.

| PREGNANCY TERMS USED IN CHAPTER | TRANSLATION |
|---|---|
| • Courtship | • Intimacy with God |
| • Embryo/Fetus/Baby | • Good Nature/Spirit/Good Character |
| • Your Womb | • Your Heart (Gods Temple) |
| • Pregnancy | • Process where Good Character is developed within you |
| • Preconception Health Care | • Preparation for pregnancy |
| • Pre-Pregnancy Requirements | • Requirements for creating a stable environment for the baby (Good Character) to grow and be developed in |
| • Prenatal Care | • Daily alone time with God |
| • Trimester | • Stages |
| • Physician/Nurse/Mid-Wife | • God/Jesus/The Holy Spirit |

# PRE-PREGNANCY HEALTH CARE

*(Preparation for Pregnancy)*

**Preconception Health Care:**

- **Center for Disease Control and Prevention:** "The medical care a woman or man receives from the doctor or other health professionals that focuses on the parts of health that have been shown to increase the chance of having a healthy baby.

  Preconception health care is different for every person, depending on his or her unique needs. Based on a person's individual health, the doctor or other health care professional will suggest a course of treatment or follow-up care as needed." (Planning for Pregnancy)

- **Flushing Hospital:** "Preconception care consists of the healthcare you receive before conceiving. During this time, your doctor will assess your health to determine if there are conditions that can affect your future pregnancy. Potential risks may be reduced or eliminated by applying interventions such as medication or lifestyle changes. Lifestyle changes that are encouraged may include eating a healthy diet, maintaining a healthy weight, taking supplements that contain folic acid, receiving pertinent vaccinations, getting mentally healthy, quitting smoking, and avoiding alcohol consumption.

  There are many benefits associated with preconception care, they include:

  - Reducing infant and maternal mortality.

- Reducing the risk of complications during pregnancy.

- Preventing certain birth defects.

Most doctors recommend receiving preconception care three to six months before the time you intend to conceive." (Malcom, 2018)

## PRE-PREGNANCY REQUIREMENTS

*(Requirements for creating a stable environment for the baby (Good Character) to be developed in)*

**Planning For Pregnancy:** "If you are trying to have a baby or are just thinking about it, it is not too early to start getting ready for pregnancy. Preconception health and health care focus on things you can do before and between pregnancies to increase the chances of having a healthy baby. For some women, getting their body ready for pregnancy takes a few months. For other women, it might take longer. Whether this is your first, second, or sixth baby, the following are important steps to help you get ready for the healthiest pregnancy possible:

1. Make a Plan and Take Action.

2. See Your Doctor.

3. Take 400 Micrograms of Folic Acid Every Day.

4. Stop Drinking Alcohol, Smoking, and Using Certain Drugs.

5. Avoid Toxic Substances and Environmental Contaminants.

6. Reach and Maintain a Healthy Weight.

7. Get Help for Violence.

8. Learn Your Family History.

9. Get Mentally Healthy.

10. Have a Healthy Pregnancy!" (Planning for Pregnancy, 2020)

**Requirements for developing Good Characteristics within you:**

- The baby (Good Character) needs to be introduced to an empty, healthy (clean), and stable environment.

- This means before committing to this pregnancy journey, you need to wait long enough for God to fix (heal and seal) the holes (wounds) that the brokenness (pain) from your past left within you.

The requirements mentioned above make your baby's growth and development, which includes the birth of a new life, a smooth and clean process, instead of a process with tons of complications.

Before you move forward, I would like to let you know that waiting to be healed, sealed, and fully filled by God is not easy. So, prepare yourself mentally for the road ahead!

## WHY IS WAITING TO BE HEALED, SEALED, AND FULLY FILLED BY GOD TOUGH?

Waiting to be healed, sealed, and fully filled by God is very tough because this stage of your journey is considered the middle of your struggles and the beginning of the wilderness (a testing ground).

"Then Moses led Israel from the Red Sea. They went into the Desert of Shur. They went three days in the desert and found no water. When they came to Marah, they could not drink the water of Marah because it was bitter. So it was given the name Marah. The people complained to Moses, saying, "What can we drink?" Moses cried to the Lord, and the Lord showed him a tree. He threw it into the water, and the water became sweet.

There the Lord made a Law for them and tested them. He said, "Listen well to the voice of the Lord your God. Do what is right in His eyes. Listen to what He tells you, and obey all His Laws. If you do this, I will put none of the diseases on you which I have put on the Egyptians. For I am the Lord Who heals you." (Exodus 15:22-26)

**The Wilderness:**

- A stage where agitation and frustrations arise because you are so close, yet it feels as if you are so far away from being *fully filled* with the Holy Spirit (fully developing one's abilities or character = (spiritually mature) and being ministered to by the angels (reaching your dreams).

- A stage where discernment, faith, patience, and love are tested so good character can be developed within you.

- A stage where focus is necessary, and your ability to survive change is tested.

- A stage where you'll encounter an unexpected new friend (your breaking point), and only one question will remain. Will you give up on your dreams, or will you keep going, allowing the pressure from your breaking point to be used as an instrument to propel you over the finish line into what you've been hoping for (a breakthrough)?

## THE BEGINNING OF THE WILDERNESS IS A PLACE WHERE IF YOU DO NOT BREAK UNDER PRESSURE, THE PRESSURE CAN BE USED TO DEVELOP YOUR BABY = CHARACTER, WHICH LEADS TO YOUR BREAKTHROUGH.

**Side Note:** *What you may think of as your breaking point is an opportunity for you to stretch, grow, and reach your full potential (spiritual maturity).*

**Breaking Point:**

- The moment of greatest strain at which someone or something gives way.

**Breakthrough:**

- A sudden, dramatic, and important discovery or development.

- An instance of achieving success in a particular sphere or activity.

**Fulfilled:**

- To carry out or bring to realization, as a prophecy or promise; completed; satisfied or happy because of fully developing one's abilities or character.

- In other words, *fulfilled* = Spiritual Maturity/*Wholeness*.

**Side Note:** *Don't give up when you are in the wilderness and it feels as though you are at your breaking point because the struggle (pressure) is what pushes you one giant step closer to being fully filled (spiritually mature).*

## SPIRITUAL MATURITY/WHOLENESS EXPLAINED:

**Got Questions:** "Spiritual maturity is achieved through becoming more like Jesus Christ. After salvation, every Christian begins the process of spiritual growth, with the intent to become spiritually mature. According to the apostle Paul, it's an ongoing process that will never end in this life. In Philippians 3:12–14, speaking of full knowledge of Christ, he tells his readers that he himself has not "already obtained all this, or have already been made perfect, but I press on to take hold of that for which Christ Jesus took hold of me. Brothers, I do not consider myself yet to have taken hold of it. But one thing I do: Forgetting what is behind and straining toward what is ahead, I press on toward the goal to win the prize for which God has called me heavenward in Christ Jesus." Like Paul, we have to press continually toward deeper knowledge of God in Christ.

Christian maturity requires a radical reordering of one's priorities, changing over from pleasing self to pleasing God and learning to obey God. The key to maturity is consistency, perseverance in doing those things we know will bring us closer to God. These practices are referred to as the spiritual disciplines and include things such as Bible reading/study, prayer, fellowship, service, and stewardship. No matter how hard we might work on those things, however, none of this is possible without the enabling of the Holy Spirit within us. Galatians 5:16 tells us that we're to "walk by the Spirit." The Greek word used here for "walk" actually means "to walk with a purpose in view." Later in the same chapter, Paul tells us again that we're to "walk by the Spirit." Here, the word translated "walk" has the idea of taking things "step by step, one step at a time." It is learning to walk under the instruction of another—the Holy Spirit. Being filled with the Spirit means we walk under the Spirit's control. As we submit more and more to the Spirit's control, we will also see an increase in the fruit of the Spirit in our lives (Galatians 5:22–23). This is characteristic of spiritual maturity." (What is spiritual maturity?, 2011)

**Growing in Faith:** "By his divine power, God has given us everything we need for living a godly life. We have received all of this by coming to know him, the one who called us to himself by means of his marvelous glory and excellence. And because of his glory and excellence, he has given us great and precious promises. These are the promises that enable you to share his divine nature and escape the world's corruption caused by human desires.

In view of all this, make every effort to respond to God's promises. Supplement your faith with a generous provision of moral excellence, and moral excellence with knowledge, and knowledge with self-control, and self-control with patient endurance, and patient endurance with godliness, and godliness with brotherly affection, and brotherly affection with love for everyone.

The more you grow like this, the more productive and useful you will be in your knowledge of our Lord Jesus Christ. But those who fail to develop in this way are short-sighted or blind, forgetting that they have been cleansed from their old sins.

So, dear brothers and sisters, work hard to prove that you really are among those God has called and chosen. Do these things, and you will never fall away. Then God will give you a grand entrance into the eternal Kingdom of our Lord and Savior Jesus Christ." (2 Peter 1:3-7)

> **Side Note:** *Because you fully developing your character (becoming spiritually mature) leads to you being more productive and useful in the Kingdom of God, the devil will, at all costs, try to use your breaking point (pressure from your circumstances and current struggles) against you.*

The devil wants to do the best that he can to tempt you to exhibit bad character (sin), which causes you to become distant from God (move backward) or, as the Church would say, backslide.

### Backslide:

- Relapse into bad ways or error.

## WHY?

The devil doesn't want you to be healed nor develop Good Characteristics within you (become spiritually mature) because that would mean he's lost you. And if he loses you, he loses them:

- Your family.

- The people you are meant to help and save.

- The people connected to your purpose. Meaning the people you can set free through the victory of your trials and tribulations.

## IF THE DEVIL LOSES YOU, HE LOSES TERRITORY.

Side Note: *The devil doesn't mind you just believing in God. However, he does mind you following through with the promises of God and teaching others how to live in the fullness of the promises of God. It's all about territory and control, which is why wars go on today.*

Territory:

- An area of land under the authority of a ruler or state.

Side Note: *Wars are all about territory. Who rules and controls what, or who rules who I should say.*

Vox: "People fight over territory all the time. Whether it's a gang war, a civil war between ethnic groups, or a big international dispute like the Russia-Ukraine crisis, people seem willing to kill and be killed over chunks of land.

Which is a little weird, if you think about it. People can seem irrationally attached to land; countries don't often gain or lose a whole lot from the territorial shifts. So why do we care so much? According to one new study by two political scientists, the answer might be in our DNA. Most of the animal kingdom has evolved a strong attachment to controlling land, and is willing to fight to hold onto it. Could this impulse also explain human war?

**Many, if not most, wars are fought over territory.**

People fight over land—a lot. The authors of the new study, the University of Oxford's Dominic Johnson and Monica Toft, reviewed two separate studies of the data on the causes of wars that occurred between 1816 and the early 21st century. In both datasets, half or a little more than half of all wars during that period were principally about land." (Beauchamp, 2014)

If the devil controls the who, he can control the what. What people do, say, and think. Mind control anyone. If the devil controls the person, he can control how they use power in their job. He can control the government as well as the images that are being placed in people's minds through the media.

## IF THE DEVIL CONTROLS THE WHO, HE CAN RULE THE WORLD!

Do you think you're important now? You are somebody, and you do have a purpose, so maybe you should start looking at yourself that way. Because trust me, this is war, and the hottest item on the block that's being fought over is not some Louis Vuitton or a Bentley; it's you!

## The Problem:

- Although you have a purpose, are important, and have been given power over the devil. He will not let you go without putting up a fight. And if he must, he will fight dirty.

**Side Note:** *To win the war to control you and your soul, the devil will fight dirty, using guerrilla warfare and strategic manipulation to try to overpower you.*

## Guerrilla warfare:

- A form of irregular warfare in which a small group of combatants, such as paramilitary personnel, armed civilians, or irregulars, use military tactics including ambushes, sabotage, raids, petty warfare, hit-and-run tactics, and mobility to fight a larger and less-mobile traditional military.

Although we (God's children) are the larger group and not easily moved, the unfairness, tipped scales, and shadiness we constantly face throughout life eventually breaks us down. That then leads to dirt being thrown in our eyes, which blinds us (guerrilla warfare), giving the enemy the perfect opportunity to "try" to attack. "Then Jesus was led by the [Holy] Spirit into the wilderness to be tempted by the devil. After He had gone without food for forty days and forty nights, He became hungry. And the tempter came and said to Him, "If You are the Son of God, command that these stones become bread." But Jesus replied, "It is written and forever remains written, 'Man shall not live by bread alone, but by every word that comes out of the mouth of God.'" (Matthew 4:1-7)

**Side Note:** *When you are at your lowest point (empty and hungry), it becomes your highest point of vulnerability because hunger weakens you and clouds your vision.*

To further illustrate, let's say you are a character in a movie and have been stuck in the desert for months with no water, no food, and no help. After some time, you begin to worry, and then boom, a mirage appears out of thin air. Now, remember, you're weak due to being hungry for a long time, so you can't think or see straight (focus). This means that when you gaze at the mirage for some time, you begin to believe it's real without even reasoning with yourself.

It's like a façade, and the devil has manipulated the circumstances, which are the struggles you face in life and the test God uses to bless you by placing a painted picture in front of you. He tells you your circumstances are who you are. It's where you'll continue to be. Or, you'll never make it out, so don't even try.

How does this help the devil?

- If you are too weak to claw away at the picture (false promises or fake circumstances) the devil places in front of you, you're never able to have the real you revealed, to have the character that sets you free from the broken systems in society revealed in you.

> **Side Note:** *While in the wilderness and going through hard times in life, there will be moments in which you will have to walk blindly. For this reason, you need to be able to trust God even when you can't see. "For we walk by faith, not by sight" (2 Corinthians 5:7)*

This is how the devil uses guerrilla warfare to take you out. He takes his shot when you are weak because he knows if he tries to tempt you while weak, your vision will be clouded. And instead of you clawing away at the picture having *Destiny Revealed*, you'll take what he has presented to you. Something that mesmerizes (comforts you) and causes you to stay stuck, fall, or backslide.

For example, let's say you just broke up with Jimmy/Jessica. Or you two have been going through some things. You're a bit down and lonely (loneliness can accentuate your feeling of emptiness, it's also the most persuasive tempter). Nevertheless, this leads you into a one-night stand (lust).

You lust for some attention, and Chris/Christina got it; lust and loneliness go hand in hand. Now, this is someone you don't even plan on being with, but you have fed your emptiness with them. And it helps for the moment, but the next day, you're empty again.

Why? Well, you fed your pain with this person, and it helped for the moment. But because "you" tried to, on your own (without God), fill the holes (brokenness) within you with something meaningless or not powerful enough to seal your broken heart, it leaked out.

## NOW, YOU'RE STUCK IN THE SAME SITUATION: DRAINED (LONELY) AND IN NEED OF MORE ATTENTION.

Now you're on a rampage and have become an addict, chasing after the lust of life. Trying to get what you want, but not having enough sense to wait on what you need.

You needed better decision-making skills (character), but the mirage of temptation convinced you otherwise.

Mirage of temptation:

- Do it.

- It will make you feel better.

- Nobody will get hurt.

This is temptation at its best, the war within. It's like being an alcoholic that gets drunk on life because the moment you use the restroom, that buzz is gone. Or for those that smoke weed, the moment you eat, that high goes down. It goes away. It leaks out. Under these circumstances, as a person, you can and will never be satisfied with anything in life. "He who loves money will not be satisfied with money, nor he who loves abundance with its income. This too is vanity." (Ecclesiastes 5:10) Nothing or no one will ever be good enough for you. You'll always need more. More money, more relationships, and more compliments because people places and things can't seal the pipes in your leaky faucet, nor can they put everlasting water in them.

"Jesus answered, "Everyone who drinks this water will be thirsty again, but whoever drinks the water I give them will never thirst.

Indeed, the water I give them will become in them a spring of water welling up to eternal life." (John 4:13-14)

**WHEN YOU THINK YOU CAN DO ALL THINGS THROUGH "YOU" AND STRENGTHEN YOUR-SELF, GOD WILL ALLOW YOU TO DO THINGS ON YOUR OWN. BUT WHAT YOU GET IN RETURN ARE THE RESULTS OF MAN AND NOT THE RESULTS FROM GOD, WHO HAS SUPERNATU-RAL POWER.**

Whenever you fill yourself on your own with the things of this world, you will continuously be thirsty because the things of this world are temporary and do not have double-acting power (healing + sealing power) as God does. Meaning eventually, the effect of said thing will leak out, and you will be left to maintain whatever area in your life you tried to fill, causing yourself stress and frustration.

To demonstrate, you can have tons of photos with a million likes on Instagram but still be frustrated and unhappy. Why? Well, the smile on your face is only "temporary" simply because it's connected to "you" using the actions of others to fill yourself. The result of which leads you to begin to feel the need to work harder than the people in the illegal sweatshops, going the extra mile to persuade people to continue to like your photos. Filter this, take off that, photoshop everything!

**Side Note:** *In life, it's said that hard work pays off. But is the work paying off if it's causing you stress and frustration because your actions are not of God. Which means the results are only "temporary".*

IIIIIIIIIIIIIIIIIIIIIIIIIIIIIIIIIIIIIIIIIIIIIIIIIIIIIIIIIIIIIIIIIIIIIIIIIIIIIIIIIIIIIIIIIIIIIIIIIIIIIIIIIIIIIIIIIIIIIIIIIIIIIIIIIIIIIIIIIIIII

"There are three things no person can ever do, simply because God has already done them.

**#1** No person can ever give you Identity.

**#2** No person can ever give you Purpose.

**#3** No person can ever Accept you."

### — *Pastor Michael Todd, Transformation Church*

IIIIIIIIIIIIIIIIIIIIIIIIIIIIIIIIIIIIIIIIIIIIIIIIIIIIIIIIIIIIIIIIIIIIIIIIIIIIIIIIIIIIIIIIIIIIIIIIIIIIIIIIIIIIIIIIIIIIIIIIIIIIIIIIIIIIIIIIIIIII

These are God holes, and if not careful, just like people who inject their bodies with substances to make themselves feel good inside, you will start filling yourself with people and things that potentially can harm you and your progress on this journey.

> **Side Note:** *If you keep doing what's hurting you (living life in the way of the world and filling yourself with the things of this world), you will cancel out any progress you have made up until now and will continue to have to repeat the process from the beginning. In the beginning there was God, and the Word was with God, Genesis type of beginning.*

This includes getting to the root of your problems and being empty repeatedly, which creates a cycle. You will need to push the junk (hurt, unforgiveness, and pride) out again. Be healed and sealed by God again, as well as build good character; again!

## WHY IS THIS?

The good character that God is trying to develop within you is built on a foundation of love. But, if your heart is broken due to you not fully completing this process, your foundation eventually becomes unstable, making it hard for you to be FULLY FILLED with the good character that enables you to reach your full potential and live a prosperous life.

To get a better illustration, take a look down below at the process that must be completed by construction workers when laying down concrete.

**WikiHow:**

1.  "Dig out the old rock (Hardened Heart = Bad Attitude).

2.  Clean the area up. (The Holy Spirit is the Cleaner, "But you

were washed, you were sanctified, you were justified in the name of the Lord Jesus Christ and by the Spirit of our God."–1 Corinthians 6:11)

3. Prepare the area in which the new concrete (Responsive Heart = Good Attitude and Character) will be placed.

4. Add reinforcements such as wire for a stronger support. (The Holy Spirit is your support system, helper, and insulation).

5. Mix the concrete.

6. Pour into the mold the new concrete.

7. Smooth the concrete out, filling any spaces, creating a new flat foundation (New You).

8. Seal the concrete to help prevent cracks. (The Holy Spirit is also the seal–Ephesians 1:1-14).

9. Let the foundation set for twenty-eight days.

10. Maintain overtime." (How to Pour Concrete, 2020)

> **Side Note:** *If you don't let concrete (your new attitude and character) set and decide to try to fill the road (your life) with cars (people, places, or things) before the appointed time, it will get messy; cracking, leaving you to start the process all over.*

**A. Pietig Concrete & Brick Paving:** "Driving on your concrete is important and convenient, but you do not want to drive on it before it is ready. There is a curing time that is needed so the concrete will fully develop. This development will create strong and durable concrete.

Knowing the steps of your concrete will help you to understand and know the importance of letting your concrete cure.

It does not take long before you can drive on your fresh concrete. The key is to be patient and let the concrete gain the strength that it needs. Keep tape across the fresh concrete to ensure that it is protected from any vehicles or people entering the driveway area." (How Long Before I Can Drive On Fresh Concrete?, 2014)

Bob Vila: "Although concrete will harden soon after pouring, it's still susceptible to damage from weight during the first four weeks. Wait at least 24 hours before allowing foot traffic, including pets, on a newly poured sidewalk or slab, and don't drive a vehicle on a new driveway for at least 10 days. After that, you can drive regular passenger cars on the concrete; heavy pickups or RVs can roll onto the driveway once the concrete reaches its full strength, at around 28 days." (The Dos and Don'ts of Curing Concrete, 2019)

**JUST LIKE CONCRETE, YOUR HEART AND CHARACTER CAN'T BE CHANGED, SET, AND FILLED (FULLY DEVELOPED AND READY TO HANDLE THE PRESSURE OF THE WORLD) OVERNIGHT. THIS PROCESS TAKES PRACTICE, PATIENCE, FORMALITY, AND ORDER. THERE ARE LEVELS TO THIS!**

As an example, we'll use the scenario of jumping from one relationship to the next to explain further.

**Example:**

- You're in a relationship with someone, but you feel they are not the right fit for you. So, you leave that relationship thinking something is wrong with the individual you were with and jump into a new relationship.

**The Problem:**

- The old saying "it's not you, it's me" actually does apply here.

> **Side Note:** *Whenever you move too fast and jump from one relationship to the next, you have no time to review the writings on the wall.*

**Writings on the wall:**

- You didn't work on nor give yourself enough time to heal before going into that new relationship.

- You didn't check or filter out the dirt and pollution (the bad attitude) in your water (yourself). Yet you blamed the individual you were in a relationship with for being the reason why things didn't work out.

> **Side Note:** *Because you are not being healed by God and working on yourself before moving on, you jump into relationships that self-destruct the moment you enter them.*

Take a look at the illustration that follows to better see how your decisions can affect your entire life.

## NEW HOUSE (NEW LIFE) + TAINTED WATER (BAD CHARACTER & ATTITUDE) + BUSTED PIPES (BROKEN HEART) = WATER DAMAGE (ISSUES THAT RUIN YOUR LIFE)

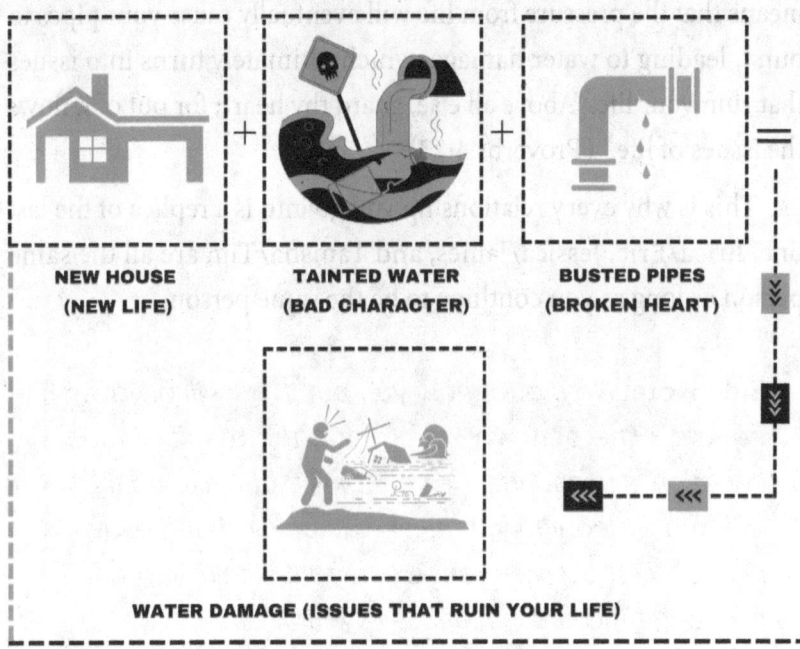

In other words, you went into a new relationship (new home), but that bad attitude (tainted water) and broken heart (busted pipes) were a deal-breaker. Now you're being evicted because you've accumulated so much debt (water damage/issues) and cannot afford the current bills in your new home. At this point, you have to find somewhere else to lay your head. This leaves you feeling unloved, a need for love, yet unfulfilled.

## HOW DID THIS HAPPEN?

Water (character) is meant to flow through your pipes (heart). But if you don't wait on God to fix them, good character will not be the water flowing through your pipes, and they cannot be filled. This means that the pressure from life will eventually cause your pipes to burst, leading to water damage, which ultimately turns into issues that ruin your life. "Above all else, guard thy heart; for out of it flows the issues of life." (Proverbs 4:23)

This is why every relationship you go into is a replica of the last one. Erica/Eric, Jessica/James, and Tanisha/Tim are all the same person as long as you continue to be the same person.

> **Side Note:** *No matter how you put it, 1+1 will always equal 2. The only way to change the result of the equation is to change the variables that make up the equation. Meaning you must wait on God and allow him to fix (heal and change you from within) in order to change the circumstances in your life.*

**YOU NEED TO WAIT ON GOD AND ALLOW HIM TO HELP YOU FIND, KNOW, AND FIX YOURSELF BEFORE FINDING OR BEING WITH ANYONE ELSE.**

One of the most important things to assess and, if necessary, have fixed before purchasing a home is the foundation.

Trulia: "The foundation is, quite literally, the base of your home. It is the bedrock upon which the whole structure rests, so it must be strong and stable enough to support the entire house. Any damage or defects that compromise the integrity of the foundation can be cause for concern—and might be a significant problem." (How to Deal with Foundation Issues When Buying or Selling a House)

And... Water damage to the foundation due to leakage can be the most dangerous problem you can encounter. It's a definite deal-breaker and must be repaired before anyone new moves in.

Triad Basement Waterproofing: "Water damage is one of the most common and worst side effects of water leakage or flooding in a basement. Water damage is also one of the leading causes of home insurance claims and it is responsible for millions of dollars in damages every year.

In addition to contributing to structural and foundation problems, basement water damage can completely destroy your personal belongings and interior decorative finishes and it also has the power to create the perfect environment for toxic mold growth." (Everything you Need to Know About Water Damage Remediation)

> **Side Note:** *If a home has suffered from water damage (structural damage). Before selling the home or people moving in, the foundation needs to be assessed and repaired to ensure the home will not fall apart when it is fully filled, and pressure arises. This means the home must be empty for some time so that someone can fix (change out) the damaged goods.*

It's the same with you. Before you move forward with your life and accomplish your dreams, you need to be empty and wait on God so He can fix (change out) the damaged goods (bad characteristics) within you.

Another way to look at it is you need to be empty long enough to be fixed (changed from within); otherwise, you'll pile up new furniture (good character) on top of old dirty furniture (bad character). How is this a problem? Well, the new furniture will only cover the old dirty furniture for a short period. Eventually, the old dirty furniture will taint your new furniture, rendering it useless. "No one puts new wine into old wineskins, or else the new wine will burst the skins, and the wine pours out, and the skins will be destroyed; but they put new wine into fresh wineskins." (Mark 2:22)

You are the wineskins, and the new attitude and good character that's being developed in you is the wine. But as mentioned previously, you don't place new good characteristics on top old bad characteristics. The old is replaced by the new.

## WHY DOES REPLACING YOUR OLD BAD CHARACTER MATTER SO MUCH?

If you don't replace your old bad habits with new good ones, you can never build healthy relationships or truly have anything in life because the bad character that lingers within you will always cause you to lose whatever you have gained.

As an example, the one thing that sets you off because you didn't deal with your inner demons could be the one thing that leads to you losing the business that you worked so hard to build. This also can lead to you losing your life because you won't have the means to take care of your family.

With that picture in mind, ask yourself, would you rather wait on God to heal you and be a strong, whole pipe with everlasting double acting water flowing through it (an individual filled with good characteristics)? Or would you rather not wait on God and be that busted pipe from earlier with tainted water that's leaking all the time, ruining everything in proximity (an individual filled with bad characteristics)?

Before deciding, remember, everything (your relationships, your job, your business) in the home (your life) can be ruined because of one broken leaky pipe.

**Side Note:** *If your heart is the pipe, you have to evaluate whether your heart can handle where God wants to take you before deciding to go to the next level, a level where pressure will make or break you.*

**GOD WILL NOT PLACE YOU IN A NEW OR HIGHER POSITION IN LIFE IF YOUR OLD BEHAVIOR AND CHARACTER WILL LEAD TO YOU THROWING EVERYTHING AWAY.**

The old version of you can't handle the great things that God has planned for you in your new life. For this reason, you need to wait on God to provide you with a new suit and tie (new attitude), which will give you the power to kill em' (the devil) in this interview (life).

**Side Note:** *It is pointless for God to bless you if you are not prepared for the blessing.*

To close, completing this stage of the journey does not mean you won't encounter trouble, pain, or won't have to deal with this particular stage ever again in life. But the first time around completing this stage is necessary because it leads to you being healed and helps create a solid foundation that can eventually withstand the pressure that comes with being filled with all of the good things God has to offer.

**FINAL WORDS: BE EMPTY AND WAIT ON GOD TO HEAL AND SEAL YOU OR DIE WITHOUT HAVING BEEN FULLY EQUIPPED TO LIVE OUT YOUR PURPOSE.**

||||||||||||||||||||||||||||||||||||||||||||||||||||||||||||||||||||||||||||||||||||||||||||||||||||||||||

"Timing is so important! If you are going to be successful in dance, you must be able to respond to rhythm and timing. It's the same in the Spirit. People who don't understand God's timing can become spiritually spastic, trying to make the right things happen at the wrong time. They don't get His rhythm – and everyone can tell they are out of step. They birth things prematurely, threatening the very lives of their God-given dreams."

— *Bishop T. D. Jakes*

||||||||||||||||||||||||||||||||||||||||||||||||||||||||||||||||||||||||||||||||||||||||||||||||||||||||||

*Dear Lord,* I pray that as I wait on you to heal my soul and fill my spirit, I receive from you the power to do so patiently and the wisdom necessary to know how.

*Crosswalk:* "I thank You that You will answer my prayers in Your perfect timing. Reveal what is in my heart, and make me ready to handle the answer in the right way when it comes. Help me to pray by faith consistently and long-term, to believe, wait, and then move forward in Your timing. Help me to be patient in prayer, not give up, and trust You even during moments when I feel negative emotions. I don't want to live by feelings but by faith. Help me not to take matters into my own hands. I choose to trust you, and I refuse to believe the lies of the enemy. I choose to be faithful in prayer (Colossians 4:2). Deepen my understanding and give me a greater knowledge of what You are doing in my life. I choose to hold unswervingly to the hope that I profess (Hebrews 10:23). Stretch my faith in the midst of the wait, just as You did with Your disciples when encountering a storm at sea (Matthew 8:23-27). I thank You that You have all wisdom and will answer my prayers in the perfect way." (Przybylski, 2018)

In Jesus' name, Amen.

# CHAPTER 16

# TIME SPENT

*You have learned how important it is for you to wait on God to heal you. Now it's time for you to find out what it means to spend time alone with Him daily in order to remain healed.*

**Ephesians 5:15-18 NLV** "So be careful how you live. Live as men who are wise and not foolish. Make the best use of your time. These are sinful days. Do not be foolish. Understand what the Lord wants you to do. Do not get drunk with wine. That leads to wild living. Instead, be filled with the Holy Spirit."

In this chapter, you will focus on what it means to daily spend time alone with God and how to maintain an intimate relationship with Him. Very similar to the previous chapters the stages of a pregnancy journey will be used to kick off this learning session, but this time around, the discussion will be centered around prenatal care.

| PREGNANCY TERMS USED IN CHAPTER | TRANSLATION |
|---|---|
| • Courtship | • Intimacy with God |
| • Embryo/Fetus/Baby | • Good Nature/Spirit/Good Character |
| • Your Womb | • Your Heart (Gods Temple) |
| • Pregnancy | • Process where Good Character is developed within you |
| • Preconception Health Care | • Preparation for pregnancy |
| • Pre-Pregnancy Requirements | • Requirements for creating a stable environment for the baby (Good Character) to grow and be developed in |
| • Prenatal Care | • Daily alone time with God |
| • Trimester | • Stages |
| • Physician/Nurse/Mid-Wife | • God/Jesus/The Holy Spirit |

## PRENATAL CARE

*(Daily alone time with God)*

**Planned Parenthood:** "Prenatal care is when you get check-ups from a doctor, nurse, or midwife throughout your pregnancy. It helps keep you and your future baby healthy.

Why is prenatal care important? Prenatal care is an important part of staying healthy during pregnancy.

Your doctor, nurse, or midwife will monitor your future baby's development and do routine testing to help find and prevent possible problems. These regular check-ups are also a great time to learn how to ease any discomfort you may be having, and ask any other questions about your pregnancy and the birth of your future baby." (Prenatal Care)

**Flushing Hospital:** "Prenatal care is healthcare you receive while you are pregnant. It is important because it helps improve your chances of having a healthy pregnancy. Your visits with your doctor may involve physical exams, imaging tests, blood tests, or screening tests to detect fetal abnormalities. It is recommended that you ask your physician lots of questions and express your concerns during these visits. Your physician will serve as a guide and source of support as your body changes.

Women who receive regular prenatal care may receive benefits that include:

- Reducing the risk of pregnancy complications.

- Managing preexisting medical conditions such as high blood pressure which can affect pregnancy.

- Receiving accurate nutritional information.

- Ensuring that medications being taken are safe.

- Physician monitoring of the baby's development.

- Decreasing the possibility of preterm labor." (Malcom, 2018)

 Before you can birth your baby and have destiny revealed, you must first settle in, get comfortable, and find out what it means to spend alone time with God.

## WHAT DOES IT MEAN TO SPEND TIME ALONE WITH GOD?

**Alone:**

- Having no one else present.

- On one's own.

First off, I would like to clarify that simply being alone and alone with God are two different things. God said it's not good for man to be alone (Genesis 2:18), but He also said to go into your closet alone to pray "But when you pray, go away by yourself, shut the door behind you, and pray to your Father in private. Then your Father, who sees everything, will reward you." (Matthew 6:6).

This means to be alone with Him so that you can maintain an intimate relationship with Him as well as on a daily ask Him to fill you with the Holy Spirit. "For everyone who asks receives, and the one who seeks finds, and to the one who knocks it will be opened. What father among you, if his son asks for a fish, will instead of a fish give him a serpent; or if he asks for an egg, will give him a scorpion? If you then, who are evil, know how to give good gifts to your children, how much more will the heavenly Father give the Holy Spirit to those who ask him!" (Luke 11:10-13)

> **Side Note:** *Spending time alone with God is not something you do for Him. It's something you do for yourself. It's you asking Him to come near to you (intimacy), which leads to Him filling you with the Holy Spirit.*

**Desiring God:** "What Is the Filling of the Holy Spirit" "But when we pray for this, what are we asking God for? In the words of Wayne Grudem, we are asking God for "an event subsequent to conversion in which a believer experiences a fresh infilling with the Holy Spirit that may result in a variety of consequences, including greater love for God, greater victory over sin, greater power for ministry, and sometimes the receiving of new spiritual gifts" (Grudem, 1,242).

Now, of course, every Christian receives the Holy Spirit upon conversion. Being born again is the greatest miracle any human being can possibly experience, and it only happens by the omnipotent power of the Holy Spirit (John 3:3–8; 1 Corinthians 12:13).

But the reason we talk about the filling of the Holy Spirit as "an event subsequent to conversion" is because that's how the New Testament usually talks about it. Paul was exhorting born-again Christians when he wrote, "be filled with the Spirit" (Ephesians 5:18). And almost all of Luke's description of Spirit-fillings occurred to people who were already born again (see Acts 2:4; 4:8, 4:31 9:17, 13:9, 13:52). And we're actually talking about events (plural) because, just like the same people received repeated fillings of the Spirit in the book of Acts, we also need to be filled repeatedly." (Bloom, Lord, Fill Me with Your Spirit, 2017)

## WHY IS IT IMPORTANT TO SPEND TIME ALONE WITH GOD DAILY AND BE REPEATEDLY FILLED WITH THE HOLY SPIRIT?

1. You need to spend time alone with God daily and be repeatedly filled with the Holy Spirit because God does not develop your character or reveal to you your purpose all at once. This means you need to continue to call on God to have Him fill you with the Holy Spirit, who, throughout your journey, reveals to you your purpose in life (who you are and what you are to do with the gifts and talents God has given to you), as well as equips you for that purpose by developing Good Characteristics within you.

"Call to me and I will answer and reveal to you wondrous secrets that you haven't known." (Jeremiah 33:3)

**Spiritual Wisdom** "Among the mature, however, we speak a message of wisdom—but not the wisdom of this age or of the rulers of this age, who are coming to nothing. No, we speak of the mysterious and hidden wisdom of God, which He destined for our glory before time began. None of the rulers of this age understood it. For if they had, they would not have crucified the Lord of glory. Rather, as it is written: "No eye has seen, no ear has heard, no heart has imagined, what God has prepared for those who love Him." But God has revealed it to us by the Spirit. The Spirit searches all things, even the deep things of

God. For who among men knows the thoughts of man except his own spirit within him? So too, no one knows the thoughts of God except the Spirit of God. We have not received the spirit of the world, but the Spirit who is from God, that we may understand what God has freely given us. And this is what we speak, not in words taught us by human wisdom, but in words taught by the Spirit, expressing spiritual truths in spiritual words." (1 Corinthians 2:6-16)

**Compelling Truth:** "Daily devotions help us learn truth. When we spend time in God's Word, we gain wisdom and understanding. It has been said that the best way to recognize a counterfeit is to study the real thing. Satan is the "father of lies" (John 8:44). If we are not steeped in God's truth, we are more easily duped. When we know the truth, we experience freedom (John 8:32)." (Why are Christians encouraged to have daily devotions or quiet times?)

**Conclusion:** *The only way to have good characteristics developed within you and fully know your true purpose in life is to spend time daily with the creator (God) who created you, gave you purpose, and fills you with the Holy Spirit who reveals Gods secrets.*

||||||||||||||||||||||||||||||||||||||||||||||||||||||||||||||||||||||||||||||||||||||||||||||||||||

"Spending time with God through prayer and His Word is a prerequisite for having a great life and fulfilling your purpose."

— *Joyce Meyer*

||||||||||||||||||||||||||||||||||||||||||||||||||||||||||||||||||||||||||||||||||||||||||||||||||||

2. You need to spend time alone with God daily and repeatedly be filled with the Holy Spirit because each day brings new challenges, and the Holy Spirit, through God, is the only one who knows what those challenges are. This means He knows what you will need to defeat whatever you come up against. Whether it's you needing strength, wisdom, or love, the Holy Spirit knows and can provide you with it.

"The steadfast love of the Lord never ceases; his mercies never come to an end; they are new every morning; great is your faithfulness. "The Lord is my portion," says my soul, "therefore I will hope in him." (Lamentations 3:22–24)

"So do not worry about tomorrow; it will have enough worries of its own. There is no need to add to the troubles each day brings." (Matthew 6:34)

**Desiring God:** "New Mercies for New Burdens" We cannot rely on yesterday's mercies for today's burdens. Go to Jesus afresh each day. Go to the word of God in prayer each day, and ask him to help you see wonders and promises that make your heart sing. Relationships take constant work and training. One of the reasons we may not feel like Jesus is with us, sitting with us when we fall asleep or when we wake up, is that we keep all of our appointments in a given week except the daily appointment we ought to prioritize with the all-powerful God of the universe. Ask him to show you more of himself, and plead with him for the new and unique grace you need today." (Zuleger, 2016)

> **Conclusion:** *Because the Holy Spirit is all things, He can provide you with all you need to conquer your day. You only need to ask.*

||||||||||||||||||||||||||||||||||||||||||||||||||||||||||||||||||||||||||||||||||||||||||||||||||||||||||

"God is able to accomplish, provide, help, save, keep, sub-
due... He is able to do what you can't. He already has a plan.
God's not bewildered. Go to Him."

— *Max Lucado*

||||||||||||||||||||||||||||||||||||||||||||||||||||||||||||||||||||||||||||||||||||||||||||||||||||||||||

3. You need to spend time alone with God daily and repeatedly
   be filled with the Holy Spirit to have Him maintain (cleanse)
   the area of your heart in which He has healed and changed by
   allowing Him to renew, regenerate, replenish, and refresh you
   on a daily.

"Now we have this treasure in jars of clay to show that this surpassingly
great power is from God and not from us. We are hard pressed on
all sides, but not crushed; perplexed, but not in despair; persecuted,
but not forsaken; struck down, but not destroyed. We always carry
around in our body the death of Jesus, so that the life of Jesus may also
be revealed in our body. For we who are alive are always consigned
to death for Jesus' sake, so that the life of Jesus may also be revealed
in our mortal body. So then, death is at work in us, but life is at work
in you. And in keeping with what is written: "I believed; therefore I
have spoken," we who have the same spirit of faith also believe and
therefore speak, knowing that the One who raised the Lord Jesus will
also raise us with Jesus and present us with you in His presence. All
this is for your benefit, so that the grace that is extending to more
and more people may overflow in thanksgiving, to the glory of God.

Therefore, we do not lose heart. Though our outer self is wasting away, yet our inner self is being renewed day by day. For our light and momentary affliction is producing for us an eternal glory that is far beyond comparison. So we fix our eyes not on what is seen, but on what is unseen. For what is seen is temporary, but what is unseen is eternal." (2 Corinthians 4:7-18)

**Renew:**

- Give fresh life or strength to; revive.

- To restore or replenish.

**Regenerate:**

- Reformed or reborn, esmanciple in a spiritual or moral sense.

- (Of a living organism) regrow (new tissue) to replace lost or injured tissue.

**Replenish:**

- Fill (something) up again.

- Restore (a stock or supply) to a former level or condition.

**Refresh:**

- Give new strength or energy to; reinvigorate.

- Revise or update (skills or knowledge).

**Desiring God:** "Do you feel dry? Are you weary? Are you tired of talking so much about glorious theology, but not experiencing the reality of it? Does your worship feel distracted and hollow? Are you lacking in gratitude to God? Do you long for more fruit, both the internal fruit of the Holy Spirit (Galatians 5:22–23) and the external fruit of empowered ministry? Then you are a good candidate for the filling of the Holy Spirit. Your dryness and discouragement may, in fact, be invitations from God to press in to him." (Bloom, Lord, Fill Me with Your Spirit, 2017)

> **Conclusion:** *When you spend time alone with God, it allows Him to fill you with the Holy Spirit, who renews, regenerates, replenishes, and refreshes you. But when you stop spending time alone with God, the area (your heart) which was healed slowly but surely reverts to its old sinful nature, and you begin to make the wrong decisions and allow the wrong people, places, or things to fill you, thus causing you to miss out on the blessings God has to offer you.*

"We need silence to be alone with God, to speak to him, to listen to him, to ponder his words deep in our hearts. We need to be alone with God in silence to be renewed and transformed. Silence gives us a new outlook on life. In it we are filled with the energy of God himself that makes us do all things with joy."

— *Mother Teresa*

4. You need to spend time alone with God daily and repeatedly be filled with the Holy Spirit to have Him protect you while your character and spirit are developing and maturing.

"Above all else, guard thy heart; for out of it flows the issues of life" (Proverbs 4:23).

Protect:

- Keep safe from harm or injury.

Because this process is very similar to a baby being developed in the womb, you must treat it as such. Meaning throughout your journey, you must call on God to fill you with the Holy Spirit to have Him help protect your developing baby (New Character) from people, places, and things that wish to tear you down and stop you from reaching your goals (abort your purpose).

People:

- False prophets and their conversations.

- Frenemies (fake friends).

- Anyone who does not edify or uplift you.

Places:

- Places that tempt you into exhibiting ungodly characteristics.

**Things:**

- Television shows

- Magazines

- Extracurricular activities

**Our Daily Bread:** "False prophets" are still with us. "Experts" dispense advice while ignoring God altogether or twisting His words to suit their purposes." (Gustafson, 2020)

"This is what the Lord Almighty says: Do not listen [to them]," He said. "They fill you with false hopes. They speak visions from their own minds, not from the mouth of the Lord" (Jeremiah 23:16). God said of them, "If they had stood in my council, they would have proclaimed my words to my people" (Jeremiah 23:22)

**Conclusion:** *When God created the world, He didn't have swarms of people around Him. Neither was He going about telling everyone His plans. He did what He had to do alone. This means you have to watch who you allow close to you while healing and developing. Everyone is not meant to know your plans, and everyone does not have your best interest at heart. To put it simply, if the people, places, and things you allow into your presence are not edifying you (instructing or improving you morally or intellectually), they should not be close to you!*

||||||||||||||||||||||||||||||||||||||||||||||||||||||||||||||||||||||||||||||||||||||||||||||||||||

"Great eagles fly alone; great lions hunt alone; great souls walk alone-alone with God. Such loneliness is hard to endure, and impossible to enjoy unless God accompanied. Prophets are lone men; they walk alone, pray alone and God makes them alone."

— *Leonard Ravenhill*

||||||||||||||||||||||||||||||||||||||||||||||||||||||||||||||||||||||||||||||||||||||||||||||||||||

5.  You need to spend time alone with God daily and repeatedly be filled with the Holy Spirit throughout your journey to remain close to God (maintain an intimate relationship with Him). Which, might I add, is the only way to survive this journey and receive what you have been hoping for.

"Yes, I am the vine; you are the branches. Those who remain in me, and I in them, will produce much fruit. For apart from me you can do nothing. Anyone who does not remain in me is thrown away like a useless branch and withers. Such branches are gathered into a pile to be burned. But if you remain in me and my words remain in you, you may ask for anything you want, and it will be granted!" (John 15:5-7)

**Conclusion:** *Our entire existence was created by God, which means we are nothing and can accomplish nothing without Him.*

||||||||||||||||||||||||||||||||||||||||||||||||||||||||||||||||||||||||||||||||||||||||||||||||||

"Moses spent forty years in the king's palace thinking that he was somebody; then he lived forty years in the wilderness finding out that without GOD he was a nobody; finally he spent forty more years discovering how a nobody with GOD can be a somebody."

— *Dwight L. Moody*

||||||||||||||||||||||||||||||||||||||||||||||||||||||||||||||||||||||||||||||||||||||||||||||||||

To conclude, spending time alone with God is a vital necessity because it is the only way to be filled with the Holy Spirit, which has and is all you need to succeed in life.

**SO, WHAT'S IT GOING TO BE? SPEND TIME ALONE WITH GOD AND BE FILLED WITH ALL YOU NEED (THE HOLY SPIRIT) TO SUCCEED IN LIFE. OR KEEP GETTING DRUNK OFF THE PLEASURES OF THIS WORLD AND RUIN YOUR LIFE?**

||||||||||||||||||||||||||||||||||||||||||||||||||||||||||||||||||||||||||||||||||||||||||||||||

"Spending time with God is the key to our strength and success in all areas of life. Be sure that you never try to work God into your schedule, but always work your schedule around Him."

— *Joyce Meyer*

||||||||||||||||||||||||||||||||||||||||||||||||||||||||||||||||||||||||||||||||||||||||||||||||

**Heavenly Father,** I come to you, as your humble servant, and ask that you fill me with the Holy Spirit so that I may learn how to seek your presence and dedicate each day to you from this day forward. Whether it be me reading your Word, doing tasks that build your Kingdom, or even spreading your Word which uplifts and edifies your children, may the days and time that I have left on this earth be dedicated to strengthening my relationship with you.

In Jesus' name, Amen.

# CHAPTER 17

# SURVIVAL OF THE FITTEST

*The wilderness stage of your journey will test your faith, and as it tests your faith, it's going to develop your character. The character traits you develop while going through the struggles of life or whatever circumstances you may be facing will become your foundation, the ground on which you stand. That same foundation will make you unshakable and unstoppable. It will give you the power to survive change. "Christ will make his home in your hearts as you trust in him. Your roots will grow down into God's love and keep you strong." (Ephesians 3:17)*

**Exodus 16:4** AMP "Then the Lord said to Moses, "Behold, I will cause bread to rain from heaven for you; the people shall go out and gather a day's portion every day, so that I may test them [to determine] whether or not they will walk [obediently] in My instruction (law)."

In this chapter, you will learn about some of the changes you can expect to go through while pregnant and how to survive them.

| PREGNANCY TERMS USED IN CHAPTER | TRANSLATION |
| --- | --- |
| • Courtship | • Intimacy with God |
| • Embryo/Fetus/Baby | • Good Nature/Spirit/Good Character |
| • Your Womb | • Your Heart (Gods Temple) |
| • Pregnancy | • Process where Good Character is developed within you |
| • Preconception Health Care | • Preparation for pregnancy |
| • Pre-Pregnancy Requirements | • Requirements for creating a stable environment for the baby (Good Character) to grow and be developed in |
| • Prenatal Care | • Daily alone time with God |
| • Trimester | • Stages |
| • Physician/Nurse/Mid-Wife | • God/Jesus/The Holy Spirit |

## WHAT TO EXPECT WHILE PREGNANT

*(What to expect when good characteristics are being developed within you)*

**Live Science:** "For a pregnant woman, feeling a new life developing inside her body is an amazing experience, even though she may not always feel her best at some points along the way.

Pregnancy can be different from woman to woman, and even for the same mother from one pregnancy to the next. Some symptoms of pregnancy last for several weeks or months, while other discomforts are temporary or don't affect all women.

"Pregnancy is a long, 10-month journey," said Dr. Draion Burch, an obstetrician and gynecologist at Magee-Women's Hospital at the University of Pittsburgh Medical Center.

A normal pregnancy usually lasts about 40 weeks, counting from the first day of a woman's last menstrual period, which is about two weeks before conception actually occurs.

Pregnancy is divided into three trimesters. Each of these periods lasts between 12 and 13 weeks. During each trimester, changes take place in a pregnant woman's body as well as in the developing fetus." (Nierenberg, 2017)

If you have not already noticed, this journey that you are on is very similar to surviving a pregnancy which includes the development and birth of a baby. How? Well, there are three parts that make up this journey, just as there are three parts that make up a pregnancy.

First, there is the start of the pregnancy. Your decision to pick up this book and read it (a desire). Secondly, there is the middle. The gap in between the start and the finish. The stage where you will be tested, and many changes will occur within you (the next section of this book—*The Process*). Third and lastly, there is the birth of your baby. Or, as I like to call it, the finish line. The line you must cross to claim victory and receive what you've been hoping for since the start of the pregnancy journey.

> **Side Note:** *The wilderness is very similar to a pregnancy journey because to make it to the end, one must go through and survive the changes that occur in the middle.*

## Survival:

- The state or fact of continuing to live or exist, typically in spite of an accident, ordeal, or difficult circumstances.

## Survival of the fittest:

- "Survival of the fittest" is a phrase that originated from Darwinian evolutionary theory as a way of describing the mechanism of natural selection. The biological concept of fitness is defined as reproductive success. In Darwinian terms the phrase is best understood as "Survival of the form that will leave the most copies of itself in successive generations." (Wikipedia)

|||||||||||||||||||||||||||||||||||||||||||||||||||||||||||||||||||||||||||||||||||||||||||||||||||||||||||||

"It is not the strongest of the species that survives, nor the most intelligent; it is the one most adaptable to change."

— *Leon C. Megginson & Charles Darwin*

|||||||||||||||||||||||||||||||||||||||||||||||||||||||||||||||||||||||||||||||||||||||||||||||||||||||||||||

Requirements for surviving the changes that occur during the middle stage of your journey:

- You must daily spend time alone with God.

- You must be able to make good decisions (discernment).

- You must have faith (trust) in God.

- You must be patient (self-disciplined).

- You must love (be faithful to) God.

**IF YOU DON'T SPEND TIME ALONE WITH GOD DAILY, YOU WON'T GROW TO LOVE HIM, WHICH MEANS YOU WILL NOT TRUST WHAT HE'S DOING WITH YOUR LIFE, OR IN HIS TIMING TO DEVELOP YOUR BABY (CHARACTER) WHILE YOU PATIENTLY WAIT ON HIM.**

Some of you may ask, umm, what exactly does that entail? In short, you are waiting for your spirit to mature, good character to be built (developed) within you, for love (God) to be filled (overflowing) within your heart, for a renewed sense of hope, and for *destiny* to be *revealed.* "Not only so, but we also glory in our sufferings, because we know that suffering produces perseverance; perseverance, character; and character, hope. And hope does not put us to shame, because God's love has been poured out into filled our hearts through the Holy Spirit, who has been given to us." (Romans 5:3-5).

> **Side Note:** *Having a baby is not simply about what you gain when you deliver (material blessings you hope for that will eventually perish). It is also about the changes you go through. The character you develop while preparing for and going through the pregnancy (spiritual blessings that will endure forever). "Everyone who competes in the games goes into strict training. They do it to get a crown that will not last, but we do it to get a crown that will last forever." (1 Corinthians 9:25)*

## NOW THE NEXT QUESTION YOU MAY HAVE IS, "HOW WILL MY CHARACTER BE BUILT (DEVELOPED) AND MY HEART FILLED"?

1. You are given a new heart and a new spirit.

"And I will give you a new heart, and I will put a new spirit in you. I will take out your stony, stubborn heart and give you a tender, responsive heart" (Ezekiel 36:26)

**Bible Study Tools:** "A "new heart" and a "new spirit" are one and the same; that is, a renewed one; renewed by the Spirit and grace of God; in which a new principle of life is put; new light is infused; a new will, filled with new purposes and resolutions; where new affections are placed, and new desires are formed; and where there are new delights and joys, as well as new sorrows and troubles; the same which in the New Testament is called the "new man", and the new creature, ( Ephesians 4:24 ) ( 2 Corinthians 5:17 )." (Bible Study Tools)

2. You are filled with the Holy Spirit, who helps lead and guide you on your journey. (Consider the Holy Spirit to be your midwife, always there when you need them).

"And I will put my Spirit in you so that you will follow my decrees and be careful to obey my regulations." (Ezekiel 36:27)

3. You will encounter trials and tribulations (testing) and be put under pressure.

**Compelling Truth:** "We should be aware that growth often comes through trials. Just as physical strength is built through exertion and straining against resistance, spiritual strength is developed in the hard times of life. "No pain, no gain," as they say." (How important is spiritual growth in Christian life?)

**OnePlace:** "God will allow pressures to come. The word tribulation literally means "pressure." It is a word that was used to describe crushing grapes in the vat for wine or crushing olives for oil. God wants the oil of gladness and the wine of joy in your character. He wants that which will sustain and give strength, but the only way that God will get it out of you is to press it out.

Is something bad happening to you right now? Are you having trouble? Are you feeling pressure? These are not obstacles; they are opportunities! They are things that God has engineered to build character into your life.

You're going to have tribulation whether you're a Christian or not, but a child of God sees what happens and can, "glory in tribulations."" (Rogers)

**Side Note:** *For good character traits to be developed and produced within you, you must be given a new heart as well as have your new spirit tested and renewed by way of trials and tribulations.*

## NEW HEART + NEW SPIRIT + TRIALS = NEW FOUNDATION/SPIRITUAL MATURITY/GOOD CHARACTER.

OnePlace: "The word experience is translated in many Bibles as character and it has to do with the idea of purity. This word was used to speak of gold that had been put in the fire and refined until it was pure. It speaks of a character that has gone through the experiences of tribulation and perseverance. And through them, God begins to burn out the dross." (Rogers)

# THE TESTING OF THE SPIRIT DEVELOPS THE CHARACTER OF THE INDIVIDUAL, FURTHERMORE REVEALING ONE'S POTENTIAL.

As you read the rest of this chapter and continue to read the next section, *The Process*, you will learn more about how the test (trials) you go through in life helps develop your character by testing your spirit.

## SPIRITUAL CHARACTER TRAITS TO BE TESTED:

Discernment (goodness):

- "Goodness displays integrity, honesty, and compassion to others, and allows us to do the right thing.

Faith (inner peace):

- Peace is surrendering and yielding to the Lord's control, for He is our ultimate peace! It is allowing tranquillity to be our tone and to control our equanimity. This will be fueled by our harmonious relationship with God so we can hand over control of our heart, will, and mind to Him. Once we make real peace with God, we will be able to make and maintain peace with others.

Self-Control:

- Allows us to have discipline, and restraint with obedience to God and others.

Patience:

- Shows tolerance and fortitude to others, and even accepting difficult situations from them and God without making demands and conditions.

Faithfulness:

- The "gluing" fruit that will preserve our faith and the other characters of the Spirit as well as identify God's Will so we can be dependable and trusting to God and others.

Altruism (Love: unselfish concern for others):

- Enables us to appreciate our brothers and sisters in the Lord, and, of course, our family, and others around us. Love is taking the initiative to build up and meet the needs of others without expecting anything in return." (Krejcir)

"But the fruit of the Spirit [the result of His presence within us] is love [unselfish concern for others], joy, [inner] peace, patience [not the ability to wait, but how we act while waiting], kindness, goodness, faithfulness, gentleness, self-control. Against such things there is no law." (Galatians 5:22-23)

## GOOD CHARACTERISTICS TO BE DEVELOPED WITHIN YOU:

**Fairness/Good decision-making skills:**

- "Using discernment, compassion, and integrity, this character trait strives to make decisions and take actions based on what you consider the ultimate best course or outcome for all involved.

**Responsibility/Accountability:**

- This exceptional quality accepts personal, relational, career, community, and societal obligations even when they are difficult or uncomfortable.

- This personal trait follows through on commitments and proactively creates or accepts accountability for your behavior and choices.

**Compassion:**

- This character traits example feels deep sympathy and pity for the suffering and misfortune of others, and you have a desire to do something to alleviate their suffering.

**Integrity:**

- Integrity is a personal trait that has strong moral principles and core values. When you have integrity, you main your adherence to it whether or not other people are watching.

**Humility:**

- You have a confident yet modest opinion of your own self-importance. You don't see yourself as "too good" for other people or situations.

- With this honorable trait you have a learning and growth mindset and the desire to express and experience gratitude for what you have, rather than expecting you deserve more.

## Authenticity:

- With this virtuous attribute you are able to be your real and true self, without pretension, posturing, or insincerity. You are capable of showing appropriate vulnerability and self-awareness.

## Honesty:

- Honesty is a good trait that is more than telling the truth. It's living the truth. It is being straightforward and trustworthy in all of your interactions, relationships, and thoughts. Being honest requires self-honesty and authenticity.

## Loyalty:

- Loyalty is an ethical trait of faithfulness and devotion to your loved ones, your friends, and anyone with whom you have a trusted relationship.

## Reliability:

- This character quality can be consistently depended upon to follow through on your commitments, actions, and decisions. You do what you say you will do.

## Politeness:

- This character trait is knowledgeable of basic good manners, common courtesies, and etiquette, and are willing to apply those to all people you encounter. You desire to learn the personal skills of politeness in order to enhance your relationships and self-esteem.

## Perseverance:

- Perseverance is a character trait of steadfast persistence and determination to continue on with a course of action, belief, or purpose, even if it's difficult or uncomfortable in order to reach a higher goal or outcome.

## Optimism:

- Optimism is a virtuous example of having a sense of hopefulness and confidence about the future. It involves a positive mental attitude in which you interpret life events, people, and situations in a promising light.

## Passion/Ambitiousness:

- When you have ambitiousness or passion, you possess the keen desire to achieve your goals. Whether you are seeking to make more money, build a business, excel in your career, or find the love of your life, your ambition and passion gives you the motivation to make it happen.

- This character trait is positive as long as your ambition doesn't overshadow your values or force you to compromise other positive character traits.

## Self-Discipline:

- With this good character trait, you are able, through good habits or willpower, to overcome your desires or feelings in order to follow the best course of action or to rise to your commitments or principles. You have a strong sense of self-control and you use it in order to reach a desired goal.

## Lovingkindness/Considerate:

- This character trait has the ability to be loving toward those you love which means showing them through your words, actions, and expressions how deeply you care about them. It includes the willingness to be open and vulnerable.

- Kindness is a positive attribute of being considerate, helpful, and benevolent to others. This virtuous trait is motivated by a positive disposition and the desire for warm and pleasant interactions. When you possess the trait of being considerate, you show an ability to think of other people as well as yourself.

## Generosity:

- This good quality is willing to offer time, energy, efforts, emotions, words, or assets without the expectation of something in return. This character trait offers these freely and often joyously.

## Respectfulness:

- With this character attribute you treat yourself and others with courtesy, kindness, deference, dignity, and civility. You offer basic respect as a sign of your value for the worth of all people and your ability to accept the inherent flaws we all possess.

## Thoroughness:

- When you are thorough, you're willing to put in the extra effort to ensure things are done completely and correctly. Others can count on you to fulfill your commitments with great care and attention to detail.

- Your ability to be thorough and consistent in your efforts means you can expect more success and respect in your personal and professional life.

## Forgiveness/Forgiving:

- You make conscious, intentional decisions to let go of resentment and anger toward someone for an offense—whether or not forgiveness is sought by the offender. Forgiveness may or may not include pardoning, restoration, or reconciliation. It extends both to others and to one's self.

- The ability to forgive yourself and others reveal that you have a balanced perspective of human nature and the flaws inherent in all of us.

## Encouraging:

- When you are encouraging, you offer hope, strength, and positive reinforcement to others. You go out of your way to give someone support and confidence.

## Courageousness:

- In spite of fear of danger, discomfort, or pain, this good human quality requires the mental fortitude to carry on with a commitment, plan, or decision, knowing it is the right or best course of action." (Davenport, 2019)

## YOU MAY BE ASKING, WHY IS CHARACTER DEVELOPMENT (SPIRITUAL MATURITY) SO IMPORTANT?

Firstly, God wants you to live a prosperous life, and the development of good characteristics within you gives you the tools necessary to do so.

**Good Character Traits:**

- "Help build respect and trust from others.

- Motivate and inspire better character from others.

- Build self-respect and confidence.

- Provide a framework for making important decisions and choices.

- Reflect leadership qualities in personal and professional endeavors." (Davenport, 2019)

Secondly, God knows that a lot of people may become discouraged when facing trials and tribulations, giving up on their hopes and dreams the moment they face opposition or a storm comes their way.

**Israel's Wilderness Detour:** "When Pharaoh finally let the people go, God did not lead them along the main road that runs through Philistine territory, even though that was the shortest route to the Promised Land. God said, "If the people are faced with a battle, they might change their minds and return to Egypt." So God led them in a roundabout way through the wilderness toward the Red Sea." (Exodus 13:17-18)

So instead of simply giving you what you desire, God uses the trials or circumstances you encounter in life to:

1.  Test your foundation and determine if you can handle the pressure of being blessed. As well as determine whether you really want or are ready for what you desire to be blessed with.

"These trials will show that your faith is genuine. It is being tested as fire tests and purifies gold--though your faith is far more precious than mere gold. So when your faith remains strong through many trials, it will bring you much praise and glory and honor on the day when Jesus Christ is revealed to the whole world." (1 Peter 1:7)

The test you go through in life allows God to evaluate where you are in the character development process. These tests also ensure your foundation is sturdy and can handle the pressure that comes with being blessed. For example, the pressure you go through as an employee working for a company allows God to see if you can withstand the pressure that comes with being a business owner. Will you snap the moment someone annoys you, or will you be professional and respectful regardless of if the customer, manager, or fellow employee is not right? The answer to that question will allow God to see whether you need to be worked on more in a particular area or if you are ready to move forward and be taken to a higher level in life (becoming a business owner).

> **Side Note:** *At each level or stage in your life, you may encounter different struggles, be held to a higher standard, or even be in a different position that comes with a new title, but the pressure, it will always be one and the same.*

2. Condition you for what you desire before you are blessed with it.

"Dear brothers and sisters, when troubles of any kind come your way, consider it an opportunity for great joy. For you know that when your faith is tested, your endurance has a chance to grow. So let it grow, for when your endurance is fully developed, you will be perfect and complete, needing nothing." (James 1:2-4)

"By your patient endurance, you will gain your souls." (Luke 21:19)

"Then you will not become spiritually dull and indifferent. Instead, you will follow the example of those who are going to inherit God's promises because of their faith and endurance." (Hebrews 6:12)

> **Side Note:** *Being conditioned before being blessed helps you grow (character-wise) and develops your ability to endure hardships (trials). Enduring hardships builds up your ability to persevere (strength to reach your dreams, take hold of your dreams, and keep what you dreamed of obtaining).*

**OnePlace:** "The Bible teaches that God wants to work a character quality in your heart known as patience. The word patient here is not one of passivity. Actually the word means "endurance or constancy." What are some reactions when troubles come?

- Some may try to escape with a plane ticket, a pill, a bottle, a needle, or even a gun.

- Others may even get cynical and shake their fist in the face of God.

- Some may recognize that God wants to teach endurance and it is His way of building Christian character.

How do you respond? One of the greatest marks of your faith and your confidence in the Almighty is your endurance, your perseverance, and your constancy when trouble comes." (Rogers)

Endurance:

- The fact or power of enduring an unpleasant or difficult process or situation without giving way.

- The ability or strength to continue or last, especially despite fatigue, stress, or other adverse conditions; stamina.

- To bear without resistance, or with patience; to tolerate.

Persevere:

- Continue in a course of action even in the face of difficulty or with little or no prospect of success.

Remember (Romans 5:3-5) perseverance develops good character, and good character helps you maintain, or should I say, keep the blessings you receive from God. Good Character is God's powerful Double Agent: Jesus and the Holy Spirit.

**GOD IS GOOD CHARACTER, AND HE HAS COME TO LIVE IN YOU (THROUGH JESUS AND THE HOLY SPIRIT). HE WANTS TO FULLY OCCUPY YOU SO YOUR CHARACTER CAN BECOME ONE WITH HIM SO THAT YOU CAN BE UNSTOPPABLE!**

The good character traits that God is developing within you along this journey are what seals your brokenness, stops the leaks (issues) in your life, and prepares you for blessings. "For God is working in you, giving you the desire and the power to do what pleases him." (Philippians 2:13)

||||||||||||||||||||||||||||||||||||||||||||||||||||||||||||||||||||||||||||||||||||||||||||||||||||

"When you center your life around God, He will repair and replace anything that's not working in your life; God is your insurance."

— *Pastor Michael Todd, Transformation Church*

||||||||||||||||||||||||||||||||||||||||||||||||||||||||||||||||||||||||||||||||||||||||||||||||||||

## STAY FOCUSED AND PAY CLOSE ATTENTION; CLASS IS IN SESSION!!!

Jesus is the foundation on which your good character is based (Ephesians 2:19-22). He is the rock on which you are built and stand (Psalm 18:2-3). The rock that gives you the power (strength) not to be shaken when pressure arises (Psalm 62:2).

**Jesus (The Foundation):**

- "Now, therefore, you are no longer strangers and foreigners, but fellow citizens with the saints and members of the household of God, having been built on the foundation of the apostles and prophets, Jesus Christ being the Chief Cornerstone, in whom the whole building, being fitted together, grows into a holy temple of the Lord, in whom you also are being built together for a dwelling place of God in the Spirit. As fellow citizens, we are part of the kingdom of God. And as members of God's household, all believers become one spiritual family; and as a holy temple, all believers together form a habitation for God." (Ephesians 2:19-22)

**Jesus (The Rock):**

- "The Lord is my rock, my fortress and my deliverer; my God is my rock, in whom I take refuge, my shield and the horn of my salvation, my stronghold." (Psalm 18:2)

- "Truly He is my rock and my salvation; He is my fortress, I will never be shaken." (Psalm 62:2)

Chron: "In every stone building, one stone is crucial. It is laid first, and it is to ensure that the building is square and stable. It is the rock upon which the weight of the entire structure rests. It is the cornerstone.

Scripture describes Jesus as the "Chief Cornerstone" of our faith. As the Chief Cornerstone, Jesus ensures the stability of the whole system of our salvation. Jesus was and is the only plan of salvation. "Therefore this says the Lord God: 'Behold, I lay in Zion a stone for a foundation, a tried stone, a precious cornerstone, a sure foundation." (Isaiah 28:16)" (Draper, 2016)

Blue Letter Bible: "Another wonderful blessing in Christ is the foundation that He provides for all who live by His grace. As with buildings, lives also need solid foundations. Our foundation is a person, Jesus. "For no other foundation can anyone lay than that which is laid, which is Jesus Christ." By the grace of God enabling him, Paul ministered the gospel of Jesus Christ. "According to the grace of God which was given to me, as a wise master builder I have laid the foundation." In doing this, he was laying the only reliable spiritual ground for living as God intended.

So many people attempt to lay other foundations for their lives. Some turn to earthly riches. Others hope in human wisdom. Others put their confidence in personal power and influence. Such vain pursuits are like attempting to construct a building upon shifting, sinking sand.

Our lives need a rock foundation. It has always been the Father's purpose to provide such for His people. David experienced this through his pilgrimage, as he trusted in the Lord. "From the end of the earth I will cry to You, When my heart is overwhelmed; lead me to the rock that is higher than I" (Psalm 61:2). In the most extreme situations on earth, when circumstances were overwhelming him, David cried out to His God. He looked to the Lord to be to him a rock upon which he could stand above the rolling waves of impossibility. "He only is my rock and my salvation; He is my defense; I shall not be moved" (Psalm 62:6). David stood on the Lord alone as his solid spiritual ground. Standing by faith he would not be destroyed." (Hoekstra)

**The Holy Spirit** is the filler and insulation (sealant and healer) (1 Corinthians 12:4-11) (Ephesians 1:13-14) who is constantly at work, equipping you with all that you need to achieve your God-ordained purpose in life. He is the helper (John 16:7) who is always on point, willing, and ready to take care of any damage that occurs (Romans 8:26-27). He is the teacher that guides you through life, helping to maintain the good character within you which eliminates stress and frustrations (John 14:26).

**The Holy Spirit (The Filler and Insulation/Sealant and Healer):**

- "There are different kinds of gifts, but the same Spirit distributes them. There are different kinds of service, but the same Lord. There are different kinds of working, but in all of them and in everyone it is the same God at work. Now to each one the manifestation of the Spirit is given for the common good. To one there is given through the Spirit a message of wisdom, to another a message of knowledge by means of the same Spirit, to another faith by the same Spirit, to another gifts of healing by that one Spirit, to another miraculous powers, to another prophecy, to another distinguishing between spirits, to another speaking in different kinds of tongues and to still another the interpretation of tongues. All these are the work of one and the same Spirit, and he distributes them to each one, just as he determines." (1 Corinthians 12:4-11)

- "And you also were included in Christ when you heard the message of truth, the gospel of your salvation. When you believed, you were marked in him with a seal, the promised Holy Spirit, who is a deposit guaranteeing our inheritance until the redemption of those who are God's possession—to the praise of his glory." (Ephesians 1:13-14)

**The Holy Spirit (Helper and Teacher):**

- "I tell you the truth, it is to your advantage that I go away; for if I do not go away, the Helper (Comforter, Advocate, Intercessor—Counselor, Strengthener, Standby) will not come to you; but if I go, I will send Him (the Holy Spirit) to you [to be in close fellowship with you]." (John 16:7)

- "And the Holy Spirit helps us in our weakness. For example, we don't know what God wants us to pray for. But the Holy Spirit prays for us with groanings that cannot be expressed in words. And the Father who knows all hearts knows what the Spirit is saying, for the Spirit pleads for us believers in harmony with God's own will." (Romans 8:26-27)

- "But the Helper, the Holy Spirit, whom the Father will send in My name, He will teach you all things, and bring to your remembrance all that I said to you." (John 14:26)

Insulation:

- Material used to insulate something, especially a building.

- Similar: protection, defense, shelter, screen, cushion, shield.

Insulate:

- To cover, line, or separate with a material that prevents or reduces the passage, transfer, or leakage of heat, electricity, or sound.

Christianity.com: "Through the power of the Holy Spirit, believers are saved, filled, sealed, and sanctified. The Holy Spirit reveals God's thoughts, teaches, and guides believers into all truth, including knowledge of what is to come. The Holy Spirit also helps Christians in their weakness and intercedes for them." (Noyes, 2019)

Crosswalk: "The Holy Spirit imparts to believers' gifts that are needed in the Church. Nobody receives all gifts, but they are distributed among the Body of Christ, each person receiving different gifts. The gift(s) that you receive will empower you for the calling God has placed on your life." (Rust, 2018)

**Christian Post:** "When Jesus walked the earth, He could be in one place at a time and He could be with the disciples. But the Holy Spirit can be everywhere, all the time, and He lives IN those who have accepted Christ as their Savior. Being with Jesus is good but having the Holy Spirit in us is even better. We don't have to go looking for God because He's as close as close can get!

See, when we receive Christ and we're born again, it literally means that God—through the power of the Holy Spirit—comes to live inside us. He makes us new on the inside, and as He works in us, the fruit of what He's doing is seen in the way we live and does some good for the people in the world around us. (See 2 Corinthians 5:17, 21; John 14:17, 26; Acts 1:8; Galatians 5:22-23.)

Think of this in the standpoint of recovering from things in the past that have hurt you. Many people come to God because their life is messed up and they don't know what to do to fix it. They've tried everything they know to do, and nothing is working. So finally, in their desperation, they ask for His help.

Thankfully, God wants to help us and heal us—spirit, soul, and body. He wants to bring restoration to us, so we won't live in a state of recovery forever. He wants us to be whole in Christ so we can help someone else. We need the Holy Spirit to lead us to truth one step at a time, and we need His strength to confront things that are hard to face so we can get victory over them." (Meyer, The Healing Power of the Holy Spirit, 2016)

**World Invisible:** "Divine healing is the work of the Holy Spirit. Christ's redemption extends its powerful working to the body, and the Holy Spirit is responsible both to transmit it to and maintain it in us." (The Holy Spirit the Spirit of Healing)

To conclude, although the tests you are facing or will face in life are meant to develop your character, they will also serve as an assessment that allows God to evaluate your faith and determine if it is genuine, which in turn determines if you are ready to be blessed, as well as if you are deserving of His blessings.

"Because of God's grace to me, I have laid the foundation like an expert builder. Now others are building on it. But whoever is building on this foundation must be very careful. For no one can lay any foundation other than the one we already have—Jesus Christ. Anyone who builds on that foundation may use a variety of materials—gold, silver, jewels, wood, hay, or straw. But on the judgment day, fire will reveal what kind of work each builder has done. The fire will show if a person's work has any value. If the work survives, that builder will receive a reward. But if the work is burned up, the builder will suffer great loss. The builder will be saved, but like someone barely escaping through a wall of flames." (1 Corinthians 3:12–15)

**FINAL WORDS: HOLD TIGHT AND EXERCISE PATIENT ENDURANCE, YOUR ABILITY TO SURVIVE THIS PREGNANCY (JOURNEY WHERE GOOD CHARACTER IS DEVELOPED WITHIN YOU) DEPENDS UPON IT. "PATIENT ENDURANCE IS WHAT YOU NEED NOW SO THAT YOU WILL CONTINUE TO DO GOD'S WILL. THEN YOU WILL RECEIVE ALL THAT HE HAS PROMISED." (HEBREWS 10:36)**

"It costs something to be a real Christian, according to the standard of the Bible. There are enemies to be overcome, battles to be fought, sacrifices to be made, an Egypt to be forsaken, a wilderness to be passed through, a cross to be carried, a race to be run. Conversion is not putting a person in an armchair and taking them easily to heaven. It is the beginning of a mighty conflict, in which it costs much to win the victory."

— *J. C. Ryle*

*Heavenly Father,* I would like to first and foremost, thank you for giving me the ability to make it this far on this journey. The road has been challenging, yet my endurance and ability to persevere have been strengthened. I can now confidently say that I have no intention of returning to who I used to be. I will persevere and see my dreams through until the end; I will survive.

In Jesus' name, Amen!

# PART SIX THE PROCESS

# CHAPTER 18

# TRIAL AND ERROR

*Decisions, Decisions, Decisions. You can't live without having to make them, and oftentimes you may feel like you can't live with the ones you've made. Either way, you have to assess; how good is your ability to make decisions?*

**Proverbs 1:1-7 NLT** The Purpose of Proverbs "These are the proverbs of Solomon, David's son, king of Israel. Their purpose is to teach people wisdom and discipline, to help them understand the insights of the wise. Their purpose is to teach people to live disciplined and successful lives, to help them do what is right, just, and fair. These proverbs will give insight to the simple, knowledge and discernment to the young. Let the wise listen to these proverbs and become even wiser. Let those with understanding receive guidance by exploring the meaning in these proverbs and parables, the words of the wise and their riddles. Fear of the Lord is the foundation of true knowledge, but fools despise wisdom and discipline."

## DISCERNMENT/DECISION-MAKING SKILLS TESTED:

*Your ability to make good decisions.*

### Discernment:

- Discernment is defined as the quality of being able to grasp and comprehend what is obscure; an act of perceiving something, a power to see what is not evident to the average mind. The definition also stresses accuracy, which is the ability to see the truth.

- Perceive or recognize (something).

- Distinguish (someone or something) with difficulty by sight or with the other senses.

"The person without the Spirit does not accept the things that come from the Spirit of God but considers them foolishness, and cannot understand them because they are discerned only through the Spirit." (1 Corinthians 2:14)

### Decision-Making:

- The thought process of selecting a logical choice from the available options. When trying to make a good decision, a person must weigh the positives and negatives of each option and consider all the alternatives.

- The action or process of making decisions, especially important ones.

"A wise man foresees evil and hides himself: the simple pass on and are punished." (Proverbs 27:12)

Decision-making is an essential part of life, and although there are times when making decisions can be tricky or confusing, there is no way around it. Whether you must decide what to eat, what to wear, when to wake up each day, or even where to work, making decisions is unavoidable. So, you should try to strengthen your ability to discern between the right and the wrong, the good and the bad, by simply doing so.

## HOW DO YOU STRENGTHEN YOUR ABILITY TO DISCERN BETWEEN RIGHT AND WRONG?

One of the best ways to improve your skills, build your character, and learn how to discern between right and wrong is through the experience you gain from living life and making decisions. This includes trials and errors.

Trial and Error:

- "A fundamental method of problem-solving. It is characterized by repeated, varied attempts which are continued until success, or until the practicer stops trying." (Trial and Error)

Side Note: *Although there is no easy way to strengthen your ability to discern between right and wrong, there are a few terms that you should learn, study, and know. You will need them not just for this chapter but throughout life.*

### Wisdom:

- "Wisdom relates to the mind, the intellect, and the control of behavior. Wisdom is a way of thinking about life and reality that enables someone to appreciate and pursue what is good in life while avoiding what is evil. God reveals life's values and how humans can achieve those." (Challies, 2005)

### Instruction:

- "Instruction is the learning of wisdom through moral and intellectual discipline." (Challies, 2005)

### Discretion:

- "Discretion is the application of insight in making good decisions." (Challies, 2005)

For me learning how to make good decisions (discern between right and wrong) didn't come easily. I had to fall quite a few times before I was able to gain the wisdom necessary to do things correctly.

## MY JOURNEY TO WISDOM AND A MORE DISCERNING SPIRIT:

I had a car, a BMW to be exact, that was constantly breaking down on me. I mean, every single time I got the car out of the shop, a new problem magically appeared. I called the situation "more money, more problems" because the more money I spent on the car, the more problems seemed to occur. This brings me to clarify. No, I am not talking about the "more money, more problems" rich people speak of.

The more money more problems I'm talking about goes a little something like this. It looks like you have more money than what you genuinely possess. For example, driving around in a brand-new BMW when you can only afford the maintenance on a Honda. This means when problems occur; you end up having to run around to get more money to fix those "more problems".

But what can I say, it was my BMW, and I loved that car. Or should I say I felt like I needed it.

Because I felt like I needed the car, I used my credit card and the money from my savings account to get it fixed three times in a row within the same month. I guess I was thinking third times a charm.

The issue, which I did not realize, was that I was simply doing what I was doing out of desperation. I was hungry, as previously mentioned in *Comfortable with Empty Part One* see also (Matthew 4:1-7). This meant I was willing to do whatever it took to get what I wanted, even if it wasn't truly what I needed.

> **Side Note:** *We live in a time where people are being taught that the fancy riches in life are a necessity and are what makes you who you are therefore tricking people into believing that wants are actually needs.*

Even though I had a ride to where I needed to go, I still used poor judgment and got the car fixed anyway. I guess you could say I didn't care about what I needed because I was so blinded by what the world told me was a necessity, and that became all that I wanted.

**SOCIETY HAS BEGUN TO TEACH PEOPLE THAT MAKING THE WRONG DECISIONS IS A GOOD THING. BECAUSE OF THIS, PEOPLE STRUGGLE WITH BEING ABLE TO MAKE THE RIGHT DECISIONS AND ARE BLINDLY BEING LED INTO ETERNAL DARKNESS.**

Because society has turned its back on what's right and has placed on a pedestal the things of this world that lead people into eternal darkness, trial and error, learning from mistakes, building character, and growing (the basis of our relationship with God) is dead. While the false promises of this world (money, cars, and clothes) are being praised instead.

"What sorrow for those who say that evil is good and good is evil, that dark is light and light is dark, that bitter is sweet and sweet is bitter. What sorrow for those who are wise in their own eyes and think themselves so clever. What sorrow for those who are heroes at drinking wine and boast about all the alcohol they can hold. They take bribes to let the wicked go free, and they punish the innocent." (Isaiah 5:20-23)

In the Bible, such acts or things are used to describe an individual who is spiritually blind.

**Spiritual Blindness:**

- **Compelling Truth:** "A condition that an individual has when they are unable to see God, or understand His message. Although God is working all around us, pursuing us and showing us His glory, some people cannot perceive His divine workings (Acts

28:26–27). A person who does not see God, does not know God, and unfortunately, they are spiritually perishing (2 Corinthians 4:3–4; Revelation 3:17). In short, those who reject Christ are spiritually blind and they are lost (John 6:68–69).

To be spiritually blind can also be translated as being spiritually undiscerning, as explained in 1 Corinthians 2:14: "The natural person does not accept the things of the Spirit of God, for they are folly to him, and he is not able to understand them because they are spiritually discerned." This means that to a spiritually blind individual, spiritual things are meaningless." (Spiritual blindness – What is it?)

**The Cause of Spiritual Blindness:**

- **Compelling Truth:** "In the Scriptures, Paul describes Satan as the cause of spiritual blindness in his letter to the Corinthians. "In their case the god of this world has blinded the minds of the unbelievers, to keep them from seeing the light of the gospel of the glory of Christ, who is the image of God" (2 Corinthians 4:4). Satan, who is the father of lies (John 8:44), aims to lead humans away from God's truth in any way he can. The Bible calls him extraordinarily evil (John 8:44), the cause of all temptations (Luke 4:2; Hebrews 4:15; 1 Corinthians 7:5), and the destroyer of flesh (1 Corinthians 5:5). He even attempts to blind believers, seeking to trap us and cause us to distance ourselves from God through temptation, fear, loneliness, worry, depression, and persecution (2 Corinthians 2:11; Ephesians 6:11; 1 Peter 5:8–9)." (Spiritual blindness – What is it?)

Because I was blinded by the promises of this world
(the thing everyone said I needed to be complete or
whole). I was led into darkness (darkness = poor decisions) and wasted thousands of dollars. The problem:
what I filled myself with (the thing I thought would make
me happy) leaked out, right along with the oil that was
leaking from the car.

So, I must ask you, does that BMW sound like a stone disguised as
bread (a want disguised as a need) or bread alone? I would say I
did not listen to the voice in the back of my head (the Holy Spirit).
Because of that, I made a poor decision and received a stone which
in the end led me to be frustrated because the money I spent on
fixing the BMW could have been used to buy a more affordable car
(what I needed) as opposed to me wasting money on the BMW
(what I wanted).

Side Note: *When you are spiritually blind, stubborn, or
have holes in you (are broken and immature), you tend
to do whatever pleases you at that moment, causing
you to make poor decisions.*

Take Jonah from the Bible as another example. God instructed Jonah
to go preach the gospel to the people in the city of Nineveh because
the people had done evil in the Lord's sight. "The Word of the Lord
came to Jonah the son of Amittai, saying, "Get up and go to the
large city of Nineveh, and preach against it. For their sin has come
up before Me." (Jonah 1:1-2)

Now, Jonah did not want to go to Nineveh because he disliked the people who lived there. He also was stubborn and wanted to do things his way (just like me). So, what did Jonah do?

Jonah refused to listen to God's voice (the Holy Spirit/the only way to discern between right and wrong) and used bad judgment (made a poor decision), deciding to go the wrong way "on purpose". "But Jonah ran away from the Lord going toward Tarshish. He went down to Joppa and found a ship which was going to Tarshish. Jonah paid money, and got on the ship to go with them, to get away from the Lord." Then the Lord sent a powerful wind upon the sea, and there was such a big storm that the ship was about to break up." (Jonah 1:3-4)

Because Jonah knowingly disobeyed God and did what he wanted to do instead of what he needed to do. He found himself in a situation where his decision would land him straight on his face and almost cost him his life.

**Jonah's decision almost cost him his life:** "Then the sailors said to each other, "Come, let us cast lots to find out who is responsible for this calamity." They cast lots and the lot fell on Jonah. So they asked him, "Tell us, who is responsible for making all this trouble for us? What kind of work do you do? Where do you come from? What is your country? From what people are you?" He answered, "I am a Hebrew and I worship the Lord, the God of heaven, who made the sea and the dry land." This terrified them and they asked, "What have you done?" (They knew he was running away from the Lord, because he had already told them so.) The sea was getting rougher and rougher. So they asked him, "What should we do to you to make the sea calm down for us?" "Pick me up and throw me into the sea," he replied, "and it will become calm. I know that it is my fault that this great storm has come upon you." Instead, the men did their best to row back to land. But they could not, for the sea grew even wilder than before. Then they cried out to the Lord, "Please, Lord, do not let us die for taking this man's life. Do not hold us accountable for killing an innocent man, for you, Lord, have done as you pleased." Then they took Jonah and threw him overboard, and the raging sea grew calm. At this the men greatly feared the Lord, and they offered a sacrifice to the Lord and made vows to him. Now the Lord provided a huge fish to swallow Jonah, and Jonah was in the belly of the fish three days and three nights." (Jonah 1:7-17)

> **Side Note:** *Don't beat yourself up thinking the poor decisions you've made in life mean your life is over. This is not true! Without those decisions you wouldn't be able to take hold of the opportunity those decisions have given you to learn and grow. To go more in-depth, the poor choices you've made in life are teachable moments, and if you allow them to, they can become valuable lessons.*

We all may find ourselves in situations that cause us to fall on our faces, just like Jonah. But there is one thing that should encourage you. Every choice you've made or will make in life can be used as a key to open a door that leads to correction, redirection, and valuable learning experiences. You just have to be willing to use that key to open the door and welcome the correction of God into your life.

**IF YOU WANT THE CHOICES YOU'VE MADE OR WILL MAKE IN LIFE TO BECOME THE KEY TO ENDLESS WISDOM, YOU MUST BE WILLING TO ALLOW GOD TO LEAD YOU THROUGH THE RIGHT AND THE WRONG, THE GOOD AND THE BAD.**

Just because you may have made a choice that God didn't originally bless doesn't mean He won't come and help you after you've done something incorrectly. Remember, God is a teaching God. He's always looking to correct you and redirect you in the event you make the right decision or even a mistake because He knows lessons are only learned through trial and error. "All Scripture is God-breathed [given by divine inspiration] and is profitable for instruction, for conviction [of sin], for correction [of error and restoration to obedience], for training in righteousness [learning to live in conformity to God's will, both publicly and privately—behaving honorably with personal integrity and moral courage]; so that the man of God may be complete and proficient, outfitted and thoroughly equipped for every good work." (2 Timothy 3:16-17)

||||||||||||||||||||||||||||||||||||||||||||||||||||||||||||||||||||||||||||||||||||||||||||||||||||||

"Experience is simply the name we give our mistakes."

— *Oscar Wild*

||||||||||||||||||||||||||||||||||||||||||||||||||||||||||||||||||||||||||||||||||||||||||||||||||||||

Although Jonah went the wrong way purposely the first time around, he was able to take the wisdom he'd gained from his experience and use it to help him get back on track with the journey (life) God had initially planned for him.

## HOW DID JONAH DO IT?

First, Jonah recognized his need for God and invited Him back into his life: "Then Jonah prayed to the Lord his God while in the stomach of the fish, saying, "I called out to the Lord because of my trouble, and He answered me. I cried for help from the place of the dead, and You heard my voice. You threw me into the deep waters, to the very bottom of the sea. A flood was all around me and all Your waves passed over me. Then I said, 'I have been sent away from Your eyes. But I will look again toward Your holy house.' Waters closed in over me. The sea was all around me. Weeds were around my head. I went down to the roots of the mountains. The walls of the earth were around me forever. But You have brought me up from the grave, O Lord my God. While I was losing all my strength, I remembered the Lord. And my prayer came to You, into Your holy house. Those who worship false gods have given up their faith in You. But I will give gifts in worship to You with a thankful voice. I will give You what I have promised. The Lord is the One Who saves." Then the Lord spoke to the fish, and it spit Jonah out onto the dry land." (Jonah 2:1-10)

Secondly, Jonah learned from his experience, and when God presented him with a second chance (correction), he took it and used it (redirection) to help him get back on track: "Then the Lord spoke to Jonah a second time: "Get up and go to the great city of Nineveh, and deliver the message I have given you." This time Jonah obeyed the Lord's command and went to Nineveh, a city so large that it took three days to see it all. On the day Jonah entered the city, he shouted to the crowds: "Forty days from now Nineveh will be destroyed!" The people of Nineveh believed God's message, and from the greatest to the least, they declared a fast and put on burlap to show their sorrow." (Jonah 3:1-5)

> **Side Note:** *Despite the poor decisions you will make or have made in life, God will continue to be with you, leading, guiding, and redirecting you if ever you fall or get off track, making sure you still end up where you need to be. Where He (God) wants you to be. So don't be afraid to try or make decisions. It is the only way to find out if your decision is even an error. It is the only way for you to become stronger. It is the only way for you to learn and grow. "The godly may trip seven times, but they will get up again. But one disaster is enough to overthrow the wicked." (Proverbs 24:16)*

Jonah probably thought he would die in the problems he created (being stuck in the whale's mouth), but he didn't because God didn't abandon him despite the poor decisions he made, nor did He use Jonah's mistakes to condemn him. God instead used the result of Jonah's decisions (trials, errors, experience) to help him become stronger, wiser. To help him learn how to discern between right and wrong.

**A LOVING PARENT MAY CHASTISE A CHILD WHEN THEY ARE WRONG, BUT INSTEAD OF CONDEMNING THEM FOR THEIR DECISIONS, THEY USE THE RESULT OF THOSE DECISIONS TO HELP BUILD THAT CHILD'S CHARACTER (SKILLS). TO REDIRECT THEM AND HELP THEM BECOME A BETTER PERSON.**

At the beginning of Jonah's journey, it may have seemed like he simply rejected God's word to go preach the gospel because he did not like the people who lived in the city of Nineveh. But really, Jonah's problem was not the people in the city of Nineveh. It was himself. Jonah was spiritually blind and needed to grow.

**Compelling Truth:** "Those who reject God's Word are spiritually blind (2 Peter 3:3). They cannot understand the truth of Scripture, which sounds foolish to them (1 Corinthians 1:18). When an individual rejects Christ's message, he is unsaved and needs his eyes to be opened to the importance of Christ in his life (John 12:48; Hebrews 2:2–4)." (Spiritual blindness – What is it?)

**Jonah's Spiritual Blindness:** "When God saw what they had done and how they had put a stop to their evil ways, he changed his mind and did not carry out the destruction he had threatened." (Jonah 3:6-10) "This change of plans greatly upset Jonah, and he became very angry. So he complained to the Lord about it: "Didn't I say before I left home that you would do this, Lord? That is why I ran away to Tarshish! I knew that you are a merciful and compassionate God, slow to get angry and filled with unfailing love. You are eager to turn back from destroying people. Just kill me now, Lord! I'd rather be dead than alive if what I predicted will not happen." (Jonah 4:1-3)

Jonah was angry with God because he was spiritually blind (couldn't understand) why God would send him to help save a wicked nation. But God knew just how to help him understand: through experience.

"The Lord replied, "Is it right for you to be angry about this?" Then Jonah went out to the east side of the city and made a shelter to sit under as he waited to see what would happen to the city. And the Lord God arranged for a leafy plant to grow there, and soon it spread its broad leaves over Jonah's head, shading him from the sun. This eased his discomfort, and Jonah was very grateful for the plant. But God also arranged for a worm! The next morning at dawn the worm ate through the stem of the plant so that it withered away. And as the sun grew hot, God arranged for a scorching east wind to blow on Jonah. The sun beat down on his head until he grew faint and wished to die. "Death is certainly better than living like this!" he exclaimed. Then God said to Jonah, "Is it right for you to be angry because the plant died?" "Yes," Jonah retorted, "even angry enough to die!" Then the Lord said, "You feel sorry about the plant, though you did nothing to put it there. It came quickly and died quickly. But Nineveh has more than 120,000 people living in spiritual darkness, not to mention all the animals. Shouldn't I feel sorry for such a great city?" (Jonah 4:4-11)

> **Side Note:** *Jonah's journey was never entirely about changing the people with the word God sent him to preach. It was about God using the situation (the experience) to build Jonah's character and change him.*

As you go through life and continue to have to make decisions, you have the opportunity to allow God to help you learn from what you do right and learn from your mistakes. As you do, your ability to discern and your connection with the Lord will continue to become stronger simply because you are gaining the wisdom (building character) that only a person who is not afraid to make decisions can gain.

**Mind Tools:** "Decision making is a skill – and skills can usually be improved. As you gain more experience making decisions, and as you become more familiar with the tools and structures needed for effective decision making, you'll improve your confidence. Use this opportunity to think about how you can improve your decision making and take your skills to the next level. Ultimately, improving your decision-making skills will benefit you." (How Good Is Your Decision Making?)

**TRYING (MAKING DECISIONS) AND DISCERNMENT (GOOD DECISION-MAKING SKILLS) GO HAND AND HAND. YOU CAN'T HAVE THE FORMER WITHOUT THE LATTER.**

||||||||||||||||||||||||||||||||||||||||||||||||||||||||||||||||||||||||||||||||||||||||||||||||||||||||||||||||||||

"The opposite of success is not failure; it's mediocrity. Failure is actually a part of the process to success. And to reach true success in our profession (or any profession worth doing), you must be willing to pay that price—the price of building skills and character."

— *Randy Gage*

||||||||||||||||||||||||||||||||||||||||||||||||||||||||||||||||||||||||||||||||||||||||||||||||||||||||||||||||||||

**Things I learned from the third fall (try):**

- The third fall (try) helped me realize that I needed to become more disciplined with money and couldn't build up the willpower to make the right decisions alone.

- The third fall (try) helped me realize that I needed to entrust my situation to God.

- The third fall (try) helped me realize that I needed to change directions, even though I was unsure of where the new path would lead me.

**Side Note:** *Although there is no way you will fully know whether or not the decisions you've made or will make are 100% correct, you can trust that either way, God will provide you with a light to lead you through the dark and show you the way. "By day the LORD went ahead of them in a pillar of cloud to guide them on their way and by night in a pillar of fire to give them light, so that they could travel by day or night." (Exodus 13:21)*

Even though I initially made the wrong decision, my falling helped me grow. And as I learned from the situation, I was able to open myself up to God, who provided me with a light and turned my mistake into a key (very valuable lesson) that opened the door to correction. Which, in the end, helped build my character.

## WHAT DOES THIS MEAN?

If you love, put your hope in, and allow the Lord into your life to lead you, the Spirit that He places within you (what you need) will become a light that in the event you make a wrong turn or even a right turn will provide you with the necessary wisdom (answers) to:

1. Help lead you to your destination (purpose) in life.

2. Help stop the leaking (issues in your life), thus eliminating stress and frustration.

To further explain, once I invited God into my problems (let down my guard and opened my heart, which means I loved Him enough to let Him in), He provided me with the Holy Spirit (wisdom/answers) to help me not only get back on track in life but also eliminate the stress (money problems) I was having.

Compelling Truth: "In Christ, we are given spiritual sight. And we can exercise this spiritual sight by allowing God to reign in our lives and by following His commands, which shield us from Satan's traps. "By this we know that we abide in him and he in us, because he has given us of his Spirit." (1 John 4:13). Although Satan aims to blind even believers to God's goodness and His promises, God has provided us with the spiritual armor that we need to be safe from the devil's schemes. "Finally, be strong in the Lord and in the strength of his might. Put on the whole armor of God, that you may be able to stand against the schemes of the devil. For we do not wrestle against flesh and blood, but against the rulers, against the authorities, against the cosmic powers over this present darkness, against the spiritual forces of evil in the heavenly places. Therefore take up the whole armor of God, that you may be able to withstand in the evil day, and having done all, to stand firm. Stand therefore, having fastened on the belt of truth, and having put on the breastplate of righteousness, and, as shoes for your feet, having put on the readiness given by the gospel of peace. In all circumstances take up the shield of faith, with which you can extinguish all the flaming darts of the evil one; and take the helmet of salvation, and the sword of the Spirit, which is the word of God, praying at all times in the Spirit, with all prayer and supplication. To that end, keep alert with all perseverance, making supplication for all the saints, (Ephesians 6:10–18). Mark 8:18 says, "Having eyes do you not see, and having ears do you not hear? And do you not remember?" We must remember that Jesus is our light, and cling to His truth so that we are never blinded to God. Jesus is the light that can save us from living a life estranged from Him." (Spiritual blindness – What is it?)

With the Holy Spirit teaching, leading, and showing me the right way to live, I learned the importance of budgeting money and how to make decisions that better suited my needs instead of decisions that suited my wants. Eventually, I got a new car (a more affordable one) and started on a journey to becoming debt-free.

To conclude, throughout life, you will have to make decisions constantly, and some may lead to you making mistakes, but the key to getting back on track is to understand that you cannot succeed in life without God.

God knows what's best for you. He knows which route you should take and which route you shouldn't take. He knows what decisions would eliminate stress in your life and what decisions would land you straight on your face causing you more stress. For this reason, you need to take time out of your life daily to get to know Him. Because to know Him is to trust Him, and trust is what you'll need to continue this journey.

**LIFE IS ALL ABOUT TRIAL AND ERROR, AND THE ONLY WAY TO MAKE IT THROUGH THE TRIALS IS WITH GOD BY YOUR SIDE, HELPING YOU CORRECT THE ERRORS.**

||||||||||||||||||||||||||||||||||||||||||||||||||||||||||||||||||||||||||||||||||||||||||||||||||||||||

"We need to accept that we won't always make the right decisions, that we'll screw up royally sometimes--understanding
that failure is not the opposite of success, it's part of success."

— *Arianna Huffington*

||||||||||||||||||||||||||||||||||||||||||||||||||||||||||||||||||||||||||||||||||||||||||||||||||||||||

*Heavenly Father,* I want to thank you for leading me through the right and the wrong, for never leaving despite my mistakes. You are my solace. The rock on which I can trust to stand. My redeemer. The one who corrects me and brings me back from the clutches of death when I am wrong. You are my Spirit. The one who gives me the ability to discern. You are my God. The one who through trial and error, will be with me forever. Thank you for all that you are, for all that I have yet to have the capacity to see or understand.

In Jesus' name, Amen!

# CHAPTER 19

# TRUST FUND

*Trusting God with our life has proven to be a struggle for many. Because of this, we are unable to either let go and not be worried about certain situations or leave behind what is not meant to be taken into the next stage of our life. Because of this, we wind up anxious or with baggage and clutter, multiple pieces (people, places, and things) where there should only be one. Or pieces in general that we are not meant to keep in life, which can lead us to live a life of mediocrity and lack.*

**Jeremiah 17:5-8 NIV** "Cursed is the one who trusts in man, who draws strength from mere flesh and whose heart turns away from the Lord. That person will be like a bush in the wastelands; they will not see prosperity when it comes. They will dwell in the parched places of the desert, in a salt land where no one lives. But blessed is the one who trusts in the Lord, whose confidence is in him. They will be like a tree planted by the water that sends out its roots by the stream. It does not fear when heat comes; its leaves are always green. It has no worries in a year of drought and never fails to bear fruit."

## FAITH/TRUST TESTED:

*Your ability to trust God.*

Faith:

- Complete trust or confidence in someone or something.

- Belief that is not based on proof.

"Now faith is the assurance of things hoped for, the conviction of things not seen." (Hebrews 11:1)

Trust:

- Reliance on the integrity, strength, ability, surety, of a person or thing; confidence.

"Trust in the Lord with all your heart; do not depend on your own understanding. Seek his will in all you do, and he will show you which path to take." (Proverbs 3:5-6)

## WHETHER OLDER OR YOUNGER, TRUSTING GOD IS ONE OF THE HARDEST THINGS FOR ANY HUMAN BEING TO DO SIMPLY BECAUSE TRUST REQUIRES A PERSON TO LET GO.

It's hard to let go and relinquish control if everyone in your life has done nothing but hurt or let you down. It's hard to trust and believe that if you give to God in return you will receive if everyone has done nothing but take from you. It's hard to trust that when God is in control of your life, everything will work out because oftentimes, you can't see His work while He's working. And let's face it, doing things on your own makes you feel as though you have more power over the outcome of your situation or circumstances. But guess what, letting go and trusting God is the only way to escape mediocrity and lack.

**Bible Study Tools:** "We live in a world where trust must be earned and seems to be in short supply. But Solomon, the famous king who wrote Proverbs, knew that trust is exactly where we must start, see above (Proverbs 3:5-6). Most of us have faced disappointments, which have taught us that we can only depend upon ourselves. But living the life God has called us to means unlearning that lesson. Instead, we're meant to rest in God's understanding." (UpChurch, 2019)

If you haven't already had the opportunity to really read and meditate on *The Purge* section of the book, you must stop, go back to that section (*The Purge*), and re-read every chapter because it is almost impossible for you to be able to learn how to trust God if you are unwilling to let go of hurt or pain.

Now, some of you may have never stopped trusting God, or maybe you have and don't know it. Some of you may have just started to trust God, and some may have never trusted Him at all. Regardless of your situation, one thing is for sure. If you want to escape mediocrity and lack, to be at peace and live a happy life, you must learn how to let go of some things.

## WHAT DOES IT MEAN TO LET GO?

The definition of what it means for an individual to let go can vary from person to person. For this reason, I have compiled some examples describing the process.

**Letting go of the past:**

- **Success Consciousness:** "Stopping the attachment to the past, especially to painful past memories, and focusing on the present. When you release the past, you can start accepting the present." (Sasson)

- **Medium:** "Letting go creates space for fresh beginnings: stripping you of what happened yesterday, and enabling the doors of brand-new opportunities to open today." (Ratliff, 2016)

- **Psychology Today:** "Letting go means being willing to allow life to carry you to a new place, even a deeper more true rendition of self. Holding on means trying to push life into the place of your making or be damned." (Andrea Mathews LPC, 2016)

**Letting go of thoughts and worries:**

- **Medium:** "Letting go is releasing all doubt, worry, and fear about a situation, person or outcome. It's releasing anything that disrupts your happiness and no longer serves you on your journey." (Ratliff, 2016)

- **Success Consciousness:** "Letting go is like lifting the anchor of your ship, so that it can sail away. In order to move on, you need to release thoughts, habits, fears and worries. These are your anchors, your shackles that tie you down to the same habits, circumstances and a certain way of life." (Sasson)

- **Medium:** "Letting go is about accepting what is happening right now and not worrying about what will come up tomorrow. It involves much more than just saying you have let go. It's an internal process that must happen for you to truly feel better and get on with life in a healthy way." (Ratliff, 2016)

**Letting go of control:**

- **Medium:** "Letting go is a choice to decide that you will no longer ruminate on things that are out of your control, and focus on what you can control, instead." (Ratliff, 2016)

- **HuffPost:** "Letting go is simply an alternative to control. Letting go is to leave things or people as they are -- letting them be. I am not advocating that we do nothing in our lives to help ourselves or our community. Quite the opposite: Letting go is the releasing of the control and the need or expectation for these things to occur. When something we desire and work hard for does not materialize in the way we had planned, we have the option to put this in perspective by ways of understanding that we are still the same person or to cultivate regrets and vow to control even more. When we are able to let go of the outcome, we are then able to start again without carrying the emotional labels of failure, fear, anger and loss. These negative emotions interfere with our ability to let go and experience the life we want." (Durnell, 2012)

**Letting go of people:**

- **Sounds of Encouragement:** "Sometimes letting go means there will be no more interaction between you and another person. This is not always the case. Letting go can also mean that although

433

there is still a relationship, you are allowing your family members or friends to make decisions for themselves." (Brennen, 2002)

## To Let Go Takes Love

### A Poem Written by an Unknown Author

- ♥ To "let go" does not mean to stop caring; it means I can't do it for someone else.

- ♥ To "let go" is not to cut myself off; it is the realization that I can't control another.

- ♥ To "let go" is not to enable, but to allow learning from natural consequences.

- ♥ To "let go" is to admit powerlessness, which means the outcome is not in my hands.

- ♥ To "let go" is not to try to change or blame another; it is to make the most of myself.

- ♥ To "let go" is not to care for, but to care about.

- ♥ To "let go" is not to "fix", but to be supportive.

- ♥ To "let go" is not to judge, but to allow another to be a human being.

- ♥ To "let go" is not to be in the middle arranging all the outcomes, but to allow others to affect their own destinies.

- ♥ To "let go" is not to be protective; it is to permit another to face reality.

♥ To "let go" is not to deny, but to accept.

♥ To "let go" is not to nag, scold, or argue, but instead to search out my own shortcomings and to correct them.

♥ To "let go" is not to adjust everything to my desires, but to take each day as it comes, and to cherish myself in it.

♥ To "let go" is not to criticize and regulate anybody, but to try to become what I dream I can be.

♥ To "let go" is not to regret the past, but to grow and to live for the future.

♥ To "let go" is to fear less and to love more.

— (Unknown)

**Side Note:** *Whether it be letting go and trusting God with a specific situation you have no control over. Or letting go of people, places, and things, trusting that God has a reason or a plan for you doing so. We all must learn how to let go.*

## WHY IS LETTING GO SO IMPORTANT?

1.  Letting go is the ultimate sign of trust, which is the ultimate sign of love.

**BibleRef:** "When you let go and give whatever it is you are letting go to God you are showing Him that you not only trust in His plans for your life, but you are also showing Him that you love Him simply because you trust Him. "Those who truly love God trust Him, and those who truly trust Him continue to obey Him even when life gets hard." (BibleRef)

If it helps, look at things this way. To let go is to trust God. To trust God is to love God. And the one who loves God receives all that He has promised.

Promises to those that love God:

♥ "He will show love to a thousand generations of those who love Him. (Exodus 20:4-6)

♥ He will send rain in its season and drive out the enemy. (Deuteronomy 11:13-15)

♥ He will become our very life. (Deuteronomy 30:19-20)

♥ He will make us like the sun when it rises in its strength. (Judges 5:31)

♥ He will turn to us and have mercy on us. (Psalm 119:132)

♥ He will watch over us. (Psalm 145:17-20)

♥ He will love us and make His home with us. (John 14:21-23)

♥ He will work all things to our good. (Romans 8:28)

♥ He will prepare for us things which are beyond what our eyes have seen, what our ears have heard, and what our minds have imagined. (1 Corinthians 2:9)

♥ He will give us all the grace we need. (Ephesians 6:24)

♥ He will give us the crown of life. (James 1:12)

♥ He will give the kingdom He has promised for those who love Him. (James 2:5)"

— What Happens to Us When We Love God (Morgan)

|||||||||||||||||||||||||||||||||||||||||||||||||||||||||||||||||||||||||||||||||||||||||||||||||||||||||||||

"The best proof of love is trust."

— *Joyce Brothers*

|||||||||||||||||||||||||||||||||||||||||||||||||||||||||||||||||||||||||||||||||||||||||||||||||||||||||||||

2. Letting go is the key to living an abundant life.

When you release worry (trust God with your life and everything in it), you receive a key that frees you from the chains of mediocrity and unlocks a door that leads to an abundant life (peace and joy). A life that God desires for all of His children. "The thief comes only to steal and kill and destroy; I came that they may have life, and have it abundantly." (John 10:10)

Abundant:

- Existing or available in large quantities; plentiful.

- Plentifulness of the good things of life; prosperity.

Abundant Life:

- Refers to life in its abounding fullness of joy and strength for mind, body, and soul. (Wikipedia)

- A peaceful life, a productive life, an extended life.

The key to an abundant life filled with peace and joy is to release worry. This means letting go of trying to control circumstances and situations that are beyond your control and releasing them to God. "Don't worry about anything; instead, pray about everything. Tell God what you need, and thank him for all he has done. Then you will experience God's peace, which exceeds anything we can understand. His peace will guard your hearts and minds as you live in Christ Jesus." (Philippians 4:6-7)

||||||||||||||||||||||||||||||||||||||||||||||||||||||||||||||||||||||||||||||||||||||||||||||||||||||

"Abundance is a process of letting go; that which is empty can receive."

— *Bryant H. McGill*

||||||||||||||||||||||||||||||||||||||||||||||||||||||||||||||||||||||||||||||||||||||||||||||||||||||

3.   Letting go is a symbolization of humility.

When you let go and let God, you are humbling yourself by admitting that you do not have all the answers. This, as previously mentioned, opens a door that allows God to bless and exalt you as He did Jesus. "The reward of humility and fear of the LORD are wealth, honor and life." (Proverbs 22:4)

**Wealth, Honor, and Life = Spiritual Wealth/Riches:**

- Wealth = Wisdom and Knowledge (Romans 11:33)

- Wealth = Love, Joy, Peace, Self-control (Galatians 5:22-23)

- Honor = Exaltation (Matthew 23:11-12)

- Life = Grace, Redemption, and Forgiveness of Sins (Ephesians 1:3-10)

- Life = Forbearance and Longsuffering (Romans 2:4)

- Life = Salvation (Isaiah 33:5-6)

**Spiritual Wealth/Riches lead to physical wealth:** "Seek first the kingdom of God and his righteousness, and all these things will be added to you." (Matthew 6:33) When you seek to have what God desires for you to have: spiritual riches (good character). He can begin to transform your spirit and mind, equipping you with all you need to obtain what you desire.

> **Side Note:** *God doesn't need to bless you with money, cars, and clothes because He can use that one thing: spiritual riches (good character = power) to change all things in your life. You just have to recognize the worth of what He has already given you.*

Spiritual riches in the Bible are likened to rubies and gold, although they are far more valuable if used in the right manner. "Blessed is the man who finds wisdom, the man who acquires understanding, for she is more profitable than silver, and her gain is better than fine gold. She is more precious than rubies; nothing you desire compares with her. Long life is in her right hand; in her left hand are riches and honor. All her ways are pleasant, and all her paths are peaceful. She is a tree of life to those who embrace her, and those who lay hold of her are blessed." (Proverbs 3:13-18)

If you take a closer look at the spiritual riches mentioned above, you'll see that these attributes are all that you need to accumulate wealth and live a prosperous life.

**This includes but is not limited to you being able to:**

- Start a business that serves a purpose and changes lives.

- Build and raise a healthy, happy family.

- Develop strong business as well as personal relationships.

- Accumulate financial wealth as well as maintain that wealth (financial stability).

||||||||||||||||||||||||||||||||||||||||||||||||||||||||||||||||||||||||||||||||||||||||||||||||||

"Humility will open more doors than arrogance ever will."

— *Zig Ziglar*

||||||||||||||||||||||||||||||||||||||||||||||||||||||||||||||||||||||||||||||||||||||||||||||||||

Trusting God is no small task, so I have broken this chapter into two parts. At this point in the chapter, I ask that you stop, take a break, and meditate on what you've just read. There is a lot more ground  to cover, and for you to understand what you are about to read, you need to fully understand what you have already read. Whenever you have finished meditating on part one of this chapter and feel as though you are ready to tackle part two, you can move forward.

In the second part of this chapter, we will discuss two ways in which you must learn to let go and trust God. Each circumstance will build your trust in God and prepare you to receive what He has in store for you. Let's dive in.

1. Let go and let God (let go of circumstances) in order to receive God's peace.

**Deep Spirituality:** "Worry often comes from trying to control things you really don't have much control over. In Matthew 6, Jesus teaches us how to let go of these kinds of worries: change your priorities. If you make God's kingdom and your relationship with him your first priority, God promises to cover everything you need." (Trusting God and Letting Go of Control, 2017)

**Jesus Teaches about Cares of Life:** "I tell you this: Do not worry about your life. Do not worry about what you are going to eat and drink. Do not worry about what you are going to wear. Is not life more important than food? Is not the body more important than clothes? Look at the birds in the sky. They do not plant seeds. They do not gather grain. They do not put grain into a building to keep. Yet your Father in heaven feeds them! Are you not more important than the birds? Which of you can make himself a little taller by worrying? Why should you worry about clothes? Think how the flowers grow. They do not work or make cloth. But I tell you that Solomon in all his greatness was not dressed as well as one of these flowers. God clothes the grass of the field. It lives today and is burned in the stove tomorrow. How much more will He give you clothes? You have so little faith! Do not worry. Do not keep saying, 'What will we eat?' or, 'What will we drink?' or, 'What will we wear?' The people who do not know God are looking for all these things. Your Father in heaven knows you need all these things. First of all, look for the holy nation of God. Be right with Him. All these other things will be given to you also. Do not worry about tomorrow. Tomorrow will have its own worries. The troubles we have in a day are enough for one day." (Matthew 6:25-34)

## TO TRUST GOD IS TO LET GO AND KNOW THAT HE'S IN CONTROL OF WHATEVER YOU'VE ENTRUSTED TO HIM.

I got injured at work and had to be off for some time. This required me to entrust my situation (bills, etc.) to God and travel into the unknown, a place that I had never experienced.

To further explain, when you work for a company, you know what you are to be paid as well as the dates on which you are to be paid. But when you are off from work for whatever reason, you may have no clue how you are to be paid, who will be paying you, or when you will be paid. This is where trusting God comes into play.

> **Side Note:** *Trusting God does not necessarily mean there is nothing to be done on your part. For instance, there are times when praying and letting go is the only thing you can do. But there are also times when you may have to take the first step and do something physically like filling out some paperwork or making a phone call.*

### Simply Praying Example:

- Simply praying means you may have to pray for something or someone and afterward leave what you've prayed for in God's hands. This could mean praying for a person you love to get well and trusting that God will take care of them because there's not much you can do physically to help.

### Physical Action Example:

- Physical action means you may have to pray about the first step you need to take. Take the first step, which could be filling out some paperwork. Then let go and trust that God will do the rest.

In my situation, I had to take some physical action before letting go and giving my circumstances to God. This was the easiest part of the process.

After notifying my employer of my injury and filling out the necessary paperwork to start my worker's compensation claim, I was placed in what seemed to be a holding pattern, where for weeks, I could do nothing but pray and wait.

## WHETHER LETTING GO REQUIRES SIMPLY PRAYING OR PHYSICAL ACTION, WAITING PERIODS ARE UNAVOIDABLE.

Whenever you pray for something to happen in your life, there will always be a waiting period. Whether it's a long or short waiting period depends on your situation and God.

Waiting Period:

- "The period of time between when an action is requested or mandated and when it occurs." (Wikipedia)

**Week One:** During the first week of my waiting period, I emailed my employer's disability department inquiring about the worker's compensation process, which included loss of wages. My case manager told me that she did not have the information I needed and I should have received a welcome package in the mail from the insurance company explaining everything that I needed to know.

At this stage in the process, I was optimistic, saying to myself, "Even though the package has not yet arrived, everything will be okay because God is working things out".

**Week Three:** By the time the third week had come around I still hadn't received any information from the insurance company. My claim, in my opinion, was in limbo.

At this stage in the process, I began to grow a little anxious and nervous because my rent would soon be due, and the welcome package I should've received still hadn't shown up.

**Week Four:** At the one-month mark (week four), I finally received a welcome package from my employer's insurance company explaining many things except for one of the most important aspects, "HOW WILL I BE PAID".

At this stage in the process, I was a little confused because not only did it take four weeks for me to receive the welcome package, but prior to there had been no attempt on the insurance companies' part to contact me about my claim or the process.

This was when I decided to email the insurance company.

**Week Five:** When week five approached, two things happened.

First, I received a letter in the mail from my employer stating that in the event my worker's compensation claim was held up, I should apply for temporary state disability benefits, which would help compensate for lost wages.

Secondly, I got a hold of the claim examiner handling my claim via telephone.

When I was finally able to speak with the claim examiner, I was told that I did not qualify for lost wage benefits through worker's compensation simply because I was quote on quote "not considered totally disabled and opted to recover/heal at home". This meant I was required to work on modified duty while being injured and in pain.

As you can imagine, at this stage in the process, I should have been upset and angry simply because I had been in a holding pattern for one whole month, and no one had explained to me before this phone call that I would not be paid if I chose to recover at home. But I wasn't angry. I was at peace.

## SOMETIMES WHEN YOU ARE IN A SITUATION AND HAVE NO CONTROL, YOU MUST SIMPLY GIVE THINGS TO GOD AND SAY TO YOURSELF, QUE SERA, SERA (WHATEVER WILL BE, WILL BE).

Although my bills were due, and I had no means (visually in the natural) to pay them, I knew I had done all I could do. This meant I had to choose to be at peace and put my situation in God's hands, trusting that He knows all of my needs and provides me with everything I need. "Don't be like them, for your Father knows exactly what you need even before you ask him!" (Matthew 6:8) "And my God will supply every need of yours according to his riches in glory in Christ Jesus." (Philippians 4:19)

> **Side Note:** *God knows everything you need before you need it, which is why it's better to rely on Him and be at peace instead of relying on yourself and being stressed or anxious.*

**Week Six:** After applying for disability and waiting for another week and a half (two days before my rent was due), I decided to go online to check my disability claim status. There was a small note which read "disqualified".

At this stage in the process I started to panic and get a little frustrated because one, I knew my rent was due, and two, I felt as though I had played the last card in the deck, and because of the very little time I had left to pay my rent, there were not many options available. So, I was still praying but frustrated.

**Side Note:** *It's okay to be a little frustrated when waiting for something you are praying for. Just make sure you don't allow those frustrations to consume you because too much frustration can turn into anger, making you lose sight of what is important, and that is not something you want to happen given how far you've come on this journey. For me, what was important was continuing to remain focused and write this book you are reading. This meant I had to put worry in the back of my mind and continue to trust God even when it didn't seem like things were working out in my favor.*

Although I was a little frustrated, this did not stop me from believing in God. It was very tough for me to do, but it was all that I could do until I was prompted via a letter or phone call to do more. Besides, I knew that because there seemed to be no other options available to me, God had to come through. My situation was entirely in His hands at this point. It was all in His timing.

## GOD MAY NOT COME IN YOUR TIMING, BUT HIS TIMING IS ALWAYS RIGHT.

After being in agony for one whole day because I read the note stating I was disqualified from receiving loss wages (disability payments), I received an email displaying the full notice.

The full notice stated that I was disqualified because I received worker's compensation benefits and had the right to appeal the disqualification online if I disagreed with the decision.

> Because I jumped the gun and wanted to know what was going on with my claim before God's timing, I read a notice that was only partially true. Had I waited until the next day to receive the entire message, I would have known that disqualified did not necessarily mean denied. It really meant delayed.

## DELAYED DOES NOT MEAN DENIED.

**Week Seven:** As week seven approached, I still hadn't received any news about the appeal I had filed a week prior. Eventually, I had to borrow money from my family to pay my rent.

At this stage in the process, you probably thought I'd say it was finally over, and I got paid. But no, that was not the case simply because trusting God builds faith and character, and that is only possible if you go through hardships. Or should I say waiting periods.

**Week Eight:** The following week, after borrowing the money to pay my rent, I received an email notification letting me know the decision to disqualify me for disability benefits was overturned, my benefits were approved, and I'd be receiving back pay from disability for all the time I had waited.

At this stage in the process, I was overjoyed. Not because I had already received the money, but simply because of the thought of me being able to get back on track with budgeting and saving. I also didn't have to worry about being in constant debt.

**Week Nine:** Finally, Finally, Finally! At the end of week nine, I received my payment from disability, and the wait was over.

> **Side Note:** *Although I could not pay my rent on time, God was still present in my situation, which means even though it may seem like to you that He's late, He's still present.*

You may be in a waiting period just as I was, but there is one thing I want you to remember. Being in a waiting period does not mean God has stopped working on your behalf. It simply means God is allowing you to demonstrate faith and grow.

**WAITING PERIODS *TEST* US, WAITING PERIODS *STRETCH* US, WAITING PERIODS *STRENGTHEN* US, WAITING PERIODS *BLESS* US.**

If I had not already mentioned this, typically, when I am writing a chapter, I often struggle or am in a situation that literally pertains to that specific chapter or topic. For instance, while writing this chapter, I was going through the situation mentioned above (trusting God with my problems which meant having my faith tested, stretched, and strengthened).

Everything that I experienced while writing this chapter helped me build up enough strength and confidence to fully believe that no matter what I am going through, if God is in control, I can let go and receive peace. "You, LORD, give perfect peace to those who keep their purpose firm and put their trust in you." (Isaiah 26:3)

|||||||||||||||||||||||||||||||||||||||||||||||||||||||||||||||||||||||||||||||||||||||||||||||||||||||

"If you let go a little you will have a little peace. If you let go a lot you will have a lot of peace. If you let go completely you will have complete peace."

— *Ajahn Chah*

|||||||||||||||||||||||||||||||||||||||||||||||||||||||||||||||||||||||||||||||||||||||||||||||||||||||

2. To leave behind what needs to be let go of in order to mature spiritually and be filled by God.

**Rizzarr:** "We spend much of our life forming attachments to things, people, places, thoughts and emotions that our lives become overburdened with trivial things that ultimately don't matter. Suffering stems from holding onto that which does not serve us—yet in a strange way, it seems comforting and familiar to hold on to these things for fear they will not be replaced or gone from our lives if we let go. The truth is: the space will be filled when we make a conscious decision to let go of that which does not serve us. Letting go of things that do not serve us is as simple as dropping the thoughts, the emotions or circumstance that take up residency within us. There is another way of looking at it, much like the toys we used to play with when we were a child. As an adult, they no longer serve us the same way as they did when we were young." (Fahkry, 2018)

"I want to know Christ—yes, to know the power of his resurrection and participation in his sufferings, becoming like him in his death, and so, somehow, attaining to the resurrection from the dead. Not that I have already obtained all this, or have already arrived at my goal, but I press on to take hold of that for which Christ Jesus took hold of me. Brothers and sisters, I do not consider myself yet to have taken hold of it. But one thing I do: Forgetting what is behind and straining toward what is ahead, I press on toward the goal to win the prize for which God has called me heavenward in Christ Jesus." (Philippians 3:10-14)

Whether it's people, places, or things, as humans, we have this tendency to believe, "if I lose what I have or give up what I want, I'll lose who I am". This way of thinking leads us to hold on to things for too long which inevitably leads to a life of mediocrity and lack simply because you can't receive the other pieces (blessings) to your puzzle (life) if you have a bunch of old baggage taking up space in the wrong areas.

**Side Note:** *Because people refuse to trust God, allowing Him to deal with the baggage and or bad debts that need to be cleared out of their lives before moving forward, they are often stuck living a life of mediocrity.*

For example, when my BMW broke down, I used poor judgment by getting it fixed multiple times. But that was not my biggest problem! After making the poor decision to waste thousands of dollars getting my car fixed repeatedly, the bigger issue I faced was that I also wanted to buy a home. And guess what, large purchases on credit cards are not preferable when doing so, or should I say debt is not preferable, period!

The worst part about the whole situation was that I knew the rules to buying a home, but I went against the grain anyway.

## BAD JUDGMENT, MUCH; DISTRACTION, MUCH; THREW OFF MY PROGRESS, VERY MUCH!

My hopes of buying a home were pushed off simply because the spot that was supposed to be empty (the amount spent on my credit card) had to be cleaned out again (paid down) before I'd be able to purchase my home.

To further explain, because I couldn't trust God and let go of what I wanted (my BMW = bad debt & baggage), I couldn't move forward (out of a life of mediocrity = lack) and receive what God had in store for me (my home = abundance).

I want to add that at this present time, I do not own a Foreign/European car, ultimately because it costs to be the boss, and I am not the boss yet! It also cost me my home, for the moment. This meant I had to choose to have faith, trust God, and "Let it Go," like Keyshia Cole.

What are you holding on to today that could be hindering you from receiving God's blessings? Is it grief, guilt, hurt, or pain? Maybe it's material possessions like cars, clothes, or money. Whatever it is, you need to take some time at this point in the chapter to figure it out because as long as you hold on to whatever "it" is, you cannot receive what He (God) has.

**For example:**

- There's a woman. We'll call her Jasmine, who wants to get married. But she continues to date the bad boy, because the immature old part of her loves him.

**The Problem:**

- God would like to bless Jasmine with Sean, who is loving, kind, and "Husband Material". But because Jasmine refuses to trust God and let go of what she wants, she does not have enough room to receive what she needs.

It's the same with you! You cannot receive God if you are unwilling to let go of the things of this world. You cannot receive a husband or a wife if you are unwilling to let go of those four men or women you are in a relationship with.

**IF YOU CANNOT SHOW GOD THAT YOU TRUST HIM BY LETTING GO OF THE FOUR PUZZLE PIECES, HE CAN'T GIVE YOU "THE ONE".**

Whenever you choose to hold on to things that are not meant for you to keep (things that no longer serve you), that says to God, "I'm not ready for the abundant life you have in store for me because I'm having a hard time trusting that if I focus on the one thing you desire for me to focus on I won't lose anything, but rather gain everything".

And this is just one example. This principle applies to many things in life. You must trust that if you lose four puzzle pieces, you'll still be able to be the masterpiece.

Take Naomi from the Bible for example. She went away with her husband and two sons thinking the place they'd be moving to would allow them to prosper and live a happy life. But the circumstances turned out to be very different than the picture she'd painted. "In the days when the judges ruled in Israel, a severe famine came upon the land. So a man from Bethlehem in Judah left his home and went to live in the country of Moab, taking his wife and two sons with him. The man's name was Elimelech, and his wife was Naomi. Their two sons were Mahlon and Kilion. They were Ephrathites from Bethlehem in the land of Judah. And when they reached Moab, they settled there. Then Elimelech died, and Naomi was left with her two sons. The two sons married Moabite women. One married a woman named Orpah, and the other a woman named Ruth. But about ten years later, both Mahlon and Kilion died. This left Naomi alone, without her two sons or her husband." (Ruth 1:1-5)

Naomi lost it all. Everything she'd worked for was gone, maybe in her mind, in the blink of an eye.

Your life due to your circumstances may make you feel like you are currently going through a similar situation as Naomi. It may seem like you are losing all you love, all you feel you need or care about. But one thing I would like you to know is that just like Naomi's story, yours doesn't end in your present pain; it ends with joy. You just need to trust God, let go of whatever you are holding on to (grief, guilt, material possessions), and remain empty long enough to be filled. "Boaz married Ruth, and the LORD blessed her with a son. After his birth, the women said to Naomi: Praise the LORD! Today he has given you a grandson to take care of you. We pray that the boy will grow up to be famous everywhere in Israel. He will make you happy and take care of you in your old age, because he is the son of your daughter-in-law. And she loves you more than seven sons of your own would love you. Naomi loved the boy and took good care of him. The neighborhood women named him Obed, but they called him "Naomi's Boy." (Ruth 4:13-17)

Initially, Naomi thought the things that she had lost (money, cars, clothes, and people) defined her. "Don't call me Naomi...Call me Mara, because the Almighty has made my life very bitter. I went away full, but the LORD has brought me back empty. Why call me Naomi? The LORD has afflicted me; the Almighty has brought misfortune upon me." (Ruth 1:20-21).

Turns out, Naomi's loss actually made room for God's blessings, making Naomi's puzzle (life/story) a work of art. A masterpiece created by God. "When Obed grew up he had a son named Jesse, who later became the father of King David." (Ruth 4:17)

> **Side Note:** *We all must be empty at one point or another, just like Naomi. But remember, the state of being empty is not what defines you. The Creator of the pieces to your puzzle (GOD) defines and makes you whole (a masterpiece).*

The pieces that you have lost or may need to give up might seem like they complete you simply because they are a part of the source. Meaning people, places, and things are what God created; therefore, they can sometimes be the wrong pieces "for you" yet temporarily make you feel whole. This is why it's very important to trust God with your life. You see, not only does He make, shape, and distribute every puzzle, but He is also the only one that can give to each individual the pieces that complete their puzzle.

**GOD IS "THE GAP FILLER", WHICH MEANS IF EVER YOU HAVE EMPTY SPACES, YOU NEED TO PUT YOUR TRUST IN HIM BECAUSE ONLY HE HAS THE ANSWERS TO FILLING YOUR VOID.**

For example, being that my loved one and I are very close when he became incarcerated, there were moments when I felt as though a piece of me was missing. And some, not all, would maybe use bad judgment by rushing to fill that space with other people or things. But what I realized is if I did not continue to trust God along this journey and rushed to try to fill that space on my own, I'd run the risk of causing myself to be stressed and frustrated simply because people, places, and things if not ordained by God are not permanent fillers, they are temporary fixes for a permanent problem.

**YOU'RE NOT EMPTY AND STILL HURTING BECAUSE YOU ARE MISSING PEOPLE, PLACES, OR THINGS. YOU'RE EMPTY AND STILL HURTING BECAUSE YOU'RE CONSTANTLY RUSHING TO FILL YOURSELF WITH THE PEOPLE, PLACES, AND THINGS "YOU" BELIEVE TO BE YOUR MISSING LINK INSTEAD OF LEANING ON AND TRUSTING IN GOD TO DO SO.**

Let's take a look at the story of Adam and Eve to get a better illustration.

At the beginning of time, before Eve was created, Adam went out looking for someone or something to suit himself, but he wound up empty-handed. "Adam gave names to all the cattle, and to the birds of the sky, and to every animal of the field. But there was no helper found that was right for Adam." (Genesis 2:20).

It was not until Adam trusted and believed that him losing what he was looking for was not as important as him gaining what God wanted for him that he'd be able to step into his purpose. "So the Lord God put the man to sleep as if he were dead. And while he was sleeping, He took one of the bones from his side and closed up the place with flesh. Then the LORD God made a woman from the rib he had taken out of the man, and he brought her to the man." (Genesis 2:21-22)

## EMPTINESS PROVOKES HEALING, HEALING PROVOKES FILLING, AND FILLING PROVOKES PURPOSE.

Once Adam decided to trust God by being comfortable with empty long enough, God was able to step in to help Adam fill his void (Adam's rib missing). This, in turn, helped Adam find his purpose in life. Meaning him becoming the head of the household and husband of Eve, who is the mother of all living. "Adam named his wife Eve, because she would become the mother of all the living." (Genesis 3:20)

> **Side Note:** *Oftentimes, you may not honestly know what you need in life. For this reason, you need to be patient and lean on God to get the answers.*

If Adam had kept trying to solve his problems alone (fill the empty space himself), he would have never received Eve (the answer to his problem, his blessing).

## EVE WAS A BLESSING. SHE WASN'T TEMPO-RARY. SHE WAS SEMI-PERMANENT.

Eve was semi-permanent because she was the rib that eventually perishes as it's a part of the body. But it sticks with you, close by your side protecting and supporting you until you leave the earth; till death do you part.

## Rib:

- The rib cage has three important functions: protection, support, and respiration.

## Semi:

- A combining form borrowed from Latin, meaning "half,".

## Permanent:

- Lasting or intended to last or remain unchanged indefinitely.

- Synonyms: lasting, enduring, indefinite, continuing, perpetual, everlasting, eternal, abiding, constant, standing, perennial, unending, endless, never-ending, immutable, undying, imperishable, indestructible.

**SEMI = (HUMAN, PARTIALLY) & PERMANENT = (SPIRIT, EVERLASTING). WE ARE SEMI-PERMANENT BECAUSE WE ARE PART HUMAN, PART SPIRIT. MEANING PART OF US (THE BODY) CAN BE DESTROYED, BUT THE OTHER PART (THE SPIRIT) IS EVERLASTING (FOREVER).**

**Side Note:** *God doesn't plan for the things in life to fill you forever because life on earth itself isn't forever. For example, we all leave this earth at one point or another. All things wither away at one time or another. For this reason, God only plans for those things or people to complement you.*

Complement:

- Add to (something) in a way that enhances or improves it; make perfect.

Eve was a complement to Adam; she was a piece of him. She could never fully-fill Adam, but she played her part and was to Adam what God predestined for her to be, the rib. Eve was "the" rib. She wasn't just "anyone". She was "the one" for Adam.

Eve was Adam's one and only, and no one could tear them apart because God had blessed them to be together. "This explains why a man leaves his father and mother and is joined to his wife, and the two are united into one.' Since they are no longer two but one, let no one split apart what God has joined together." (Mark 10:7-8)

It may seem like a piece of you is missing just as Adam was missing his rib, but remember, if you trust God with your emptiness and give to Him what you feel is missing, He will transform that piece making it more beautiful than what it originally was when He received it. "Take delight in the Lord, and he will give you the desires of your heart." (Psalm 37:4) But you have to let it go, trust God, be patient, and stop trying to fill that space long enough for God to work on it; for Him to work on you!

## GOD IS NOT ONLY WORKING ON THE PIECES TO YOUR PUZZLE, BUT HE'S ALSO WORKING ON YOU!

The long, tough road of my loved one's incarceration has allowed each of us to, in different ways, experience God's work. For instance, God has used our individual and combined circumstances to strengthen our relationship and strengthen us by turning what used to be fussing and fighting between my loved one and me into us learning how to fight for one another.

I no longer nag and complain about what he does wrong, but I've learned to uplift and motivate him in every circumstance. I love him no matter what. And if ever I'm upset with him, I remember neither of us or should I say nobody in this world is perfect; we are all *Only Human.* That is the result of God's work in me. It's the work He's done on my empty space.

And as for my loved one, God has worked on him as well, transforming him into a beautiful person.

To conclude, although there are certain people, places, and things that are not meant to be taken into the next stage of your life, it's not the end of your story. It's the beginning of you trusting God, the beginning of knowing that through Him, a new life, a more abundant life awaits.

**YOU ARE THE ONLY ONE WITH THE POWER TO DECIDE HOW LONG YOU WILL BE STUCK LIVING A LIFE OF MEDIOCRITY. THE MOMENT YOU LET GO IS THE MOMENT YOU WILL BE FREE. THE CHOICE IS YOURS: TRUST GOD (RECEIVE AN ABUNDANCE OF PEACE AND JOY) AND LET GO. OR BE STUCK (CARRYING BAGGAGE, CLUTTER, AND BAD DEBTS) AND NEVER GROW.**

"Faithless is he that says farewell when the road darkens."

— *J.R.R. Tolkien*

***Serenity Prayer:*** God grant me the serenity to accept the things I cannot change, Courage to change the things I can, and the wisdom to know the difference. Living one day at a time; Enjoying one moment at a time, Accepting hardship as the pathway to peace. Taking, as Jesus did, this sinful world as it is, not as I would have it. Trusting that You will make all things right, If I surrender to Your will, So that I may be reasonably happy in this life, And supremely happy with You forever in the next.

In Jesus' Name, Amen.

# CHAPTER 20

# STUCK IN THE WAIT: 40 DAYS VS 40 YEARS

*You thought you were whole already, didn't you, but you wound up stuck. Most tend to hit a snag when working towards becoming spiritually mature, so they wind up stuck in the wait. The journey that leads to you developing good characteristics is not perfect, so I had to throw in a wrench to show you how imperfect your journey in life could be. How imperfect people could be.*

**Joshua 5:6 ESV** "For the people of Israel walked forty years in the wilderness, until all the nation, the men of war who came out of Egypt, perished, because they did not obey the voice of the LORD; the LORD swore to them that he would not let them see the land that the LORD had sworn to their fathers to give to us, a land flowing with milk and honey."

This section of the book (*The Process*) has been a lot so far. So, I want you to reflect on the previous chapters you have read and evaluate what you've been letting fill you that needs to be let go.

## WHY?

Well, you can come to God with baggage and be saved, but you cannot continue with Him on this journey with baggage and still be able to receive the blessings He has in store for you. "Then Jesus said to his disciples, "If any of you wants to be my follower, you must give up your own way, take up your cross, and follow me." (Matthew 16:24) Every disciple had to let go of something to follow Jesus, and so do you.

## IF YOU DIDN'T ALREADY KNOW, THIS IS WAR, WHICH MEANS YOUR BAD ATTITUDE MUST BE LET GO!

There's a war of two world's going on inside of you. The old you is fighting with the new you, the flesh is fighting with the Spirit, the past fighting the future, and the devil fighting the Lord. One fighting the other for who will have control over you. For this reason, issues from your past, such as anger and frustration, may be trying to become present again. Causing you to feel torn. "I don't really understand myself, for I want to do what is right, but I don't do it. Instead, I do what I hate. But if I know that what I am doing is wrong, this shows that I agree that the law is good. So I am not the one doing wrong;

it is sin living in me that does it. And I know that nothing good lives in me, that is, in my sinful nature. I want to do what is right, but I can't. I want to do what is good, but I don't. I don't want to do what is wrong, but I do it anyway. But if I do what I don't want to do, I am not really the one doing wrong; it is sin living in me that does it." (Romans 7:15-20)

Your body is a battle zone, and the bad must die for the good in you to live. Meaning death to the flesh (sin) because only one can reign on the throne of your heart, and that's God.

The Spirit will win, but before you can make it to the finish line, you must first recognize and deal with the things that can keep you stuck in the wait.

Things that will keep you stuck in the wait:

1. Disbelief and Complaining

2. Ungratefulness

3. Being afraid of making a mistake

4. Not the right time

5. God is still developing your character

6. God is positioning you

## 1. Disbelief and Complaining

**Disbelief:**

- Inability or refusal to accept that something is true or real; lack of faith.

**Complain:**

- To express dissatisfaction or annoyance about something.

"One day the Israelites started complaining about their troubles. The Lord heard them and became so angry that he destroyed the outer edges of their camp with fire. When the people begged Moses to help, he prayed, and the fire went out. They named the place "Burning," because in his anger the Lord had set their camp on fire." (Numbers 11:1-3)

When you are on the brink of being fully filled (spiritually mature), the devil gets desperate. Using minor things like your appearance, the people around you that you find annoying, or traffic to get you to become frustrated and complain.

> **Side Note:** *Complaining leads to you being stuck in the wait.*

**Stuck:**

- Synonyms: fixed, fastened, attached, glued, pinned.

The funny part is you've already conquered the more significant obstacles: recognizing your sin, repenting, being broken down, and forgiveness. But it's those minor things that seem to give us more problems than them all.

**BEING IN THE FIGHT, IN THE WAIT, IN THE STRUGGLE FOR SO LONG CAN MAKE YOU LOSE HOPE. FURTHERMORE, LEADING TO DISBELIEF, WHICH EVENTUALLY LEADS TO COMPLAINTS.**

Disbelief and complaining are intertwined because disbelief stems from doubt, which stems from unfulfilled desires. Unfulfilled desires then lead you to complain about the things you have yet to receive, why you have yet to receive them, or why you deserve to receive them.

> **Side Note:** *The Me Me Me song of life comes to play its tune when you constantly complain about things in life.*

**The People Grumble about Being Hungry:** "One day some worthless foreigners among the Israelites became greedy for food, and even the Israelites themselves began moaning, "We don't have any meat! In Egypt we could eat all the fish we wanted, and there were cucumbers, melons, onions, and garlic." (Numbers 11:4-5)

The Israelites were stuck wandering in the wilderness for 40 years because they fought many battles, yet the victory did not come as quickly as they thought it would. This caused them to believe that what they were promised, what they were hoping and believing for, would never happen. Ultimately leading to them complaining about their future while living on the border of their past.

"They said, "If we have found favor in your sight, let this land be given to your servants as a possession. Do not take us across the Jordan [River]." But Moses said to the sons of Gad and the sons of Reuben, "Shall your brothers go to war while you sit here? Now why are you discouraging the hearts of the Israelites from crossing over into the land which the Lord has given them? This is what your fathers did when I sent them from Kadesh-Barnea to see the land! For when they went up to the Valley of Eshcol and saw the land, they discouraged the hearts of the Israelites so that they did not go into the land which the Lord had given them." (Numbers 32:5-9)

The Israelites figured if they did not move forward, they would not have to confront nor deal with the problems that looked bigger than them. The funny part about it all was that the problems they faced were themselves. The problems they faced were because of their mindset; their belief system.

## WHEN YOU ARE SO BUSY FOCUSING ONLY ON THE THINGS YOU BELIEVE TO BE PROBLEMS (OUTWARDLY), YOU BEGIN TO LOSE THE WAR GOING ON INSIDE OF YOU.

**Side Note:** *Complaining causes you to exert all of your energy on your problems, and when it comes time for you to fight the real war, you're too weak to do so.*

You see, the war is not simply about the people you don't like or your circumstances. The war is actually within you. It's how you let your circumstances and the people you don't like get under your skin and into your spirit.

## THE ISRAELITES WERE SO FOCUSED ON THEIR PROBLEMS THAT THEY BECAME BLINDED, NOT REALIZING THEY WERE LOSING THE REAL WAR. THE WAR WITHIN. "FOR OUR STRUGGLE IS NOT AGAINST FLESH AND BLOOD, BUT AGAINST THE RULERS, AGAINST THE AUTHORITIES, AGAINST THE POWERS OF THIS DARK WORLD AND AGAINST THE SPIRITUAL FORCES OF EVIL IN THE HEAVENLY REALMS." (EPHESIANS 6:12)

Eventually, the Israelites started to become the very thing they despised; the broken system of hatred they were supposed to leave in Egypt.

We have been fighting a similar battle for over one hundred and fifty years.

HuffPost: "On Dec. 18, 1865, slavery ended in the United States. Secretary of State William Seward issued a statement verifying the ratification of the 13th Amendment to the U.S. Constitution making the end of slavery official eight months after the end of the Civil War." (Voices)

Today we focus on and complain about the politics in life, not realizing the problems created by politics are often distractions.

These distractions disable us from seeing that we are starting to become them. The government, the criminal justice system, and the hateful people of this world. For example, African Americans are constantly being stereotyped. Some people even say every Black person who dresses or looks a certain way is a criminal. This, in turn, leads Black people to make similar statements, stereotyping every White person as a racist. Neither statement is true, but you get the point.

> **Side Note:** *We need to be better and do better to win the fight that's in front of us. We do not need to be the people we dislike to beat them; we only need to know our opponent to win.*

## HAVE YOU BEEN STRUGGLING TO PROGRESS IN LIFE BECAUSE YOU'RE LIVING ON THE BORDER OF LOVE AND HATE?

Some of us want to live on the border of our past because we don't want to change, and it's impossible. For example, Lot could've chosen anywhere to live; anyone to be. "The whole countryside is open to you. Take your choice of any section of the land you want, and we will separate. If you want the land to the left, then I'll take the land on the right. If you prefer the land on the right, then I'll go to the left." (Genesis 13:9)

But Lot chose a place that was right on the border of where he was delivered from; a city filled with wickedness; a city similar to his past. "Lot looked around and saw that the whole plain of the Jordan toward Zoar was well watered, like the garden of the Lord, like the land of Egypt. (This was before the Lord destroyed Sodom and Gomorrah.) So, Lot chose for himself the whole plain of the Jordan and set out toward the east. The two men parted company: Abram lived in the land of Canaan, while Lot lived among the cities of the plain and pitched his tents near Sodom. Now the people of Sodom were wicked and were sinning greatly against the Lord." (Genesis 13:10-13)

Lot caused his family to be ruined because he wanted to secretly still be in the game like Ghost off of the television show Power, making dirty money while also leading a legit business with a happy family life at the same freaking time. A little bit of good character, a little bit of bad. "At dawn the next morning the angels became insistent. "Hurry," they said to Lot. "Take your wife and your two daughters who are here. Get out right now, or you will be swept away in the destruction of the city!" When Lot still hesitated, the angels seized his hand and the hands of his wife and two daughters and rushed them to safety outside the city, for the Lord was merciful. When they were safely out of the city, one of the angels ordered, "Run for your lives! And don't look back or stop anywhere in the valley! Escape to the mountains, or you will be swept away!" "Oh no, my lord!" Lot begged. "You have been so gracious to me and saved my life, and you have shown such great kindness. But I cannot go to the mountains. Disaster would catch up to me there, and I would soon die. See, there is a small village nearby. Please let me go there instead; don't you see how small it is? Then my life will be saved." "All right," the angel said, "I will grant your request. I will not destroy the little village. But hurry! Escape to it, for I can do nothing until you arrive there." (This explains why that village was known as Zoar, which means "little place.") Lot reached the village just as the sun was rising over the horizon. Then the Lord rained down fire and burning sulfur from the sky on Sodom and Gomorrah. He utterly destroyed them, along with the other cities and villages of the plain, wiping out all the people and every bit of vegetation. But Lot's wife looked back as she was following behind him, and she turned into a pillar of salt." (Genesis 19:15-26)

If it weren't for Abraham begging God to save Lot when destruction came to the city, Lot's past would've killed him. "And the prayer offered in faith will make the sick person well; the Lord will raise them up. If they have sinned, they will be forgiven. Therefore, confess your sins to each other and pray for each other so that you may be healed. The prayer of a righteous person is powerful and effective." (James 5:15-16)

**ARE YOU SO DESPERATELY TRYING TO HANG ON TO YOUR PAST THAT YOU'RE WILLING TO STAY STUCK IN THE WAIT, POSSIBLY KILLING YOURSELF?**

I possibly could've died when I got sick (started rapidly losing weight and declining in health due to unexplained illnesses). And at first, I was filled with complaints, but eventually, I fell to my knees. I started asking God, "what's next, what's Your plan". But sometimes, nobody can tell you to let go of your past behaviors, to have faith and believe. Sometimes when you get to a point where enough is enough, you'll see the big picture. Whether you wait for things to get so hard and stay in the wait longer than was planned for you to change your ways or chose to do so on your own, that's something you decide. Because the war going on around you is just a distraction to make

474

you give up not only on receiving the promise but distract you from conquering and changing the problems that you face within.

So granted, the Israelites were going through some things just as you may be today but what's failed to see is the Israelites kept complaining yet refused to see their need to change. Look at it this way; the Israelites wanted something, and God wanted to give it to them, but they wanted something for nothing. They didn't want to change their mindset and belief system, but they wanted the blessings that come from changing. The blessings that are reaped when a changed heart and soul (mind, will, and emotions) are sowed.

## COMPLAINING HIDES THE TRUTH. IT DISTRACTS YOU FROM THE TRUTH, CAUSING YOU TO BECOME UNGRATEFUL.

### 2.   Ungratefulness

**Ungratefulness:**

- Not feeling or exhibiting gratitude, thanks, or appreciation.

"But we're starving out here, and the only food we have is this manna." (Numbers 11:6)

When the material things in life blind you, you can easily miss seeing the true blessings or gifts from God, such as breath and life; thus, causing you to take these things for granted. The Israelites battled with this same problem. See, not only did they complain all the time, but they were mad ungrateful, just like we are today.

Instead of counting the progress we have made in life as a blessing, we continue to complain about what we have yet to receive. For example, a Black President is elected to office, but some feel that Black President hasn't done enough. Yet when the opposite of Obama, which is Trump, gets elected as President, people still aren't happy.

## WILL YOU EVER BE GRATEFUL FOR WHAT YOU HAVE?

Often we receive so much yet are grateful for so little, or should I say are grateful for all the wrong things. For instance, you may be praising God for your new house, but have you forgotten to thank Him for your new day? You may be praising God for your new job, but have you forgotten to thank him for the breath you used to speak in the interview to get it?

You see, some of you think you're praising the Lord, but in reality, you may be worshiping the devil. And no, it's not one hundred percent your fault because the devil is crafty. He can make you believe that everything you have been given in life is such a blessing when it can actually be a curse. Because by nature, we covet. By nature, we idolize. By nature, we complain. And by nature, we always want more than what God has given us. So, life and a new day become less important than a new Bentley. So, the breath that you breathe becomes less important than a new body. But do you not realize that if you didn't have life and a new day or breath to breathe, you wouldn't be able to enjoy any of these things in the first place?

## I URGE YOU TO TAKE A STEP BACK AND DIG DEEP, REAL DEEP, THINK AND MEDITATE ON WHAT YOU ARE UNGRATEFUL FOR.

I sit back and see some people complain about the parents they do have, failing to realize I only have a memory of the parent I don't. The same goes for material things. We all complain about what we have, "I hate this job; this house is too small". Failing to see, some don't have what we have at all, or some people wish they had what we have.

3. Being afraid of making a mistake

**Afraid:**

- Feeling fear or anxiety; frightened.

**Israel Refuses to Enter Canaan:** "That night all the members of the community raised their voices and wept aloud. All the Israelites grumbled against Moses and Aaron, and the whole assembly said to them, "If only we had died in Egypt! Or in this wilderness! Why is the Lord bringing us to this land only to let us fall by the sword? Our wives and children will be taken as plunder. Wouldn't it be better for us to go back to Egypt?" And they said to each other, "We should choose a leader and go back to Egypt."

Then Moses and Aaron fell facedown in front of the whole Israelite assembly gathered there. Joshua son of Nun and Caleb son of Jephunneh, who were among those who had explored the land, tore their clothes and said to the entire Israelite assembly, "The land we passed through and explored is exceedingly good. If the Lord is pleased with us, he will lead us into that land, a land flowing with milk and honey, and will give it to us. Only do not rebel against the Lord. And do not be afraid of the people of the land, because we will devour them. Their protection is gone, but the Lord is with us. Do not be afraid of them." (Numbers 14:1-9)

Because life has so many variables, which can be confusing, life sometimes can make you afraid. Afraid to change, afraid to live, and afraid to make simple everyday decisions.

> **Side Note:** *When you are in a battle that seems like you're warring for your life, making decisions can become tough. Not just tough for you to make but make you tough on yourself in general. Thus, leading to you not making decisions at all. Stuck still is what you are. Some may even be wondering; will I ever be good enough?*

You may not want to change because you're afraid to make a mistake or think you'll look foolish, so you complain about your problems instead of taking action to be different in a world where people are conforming day by day. Another reason for not changing is because you don't want to be the change. You'd rather complain about how you want things to change while waiting for someone else to invest in the future you complain about as opposed to investing in it yourself.

See, you say you want to change but are afraid to change. You say you want the world to be different, yet you are afraid to be the difference. But get this; if you continue to fear change, you will always be waiting for someone who doesn't care about you to change your circumstances.

"People who never dream, or never set goals, let life go by day by day letting others determine their destiny. Without advancing your dream through the process of setting plans to reach your goal, you are forced to accept what you have today."

— *Catherine Pulsifer*

**WHEN YOU ARE AFRAID OF MOVING FORWARD, YOU RELY ON OTHERS TO CHANGE YOUR CIRCUMSTANCES, THEREFORE, PLACING WHETHER OR NOT YOUR LIFE GETS BETTER IN THEIR HANDS INSTEAD OF YOUR OWN.**

I'll use myself as an example. I quit pursuing my college education multiple times because I was afraid of making a mistake, such as choosing the wrong major. Doing this caused me to overthink the process, which prolonged the process. Eventually, I became depressed and frustrated, wanting to give up on college altogether simply because I was too afraid to try. The issue with that is that nobody will do the footwork for you. If you want to reach your dreams or destiny, you must be willing to do the work, stepping out in faith.

## FAITH WITHOUT WORKS IS DEAD BECAUSE YOU CAN'T BUILD FAITH WITHOUT AT LEAST TRYING.

When you take the first step and try to progress in life, God can lead and direct you through the answers you receive. A yes, could mean you're on the right path. A no could mean you need to be redirected or need to re-evaluate your plans.

## EVERYONE HAS THEIR OWN FIRST STEP EVERY DAY. NO ONE PERSON'S FIRST STEP IS THE SAME.

The first step for you could be simply getting up in the morning. It could also be filling out an application for a job you don't feel qualified for. We all have different battles, but we also all have a decision to make each day, and that's whether or not we'll take our first step. Not the person's first step next door, but ours.

## GOD WANTS TO BUILD YOUR FAITH THROUGH "YOUR" STEPS.

For example, if you want to buy a house, your first step is to pray and ask God for it. After asking for the home, your job is to apply for it and get direction from the lender on where you are in the process of being able to purchase. The lender may say yes, you are ready to buy now. Or the lender may say no, you still have some work to do, such as saving money for a down payment or creating a budget.

Now yes can be exciting while no may be discouraging. But guess what. Because you at least tried, you now know a lot more than what you would have known if you did not try at all.

> **Side Note:** *The no's in life tell you what you need to do to get to where you want to go. The no's in life tell you how to re-evaluate your plan in order to move forward.*

## ARE YOU ABLE TO ACCEPT THAT THERE'S POWER IN GOD'S YES' BUT ALSO LEARNING EXPERIENCES IN HIS NO?

Some of you are still waiting for your answer. Some of you have already gotten your answer and have to change your plans. A lot of you don't even know where to begin. The best advice I can give you is not to be afraid to start with the first step. Because only after the first step is taken can the next step be revealed.

### 4.  Not the right time

Timing:

- A particular point or period of time when something happens.

"There is a season (a time appointed) for everything and a time for every delight and event or purpose under heaven—

A time to be born and a time to die;

A time to plant and a time to uproot what is planted.

A time to kill and a time to heal;

A time to tear down and a time to build up.

A time to weep and a time to laugh;

A time to mourn and a time to dance.

A time to throw away stones and a time to gather stones;

A time to embrace and a time to refrain from embracing.

A time to search and a time to give up as lost;

A time to keep and a time to throw away.

A time to tear apart and a time to sew together;

A time to keep silent and a time to speak.

A time to love and a time to hate;

A time for war and a time for peace." (Ecclesiastes 3:1-8)

Being stuck in the wait does not always mean you have done something wrong. Although disbelief and complaining are issues you have to work with God to change. Timing is just that, timing. Your destiny is in God's hands, and it just may not be the right time.

**GOD HAS A TIME AND A PLAN. YOU WILL RE-CEIVE WHAT YOU DESIRE IN DUE TIME WHEN YOUR CHARACTER CAN HANDLE YOU HAVING IT.**

For instance, there may be some things God needs to instill in you before revealing you to the world.

God could be lining certain people, places, and things up so that He can bless you in the way He wants to. Or, most importantly, He could still be changing your mind, renewing it.

5. God is still building your character

Building:

- The process of creating or developing something, typically a system or situation, over a period of time.

"Now Jesse said to his son David, "Take this ephah of roasted grain and these ten loaves of bread for your brothers and hurry to their camp. Take along these ten cheeses to the commander of their unit. See how your brothers are and bring back some assurance from them. They are with Saul and all the men of Israel in the Valley of Elah, fighting against the Philistines." Early in the morning David left the flock in the care of a shepherd, loaded up and set out, as Jesse had directed. He reached the camp as the army was going out to its battle positions, shouting the war cry. Israel and the Philistines were drawing up their lines facing each other. David left his things with the keeper of supplies, ran to the battle lines and asked his brothers how they were." (1 Samuel 17:17-22)

The battles that you currently face in life are not all physical. Now, this can seem confusing because the struggles in your life are very much present and real, but they are not the focus. Let me explain it this way. When David fought Goliath and won, it was not about the physical giants in front of or ahead of him. It was about the journey and the character he developed along the way.

Throughout David's journey, he remained humble, did not complain, and was committed to what was asked of him. When God saw this, He knew He could trust David to be King over His people.

### 6.   God is positioning you

Positioning:

- Put or arrange (someone or something) in a particular place or way.

"But now your kingdom will not endure; the Lord has sought out a man after his own heart and appointed him ruler of his people, because you have not kept the Lord's command." (1 Samuel 13:14)

This statement from the previous scripture was made to Saul, who was King over Israel at the time. It did not reference David's name but was about David becoming king. This statement was also made before David set out on his journey to beat Goliath. This further confirms that David's journey was simply a testing or training ground used to build his character, his platform, and position him to become King.

Once God saw David's heart posture was in line with His own, He knew He could then use David's circumstances to position him to become King.

**TO SUM IT UP, YOU MUST CHECK YOUR ATTITUDE AND BEHAVIOR IN THE SPIRITUAL WAR IF YOU WANT GOD TO BLESS YOU TO CONQUER THE PHYSICAL BATTLE.**

David did not have to fight the physical battle that led to him becoming King because he had already won and conquered the war that he was supposed to fight, which was the battle of him having the correct heart posture. The spiritual war. "Now the Philistines attacked Israel, and the men of Israel fled before them. Many were slaughtered on the slopes of Mount Gilboa. The Philistines closed in on Saul and his sons, and they killed three of his sons—Jonathan, Abinadab, and Malkishua. The fighting grew very fierce around Saul, and the Philistine archers caught up with him and wounded him severely. Saul groaned to his armor bearer, "Take your sword and kill me before these pagan Philistines come to run me through and taunt and torture me." But his armor bearer was afraid and would not do it. So Saul took his own sword and fell on it. When his armor bearer realized that Saul was dead, he fell on his own sword and died beside the king. So Saul, his three sons, his armor bearer, and his troops all died together that same day." (1 Samuel 31:1-6).

David did not kill Saul, Saul essentially killed himself, and David only had to come in afterward to claim his title as King.

In other words, your battle is not with the Old Testament (the physical). It's with the New Testament (the spirit). Today, your job is to fight your spiritual issues, which are the things you cannot see, your emotions, anger, mind frame, and belief system. Once you learn what battle is yours to fight, you can focus on it, thus allowing God to come in and conquer your physical fights.

**I'LL PUT IT THIS WAY, WHY WOULD YOU LEARN HOW TO FIGHT A PHYSICAL BATTLE IF YOUR SPIRIT IS WHAT WILL REMAIN EVEN AFTER DEATH? SHOULDN'T THE SPIRIT BE WHAT YOU LEARN HOW TO FIGHT IN, TO FIGHT FOR?**

**Side Note:** *Your physical body will not last after you die, but your spirit, which is what you cannot see, will.*

To conclude, the struggle, the wait, is however long it takes for you to decide to move closer to your future. However long it takes for you to decide to start on the journey with mercy and grace to be made different. However long it takes for you to start to change your mind. The keyword is start; you don't have to be perfect.

**40 DAYS; JESUS, OR 40 YEARS; ISRAELITES, BETTER YET 150 YEARS OUT OF SLAVERY; US!**

Jesus made it through the wilderness in 40 days without getting stuck because Jesus chose to wait on the Lord. "Jesus said to them, "The right time for me has not yet come. Any time is right for you." (John 7:6)

Jesus chose to use his alone time to be alone with God. "After He had sent the crowds away, He went up on the mountain by Himself to pray; and when it was evening, He was there alone." (Matthew 14:23)

Jesus chose to face his fears because He trusted the Lord and what He was doing through Him. "He told them, "My soul is crushed with grief to the point of death. Stay here and keep watch with me." He went on a little farther and bowed with his face to the ground, praying, "My Father! If it is possible, let this cup of suffering be taken away from me. Yet I want your will to be done, not mine." (Matthew 26:38-39)

Jesus didn't need all of the things the world said He needed to become whole or complete. He didn't need to fix himself; because, ultimately, Jesus knew He needed to be changed by God, to be empty then filled, to be tempted and resist.

The Israelites, on the other hand, couldn't even resist the temptation to complain.

**THE JOURNEY THAT TOOK THE ISRAELITES 40 YEARS COULD HAVE BEEN 11 DAYS. "NORMALLY IT TAKES ONLY ELEVEN DAYS TO TRAVEL FROM MOUNT SINAI TO KADESH-BARNEA, GOING BY WAY OF MOUNT SEIR." (DEUTERONOMY 1:2) MOTIVATION ENOUGH TO ASK GOD TO HELP YOU CHANGE YOUR WAYS?**

God is waiting on you to come to Him and ask for his grace to be changed; because you are the modern-day Israelites. And you do need to change from within (attitude/character) to conquer and defeat your problems and the problems in this world.

**LISTEN, DESTINY IS FOR THE TAKING! YOU ARE NOT STUCK AND WAITING ON GOD TO CHANGE THE WORLD. GOD'S WAITING ON YOU TO CHANGE SO THAT HE CAN WORK THROUGH YOU, ENABLING YOU TO BE THE CHANGE THIS WORLD NEEDS.**

"The main theme of the Bible is the restoration of humanity and, through humanity, of the whole of creation to its original harmony."

— *Bede Griffiths*

*Heavenly Father,* thank you for sending the Holy Spirit to give me the grace to be a better person. I recognize that I cannot change myself, and it's only by Your grace and mercy that I can do better. So, I invite you in. I ask you to change me, shape me, make me, and mold me into who you desire for me to be. Help me change and get rid of this bad attitude so that my attitude doesn't take control of me. Change me Lord, so that I can change the world we live in.

In Jesus' name, Amen!

# CHAPTER 21

# VIRTUAL REALITY OF PATIENCE

*In the world we live in today, almost everyone's value of patience is out of order. There's a sign that reads "closed for an hour; please come back later" hanging on a door that, when opened, reveals a blessing. The problem: most never make it back around to the door which holds said blessing, simply because the moment something is not "right now", one moves to get the next best thing that allows them to skip ahead; or should I say move two spaces forward.*

**Psalm 37:7-11** GNT "Be patient and wait for the Lord to act; don't be worried about those who prosper or those who succeed in their evil plans. Don't give in to worry or anger; it only leads to trouble. Those who trust in the Lord will possess the land, but the wicked will be driven out. Soon the wicked will disappear; you may look for them, but you won't find them; but the humble will possess the land and enjoy prosperity and peace."

## PATIENCE, SELF-CONTROL/SELF-DISCIPLINE TESTED:

*Your ability to be self-disciplined.*

Patience:

- The capacity to accept or tolerate delay, trouble, or suffering without getting angry or upset.

- Not the ability to wait, but how we act while waiting.

- Quiet, steady perseverance; even-tempered care; diligence.

"For in this hope we were saved. But hope that is seen is no hope at all. Who hopes for what they already have? But if we hope for what we do not yet have, we wait for it patiently." (Romans 8:24-25)

Self-Control:

- The ability to control oneself, in particular one's emotions and desires or the expression of them in one's behavior, especially in difficult situations.

"For the grace of God has appeared that offers salvation to all people. It teaches us to say "No" to ungodliness and worldly passions, and to live self-controlled, upright and godly lives in this present age." (Titus 2:11-12)

Self-Discipline:

- The ability to control one's feelings and overcome one's weaknesses.

- The ability to pursue what one thinks is right despite temptations to abandon it.

- Self-discipline often means putting off your immediate comfort or wishes in favor of long-term success.

- Similar; self-control, will power, persistence.

"For the moment all discipline seems painful rather than pleasant, but later it yields the peaceful fruit of righteousness to those who have been trained by it." (Hebrews 12:11)

People are capitalizing on our inability to be patient. For example: on Pandora (Music Service), you can pay to remove all commercials. On the freeway, there are express lanes that rake in tons of money by promising a quicker commute. Why is this?

## NO ONE WANTS TO BE PATIENT NOR WORK FOR WHAT THEY DESIRE ANYMORE.

For instance:

- You may want a nice body but would rather get surgery because you don't want to do the necessary work to get a nice body.

- You may want a better job but would rather skip the interview.

## *THE PROBLEM...* ANYTHING YOU DON'T WORK FOR IS NEVER TRULY YOURS.

When you don't have to work or fight for something you desire, you often won't value or appreciate it. This means it will rapidly depreciate.

Depreciate:

- Diminish in value over a period of time.

In other words, as soon as you get whatever it is you desire, it'll be gone.

For instance, working out and getting fit requires endurance, self-discipline, patience, and dedication. But to get surgery, all you need is the right amount of money and a doctor who's mastered duplication.

> **Side Note:** *Anything being duplicated oftentimes does not last long. The effect will soon fade (depreciate), leaving you to eventually need a re-up.*

Why? If you don't master being patient or self-discipline in the first place, you won't have an incentive (motivation) to maintain what you've gained.

## ON THE OTHER HAND, WHEN YOU INVEST IN WHAT YOU DESIRE, THE VALUE OF THE THING YOU INVESTED IN INCREASES.

It's known that when you work for or invest in something you desire, the value is increased. Externally (to others), as well as internally (to you). As a result, you are more likely to appreciate, take care of (maintain), and put up a fight to keep whatever it is you've gained.

For example, there's a program called Sweat Equity. It acts as a form of assistance to people who cannot afford the down payment on a home. How does it work? I'm glad you asked!

- The person applying for the assistance must earn it by working on the home they wish to purchase.

- The work that person puts into renovating the home increases the home's value.

- The home's increased value later becomes a credit (equal to money) to be used as a down payment for the home.

**Nerd Wallet:** "Sweat equity allows buyers to "earn" their entire down payment by improving a home before purchase, says Danny Gardner, senior vice president of affordable lending at Freddie Mac. Buyers do the work themselves, and the change in appraised value after the renovations becomes a credit they can apply to the purchase." (Buczynski, 2019)

**Sweat Equity:**

- An interest or increased value in a property earned from labor toward upkeep or restoration.

- A party's contribution to a project in the form of labor, as opposed to financial equity such as paying others to perform the task.

To go more in-depth, because the person in the above-referenced example valued their dream of owning a home, they invested in it (fought for it). In return, the value of the home itself increased. Externally (to the loan advisors/appraiser), as well as internally (to the one purchasing the home).

Why is all of this so important?

## SIMPLE ANSWER: ANYTHING WORTH FIGHTING FOR IS WORTH KEEPING!

When you've worked hard, putting blood, sweat, and tears into something, it gives you an incentive (motivation) to fight if opposition comes your way or someone tries to take what you've worked for.

> **Side Note:** *God wants you to learn how to persevere no matter what comes your way. Earning or working for what you desire teaches you how to do just that!*

## HAVE YOU BEEN MOVING TOO FAST TRYING TO GET WHAT YOU WANT WITHOUT HAVING THE NEW HEART AND GOOD CHARACTER THAT'S NEEDED TO TAKE HOLD OF AND KEEP WHAT YOU'VE WORKED HARD FOR (TO PERSEVERE)?

So many people miss out on the blessings God wants to give them simply because, as humans, we oftentimes move too fast and are impatient. It was the same with Moses. He died before entering the promised land (receiving the blessing) because he ignored God's command and rushed, striking a rock out of anger, which are signs of impatience.

"Take the rod; and you and your brother Aaron assemble the congregation and speak to the rock in front of them, so that it will pour out its water. In this way you shall bring water for them out of the rock and let the congregation and their livestock drink [fresh water]." So Moses took the rod from before the Lord, just as He had commanded him; and Moses and Aaron gathered the assembly before the rock. Moses said to them, "Listen now, you rebels; must we bring you water out of this rock?" Then Moses raised his hand [in anger] and with his rod he struck the rock twice [instead of speaking to the rock as the Lord had commanded]. And the water poured out abundantly, and the congregation and their livestock drank [fresh water]. But the Lord said to Moses and Aaron, "Because you have not believed (trusted) Me, to treat Me as holy in the sight of the sons of Israel, you therefore shall not bring this assembly into the land which I have given them." (Numbers 20:8-12)

**Signs of Impatience:**

- **Mind Tools:** "How do you know when you're being impatient? You will probably experience one or more of the following symptoms:

  - Shallow breathing (short breaths).

  - Muscle tension.

  - Hand clenching/tightening.

  - Jiggling/restless feet.

  - Irritability/anger.

- Anxiety/nervousness.

- Rushing.

- Snap/quick decisions." (How to Be Patient; Staying Calm Under Pressure)

**The Problem:**

• Things had changed. God no longer wanted Moses to perform miracles (strike the rock) as he had done before. He wanted Moses to be the blessing he was called to be (speak to the rock in front of a large crowd).

**Here's a little background on Moses to help you further understand the illustration:** When God told Moses to go to Egypt and speak to Pharaoh, demanding he set the Israelites free, Moses did not want to go. His reasoning: he had a problem—speaking in front of large crowds. "Look! "The cry of the people of Israel has reached me, and I have seen how harshly the Egyptians abuse them. Now go, for I am sending you to Pharaoh. You must lead my people Israel out of Egypt." (Exodus 3:9-10) "But Moses pleaded with the LORD, "O Lord, I'm not very good with words. I never have been, and I'm not now, even though you have spoken to me. I get tongue-tied, and my words get tangled." Then the Lord asked Moses, "Who makes a person's mouth? Who decides whether people speak or do not speak, hear or do not hear, see or do not see? Is it not I, the Lord? Now go! I will be with you as you speak, and I will instruct you in what to say." But Moses again pleaded, "Lord, please! Send anyone else." (Exodus 4:10-13)

This means God was all along trying to get Moses to face and conquer the thing he was most afraid of, speaking, not necessarily to the rock, but in front of a large crowd.

God was trying to make Moses "the" blessing by using the wilderness as a testing ground to build his character for who he was initially called to be.

If Moses had done as the Lord had commanded, he would have had the opportunity to show the people of Israel what it meant to be a living example of Deuteronomy 31:6. "Be strong and courageous, do not be afraid or tremble in dread before them, for it is the Lord your God who goes with you. He will not fail you or abandon you." (Deuteronomy 31:6).

## ARE YOU LIKE MOSES, ONLY SEEKING MIRACLES WHEN GOD'S TRYING TO MAKE YOU A BLESSING? "I WILL MAKE YOU INTO A GREAT NATION, AND I WILL BLESS YOU; I WILL MAKE YOUR NAME GREAT, AND YOU WILL BE A BLESSING." (GENESIS 12:2)

I was the same as Moses at one point in time. In fact, it was while I was writing this very book. I didn't know what to do. I didn't believe I was a "real" writer. But I believed God had called me to do it, so I did it. I sat in a room at my grandmother's home, pulled out my iPhone 6, and simply started writing about the things God had placed on my heart. And yes, you read that right. This book was drafted on an iPhone 6, which means anything is possible.

After only writing the first draft, I thought it was time to publish the book. I thought my work was done!

I figured I'd get someone else to do the rest of the work. Throw the book out there. And God would send me a miracle. Enabling the book to miraculously, without much effort, do well and sell. But this was not the case!

I presented the book to the world by creating a crowdfunding campaign, and the campaign flopped. I was frustrated and didn't understand why this had happened. Everything people had preached about said God will provide a miracle; you need only to believe.

Well, I know now that is not the whole story because it is not how my story ended.

After I had finished the first draft of the book and put it out there for the world to see, there was still a lot of work needing to be done, and I had to be the one to do it. I had to become the blessing God called me to be by being consistent and writing on the days I had scheduled for myself to do so, even when I had anxiety and felt like I was not good at it.

‖‖‖‖‖‖‖‖‖‖‖‖‖‖‖‖‖‖‖‖‖‖‖‖‖‖‖‖‖‖‖‖‖‖‖‖‖‖‖‖‖‖‖‖‖‖‖‖‖‖‖‖‖‖‖‖‖‖‖‖‖‖‖‖‖‖‖‖‖‖‖‖‖‖

"Potential is revealed in the process."

— *Steven Furtick*

‖‖‖‖‖‖‖‖‖‖‖‖‖‖‖‖‖‖‖‖‖‖‖‖‖‖‖‖‖‖‖‖‖‖‖‖‖‖‖‖‖‖‖‖‖‖‖‖‖‖‖‖‖‖‖‖‖‖‖‖‖‖‖‖‖‖‖‖‖‖‖‖‖‖

When I first began writing, I had terrible anxiety. But as I continued to write, I became hopeful and confident in myself, confident in God. The journey, or should I say the process of me having to draft, revise, and edit this book is what helped develop my character (my confidence and skills as a writer), making myself and this book more than a miracle. This process has prepared each to be a blessing.

> **Side Note:** *You must stick with God throughout your journey and be planted and rooted (dedicated) to the thing you are hoping for to produce the results you desire. For example, I had to continuously spend time alone with God to have the chapters and purpose of this book be revealed to me over time. I also had to become dedicated to progressively becoming a better writer to finish each chapter and complete this book. In the Bible, this process is called sowing and reaping. "Do not be deceived: God cannot be mocked. A man reaps what he sows." (Galatians 6:7)*

## THERE IS A PROCESS TO PROMISE, BUT YOU MUST BECOME A BLESSING INSTEAD OF ONLY SEEKING MIRACLES IN ORDER TO RECEIVE WHAT YOU DESIRE.

Some of you may be reading the last passage and thinking, "what's the difference? I thought miracles and blessings were both gifts given to us by God!"

In short, a miracle is often short-lived or temporary. Blessings, on the other hand, are prepared over time before being received; they are "long-lasting".

> **Side Note:** *Being Saved or Salvation is a miracle because it happens instantly. Sanctification is a blessing because it's an ongoing process.*

To explain further, a miracle comes instantly, but it often does not produce long-lasting results. Why? Well, the issue is not with God; His miracles and blessings are both wonders of this world. The problem lies with the person receiving the miracle.

When a person does not go through the proper steps which would teach them how to maintain the miracle they've received from God, the results are often temporary or short-lived. As a result, that person ends up needing God to constantly do all of the work for them, as opposed to working with God to get the job done.

Below, I have prepared some examples to give you an in-depth explanation of the difference between God doing everything for you and you working with God to get things done.

## EXAMPLE OF A MIRACLE:

You want to buy a home. So, you pray to God and say, "Lord, I need some extra money to pay off my current credit card debt so I may be able to afford this home". The next thing you know, God miraculously sends a lump sum of money your way. The money helps you pay off all your current credit card debt. Paying off your existing debt helps bring down your debt-to-income ratio, which ultimately allows you to close the deal on the home of your dreams.

But what happens next is something you did not expect. You never learned how to budget, which means your finances are out of control. You do not know what to do. You also do not know how to or have the determination to fight for the home. After all, it was a miracle, and you did not even have to fight to get it, which means you are not dedicated to it and won't fight to keep it. At this point, you have no choice but to foreclose; you lose the home.

"Why did God let this happen to me?" is probably what you're thinking.

Well, why did this happen to you? It's simple; you received a miracle, but that miracle did not require you to go through a process that would have not only prepared you for that home but also taught you how to maintain and keep it.

What does this mean? God didn't lose the home. You did!

GOD WANTS A PARTNERSHIP WITH YOU. ONE WHERE YOU WORK WITH HIM TO PERFORM BLESSINGS. NOT YOU SIT DOWN BEING LAZY, HAVING HIM DO ALL THE WORK FOR YOU. "BUT BY THE [REMARKABLE] GRACE OF GOD I AM WHAT I AM, AND HIS GRACE TOWARD ME WAS NOT WITHOUT EFFECT. IN FACT, I WORKED HARDER THAN ALL OF THE APOSTLES, THOUGH IT WAS NOT I, BUT THE GRACE OF GOD [HIS UNMERITED FAVOR AND BLESSING WHICH WAS] WITH ME." (1 CORINTHIANS 15:10)

Next, we'll take a deeper look at a blessing.

A blessing prepares you to receive what you are hoping for as well as teaches you how to continue using the methods you learn along the way to produce "long-lasting" results.

We'll use the same scenario as we did when explaining a miracle, purchasing a home. But this time, the illustration will give you a complete view of what it looks like to work with God to achieve the results you desire.

## EXAMPLE OF A BLESSING:

You want to buy a home. The keyword is "want to".

> **Side Note:** *The word "want to" is mentioned in quotation marks because often, when working towards a blessing, you don't always get what you want when you want it. You get what you need to be able to achieve the results that you want.*

So, what is your first step? Well, first, you get your priorities in order. This includes creating a budget that breaks down how you will need to spend your money monthly if you were to purchase a home.

- This method requires patience as it includes paying off your current debt as well as calculating how much money you need in addition to what you already pay in rent to be able to afford the monthly mortgage amount you desire.

So, what does this look like? Well, as I mentioned before, the first thing you should do is create a budget.

Step 1.

Your budget should look something like this:

**December 6ᵗʰ Check: $1,750**

- $25 *Discover Credit Card*

- $50 *Chase Credit Card*

- $100 *American Express Credit Card*

- $100 *Gas*

- $150 *Electricity Bill*

- $75 *Water Bill*

- $150 *Cell Phone Bill*

- $200 *Food*

- $200 *Car Payment*

- $50 *Car Insurance*

- $50 *Hair Cut/ Hair Stylist*

- $25 *Miscellaneous/Home Supplies*

- $100 *Self-Care (something special for yourself - Ex: massage)*

- $50 *Emergency Fund (Ex: car repair, traffic ticket)*

*Money Leftover: $425*

**December 20th Check: $1,750**

- $1,500 *Rent*

- $100 *Gas*

*Money Leftover:* $150

## Step 2.

After you have your budget in place, you can calculate how much money you have in total leftover from your checks for the month.

» In this case, you have $575 leftover for December.

» Write that number down. It will help you keep track of everything you are doing.

## Step 3.

Your next step is to access your credit card portal and write down the total amount owed for each credit card.

» Keep a log of these amounts. You will need them for future reference.

$1,500 **Discover Credit Card**
$1,700 **Chase Credit Card**
$2,500 **Amex Credit Card**

Step 4.

Add the amounts up from step 3 to get a visual of how much money in total you owe in credit card debt.

» For this method, you will only focus on credit card debt, not your car loan or student loans which would take a lot longer to pay off.

$1,500 **Discover Credit Card**
$1,700 **Chase Credit Card**
+ $2,500 **Amex Credit Card**

_____

$5,700 **Total Debt Owed**

**Side Note:** *Remember you do not want to take old baggage into your new home (new life). You want to first clear out the old baggage and then move forward. This enables you to live your new life starting with a clean slate instead of having a road filled with potholes.*

Step 5.

Now that you have figured out the total amount you owe in credit card debt, you can begin to save up to pay off those debts.

» As the money in your savings account accumulates, you can take it and pay each of your debts off one by one, starting with the smallest balance and working your way up.

» For example, if you owe $1,500 on your Discover credit card, you can take whatever you have saved from the additional money you have leftover monthly and pay off that debt.

» In my case, I took the additional money I had leftover from my paychecks every month and put it into a high-yielding savings account (one that gains interest). When the amount totaled, for instance, the $1,500 owed on the Discover credit card, I used the money to pay off that debt in full.

## DEBT CRUSHER FORMULA

| MONTH | INCOME | PREVIOUS SAVINGS + CURRENT SAVINGS | CURRENT SAVINGS - DEBT PAID | SAVINGS TOTAL |
|-------|--------|-----------------|-----------------|---------|
| JAN #1 | $1,750 | $0 + $425 = $425 | N/A | $425 |
| JAN #2 | $1,750 | $425 + $150 = $575 | N/A | $575 |
| FEB #1 | $1,750 | $575 + $425 = $1,000 | N/A | $1,000 |
| FEB #2 | $1,750 | $1,000 + $150 = $1,150 | N/A | $1,150 |
| MAR #1 | $1,750 | $1,150 + $425 = $1,575 | $1,575 - $1,500 (Discover) = $75 | $75 |

As you can see in this scenario, it would take two and a half months to pay off a debt of $1,500. You would continue using this method for however long it takes to pay off all debts.

> **Side Note:** *When using this method, you will not be stressed or overwhelmed because you are not trying to pay off all of your credit card debt at once. You are building momentum by taking small steps and overcoming smaller obstacles as you progress towards a bigger goal (blessing).*

Step 6.

Now for the fun part. After paying off your credit card debt, you can calculate how much you can afford monthly in mortgage payments.

   6a.  Assess your budget to see how much excess money you have leftover per month.

     »  In this case, after paying off all of your credit card debts, you now have $750 leftover per month. How did we get this?

     »  Your savings used to total $575 per month. But, because you've paid off the following credits cards: **Discover** $25 per month, **Chase** $50 per month, and **AMEX** $100 per month, you now have an extra $175 per month that can be used as savings.

6b. Determine how much of the excess money you would like to spend monthly on your mortgage. And how much you would like to keep as permanent savings (investments) for your future.

» In this case, we will say you wouldn't mind spending an extra $400 a month for monthly mortgage purposes.

» This leaves you with $350 per month, which can be used to build a permanent savings account or for investments.

## Step 7.

Now that you know you want to spend $400 per month in addition to the $1,500 you are already paying in rent; you must then put that $400 into a savings account every month; **not touching that money at all.**

» Do this for at least 3-6 months, giving yourself enough time to become disciplined with putting aside the amount of money you've chosen for your desired monthly mortgage.

## Formula:

$1,900 / per month **Desired Mortgage Payment**

- $1,500 / per month **Current Rent Payment**

---

$400 per month **Difference to be put away each month to total "future mortgage payments"**

» If you cannot save the additional amount of money necessary to afford the monthly mortgage (be disciplined), then you should not be purchasing a home for that amount.

**Side Note:** *Purchasing a home is just one scenario. This principle applies to many things you may be trying to accomplish. For example, if you are trying to start a business but cannot set aside the time necessary to work on your business plans, you should not be starting a business.*

Step 8.

Find the perfect home, close the deal, and move in!

**Disclaimer:** I am not a licensed financial counselor; I am speaking from personal experience; experiences that have helped me learn how to be disciplined and consistent with budgeting. This is also the process that helped me prepare to purchase a home.

**THIS PROCESS MAY SEEM LENGTHY, BUT IF YOU ARE PATIENT AND GRATEFUL FOR THE SMALL VICTORIES, THE RESULTS WILL BE WORTH IT BECAUSE THEY ARE "LONG-LASTING".**

Therefore, "do not despise these small beginnings" (Zechariah 4:10), for they fill you with hope which gives you the strength to continue to work toward and fight to keep whatever you are hoping for.

Small victories are very important when it comes to accomplishing anything in life because they not only help you make lifestyle changes as opposed to temporary changes that only last for the moment, but they also produce perseverance, character, and hope (see Romans 5:3). For example, every pound you lose (small victory) while working out will produce hope. That hope will give you the strength to continue to see your way through (persevere) until you reach your weight goal (blessing). It also gives you an incentive (motivation) to maintain your weight (long-lasting results that build character).

**Develop Good Habits:** "Small wins help you feel like you're accomplishing something. If we focus too much on the bigger goals, we'll feel like we will never get there. That's why smaller wins are so important. They give us the motivation to keep on going where it snowballs into the development of the bigger goals." (Scott)

## BLESSINGS ARE BUILT UPON SMALL VICTORIES; SMALL VICTORIES REQUIRE YOU TO BE CONSISTENT, PATIENT, AND DISCIPLINED.

Repetition, discipline, and being consistent over forty years are what prepared the Israelites for the blessings God had in store for them.

Repetition:

- The recurrence of an action or event.

Consistency:

- Steadfast adherence to the same principles, course, form, etc.

"Then the Lord said to Moses, "Behold, I will cause bread to rain from heaven for you; the people shall go out and gather a day's portion every day, so that I may test them [to determine] whether or not they will walk [obediently] in My instruction (law). And it shall be that on the sixth day, they shall prepare to bring in twice as much as they gather daily [so that they will not need to gather on the seventh day]." (Exodus 16:4-5)

The Israelites didn't eat manna (bread) for forty years in the wilderness because God wanted to torment them. "The Israelites ate manna forty years, until they reached an inhabited land; they ate the manna until they came to the border of the land of Canaan." (Exodus 16:35)

They ate manna for forty years in the wilderness because God was taking them through a process that would teach them the importance of patience. This included them being consistent as they listened to His voice, followed His commands, and worked for what they wanted.

**Side Note:** *God's children are not exempt from going through the processes of life, although they are guaranteed victory. To explain further, no matter what you may be trying to accomplish in life; start a business, get a promotion at work, acquire a bachelor's degree, or even write a book, you must still go through whatever process is required to accomplish said thing, just as everyone else. The only difference is that you know who's in control of your story (God), which means you know how your story ends (in victory).*

## GOD SENT THE ISRAELITES OUT TO THE BASKETBALL COURT TO PRACTICE BEFORE HE SENT THEM OUT TO PLAY FOR AND WIN THE CHAMPIONSHIP RING; IT WAS A PROCESS.

The Israelites may not have known it, but each battle they fought while journeying through the wilderness was a part of a process that prepared them to knock down the walls of Jericho and take hold of their blessings.

They went out for six days to pick up manna. They rested on the seventh day. When it was time to knock down the walls of Jericho, they did something very similar. They marched in silence for six days and screamed on the seventh day, knocking down the wall that separated them from their blessings.

"Now Jericho [a fortified city with high walls] was tightly closed because [of the people's fear] of the sons of Israel; no one went out or came in. The Lord said to Joshua, "See, I have given Jericho into your hand, with its king and the mighty warriors. Now you shall march around the city, all the men of war circling the city once. You shall do this [once each day] for six days. Also, seven priests shall carry seven trumpets [made] of rams' horns ahead of the ark; then on the seventh day you shall march around the city seven times, and the priests shall blow the trumpets. When they make a long blast with the ram's horn, and when you hear the sound of the trumpet, all the people shall cry out with a great shout (battle cry); and the wall of the city will fall down in its place, and the people shall go up, each man [going] straight ahead [climbing over the rubble]." (Joshua 6:1-5)

"Then on the seventh day they got up early at daybreak and marched around the city in the same way seven times; only on that day they marched around the city seven times. And the seventh time, when the priests had blown the trumpets, Joshua said to the people, "Shout! For the Lord has given you the city. The city and everything that is in it shall be under the ban [that is, designated to be destroyed as a form of tribute] to the Lord; only Rahab the prostitute and all [the people] who are with her in her house shall [be allowed to] live, because she hid and protected the messengers (scouts) whom we sent. But as for you, keep yourselves [away] from the things under the ban [which are to be destroyed], so that you do not covet them and take some of the things under the ban [for personal gain], and put the camp of Israel under the ban (doomed to destruction), and bring disaster upon it. All the silver and gold and articles of bronze and iron are holy (consecrated) to the Lord; they shall go into the treasury of the Lord." So the people shouted [the battle cry], and the priests blew the trumpets. When the people heard the sound of the trumpet, they raised a great shout and the wall [of Jericho] fell down, so that the sons of Israel went up into the city, every man straight ahead [climbing over the rubble], and they overthrew the city. Then they utterly destroyed everything that was in the city, both man and woman, young and old, and ox and sheep and donkey, with the edge of the sword." (Joshua 6:15-21)

> **Side Note:** *Once the Israelites knocked down the walls which separated them from their blessing (the promised land), they did not immediately fully receive the blessing. They had to continue to use the tools they had learned along the way to clear out the land, city by city.*

When the Israelites entered into their blessing (the promised land), people were still living in the land. This meant that even though the blessing was theirs, they still had to possess it.

"Now Joshua was old and advanced in years, and the Lord said to him, "You have grown old and advanced in years, and very substantial portions of the land remain to be possessed. This is the land that remains: all the regions of the Philistines and all those of the Geshurites; from the Shihor [waterway] which is east of Egypt [at the southern end of Canaan], northward to the border of Ekron (all of it regarded as Canaanite); the five rulers of the Philistines: the Gazite, Ashdodite, the Ashkelonite, the Gittite, the Ekronite; and the Avvite in the south, all the land of the Canaanite, and Mearah that belongs to the Sidonians, as far as Aphek, to the border of the Amorite; and the land of the Gebalite, and all Lebanon, toward the east, from Baal-gad below Mount Hermon to the entrance of Hamath." (Joshua 13:1-5)

**Posses:**

- Have as belonging to one; have as property; to own.

- To control.

- To dominate.

This is why you need to make lifestyle changes that are long-lasting as opposed to making temporary changes that last for a moment. You never know when the skills you have previously learned will come in handy.

Look at it this way: the Israelites are the basketball team the Golden State Warriors. The teams they have to face in the Playoffs are the walls of Jericho. And the Finals is the Promised Land, the reward.

Now even though the Golden State Israelite Warriors have won many Basketball Championships, they still have to continue to practice as well as use the tools they've gained each year to tear down the walls (teams) that separate them from making it to the Finals where they can fully take control of the land (dominate and rule the basketball league).

**To do this, they must:**

- Practice to qualify for the playoffs (be consistent and disciplined)

- During the Playoffs, go city to city using the skills they've gained while practicing to beat every team that stands in the way of them making it to the semi-finals (break through the walls of the promised land).

- Win the semi-finals by beating more teams to advance to the Finals (possess the land).

- Play for and win the Finals. Taking home the title and the ring (fully possess = dominate and rule the land).

> **Side Note:** *After winning the Championship, the Golden State Israelite Warriors can rest until it's time to use those same skills to fight again.*

"So the LORD gave to Israel all the land he had sworn to give their ancestors, and they took possession of it and settled there. And the LORD gave them rest on every side, just as he had solemnly promised their ancestors. None of their enemies could stand against them, for the LORD helped them conquer all their enemies. Not a single one of all the good promises the LORD had given to the family of Israel was left unfulfilled; everything he had spoken came true." (Joshua 21:43-44)

## WHAT ARE YOU DOING IN YOUR DAY-TO-DAY LIFE THAT SEEMS MUNDANE OR IRRELEVANT BUT CAN BE A BLESSING THAT CONTINUES TO KEEP ON BLESSING YOU?

There are many things in life you may be overlooking, thinking they are meaningless. For example, paying your rent on time. It may seem like just another daily duty, but if you are someone who wants to purchase a home, it allows you to practice and prove that you can pay your bills on time.

And we all know practice makes what perfect!

## Practice Makes Perfect:

- Used to convey that regular exercise of an activity or skill is the way to become proficient in it, especially when encouraging someone to persist in it.

By practicing paying your bills on time, you not only prove that you can maintain your finances but you also prove that you are hard-working and dedicated to whatever you choose to set your mind to do. This opens the door for you to successfully start and run your own business, as you can now put to work the skills you've acquired in the previous battle to do so.

> **Side Note:** *Whenever you fight and conquer something in life, there is always something to be gained, which in turn can be used to win the next battle you may come up against.*

David, for example, took Goliath's sword after beating him in a battle. He then used that same sword to win the next battle he had to fight.

**David fights Goliath and wins:** "Then David ran over and pulled Goliath's sword from its sheath. David used it to kill him and cut off his head. When the Philistines saw that their champion was dead, they turned and ran." (1 Samuel 17:51)

**David takes and stores away what he has gained:** "David took the Philistine's head and brought it to Jerusalem; he put the Philistine's weapons in his own tent." (1 Samuel 17:54)

**David uses the weapon he acquired after winning his previous battle to fight his next battle:** "David asked Ahimelech, "Do you have a spear or sword? The king's business was so urgent that

I didn't even have time to grab a weapon!" "I only have the sword of Goliath the Philistine, whom you killed in the valley of Elah," the priest replied. "It is wrapped in a cloth behind the ephod. Take that if you want it, for there is nothing else here." "There is nothing like it!" David replied. "Give it to me!" (1 Samuel 21:8-9)

**BE CAREFUL TO PAY ATTENTION TO, AS WELL AS BE GRATEFUL FOR THE TEST AND BATTLES YOU FACE IN LIFE—THEY ALWAYS HAVE SOMETHING TO GIVE.**

As you can see, learning how to endure, be patient, self-disciplined, consistent, and work for what you desire before being blessed is not easy; but it has its perks.

**WORDS OF WISDOM: STOP TRADING YOUR CURRENT REALITY FOR INSTANT GRATIFICATION AND IMMORTALITY; BE PATIENT AND WAIT ON THE LORD.**

||||||||||||||||||||||||||||||||||||||||||||||||||||||||||||||||||||||||||||||||||||||||||||||||

"Willpower is what separates us from the animals. It's the capacity to restrain our impulses, resist temptation – do what's right and good for us in the long run, not what we want to do right now. It's central, in fact, to civilization."

— *Dr. Roy Baumeister, Ph.D.*

||||||||||||||||||||||||||||||||||||||||||||||||||||||||||||||||||||||||||||||||||||||||||||||||

*Heavenly Father,* I want to first thank you for choosing to work with me. For giving me your grace, and the wisdom necessary to continue to fight each day. Through the ups, through the downs, through the times I've wanted to give up, you've stuck by my side, continuously providing me with just the right amount of strength to continue. Because of you, I have not only grown tremendously, but I've also learned how to persevere and conquer any problem I come up against. For that, I am forever grateful. For you, I am forever grateful.

Without you Lord, I don't know where I would be. So I would like to end this prayer by thanking you for teaching me how to endure patiently.

In Jesus' name, Amen.

# CHAPTER 22

# PROPHETS AND LOSSES

*Many people today have a weakness when it comes to money. "Money hungry" is the term used frequently in today's culture to describe the individual who'd do anything for it. For this reason, God wants to test you on the subject matter of loyalty, greed, and power before allowing you to minister to, help, or serve others. When you emerge from the fire, you will find out whether you're a Prophet or a loss.*

**Matthew 16:26** AMP "For what will it profit a man if he gains the whole world [wealth, fame, success], but forfeits his soul? Or what will a man give in exchange for his soul?"

## ALTRUISM (LOVE), FAITHFULNESS/LOYALTY TESTED:

*God's ability to trust you.*

Altruism:

- Showing a disinterested and selfless concern for the well-being of others.

- Unselfish, self-sacrifice, self-denial, consideration, compassion.

"Therefore, if you have any encouragement from being united with Christ, if any comfort from his love, if any common sharing in the Spirit, if any tenderness and compassion, then make my joy complete by being like-minded, having the same love, being one in spirit and of one mind. Do nothing out of selfish ambition or vain conceit. Rather, in humility value others above yourselves, not looking to your own interests but each of you to the interests of the others." (Philippians 2:1-4)

Faithfulness:

- The quality of being faithful; fidelity.

- Reliable, trusted, or believed.

"Finally, the devil took Jesus up on a very high mountain and showed him all the kingdoms on earth and their power. The devil said to him, "I will give all this to you, if you will bow down and worship me." Jesus answered, "Go away Satan! The Scriptures say: 'Worship the Lord your God and serve only him.' Then the devil left Jesus, and angels came to help him." (Matthew 4:8-11)

**Loyalty:**

- A strong feeling of support or allegiance.

- Faithfulness to commitments or obligations.

"Never let go of loyalty and faithfulness. Tie them around your neck; write them on your heart." (Proverbs 3:3)

When a person is not tested, or their character has not been fully developed before they become successful, they are more prone to making bad decisions when opposition comes their way. For example, if a person who lacks love (is not fully developed) is at risk of losing their riches and a shady deal is presented to them, they are more likely to take it. Why? Because the people whose empires (hearts) are ruled and developed by man as opposed to God will chop down any tree or barter any piece of land to get what they want, to keep what they have.

The thought of that person losing what they have may scare them so much that they'd be willing to do whatever must be done to keep their riches. And I don't mean that in a good way, as in fight for what you have, but kill for what you want.

Some will harm their brother or kill their sister just to keep a piece of a pie that was never truly theirs to begin with. Hunger, which will be discussed more later on in this chapter, can be dangerous. This is why God is testing your heart, your ability to love, your ability to be loyal before allowing you to advance to a place where money, power, and greed can control you and ruin the lives of others.

"Moses said to the people, "Do not be afraid; for God has come in order to test you, and in order that the fear of Him [that is, a profound reverence for Him] will remain with you, so that you do not sin." (Exodus 20:20)

**YOU HAVE MADE IT TO THE END OF THE WILDERNESS. AND ALTHOUGH THE TESTS WHICH ARE MEANT TO DEVELOP YOUR CHARACTER ARE NOT OVER, THE BLESSINGS IF THE RIGHT CHOICES ARE MADE ARE GUARANTEED.**

Let's continue to move forward so you can be blessed and filled with a new character.

The devil knows you pledging allegiance to God means you must distance yourself from him. "No one can serve two masters. For you will hate one and love the other; you will be devoted to one and despise the other. You cannot serve God and be enslaved to money." (Matthew 6:24) For this reason, right at the moment when your testimony is getting ready to be used. When God sees He can trust you to go out and be helpful to other people, the devil will come and try to tempt you with false blessings.

False Blessings:

- A blessing that is rightfully yours to claim but is presented by the wrong person or people, and if accepted, it's for the wrong reasons (selfish gain).

You may be thinking, "Why now? I've already reached the end of the road".

The simple answer is oftentimes when you have fought a long battle and have been hungry for so long (hoping for a dream to come true), there is a tendency for your patience to at the end of the road begin to wear thin. As a result, desperation can creep in, making it easier for you to be manipulated into thinking you only have two options available to choose from.

- **Option #1:** Stop caring whether you eat (possess your dreams) and give up.

- **Option #2:** Do whatever you have to do to be fed (make it to the top), even if that means stepping over and harming others.

**Side Note:** *Hunger can make it easier for an individual to be manipulated into choosing an option that's harmful to themselves and others because they are often weak and or have become numb due to fighting a battle for so long.*

## LONG BATTLE ---> HUNGER ---> WEAKNESS/ NUMBNESS ---> DESPERATION

Hunger:

- A feeling of discomfort or weakness caused by lack of food, coupled with the desire to eat.

- A strong desire or craving.

**Weak:**

- Lacking physical strength and energy.

- Liable to break or give way under pressure.

**Numb:**

- Deprived of the power of sensation.

- Unable to think, feel, or respond normally.

**Desperation:**

- A state of despair, typically one which results in rash or extreme behavior.

To further illustrate, let's say you are a singer, and you are really good at it. But your dream is to be on a stage in front of millions of people, singing uplifting and motivational songs.

Although you have been working hard, trying to get to that stage where you are singing in front of millions, you haven't quite reached your goal.

At this point, you are discouraged and begin to feel as though you will never possess your dreams because every single time you take one step closer, it seems as if opposition always comes knocking at your door: kicking you down.

**Side Note:** *Constantly battling back and forth with opposition can lead to your ability to be patient to decrease as your hunger (level of desperation) rises.*

The next thing you know, a record label comes along and says, "I will give you ten million dollars if you allow XYZ Record Label to take over all creative aspects of your work, including your image".

Now, you don't want to take this deal because deep down inside you know this record label is shady. And let's face it, there are children as well as many other people who look up to you, people who want to be just like you, people who will follow your every move that could be led in a direction that leads to destruction if you were to take this deal.

You take a moment and think to yourself, "if I take this deal, what happens to them; the people that started from the bottom with me, the people who have high hopes of me changing the music industry for the better? If I take this deal, what happens to me?"

You are now at a crossroad, and with only a couple of hours left to deliberate, thoughts, or should I say, temptations start to race through your head. "This may be your only opportunity to get to where you want to be. Take the deal! If anybody gets hurt, it's not your fault. It's the parents' fault who allow their children to follow and look up to you. If you don't take this deal, your dreams will go down the drain. You will have no choice but to give up. You can't make it to where you want to be simply by the grace of God! Just look at how much time and effort you've already invested into your career, yet the results are non-existent. There is no proof that God will bless you now or ever! TAKE THE DEAL!"

In the end, you convince yourself that the only person being harmed if this deal is not taken is you. So, you pick up the pen, sign your name on the dotted line, and take the deal, selling yourself short for the almighty dollar.

## The Problem:

- Because you were so hungry or, as people today would call it, "thirsty" for money, fame, and fortune, you didn't take the time to read the contract's fine print.

### *Fine Print:*

- XYZ Record Label has the authority to change and or manipulate your persona in any way they see fit.

- XYZ Record Label can make you sing songs that are degrading.

- XYZ Record Label can make you dress in provocative clothing.

- XYZ Record Label can use your image to build hatred, create dysfunction and disunity.

- XYZ Record Label **OWNS YOU!**

All of the music you make, the home you live in, and all of the clothes you have are essentially owned by XYZ Record Label. You are living a borrowed life, and for you to keep the home and money you have been given, you must continue to sell yourself, doing exactly what XYZ Record Label says. Living a life they control.

**MANY PEOPLE ARE TRICKED INTO TAKING A DEAL. NOT KNOWING THE CONTRACT ALLOWS THE DEVIL TO CONTROL THEM FOR A LIFETIME.**

Thousands of people are tricked into taking deals from the devil every day. The thought that person may have is, "if I take this deal that makes me rich, the money or fame I gain will solve all of my problems".

Truth is, money, cars, clothes, and fame do not solve all of the problems you face in life. In fact, in many cases, if your mind is corrupt and you can't make good decisions, or you are not disciplined, everything you wished for can quickly become a curse and create more problems.

Look at it this way, if, in the end, you have to slave and work ten times as hard to keep what's been given to you, having no time for your kids or family, money, nor any of the treasures of this world the devil offers to you is the solution. It's the exact opposite. The problem. This is because you've become a slave to those things. Meaning the more you feel like you need money, cars, clothes, and fame, the more power they have over you. As a result, those things begin to control you and your actions. "Don't you realize that you become the slave of whatever you choose to obey? You can be a slave to sin, which leads to death, or you can choose to obey God, which leads to righteous living." (Romans 6:16)

> **Side Note:** *It may take a little longer to get to where you want to go when working with God simply because He prepares those He blesses, and that takes time. But a good thing to remember is that when God prepares you, you don't have to jump through hoops to keep what He has given you, unlike if the devil promises you things in life.*

Words of encouragement: enter by the narrow gate; otherwise, you will take a deal (sell your soul for a shortcut to a better life) and be led down a road that leads to destruction (worshiping the devil). "For the gate is wide and the way is easy that leads to destruction, and those who enter by it are many. For the gate is narrow and the way is hard that leads to life, and those who find it are few." (Matthew 7:13-14)

## WHENEVER YOU TAKE A DEAL FROM THE DEVIL, YOU INADVERTENTLY TAKE A DEAL THAT REQUIRES YOU TO WORSHIP HIM, THUS GIVING HIM THE POWER TO CONTROL YOUR SOUL: MIND, WILL, AND EMOTIONS.

Whenever the devil controls your soul, he controls you, and as a result, he has the authority to use your image (which is power) in any way he sees fit.

Image:

- A physical likeness or representation of a person, animal, or thing, photographed, painted, sculptured, or otherwise made visible.

Power:

- The capacity or ability to direct or influence the behavior of others or the course of events.

- The ability to do something or act in a particular way, especially as a faculty or quality.

> **Side Note:** *People who abuse their power are often being used.*

Some people are not in a place of power because they fought hard to get to where they are or are the right fit for the position. They are in a place of power simply because the devil knows he can easily use them or what they look like to control, influence, or manipulate others.

## THE DEVIL IS AFTER AND WANTS TO CONTROL YOUR IMAGE.

The devil wants the authority to control your image because it is powerful and possesses the ability to influence others. For example, if the devil would've gotten Jesus to worship him (take the deal) as he tried to do in the scripture Matthew 4:8-11, this would have given him the ability to use Jesus' image for evil. Such an act would have caused everyone who looked up to Jesus to be led down the same evil road: worshiping the devil.

What does this have to do with you? Well, if people look up to you, but you are reckless, making decisions solely based on the fact that you are thirsty for money, fame, and fortune, God cannot trust you to lead His people.

As an example, if you have a social media account. Or, say for instance, a YouTube account, and you receive money (take deals) in exchange for you posting videos, influencing people who look up to you into buying a product you have never tried or a product you know does not work means you are untrustworthy.

Side Note: *#Sponsored/#Ad is what some may call it today (using your image for selfish gain), but in the Bible, this little act that may seem harmless is called selling your soul and or leading people astray. Actions such as these will not lead to a blessing from God, nor will they get you into heaven.*

## GOD WILL NOT BLESS THE ACT OF YOU USING THE GIFTS AND TALENTS HE HAS PROVIDED YOU WITH TO BUILD YOUR EMPIRE STATE OF MIND IF IT MEANS THAT IN THE LONG RUN, EVERYONE WHO LOOKS UP TO YOU DIES.

What does this mean? Just as Jesus was led into the wilderness by the Holy Spirit, having to prove His loyalty before He started His ministry, so will you. "Then Jesus, full of the Holy Spirit, returned from the Jordan and was led by the Spirit into the wilderness, where for forty days He was tempted by the devil. He ate nothing during those days, and when they had ended, He was hungry." (Luke 4:1-2)

## GOD HAS TO ALLOW YOU TO BE EMPTY, TO BE HUNGRY, IN ORDER TO SEE WHAT YOU WILL DO TO BE FED.

The wilderness, which includes the good, the bad, and the ugly things you come up against in life, allows God to see if or what you would sell yourself short for.

Will you use what you got to get what you want or consult God to receive what you need? Will you take anything that comes your way simply because there's a dollar sign connected to it? Will you utilize shortcuts to beat the others in the race? Will you use bad judgment and take bribes in exchange for the blessings, talents, and gifts God has given you?

Or, will you be faithful, exhibit good character, and be a good steward, even when you're hungry?

God wants to know prior to Him blessing you how you will use the gifts and talents He's given to you. Will you be selfish, only seeing yourself and what you can gain out of the deals presented to you, or will you be selfless and think of how your decisions could harm or affect others?

**THE DEVIL PRESENTED JESUS WITH A DEAL TO RULE THE WORLD, BUT JESUS WAS MORE CONCERNED ABOUT SAVING THE PEOPLE WHO OCCUPIED THE WORLD. JESUS WAS AND IS ALTRUISTIC.**

When Jesus was at His lowest and very vulnerable (Him being hungry), the devil came and tried to tempt him with false blessings.

**The devil's Plan:** Get Jesus to use the gifts and talents God blessed Him with to lead a Nation of people astray.

**The devil's Reward:** Blessings that God had already promised to Jesus prior to Him even being born. "Listen! You will become pregnant and give birth to a son, and you will name him Jesus. He will be great and will be called the Son of the Most High. The Lord God will give him the throne of King David, his ancestor. He will rule over the people of Jacob (Israel) forever, and his kingdom will never end." (Luke 1:31-33)

**Jesus' Triumph:** Jesus passed the tempting test the devil threw at Him because:

1. He knew right from wrong (discernment). *Chapter Sixteen: Trial and Error*

2. He trusted God (faith). *Chapter Seventeen: Trust Fund*

3. He was disciplined (patient). *Chapter Nineteen: Virtual Reality of Patience*

4. He was loyal to His mission to save the world and be a benefit to humanity (altruistic—concerned about others). *Chapter Twenty: Prophets and Losses*

"Jesus answered, "Go away Satan! The Scriptures say: 'Worship the Lord your God and serve only him.'" Then the devil left Jesus, and angels came to help him." (Matthew 4:10-11)

Instead of Jesus giving in to selfish desires and taking something that would relieve His stress at that moment (benefit Him and Him only). He waited on God to give Him what was rightfully His and for the right reasons (to benefit/save the world).

**Side Note:** *Right after Jesus passed the test of loyalty, greed, and power, He was then helped by the angels and could go about being the blessing He was always destined to be.*

**The Ministry of Jesus Begins:** "When Jesus heard that John had been put in prison, he went to Galilee. But instead of staying in Nazareth, Jesus moved to Capernaum. This town was beside Lake Galilee in the territory of Zebulun and Naphtali. So God's promise came true, just as the prophet Isaiah had said, "Listen, lands of Zebulun and Naphtali, lands along the road to the sea and across the Jordan. Listen Galilee, land of the Gentiles! Although your people live in darkness, they will see a bright light. Although they live in the shadow of death, a light will shine on them." Then Jesus started preaching, "Turn back to God! The kingdom of heaven will soon be here." (Matthew 4:12-17)

As you continue to journey through life, there will be deals presented to you by the wrong people. And although it may seem like the right decision to take the deal, because the blessings are rightfully yours, you need to ask yourself before making your decision. Will this deal only benefit me (lead others into darkness), or will this deal help save lives (free others from darkness)?

Before you decide, there is one last thing you need to know. Your choice determines your eternity.

## TAKE THE DEAL: GAIN THE WORLD YET LOSE YOUR SOUL (LOSS). OR BE ALTRUISTIC LIKE JESUS: RECEIVE THE KINGDOM AND THE CROWN OF LIFE (PROPHET).

||||||||||||||||||||||||||||||||||||||||||||||||||||||||||||||||||||||||||||||||||||||||||||||||

"Every man must decide whether he will walk in the light of creative altruism or in the darkness of destructive selfishness."

**— *Dr. Martin Luther King Jr.***

||||||||||||||||||||||||||||||||||||||||||||||||||||||||||||||||||||||||||||||||||||||||||||||||

*Heavenly Father,* I would like to thank you for allowing me to struggle through these trials that I have faced. I can see how every obstacle has developed my character, making me stronger than ever. I am not who I once was, and that is because you believed in me. You saw my potential when no one else did. You've helped me unearth a person I never knew I could be. As I continue on this journey that develops my character, I pray that I remain loyal to you and the purpose you have placed in my heart.

In Jesus' name, Amen.

# PART SEVEN THE PURPOSE

# CHAPTER 23

# HEALING AGENT OF LIGHT: FOR BETTER OR WORSE

*You've come a long way, and the journey has not been easy. Whatever your situation is and whatever you have been through, know it has prepped and prepared you to become a better person. But before you can create a better future for yourself and the world we live in, you need to first change how you think about the things you see or have seen in life.*

**Luke 11:34-35** NLT "Your eye is like a lamp that provides light for your body. When your eye is healthy, your whole body is filled with light. But when it is unhealthy, your body is filled with darkness. Make sure that the light you think you have is not actually darkness."

 In this chapter, you are going to be working backward again. This time, you'll focus on your mind because it is a terrible thing to waste, right?

Throughout this journey, God has been working on and changing your heart. The reason for this was so He'd be able to transform your mind and your perspective, thus changing your life and the world.

## HEALTHY VISION (MINDSET) = HEALTHY THOUGHTS (OUTLOOK) = PROSPEROUS LIFE

Perspective:

- An attitude toward or way of regarding something; a point of view.

All aspects of your life need to be changed; meaning heart and mind, because the way you feel (heart posture) often leads to how you think (mindset), which leads to the way you see things in life (perspective), eventually leading to the words you speak and actions you produce. For this reason, you needed the light, which is God's vision. And truth, to expose your old flawed mindset, to change your negative outlook to a positive one.

||||||||||||||||||||||||||||||||||||||||||||||||||||||||||||||||||||||||||||||||||||||||||||||||||||||

"Darkness cannot drive out darkness only light can do that."

— *Dr. Martin Luther King Jr.*

||||||||||||||||||||||||||||||||||||||||||||||||||||||||||||||||||||||||||||||||||||||||||||||||||||||

Over the years, society has developed new ways to teach people how to be masterful in covering up bad behaviors and old flawed mindsets. "But everything exposed by the light becomes visible, for everything that is illuminated becomes a light itself." (Ephesians 5:13) That's one of the many purposes of this book. To reveal your sinful nature, which, in turn, helps you turn your sinful nature into righteous behavior.

### TRUTH AND LIGHT ARE NOT MEANT TO HARM YOU. THEY'RE MEANT TO HELP YOU.

Truth is love, so it does not tell the world about your flaws nor expose your mistakes or problems like the tabloid and gossip columns do. Instead, this truth helps you change from within. That's what any good sermon, pastor, spiritual book, or friend would do. If the light lives within them, in the work they do, or even in you, it will reveal truth and help others who are on a dark road become a light of hope.

### THE DEVIL IS AFTER YOUR LIGHT!

Often, we don't realize the obstacles we currently face in life are due to a foundation of bad mindsets that were created before we were born. The matters of the heart, your belief system that's tainted. You didn't even realize that the devil was working on you at a young age, trying to sift you from the start. "Simon, Simon (Peter), listen! Satan has demanded permission to sift [all of] you like grain; but I have prayed [especially] for you, that your faith [and confidence in Me] may not fail; and you, once you have turned back again [to Me], strengthen and support your brothers [in the faith]." (Luke 22:31-32).

The frame of mind I developed that made me think love didn't exist in this world started when I lost my dad at the age of four. This same mindset which continued for nearly twenty years, changed my whole outlook on life as it eventually led to fear, anger, and hate towards others.

With that being said, it's important for you to understand you will need time to develop new positive thoughts because the work that has been done, the imaginations in the mind, didn't just pop up nor magically appear yesterday.

**THE DEVIL PLACED DOUBT IN YOUR MIND BEFORE YOU EVEN KNEW IT. HE PLACED HURT AND HATRED IN YOUR HEART BEFORE YOU WERE OLD ENOUGH TO BE TAUGHT HOW TO LET GO, HOW NOT TO CONSUME IT.**

Final Call – Willie Lynch Letter: "Gentlemen, you know what your problems are; I do not need to elaborate. I am not here to enumerate your problems, I am here to introduce you to a method of solving them. In my bag here, I have a full proof method for controlling your black slaves. I guarantee every one of you that, if installed correctly, it will control the slaves for at least three hundred years. My method is simple. Any member of your family or your overseer can use it. I have outlined a number of differences among the slaves; and I take these differences and make them bigger. I use fear, distrust, and envy for control purposes.

These methods have worked on my modest plantation in the West Indies and it will work throughout the South. Take this simple little list of differences and think about them. On top of my list is "AGE," but it's there only because it starts with an "a." The second is "COLOR" or shade. There is intelligence, size, sex, sizes of plantations, status on plantations, attitude of owners, whether the slaves live in the valley, on a hill, East, West, North, South, have fine hair, course hair, or is tall or short. Now that you have a list of differences, I shall give you an outline of action, but before that, I shall assure you that distrust is stronger than trust and envy stronger than adulation, respect, or admiration. The Black slaves after receiving this indoctrination shall carry on and will become self-refueling and self-generating for hundreds of years, maybe thousands. Don't forget, you must pitch the old black male vs. the young black male, and the young black male against the old black male. You must use the dark skin slaves vs. the light skin slaves, and the light skin slaves vs. the dark skin slaves. You must use the female vs. the male, and the male vs. the female. You must also have white servants and overseers [who] distrust all Blacks. But it is necessary that your slaves trust and depend on us. They must love, respect, and trust us only. Gentlemen, these kits are your keys to control. Use them. Have your wives and children use them, never miss an opportunity. If used intensely for one year, the

slaves themselves will remain distrustful. Thank you, gentlemen."
(Willie Lynch Letter: The Making of a Slave)

This letter was said to be written in the year 1712 by Willie Lynch, a British slave owner. He used these methods to develop certain mindsets within the Black race, leaving a nation of people damaged for many years to come.

Mindset:

- The established set of attitudes held by someone. A set of assumptions, methods, or notations held by one or more people or groups of people. A mindset can also be seen as incident of a person's worldview or philosophy of life.

Frame of Mind:

- A particular mood that influences one's attitude or behavior. Mental attitude or outlook. Synonyms: mood, state of mind, emotional state, temper, spirit, vein, attitude, perspective, condition, persuasion.

Some of the mindsets we struggle with today can be classified as assumptions, pessimism, doubt, and unbelief, which eventually lead to envy, hate, anger, entitlement, disappointment, or fear.

These things can not only live in your heart but can also take over your mind. Tricking you into believing that anger and hatred are justifiable if you have been wronged. Or make you hate one another in general.

**SOCIETY HAS DESENSITIZED US!**

**Desensitized:**

- Having been made less sensitive.
- Having been made less likely to feel shock or distress at scenes of cruelty or suffering by overexposure to such images.

You were taught to fight one another and take what someone else has but little do you know. We are all caught up in the same system called the caste.

**Caste:**

- Synonyms: class, social class, order, social order, social division, grade, grading, group, grouping, station, stratum, echelon, rank, level, degree, set, place, standing, position, status, varna, estate, sphere.

The craziest part about it all is the oppressors and hateful people such as Willie Lynch, the people who set up certain systems designed for you to fail, don't even have to do much work now. The Thirteenth Amendment, The Making of a Slave, and Jim Crow Laws have already made the slave and branded them.

But that's all about to change because you will be the one to change it! Let's get down to business. You have some digging to do!

## THE IMPORTANCE OF GOD HAVING ACCESS TO AND TRANSFORMING YOUR MIND EXPLAINED:

"A good tree produces good fruit, and a bad tree produces bad fruit. A good tree can't produce bad fruit, and a bad tree can't produce good fruit. So, every tree that does not produce good fruit is chopped down and thrown into the fire. Yes, just as you can identify a tree by its fruit, so you can identify people by their actions." (Mathew 7:17-20)

## THE FRUIT OF THE LABORER LEADS TO THE DEVELOPMENT OF A LEADER.

Did you know your vision is light to your path but can also be darkness depending upon how you think about the things you see? It's what leads you to become a great leader or a bad leader.

To explain further, your mind leads to the production of fruit. That fruit is your actions. This means when a seed (word) is planted in the soil (your mind) (Matthew 13:1-23) positive perspective (light) or negative perspective (darkness) develops into good actions or bad actions.

> **Side Note:** *When you give a seed water (your tears, struggles, and pain) along with light (vision, perspective), it grows, but bad soil and darkness cannot produce good fruit.*

The soil is the environment the seed is planted in; therefore, the soil needs to be turned over or dug up and replaced before being able to yield good crops.

To explain further, if the seed is planted in bad soil, good actions/fruit cannot be produced. This means, your mind must be changed before you can start to produce good actions. The reason for this is that no matter how much you receive the Word of God if your mindset is tainted or flawed, you will not be able to properly act upon what's been given to you.

To sum it up, if your outlook on life is negative, no matter how much good is shown or given to you, you will never be able to receive the ultimate blessings God has in store for you simply because darkness will not allow you to see it thus canceling out your ability to accept and receive it.

## WHY IS THIS IMPORTANT? WELL, IT'S BIGGER THAN YOU!

Your ability to receive the Word, produce good fruit (actions), and become a positive role model is vital to the reproduction process of the people who occupy this world. Whatever fruit you produce will lead those that follow you to reproduce that same fruit. If you produce hate because you have a hateful heart or hateful mind, then that hate is what will be reproduced.

Why do you think racism has lasted for so long? It's a mindset or fruit (action) that has been reproduced repeatedly. Eventually, the person who handed down that way of thinking dies but the hate they produced lives on.

To further illustrate, the writings within this book can become a source of good or bad. If I think positively and set my mind on God, the writings will produce positive thoughts and actions within you. But if my thoughts are negative, I can lead you to become a negative person simply because you have read, believed, and followed what I have written. "The unfolding of your words gives light; it imparts understanding to the simple." (Psalm 119:30)

Hence the importance of generational mindsets needing to be torn down before you become a leader.

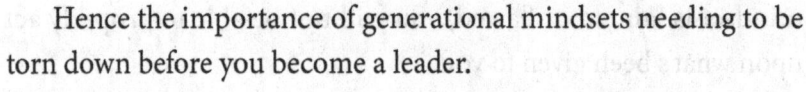

"You can teach what you know but you can only reproduce what you are."

— *Pastor Touré Roberts*

## THE WORD HAS BECOME A LAMP TO GUIDE YOUR FEET. NOW IT'S TIME FOR YOU TO ALLOW IT TO BE A LIGHT FOR YOUR PATH.

**Side Note:** *When your mind is clear, it's because you've set your sight on the truth on positive thoughts. But when your sight is foggy, or you are confused, it's because you've set your mind on false things, such as negative thoughts. Therefore, darkness can take over.*

What thoughts are in your mind that's been taunting you or haunting you? It's time to shine a light on them so that your path can become clear and visible, enabling you to take off towards your hopes and dreams.

We all have problems haunting us. Some people are pessimistic. You only and always see the worst. Or there are the assumers, the individual who judges someone or something without having proof.

**Pessimistic:**

- Tending to see the worst aspect of things or believe that the worst will happen.

**Assumer:**

- Supposed to be the case, without proof.

Or maybe you are someone who's been hurt. Someone who has allowed their past experiences to creep back in and shape the way they see their current situations. You are afraid of your own progress, so you keep taking ten steps back instead of moving forward. You just can't fully believe that God is in control. That He is working things out for your good. That the matters of the past have been washed away.

Maybe it's hard to believe it because the way your life was growing up, you couldn't see it.

Isn't it funny that no matter how much good God produces in your life, there's always this tendency to immediately refer to the past and assume the worst? And not necessarily refer to the past because the past has great deeds in it, but refer to that one tragedy that has happened, overlooking all the progress God has made in you.

"Then Jesus told them, "You are going to have the light just a little while longer. Walk while you have the light, before darkness overtakes you. Whoever walks in the dark does not know where they are going. Believe in the light while you have the light, so that you may become children of light." When he had finished speaking, Jesus left and hid himself from them." **Belief and Unbelief Among the Jews:** Even after Jesus had performed so many signs in their presence, they still would not believe in him." (John 12:35-37) "The Lord said to Moses,

"How long will these people treat me disrespectfully and reject Me? And how long will they not believe in Me, despite all the [miraculous] signs which I have performed among them?" (Numbers 14:11)

**DON'T SET YOURSELF UP FOR FAILURE BECAUSE YOU REFUSE TO SEE THAT THINGS IN LIFE COULD BE DIFFERENT FOR YOU, SIMPLY BECAUSE YOU ARE DIFFERENT, SIMPLY BECAUSE YOU BELONG TO GOD.**

**Side Note:** *Belief opens the door for the Holy Spirit to move in your life. But the Holy Spirit cannot manifest God's Will if you keep allowing your negative perspective to kill what He has instilled.*

The Israelites wandered for 40 years in the wilderness because even though they had been rescued from slavery, their frame of mind remained the same. They lived in poverty for so long; therefore, they had a tough time believing in the fullness of God's blessings. They'd been oppressed, beaten, overlooked, and undervalued, so it was hard for them to envision themselves overcoming their problems and claiming victory. The Israelites were "free slaves"! Meaning their bodies were no longer bound and in chains, but their minds were. Therefore, when their vision became clouded with problems, they could no longer see what they hoped for. This led them to stop dreaming, stop believing, and lose hope.

Some of you have developed this same astigmatism.

Astigmatism:

- A common vision condition that causes blurred vision.

The Israelites focused solely on their circumstances and all of the reasons why they thought they could not move forward in life. Every time God strengthened their faith, they found another reason not to believe.

> **Side Note:** *Roadblocks become steppingstones for you to place your foot on and elevate upwards. But if you focus solely on the roadblock, it will become a blur as you move closer to it. Instead of the roadblock becoming a steppingstone, it will become a stumbling block leading you to fall. "But he turned and said to Peter, "Get behind me, Satan! You are a stumbling block to me, because you are not setting your mind on God's interests, but on man's." (Matthew 16:23)*

## ARE YOU STILL ALLOWING THE PAIN OF YOUR PAST TO OVERSHADOW AND FALSELY WHISPER SWEET NOTHINGS INTO YOUR FUTURE?

"After exploring the land for forty days, the men returned to Moses, Aaron, and the whole community of Israel at Kadesh in the wilderness of Paran. They reported to the whole community what they had seen and showed them the fruit they had taken from the land. This was their report to Moses: "We entered the land you sent us to explore, and it is indeed a bountiful country—a land flowing with milk and honey. Here is the kind of fruit it produces. But the people living there are powerful, and their towns are large and fortified. We even saw giants there, the descendants of Anak! The Amalekites live in the Negev, and the Hittites, Jebusites, and Amorites live in the hill country. The Canaanites live along the coast of the Mediterranean Sea and along the Jordan Valley." But Caleb tried to quiet the people as they stood before Moses. "Let's go at once to take the land," he said. "We can certainly conquer it!" But the other men who had explored the land with him disagreed. "We can't go up against them! They are stronger than we are!" So they spread this bad report about the land among the Israelites: "The land we traveled through and explored will devour anyone who goes to live there. All the people we saw were huge. We even saw giants there, the descendants of Anak. Next to them we felt like grasshoppers, and that's what they thought, too!" (Numbers 13:25-33)

> **Side Note:** *The Israelites saw giants and immediately forgot God! You see problems and immediately forget God! Problems are overshadowing your view of who God is.*

The physical giants the Israelites saw reminded them of their bad days in Egypt. Therefore they thought they were fighting battles on the battlefield again. And because of their problems, they didn't see they were really fighting battles within the mind. It's the same with you today. The good report is fighting with the bad report. If not careful, the sight of problems can make you double-minded. And, "That person should not expect to receive anything from the Lord. Such a person is double-minded and unstable in all they do." (James 1:7-8).

"Elijah came near to all the people and said, "How long will you hesitate between two opinions? If the LORD is God, follow Him; but if Baal, follow him." But the people did not answer him a word." (1 Kings 18:21)

## APART OF YOU WOULD LIKE TO BELIEVE THE GOOD REPORT, BUT IT SEEMS THE ODDS ARE STACKED IN THE BAD REPORT'S FAVOR, THUS MAKING YOU THINK THE NEGATIVE IS WHAT YOU SHOULD ACCEPT.

Twelve Israelite men were sent out to explore the promised land. Ten brought back a bad report, while only two brought back good. But get this, the ten men who believed the bad report, bringing back bad news, died in their circumstances. "As for the men whom Moses sent to spy out the land, and who returned and made all the congregation murmur and complain against him by bringing back a bad report concerning the land, even those [ten] men who brought back the very bad report of the land died by a plague before the Lord." (Numbers 14:36-37)

The ten Israelite men who brought back bad news did not make it to the promised land simply because they became a stumbling block (distraction) and darkness to the people of Israel instead of a light of hope.

Remember, to become a positive role model and leader; you need light which is a positive perspective. Without it, you'll kill everything around you, including yourself.

## Thinking Poem by Walter D. Wintle

*"If you think you are beaten, you are*

*If you think you dare not, you don't,*

*If you like to win, but you think you can't*

*It is almost certain you won't.*

*If you think you'll lose, you're lost*

*For out of the world we find,*

*Success begins with a fellow's will*

*It's all in the state of mind.*

*If you think you are outclassed, you are*

*You've got to think high to rise,*

*You've got to be sure of yourself before*

*You can ever win a prize.*

*Life's battles don't always go*

*To the stronger or faster man,*

*But soon or late the man who wins*

*Is the man WHO THINKS HE CAN!"*

**THE KNIFE IN YOUR CHEST WILL ONLY CON-TINUE TO HURT YOU IF YOU REFUSE TO TAKE IT OUT. GOD CAN STOP THE BLEEDING, BUT YOU MUST FIRST REMOVE THE KNIFE.**

Because your life started out rocky and statistics say you won't make it, it can make every decision or thought an assumption of the worst, disbelief. Assumptions is the knife in your chest because disbelief kills dreams and hope. When hope is lost, that leads to complaints and anger, which leads to the walls in your heart being built up again.

This will either prolong the dreams of your future or make you give up, killing those dreams altogether. "And "don't sin by letting anger control you." Don't let the sun go down while you are still angry, for anger gives a foothold to the devil." (Ephesians 4:26-27)

Sometimes heartache can make you angry and bitter, but that's a trap. Because anger will only cause you to begin to inflict the same pain you've suffered onto others, turning you into a hypocrite.

**ASSUMPTIONS AND DWELLING ON THE PAST WILL MAKE YOU ANGRY, KILLING THE LIGHT OF YOUR FUTURE.**

Let's look at it this way. You assume someone is cheating on you; therefore, all you think and talk about is the assumption of that such thing. The light that you give that assumption brings it to life, and eventually, what you assumed the devil tries to use against you. The assumption may not even be valid or relevant. That's why it's called an assumption. But because you gave it breath, you gave it life. "The tongue can bring death or life; those who love to talk will reap the consequences." (Proverbs 18:21)

> **Side Note:** *You can kill your chances of a good relationship simply because you have a negative way of seeing things in life. That way of seeing things eventually leads to disbelief and negative words being spoken.*

## ARE YOU TRADING YOUR POWER FOR THE PAIN OF YOUR PAST?

God has given you power, and that power lies within the choices you make; it's in the words you speak. In other words, there is life in the light of Jesus, which is in you. So if you are bringing light to your negative thoughts by the way you speak, you give negativity power to live.

The only way the devil can have your power is if you willingly give it up.

It's not easy to choose to put away negative words, assumptions, and thoughts, but it is possible.

**WHEN CHOOSING TO FIGHT NEGATIVITY AND TAKE BACK YOUR POWER, YOU MUST DO MORE THAN BEAT THE ODDS. YOU NEED TO CHANGE THEM!**

The first thing you need to do to change the odds is allow your trials to help you be better than your past self, changing inwardly.

You can accomplish changing inwardly by:

- Continuing to talk about the negative thoughts you've been having with God.

- Continuing to read the Word, which is not just the Bible. It's books that people have written through the power of the Holy Spirit.

- Continuing to stay connected to God by being in His presence (abide in Him, and He'll abide in you).

- Continuing to call on the Holy Spirit (the Spirit of ease and helper) to be directed towards what you need to change.

- Continuing to pray.

For further encouragement, let the life you have left be the motivation that helps you choose to change within.

Secondly, to change the odds, you need to take and use what the devil has been trying to use against you and turn it around for good. For me, it's the loss of my dad, the incarceration of my loved one, and my family's pain that the devil has been trying to use against me.

As you can see, the devil wanted to try to use the problems and pain mentioned above to take me out. But because God allowed me to see my problems differently, the pain has been used to first off and, most importantly, develop a loving heart towards others in me. Secondly, the problems and pain motivated me to create the concept for Destiny Revealed, a training and re-entry program for individuals impacted by incarceration, unemployment, homelessness, and broken homes. Thirdly, the problems and pain have lit a fire in me. That fire has fuelled me with enough strength to produce this book which helps others overcome their pain. To sum it up...

## YOU HAVE TO CHANGE THE WAY YOU SEE YOUR PROBLEMS, SO YOU CAN CHANGE THE WAY YOU BEAT YOUR PROBLEMS!

"The Lord took hold of me, and I was carried away by the Spirit of the Lord to a valley filled with bones. He led me all around among the bones that covered the valley floor. They were scattered everywhere across the ground and were completely dried out. Then he asked me, "Son of man, can these bones become living people again?" "O Sovereign Lord," I replied, "you alone know the answer to that." Then he said to me, "Speak a prophetic message to these bones and say, 'Dry bones, listen to the word of the Lord! This is what the Sovereign Lord says: Look! I am going to put breath into you and make you live again! I will put flesh and muscles on you and cover you with skin. I will put breath into you, and you will come to life. Then you will know that I am the Lord.'" So I spoke this message, just as he told me. Suddenly as I spoke, there was a rattling noise all across the valley. The bones of each body came together and attached themselves as complete skeletons. Then as I watched, muscles and flesh formed over the bones. Then skin formed to cover their bodies, but they still had no breath in them. Then he said to me, "Speak a prophetic message to the winds, son of man. Speak a prophetic message and say, 'This is what the Sovereign Lord says: Come, O breath, from the four winds! Breathe into these dead bodies so they may live again.'" So I spoke the message as he commanded me, and breath came into their bodies. They all came to life and stood up on their feet—a great army." (Ezekiel 37:1-10)

Notice that what the prophet saw was negative. The bones were already dead. But because he chose to believe in what the Lord told him was true, it allowed him to speak positively, allowing the bones to come to life.

**Side Note:** *Your situation may look dead, but if you believe in what God has told you, it will give you the strength to continue to call the things in your life which look like they are dead what God told you they would be.*

## CONTINUE TO FOCUS ON YOUR GOALS AND WHAT YOU ARE HOPING FOR. SPEAK POSITIVE WORDS INTO YOUR SITUATION.

If you focus on the goal ahead of you, you will grow closer to it. If you focus on what's behind you or your problems, you will continuously be pulled back and away from your goal. "Look straight ahead and fix your eyes on what lies before you. Mark out a straight path for your feet; stay on the safe path. Don't get sidetracked; keep your feet from following evil." (Psalm 4:25-27)

For instance, don't look at your current living situation look at the goal of buying a home. Don't look at the circumstances on the job look at the goal of you owning your own business. Tell yourself. I am a homeowner; I am a business owner. Tell yourself other people may not believe they can make it through the struggle, but I am a child of God, so I know I will make it; I know I will win. I may be incarcerated, but I am free. I may not have money, but I am rich through Christ. I may have a drug addiction, but I am healed.

This will lead to your circumstances becoming less visible simply because you're not solely focusing on them. That's how you bring positive light to a situation. By admitting where you are but also confirming where God said you would be. The prophet said dry bones. That was him admitting what the situation looked like on the surface. Then he said you will live. That was him confirming and believing what God told him was true.

In other words, don't simply believe in what you see on the surface. And remember, God works through the one who has faith in the unseen. Don't lose hope either whatever you are hoping for is closer than you think. Start to focus on the good report. The people who have gone before you and won their battles. They are the light and the truth simply because their victories are proof of God's miracles.

You may look at your circumstances and think your prayers are not working or have not been answered, causing you to focus more on your problems, trying to solve them all on your own because you believe God won't. But the progress is not on the outside. The progress is within you. It's your heart posture, character, and faith that have evolved along this journey.

> **Side Note:** *Once you've conquered the spiritual and mental roadblocks in life, becoming faith-full. Then and only then will you be able to see the financial and physical blessings come to pass.*

The prophet was filled with faith which is why he was able to speak the way he did about what he saw. This ultimately led to the blessings forming and coming alive right before his eyes, physical blessings.

So, continue to abide in the Lord and allow your pain to become a healing agent of light throughout the earth, just like the people before you. "For at one time you were darkness, but now you are light in the Lord. Walk as children of light." (Ephesians 5:8) This doesn't mean you necessarily have to be a leader in the area where you had trouble, pain, or problems. It's just saying allow your trouble, pain, and problems to make you humble enough to know that we all suffer and go through trials. Not one person is greater than the other. Also...

## SOMETIMES GOD MUST BREAK YOUR HEART TO SAVE YOUR SOUL, TO SAVE THEIR SOULS; THE PEOPLE CONNECTED TO YOUR DESTINY!

Often God allows you to go through certain trials in life so that when others are faced with those same troubles, you would have the wisdom needed to help. Knowing what it feels like to be them develops compassion in you, empathy, and a good heart. A good heart that you would not be able to obtain if you had not gone through trials and tribulations. I knew what it felt like to be left alone while facing adversity. So, I said to myself, if someone is left alone hurting, I'd be there for them.

> **Side Note:** *God was not trying to harm you by allowing you to face adversity; He wanted to humble you so that He could heal you.*

God knows more than any of us could ever imagine knowing; therefore, He knows that even though hurt people hurt people, and broken people break people, healed people possess the power to heal people! "Because He Himself [in His humanity] has suffered in being tempted, He is able to help and provide immediate assistance to those who are being tempted and exposed to suffering." (Hebrews 2:18)

My heart was broken in so many ways seeing my family members in pain. Knowing there was nothing I could do about it caused me pain. Yet what I didn't realize because the pain was blocking my view is that we often learn through our heartache. In particular, I learned how it felt to be on the other side of the stick—to be the one in need. I learned how it felt to call out, but nobody be there. This, in turn, made me more aware. It showed me how desperately others needed help, how desperately God was needed in this world. It's funny because now someone can look a certain way, and I don't even need to hear them speak, but I can feel the pain. That is what leads to the making of a great leader.

## A GREAT LEADER CAN BE FROM PAIN (HAVE GONE THROUGH IT), SENSE PAIN, AND BE THE SOLUTION TO THE PAIN ALL AT THE SAME TIME.

Trials and tribulations allowed me to see pain in a different light. Pain helps to purge; It's meant to push out pride and hatefulness.

I, at this point, can't look at someone hurting and not see myself (depressed and anxious), my loved one (incarcerated), my mother (a single parent), my brother (suffering with mental health issues), or my grandmother (constantly ill). Because when hurt hits close to home, everyone in the world becomes them. I see them when I see other people hurt. I see me when I see other people hurt. I see our struggles, which makes me want to help and be compassionate towards others. It helps me understand others and them understand me.

## JUST AS GAME RECOGNIZES GAME, PAIN RECOGNIZES PAIN.

It was the same with David before he became king. The Israelites needed to be saved, and trials helped develop a pure heart in David, making him a great king. "But God removed Saul and replaced him with David, a man about whom God said, 'I have found David son of Jesse, a man after my own heart. He will do everything I want him to do." (Acts 13:22) "Then all the tribes of Israel came to David at Hebron and said, "Behold, we are your bone and flesh. In times past, when Saul was king over us, it was you who led out and brought in Israel. And the Lord said to you, 'You shall be shepherd of my people Israel, and you shall be prince over Israel.'" So all the elders of Israel came to the king at Hebron, and King David made a covenant with them at Hebron before the Lord, and they anointed David king over Israel." (2 Samuel 5-8)

David was able to lead the people because he knew what it felt like to run, fight, and struggle. His trials helped him, help them. David would have never wanted to do anything to hurt the people he led, simply because he didn't like how it felt when the pain hit close to home.

And, "No one hates his own body but feeds and cares for it, just as Christ cares for the church." (Ephesians 5:29)

This means if you see yourself in others, the love you have for yourself will manifest into love for them. And in the world that we live in today, I know there are a lot of self-loving people. So, it's not hard to love others. People just choose not to.

To recap, God had to change your heart so that he could change your perspective and your life. How you think determines who you'll become. Another thing I want to leave you with is, do not let other people's actions or your circumstances control your progress with God. Their actions are their own. Let your actions be of God.

God wants you to do better than the people that hurt you. He wants you to be merciful to the people that curse you. "Bless those who curse you, pray for those who mistreat you." (Luke 6:28) Because in the end, you're just a sinner in the hands of a merciful and gracious God just like me, just like them.

||||||||||||||||||||||||||||||||||||||||||||||||||||||||||||||||||||||||||||||||||||||||||||||||||||

"As my sufferings mounted I soon realized that there were two ways in which I could respond to my situation—either to react with bitterness or seek to transform the suffering into a creative force. I decided to follow the latter course."

— *Dr. Martin Luther King Jr.*

||||||||||||||||||||||||||||||||||||||||||||||||||||||||||||||||||||||||||||||||||||||||||||||||||||

## THE LORD HAS USED A FIRE OF INJUSTICES TO LIGHT A LIGHT ON THE INSIDE OF YOU. THROUGH THIS LIGHT, YOU HAVE AN OPPORTUNITY TO BRING HOPE, JOY, AND LOVE TO OTHERS, TO SAVE THE SOULS OF THE LOST.

Will you turn away from bad thoughts or continue to move towards what God is calling you away from. Darkness everybody darkness! Be the light in it, don't let it (darkness) be a spirit that turns into a demon in you.

"You are the light of the world. A town built on a hill cannot be hidden. Neither do people light a lamp and put it under a bowl. Instead they put it on its stand, and it gives light to everyone in the house. In the same way, let your light shine before others, that they may see your good deeds and glorify your Father in heaven." (Matthew 5:14-16)

# HOW WILL YOU USE THE POWER OF YOUR LIGHT—FOR BETTER OR WORSE?

—————————————————————————————————————————

"Your work is to discover who you are and then with all your heart give your light to the world."

— *Jennifer Williamson*

—————————————————————————————————————————

*Heavenly Father,* thank you for healing my mind and giving me the right perspective. "Your word is a lamp for my feet, a light on my path. I have taken an oath and confirmed it, that I will follow your righteous laws. I have suffered much; preserve my life, Lord, according to your word. Accept, Lord, the willing praise of my mouth, and teach me your laws. Though I constantly take my life into my hands, I will not forget your law. The wicked have set a snare for me, but I have not strayed from your precepts. Your statutes are my heritage forever; they are the joy of my heart. My heart is set on keeping your decrees to the very end." (Psalm 119:105-115) May your grace be upon this world, and may the light you have given me be a blessing within it.

In Jesus' name Amen.

# CHAPTER 24

# MASTER PLAN

*Thinking of a master plan, you know everything you need*
*you can ask the man (up above, that is).*

**2 Corinthians 1-10 AMP** "For we know that if the earthly tent [our physical body] which is our house is torn down [through death], we have a building from God, a house not made with hands, eternal in the heavens. For indeed in this house we groan, longing to be clothed with our [immortal, eternal] celestial dwelling, so that by putting it on we will not be found naked. For while we are in this tent, we groan, being burdened [often weighed down, oppressed], not that we want to be unclothed [separated by death from the body], but to be clothed, so that what is mortal [the body] will be swallowed up by life [after the resurrection]. Now He who has made us and prepared us for this very purpose is God, who gave us the [Holy] Spirit as a pledge [a guarantee, a down payment on the fulfilment of His promise].

So then, being always filled with good courage and confident hope, and knowing that while we are at home in the body we are absent from the Lord—for we walk by faith, not by sight [living our lives in a manner consistent with our confident belief in God's promises]—we are [as I was saying] of good courage and confident hope, and prefer rather to be absent from the body and to be at home with the Lord. Therefore, whether we are at home [on earth] or away from home [and with Him], it is our [constant] ambition to be pleasing to Him. For we [believers will be called to account and] must all appear before the judgment seat of Christ, so that each one may be repaid for what has been done in the body, whether good or bad [that is, each will be held responsible for his actions, purposes, goals, motives—the use or misuse of his time, opportunities and abilities]."

When working in my creative element, I learned early on that creating the book's content would be the most important of all. Why? Because the content, as opposed to the beauty of the presentation, would be the thing that eventually kept people coming back.

## FOR EXAMPLE:

### Female Perspective:

- It doesn't matter how good the container a bundle of hair comes in looks when it arrives in the mail. If the hair naps up in less than a week, you will not be a repeat customer.

### Male Perspective:

- If you married a woman because her beauty was music to your eyes, yet she had the worst attitude in the world. That beast within that beauty would overshadow what you thought looked good. The music you once saw eventually becomes death to your ears, which would ultimately lead to divorce because no matter how beautiful she is, if her nagging is UNFORGETTABLE (Nat King Coles Voice), you wouldn't want to stick around.

For this very reason, I learned to first focus on the content that was in the container, more or less what housed it. I had to make sure that the product on the inside of the book had substance before I started to make it look pretty and could present it to the world.

So, what did I do? I wrote (drafted the book), fine-tuned every chapter (edited and revised the book), and after that, I added the pretty pictures that captivate the eye (formatted and did a makeover on the book).

**Side Note:** *What a person looks like is not what pleases the Lord. It's the quality; what's inside that individual's heart that He's concerned with. "But the LORD said to Samuel, "Do not look on his appearance or on the height of his stature, because I have rejected him. For the LORD sees not as man sees: man looks on the outward appearance, but the LORD looks on the heart." (1 Samuel 6:17)*

## HOW DOES THIS RELATE TO YOUR JOURNEY AND GOD'S PURPOSE FOR THE PLANS HE CREATED FOR YOUR LIFE?

Well, if something looks good but functions horribly, it's useless. Stay with me; I'm going somewhere with this.

## GOD DOES NOT CREATE USELESS THINGS!

For this reason, God had to test you before putting you out to see how well you'd function under different types of pressure and in different circumstances. It's the same reason why car manufacturers require their cars to undergo various kinds of tests before a vehicle is sold. They have a two hundred-point checklist. I'm not sure if that's correct; I'm just exaggerating. But why do you think manufacturers try to make the best product possible?

Because you lose money when you put out a bad product, it's a waste of time and energy.

> **Side Note:** *When God is shaping you, He makes sure you have all that you need to function properly in your blessings (family, businesses, finances, etc.) because it's not a waste of His time if you're not ready for your blessings; it's a waste of yours.*

## HOW DOES GOD'S PLAN START?

When God created you and your life, heck, when God created the world, He used a master plan. "For I know the plans I have for you, declares the Lord, plans to prosper you and not to harm you, plans to give you hope and a future." (Jeremiah 29:1)

He mapped out things in such a way that if we as people had followed His instructions, we'd be set for greatness.

**Day 1.** The earth is formless.

"In the beginning God created the heavens and the earth. The earth was formless and empty, and darkness covered the deep waters. And the Spirit of God was hovering over the surface of the waters.

Then God said, "Let there be light," and there was light. And God saw that the light was good. Then he separated the light from the darkness. God called the light "day" and the darkness "night."

And evening passed and morning came, marking the first day." (Genesis 1:1-3)

**Day 2.** God made space to separate heaven and earth.

"Then God said, "Let there be a space between the waters, to separate the waters of the heavens from the waters of the earth." And that is what happened. God made this space to separate the waters of the earth from the waters of the heavens. God called the space "sky."

And evening passed and morning came, marking the second day." (Genesis 1:6-8)

**Day 3.** Fruit is planted, and new creations are developed.

"Then God said, "Let the waters beneath the sky flow together into one place, so dry ground may appear." And that is what happened. God called the dry ground "land" and the waters "seas." And God saw that it was good. Then God said, "Let the land sprout with vegetation—every sort of seed-bearing plant, and trees that grow seed-bearing fruit. These seeds will then produce the kinds of plants and trees from which they came." And that is what happened. The land produced vegetation—all sorts of seed-bearing plants, and trees with seed-bearing fruit. Their seeds produced plants and trees of the same kind. And God saw that it was good.

And evening passed and morning came, marking the third day." (Genesis 1:9-13)

**Day 4.** God calls you to rule over the day. To separate the light from darkness by helping others find the light and purpose that has been placed in them.

"Then God said, "Let lights appear in the sky to separate the day from the night. Let them be signs to mark the seasons, days, and years. Let these lights in the sky shine down on the earth." And that is what happened. God made two great lights—the larger one to govern the day, and the smaller one to govern the night. He also made the stars. God set these lights in the sky to light the earth, to govern the day and night, and to separate the light from the darkness. And God saw that it was good.

And evening passed and morning came, marking the fourth day." (Genesis 1:14-19)

**Day 5.** God provides all that you need to survive.

"Then God said, "Let the waters swarm with fish and other life. Let the skies be filled with birds of every kind." So God created great sea creatures and every living thing that scurries and swarms in the water, and every sort of bird—each producing offspring of the same kind. And God saw that it was good. Then God blessed them, saying, "Be fruitful and multiply. Let the fish fill the seas, and let the birds multiply on the earth."

And evening passed and morning came, marking the fifth day." (Genesis 1:20-23)

**Day 6.** God saw everything He made and said it was very good.

"Then God looked over all he had made, and he saw that it was very good! And evening passed and morning came, marking the sixth day." (Genesis 1:31)

**Day 7.** God rests.

"So, the creation of the heavens and the earth and everything in them was completed. On the seventh day God had finished his work of creation, so he rested from all his work. And God blessed the seventh day and declared it holy, because it was the day when he rested from all his work of creation. This is the account of the creation of the heavens and the earth." (Genesis 2:1-4)

## THEN SOMETHING WENT WRONG.

**The Man and Woman Sin:** "The serpent was the shrewdest of all the wild animals the Lord God had made. One day he asked the woman, "Did God really say you must not eat the fruit from any of the trees in the garden?"

"Of course, we may eat fruit from the trees in the garden," the woman replied. "It's only the fruit from the tree in the middle of the garden that we are not allowed to eat. God said, 'You must not eat it or even touch it; if you do, you will die.'"

"You won't die!" the serpent replied to the woman. "God knows that your eyes will be opened as soon as you eat it, and you will be like God, knowing both good and evil."

The woman was convinced. She saw that the tree was beautiful and its fruit looked delicious, and she wanted the wisdom it would give her. So, she took some of the fruit and ate it. Then she gave some to her husband, who was with her, and he ate it, too. At that moment their eyes were opened, and they suddenly felt shame at their nakedness. So, they sewed fig leaves together to cover themselves.

When the cool evening breezes were blowing, the man and his wife heard the Lord God walking about in the garden. So they hid from the Lord God among the trees. Then the Lord God called to the man, "Where are you?"

He replied, "I heard you walking in the garden, so I hid. I was afraid because I was naked."

"Who told you that you were naked?" the Lord God asked. "Have you eaten from the tree whose fruit I commanded you not to eat?"

The man replied, "It was the woman you gave me who gave me the fruit, and I ate it."

Then the Lord God asked the woman, "What have you done?" "The serpent deceived me," she replied. "That's why I ate it."

Then the Lord God said to the serpent, "Because you have done this, you are cursed more than all animals, domestic and wild. You will crawl on your belly, groveling in the dust as long as you live. And I will cause hostility between you and the woman, and between your offspring and her offspring. He will strike your head, and you will strike his heel."

Then he said to the woman, "I will sharpen the pain of your pregnancy, and in pain you will give birth. And you will desire to control your husband, but he will rule over you."

And to the man he said, "Since you listened to your wife and ate from the tree whose fruit I commanded you not to eat, the ground is cursed because of you. All your life you will struggle to scratch a living from it. It will grow thorns and thistles for you, though you will eat of its grains. By the sweat of your brow will you have food to eat until you return to the ground from which you were made. For you were made from dust, and to dust you will return." (Genesis 3:1-19)

> **Side Note:** *Although God's plans for perfection are still in full effect, those plans have been delayed because of sin and evil. What does this mean? There were and still are some things that must be done before God's plans are fully presented and revealed to the world. What does this have to do with you? Sin leads to hardened hearts. Therefore before revealing you to the world, God had to allow you to be broken so that He could rebuild you.*

Notice in the Old Testament of the Bible, the tablet on which the commandments had been written was broken before the commandments would be put into place, presented to the people (presented as an example to be followed), and used. "When Moses approached the camp and saw the calf and the dancing, his anger burned and he threw the tablets out of his hands, breaking them to pieces at the foot of the mountain." (Exodus 32:19)

The tablet of stone in the Old Testament is a symbolization of your hardened heart in the New Testament of today. "My son, do not forget my teaching, but keep my commands in your heart, for they will prolong your life many years and bring you peace and prosperity.

Let love and faithfulness never leave you; bind them around your neck, write them on the tablet of your heart." (Proverbs 3:1-3)

It symbolizes the temple that needed to be destroyed and rebuilt. "Jesus answered them, "Destroy this temple, and in three days I will raise it up." The Jews then said, "It has taken forty-six years to build this temple, and will you raise it up in three days?" But he was speaking about the temple of his body." (John 2:19-21)

> **Side Note:** *Hardened hearts have to be broken or chiseled by the hand of the Lord just as the commandments were on the tablet before the people could see it and allow it to be used as a source to lead them. Because of this, your hardened heart may have had to experience some pain due to the work God had to perform on your heart.*

## BUT IT'S ALL A PART OF HIS MASTER PLAN. I'M STILL GOING SOMEWHERE WITH THIS!

God had to break you because there was a recall on the you that you created. How did He do this?

Looking at each piece individually, God decided what needed the most attention and what went where. The plan He wrote was studied carefully, skillfully, and thoughtfully. "I knew you before I formed you in your mother's womb. Before you were born I set you apart and appointed you as my prophet to the nations." (Jeremiah 1:5)

Once God finishes evaluating the plan He created for your life, He starts to work on your foundation or the product's base.

**Side Note:** *The hurt, the pain, and the agony that you've been through starts to build your character, and as God refines and reshapes you, you become in the image He desires. A more "like Him" product starts to form.*

## AT THIS POINT IN THE PROCESS, YOUR HEART IS TESTED WHILE YOUR SPIRIT IS TRAINED TO STAY CALM AND RESTED.

The going gets tougher the closer you get to the finished product. But because God wants to make sure that the tough won't make you get going if faced with it again, He starts to pull out all the stops; to make sure that your heart, soul, mind, and spirit are one with Him, one like Him. "But whoever is united with the Lord is one with him in spirit." (1 Corinthians 6:17)

As your new walls start to go up, your insecurities begin to fall away. You no longer have to defend who you are, and you've come a long way, so you trust who God has created you to be. But things still don't look perfect, and the pain hasn't entirely gone away. Now, God has to put pressure on you to be sure that the foundation that was laid will be able to withstand and hold up the walls that He's started to put in place.

So, He shakes the building with an earthquake measuring 7.0. Whether you buckle or fold determines whether He can keep going, keep building. Next, a building inspection is done. You are halfway through. How many cracks have manifested from that broken heart that's still present, if any at all? This determines whether God needs to go back and do a little this or that, but eventually, when you pass the test, He can move forward.

As your foundation continues to be built on love, it explodes inside of you. The vibrant glow of colors and paint begin to show a glimmer of the effect that starts to reflect on the outside of you. Even though the windows are not yet installed, the light still prevails and shines through the walls of darkness. "The light shines in the darkness, and the darkness has not overcome it." (John 1:5)

## GOD'S PLAN IS ALMOST COMPLETE.

It's now time to build and mount the roof. The roof, which are the wings of the Lord, will now be put in place to cover and protect you from the storms and rains that will still be present but not have the ability to break you. "He will cover you with his feathers. He will shelter you with his wings. His faithful promises are your armor and protection." (Psalm 91: 4)

> **Side Note:** *Because your foundation was made from rock (love), and your roof from the wings of the Lord, they now cover you and keep you grounded. This has made you unstoppable.*

The pieces of the plan can now come together without a problem. Left and right, the inside of you starts to take shape. No weapon formed against you can prosper. And now that the big projects are out of the way, the small minor touches of excellence can be put into motion.

Your carpet is laid, and your windows are installed, allowing the world to see what glory now shines from inside of you. "In the same way, let your light shine before others, that they may see your good deeds and glorify your Father in heaven." (Matthew 5:16)

The final inspection is underway but not yet completed before another disaster hits, testing your foundation, your faith. But this time, you stand strong and tall because the master plan the Lord created has finally passed the test. The test of time, the test of patience, and, most of all, the test of love.

And to think all of this was possible because of He who would never leave you nor forsake you, because of He who vowed to finish constructing His good work in you until the day of Jesus Christ.

To close, as life goes on, the home (your temple, heart) will continue to be decorated with the beauty of God's work. Never to stay, nor be the same. Always progressing into something more beautiful than what the last renovation brought forth. Ever-changing and everlasting is what you are. Built to stand and sure to last.

You are a miracle. A home people never thought would make it through the storm due to the conditions (circumstances) you were in.

The dusty little shack at the end of the road that people doubted and thought the blueprint had been lost, never to be found or completed. A home that was laughed at because it hadn't yet become what its master plan boasted of it being.

The most significant mistake people made was overlooking the contents of your character (what's inside of you). And most importantly, the God that created you.

**EVEN IN THE MIDST OF ALL THE PAIN, BECAUSE OF WHO YOUR MAKER IS, BECAUSE OF THE MASTER PLAN HE HAD ALREADY CREATED, YOU'VE BECOME A PLACE THAT CAN HOLD UP WHERE THE BILLION-DOLLAR HOUSES COULD NOT.**

You possess more inside of you than the worth of any of the gold-plated toilets and marble floors that any of the other houses contain. The most beautiful home on the block is what you are. In fact, you have become the block—the home that everyone wants to pass by, see, and try to become.

## THE AFTERMATH.

After God's work is complete, the blueprints are eventually tossed out, becoming worthless. Why? Because there will never be another you, and nothing on paper can compare to a living, breathing, walking work of art.

Side Note: *You have come a long way going from what was once just a blueprint, a skillfully thought-out master plan, to someone ready to be showcased to the world as the masterpiece you were always created to be.*

"Then it shall come about when the Lord your God brings you into the land which He swore (solemnly promised) to [give] your fathers—

to Abraham, Isaac, and Jacob—to give you, [a land with] great and splendid cities which you did not build, and houses full of all good things which you did not fill, and hewn (excavated) cisterns (wells) which you did not dig out, and vineyards and olive trees which you did not plant, and you eat and are full and satisfied, then beware that you do not forget the Lord who brought you out of the land of Egypt, out of the house of slavery." (Deuteronomy 6:10-12)

**GOD SAID YOU WOULD LIVE IN CITIES YOU DID NOT BUILD. IN HOMES (TEMPLES) YOU DID NOT FILL. LOOK CLOSELY. YOU ARE THE CITY YOU DID NOT BUILD—THE HOME YOU DID NOT FILL!**

"The art of achievement is the art of making life - your life - a masterpiece."

— *Wilferd Peterson*

*Heavenly Father,* I thank you for showing me that's it's not always about the glitter on the outside of the presentation but about the glory, the beauty, and preparation of the inside that matters most. I must admit that, at times, I looked and judged but did not understand the innermost parts of things or people. Lord, help me to be humble in all my ways, understanding that inside every person, there's a struggle. As I fight to give up what my flesh has tried to make me believe I am and what it has tried to make me become, I pray that you give me the courage to take back what you have already planned to be mine. I know that I will always be victorious because of your righteousness and not my man-made righteousness. My house was built but not quite well. Because of you and your construction team, you've allowed not only me but others to see the beauty you have created in me from within. As I strive to be a great example to your people, I pray that you enable me to allow you and your army of those who fight to protect me to be the only fix to all my problems. Your plans are great, and your love is even greater. I know I won't be shaken because of who has the last say in my making. Thank you, Lord, for all that you have allowed me to be and for the work you're still doing for who I have yet to become.

In Jesus' name, Amen.

# CHAPTER 25

# DEATH, BURIAL, RESURRECTION

*Being in the wilderness, in the struggle, a place where life seems to be unknown, and you have no control, can be scary. It can make you believe that you are being punished or that God is no longer with you. But you were never alone on this journey, neither are you the first to walk on this road.*

**Isaiah 43:18-19 GNT** "But the Lord says, "Do not cling to events of the past or dwell on what happened long ago. Watch for the new thing I am going to do. It is happening already—you can see it now! I will make a road through the wilderness and give you streams of water there."

The wilderness is where Jesus struggled with being tempted. The road the woman with the issue of blood took to be cleansed. This path led to each of them being purified, transformed, whole, and filled with the character needed for God to present them to the world; confident, courageous, and comfortable in their skin.

**THE WILDERNESS IS NOT A DEATH SENTENCE. IT'S JUST A DARK PLACE THAT GOD USES TO PURIFY YOU, NURTURE YOU, FEED YOU, GROW YOU, TO *TRANSFORM YOU*.**

As an example, look at the caterpillar. When it goes into a dark place, it changes and evolves into something beautiful; being reborn or resurrected, one could say. With wings it flies like angels in the sky. But is the caterpillar the only creature known to man for its evolution and beauty?

God put you in a dark place to work on you, just like He does with the caterpillar. The caterpillar started as an egg. You started as a seed, as a Word. "In the beginning was the Word, and the Word was with God, and the Word was God." (John 1:1)

**Side Note:** *In the beginning stages of its transformation, the caterpillar goes into a dark place, the cocoon. You went into the wilderness through trials and tribulations.*

Inside of the cocoon, all nutrients needed for the transformation are provided. How? They are already within the caterpillar.

**THE HOLY SPIRIT AND GOD'S NATURE HAVE ALWAYS BEEN WITHIN YOU.**

To release the nutrients, the caterpillar digests itself (dies to its old self). Only the important parts that are needed for the caterpillar to continue its transformation can survive the process. You had to die to sin to be free from it and survive.

"For if we have been united with Him like this in His death, we will certainly also be united with Him in His resurrection. We know that our old self was crucified with Him so that the body of sin might be rendered powerless, that we should no longer be slaves to sin. For anyone who has died has been freed from sin." (Romans 6:5-7)

**YOUR PAST MESS OR PAIN DOES NOT SURVIVE THIS PROCESS, BUT LOVE, FAITH, HOPE, PATIENCE, AND KINDNESS DO.**

What remains within the cocoon after the digestion stage of the caterpillar is eventually used to develop the new creature. What emerges after the metamorphosis is the butterfly.

Metamorphosis:

- (In an insect or amphibian) the process of transformation from an immature form to an adult form in two or more distinct stages.

- A change of the form or nature of a thing or person into a completely different one, by nature or supernatural means.

The caterpillar's past was not killing its future. It may have looked that way when it digested itself, but God had already worked everything together. Therefore the past was only used to transform the future by creating a new creature—a new you.

**WHAT YOU NEEDED TO TRANSFORM AND TO CHANGE HAS ALWAYS BEEN IN YOU. YOU ONLY NEEDED TO TAKE THE FIRST STEP AND DIE TO YOUR OLD WAYS OF SIN FOR THE TRUE TRANS-FORMATION TO BEGIN.**

Sometimes you must go to a dark place alone and shed everything that you are so that you can evolve and come out a better person. The caterpillar is the physical representation of the intangible change that happens within you. Consider this, "your present sufferings are not worth comparing with the glory that will be revealed in you." (Romans 8:18)

## ALONE BUT NOT AFRAID.

Did you become afraid thinking that dark place you were in meant you were dying when all along you were being recreated?

While in the cocoon, the caterpillar is alone but not afraid because it knows it's being transformed, not dying. That should give you hope! If God nourishes and provides a caterpillar with all it needs to transform while in a dark place, what makes you think He hasn't already done the same for you?

## YOU MUST STOP LOOKING FOR WHAT'S WRONG IN YOUR LIFE IN ORDER TO START SEEING WHAT'S RIGHT.

The moment the devil goes to take his victory leap of joy, thinking you are dead, is the moment the Lord will jump in and snatch his breath away. The enemy won't make it to the finish line, but you will. Your dying to your old self just makes way for your burial which means you're even closer to your resurrection.

> **Side Note:** *Try taking a deeper look into your pain, and you will begin to see how God has used problems and trials to change and transform your life for the better.*

## GOD'S PURPOSE BEHIND YOUR PROBLEMS

1. "God uses problems to **DIRECT** you - Sometimes God must light a fire under you to get you moving.

Problems along with painful situations often point you in a new direction and motivate you to change. Problems also allow you to see your true nature. You get a glimpse of who you are currently but also the power to see who you can become. This can take you from walking down a road that ends in destruction. To walking down a road that leads to righteousness. How has God used problems to get your attention, to help you change?

2. God uses problems to **INSPECT** you - People are like teabags. If you want to know what's inside of them, you drop them into hot water!

God uses problems to bring out the best and the worst in you. To see whether you are only capable of being called or if you have the potential to become one of the chosen few. It takes a strong warrior to fight in this war, and one cannot reign with Jesus if you have not suffered with Him. Has God ever tested your faith with a problem? What do your problems reveal about you?

3. God uses problems to **CORRECT** you - Some lessons are only learned through pain and failure. God corrects you by chastising you when you make mistakes.

Mistakes are made because life is learned through them. Making a mistake can be considered progress because it teaches you something. Sometimes you only learn the value of something—health, money, a relationship—by losing it, or maybe even just the mere thought of losing it. How has God used problems to give you a lesson on this thing we call life?

4. God uses problems to **PROTECT** you - A problem can be a blessing in disguise. Oftentimes problems prevent you from being harmed in a more serious way.

Sometimes problems can be seen as nuisances, but are they really if they save your soul? Look back on your life. How has God used problems to protect you from yourself, to save your soul from eternal death?" (Warren)

## GOD USES PROBLEMS TO HELP YOU DEVELOP SURVIVAL SKILLS.

### 1. Character

While going through the trials you have gone through. Your character has been transformed. Unforgiveness, bitterness, rage, and anger have been replaced with patience, kindness, and love. Utilizing these new attributes gives you the ability to conquer any dream you can think of.

- "Love is patient, love is kind. It does not envy, it does not boast, it is not proud. It does not dishonor others, it is not self-seeking, it is not easily angered, it keeps no record of wrongs. Love does not delight in evil but rejoices with the truth. It always protects, always trusts, always hopes, always perseveres. Love never fails. (1 Corinthians 13:4-8) "The fear of the Lord is the beginning of wisdom; all who follow his precepts have good understanding. To him belongs eternal praise." (Psalm 111:10)

Because your soul is no longer sour, you hold the key to life along with the power.

### 2. Shelter

You have learned who your true shelter is. The one who protects you when faced with adversity and loves you simply because He is love.

- "God is our shelter and strength, always ready to help in times of trouble. So, we will not be afraid, even if the earth is shaken and mountains fall into the ocean depths; even if the seas roar and rage, and the hills are shaken by the violence. There is a river that brings joy to the city of God, to the sacred house of the Most

High. God is in that city, and it will never be destroyed; at early dawn he will come to its aid." (Psalm 46:1-5)

You will never be left without because God is not like your job or man. He covers you without a doubt.

### 3. Water

You've found the well that leads to everlasting life. It flows in and through you simply because of Christ.

- "Now on the last and most important day of the feast, Jesus stood and called out [in a loud voice], "If anyone is thirsty, let him come to Me and drink! He who believes in Me [who adheres to, trusts in, and relies on Me], as the Scripture has said, 'From his innermost being will flow continually rivers of living water.'" (John 7:37-38)

You will never be thirsty like those around you because the water you have will always flow through you and surround you.

### 4. Food

Your discovery of the Word of God has opened up your eyes, thus giving you the ability to see clearly.

- "Do not work for food that spoils, but for food that endures to eternal life, which the Son of Man will give you. For on him God the Father has placed his seal of approval." Then they asked him, "What must we do to do the works God requires?" Jesus answered, "The work of God is this: to believe in the one he has sent." So they asked him, "What sign then will you give that we may see it and believe you? What will you do? Our ancestors ate the manna in the wilderness; as it is written: 'He gave them bread from heaven to eat." Jesus said to them, "Very truly I tell you, it is not Moses who has given you the bread from heaven, but it is my Father who gives you the true bread from heaven. For the bread of God is the bread that comes down from heaven and gives life to the world." "Sir," they said, "always give us this bread." Then Jesus declared, "I am the bread of life. Whoever comes to me will never go hungry, and whoever believes in me will never be thirsty." (John 6:28-35)

When walking with God you'll never go hungry because God always feeds those he leads.

## GOD USES TRIALS TO SAVE YOU FROM YOURSELF.

The whole purpose of this journey of struggle and pain was for God to use your pain to push you closer toward Him. By doing this, He granted you the opportunity to see your sin and become reformed, thus allowing you to reap the benefits of everlasting life. "As surely as I live says the Sovereign Lord, I take no pleasure in the death of wicked people. I only want them to turn from their wicked ways so they can live." (Ezekiel 33:11)

## THERE'S LIFE FOR ALL WHO CHOOSE IT AND FORGIVENESS FOR ALL WHO SEEK GOD.

When reading the Bible, you can repeatedly see God using trials to save people's souls. God took people who were not believers, people who were sinners, and turned them away from their sin. These same people became some of the most important, influential, and wise leaders of all time.

For example, the Apostle Paul was originally Jewish and despised Christians. He even went so far as killing them simply because of their beliefs. "I thank Christ Jesus our Lord, who has strengthened me, that He considered me faithful and appointed me to service. I was formerly a blasphemer, a persecutor, and a violent man; yet because I had acted in ignorance and unbelief, I was shown mercy. And the grace of our Lord overflowed to me, along with the faith and love that are in Christ Jesus." (1 Timothy 1:12-14)

The city of Nineveh is another example. The whole city did terrible things in the Lord's sight, so God sent Jonah to preach the gospel to them. That message ended with suffering and famine. This led the city to see their need for change and God, ultimately causing them to cry out to Him. "And the people of Nineveh believed the word of the Lord as spoken by Jonah. They turned away from their sins and fasted and sought the Lord, from the greatest of them even to the least." (Jonah 3:5)

The suffering and famine the city of Nineveh endured had been a wake-up call that showed them what destruction could look like if they continued to live sinful lives.

The beauty of this story is that God saw their desire to change, so He did not bring destruction upon them. "When God saw what they had done and how they had put a stop to their evil ways, he changed his mind and did not carry out the destruction he had threatened." (Jonah 3:10)

The people living in the City of Nineveh did not become influential leaders like the Apostle Paul who physically went about preaching the gospel. But they did become living proof of the gospel and the true power of God.

> **Side Note:** *The city of Nineveh cried out to God, and He saved a whole city of sinners. Now that's power, along with forgiveness, grace, and mercy! "Don't you see how wonderfully tolerant, and patient God is with you? Can't you see that his kindness is intended to turn you from your sin?" (Romans 2:4)*

Even though God's kindness can hurt, it's still tolerant and patient. Look at it this way God's plan has always been to draw you away from eternal death with the pain of His love because...

## SOMETIMES YOU MUST STRUGGLE TO LIVE.

The trickiest part about the transformation of the caterpillar is timing and struggles. Without the right timing and struggles, the caterpillar is not able to become the new creature it was destined to be. And you are no different.

*Struggle is Good if you Want to Fly!* – Words of encouragement for future students written by the leaders and instructors at Mid-State Technical College

"Once a little boy was playing outdoors and found a fascinating caterpillar. He carefully picked it up and took it home to show his mother. He asked his mother if he could keep it, and she said he could if he would take good care of it.

The little boy got a large jar from his mother and put plants to eat, and a stick to climb on, in the jar. Every day he watched the caterpillar and brought it new plants to eat.

One day the caterpillar climbed up the stick and started acting strangely. The boy worriedly called his mother who came and understood that the caterpillar was creating a cocoon. The mother explained to the boy how the caterpillar was going to go through a metamorphosis and become a butterfly.

The little boy was thrilled to hear about the changes his caterpillar would go through. He watched every day, waiting for the butterfly to emerge. One day it happened, a small hole appeared in the cocoon and the butterfly started to struggle to come out.

At first, the boy was excited, but soon he became concerned. The butterfly was struggling so hard to get out! It looked like it couldn't break free! It looked desperate! It looked like it was making no progress!

The boy was so concerned he decided to help. He ran to get scissors, and then walked back (because he had learned not to run with scissors). He snipped the cocoon to make the hole bigger and the butterfly quickly emerged!

As the butterfly came out the boy was surprised. It had a swollen body and small, shriveled wings. He continued to watch the butterfly expecting that, at any moment, the wings would dry out, enlarge, and expand to support the swollen body. He knew that in time the body would shrink, and the butterfly's wings would expand.

But neither happened!

The butterfly spent the rest of its life crawling around with a swollen body and shriveled wings.

It never was able to fly…

As the boy tried to figure out what had gone wrong his mother took him to talk to a scientist from a local college. He learned that the butterfly was SUPPOSED to struggle. In fact, the butterfly's struggle to push its way through the tiny opening of the cocoon pushes the fluid out of its body and into its wings. Without the struggle, the butterfly would never, ever fly. The boy's good intentions hurt the butterfly.

As you go through school, and life, keep in mind that struggling is an important part of any growth experience. In fact, it is the struggle that causes you to develop your ability to fly." (Struggle is Good! I Want to Fly!)

All the pain I have gone through in life has taught me things I could not have learned without having gone through the struggle. It's allowed me to learn about forgiveness and see who I am on a deeper level. It taught me what it means to love and be loved. Most importantly, this pain has allowed me to gain what God wanted for me all along. A faith and character that is powerful, unexplainable, and only obtainable through Him, through love.

I can now look at all I have been through and say how grateful I am for the struggle. My faith and character grew stronger because of it.

**WHEN YOU'VE MADE IT TO A PLACE WHERE YOU CAN SAY YOU'RE GRATEFUL FOR YOUR STRUGGLES AND SEE HOW MUCH OF A BLESSING THEY HAVE BEEN, YOU KNOW THAT YOU'VE MATURED, YOU'VE GROWN, AND ARE READY TO FLY.**

God's plan was not to punish you for the mistakes you've made in life. His plans were to plant you so that He could grow your faith in Him. So that you could fly. "Those who trust in the Lord will renew their strength. They will soar high on wings like eagles. They will run and not grow weary. They will walk and not faint." (Isaiah 40:31)

Sometimes you may have to go through hard times because of your decisions, but the outcome if the right choices are made leads to prosperity. Prosperity does not just speak in terms of wealth. It also speaks in terms of within. God doesn't just change your life by allowing you to struggle. He also changes you.

**DON'T TURN AWAY WHEN THE LORD IS CALLING, FOR THOSE WHO ARE CALLED STILL HAVE TO GO THROUGH TRIALS TO BE APPROVED AS GOD'S CHOSEN.**

The trials you've overcome. The pain you've endured was just a road you had to pass through to reach the greatness that lives within you, to reach the promised land. "And I have promised to bring you up out of your affliction in Egypt, into the land of the Canaanites, Hittites, Amorites, Perizzites, Hivites, and Jebusites—a land flowing with milk and honey." (Exodus 3:17)

## YOU DON'T NEED TO DO THINGS TO BE RESURRECTED AND REACH THE PROMISED LAND. BUT YOU DO NEED TO BELIEVE IN THE GOD OF ALL THINGS.

Greatness is getting ready to be revealed within you and through you, but your resurrection is not something you can make happen physically. It is in the hands of the Lord, and His power is released when you believe in Him. "Lord, have mercy on my son, He has seizures and suffers terribly. He often falls into the fire or into the water. So I brought him to your disciples, but they couldn't heal him." Jesus said, "you faithless and corrupt people! How long must I put up with you? Bring the boy here to me." Then Jesus rebuked the demon in the boy, and it left him. From that moment the boy was well. Afterward the disciples asked Jesus privately, "Why couldn't we cast out that demon?" "You don't have enough faith," Jesus told them. "I tell you the truth, if you had faith even as small as a mustard seed, you could say to this mountain, 'Move from here to there,' and it would move. Nothing would be impossible." (Matthew 17:15-20)

What are you hoping for? Is it something huge? Whatever you are hoping for now, that very thing is what has been used to test your faith. To give you the strength and the power needed to take hold of the blessing. To further clarify, your faith faces many trials before laying hold of the blessing simply because to whom much is given, much faith is required.

> **Side Note:** *God keeps his promises. You only need to keep your faith. By keeping faith, you choose life.*

## FAITH AND BELIEF HAVE RESURRECTING POWER. IT BREAKS BARRIERS, CURSES, AND CHAINS.

**Sin's Power Is Broken:** "What does this mean? Are we to keep on sinning so that God will give us more of His loving-favor? No, not at all! We are dead to sin. How then can we keep on living in sin? All of us were baptized to show we belong to Christ. We were baptized first of all to show His death. We were buried in baptism as Christ was buried in death. As Christ was raised from the dead by the great power of God, so we will have new life also. If we have become one with Christ in His death, we will be one with Him in being raised from the dead to new life. We know that our old life, our old sinful self, was nailed to the cross with Christ. And so the power of sin that held us was destroyed. Sin is no longer our boss. When a man is dead, he is free from the power of sin. And if we have died with Christ, we believe we will live with Him also. We know that Christ was raised from the dead. He will never die again. Death has no more power over Him. He died once but now lives. He died to break the power of sin, and the life He now lives is for God. You must do the same thing! Think of yourselves as dead to the power of sin. But now you have new life because of Jesus Christ our Lord. You are living this new life for God. So do not let sin have power over your body here on earth. You must not obey the body and let it do what it wants to do. Do not give any part of your body for sinful use. Instead, give yourself to God as a living person who has been raised from the dead. Give every part of your body to God to do what is right. Sin must not have power over you. You are not living by the Law. You have life because of God's loving-favor." (Romans 6:1-14)

You've reached destination resurrection. That means the point of being in this world but not of it. You've been remade of the Spirit and are now living through the power of God. But remember, this is a battle, so you must keep fighting because you dying to your old self does not mean continuing to live in sin. It means this is the beginning of you living for God. Stay humble, stay focused, remain steadfast, and unmovable. Oh, and it's ok to stop digging. You're no longer buried. You have been resurrected. It's time to fly.

**A NEW LIFE AWAITS. YOU HAVE SUFFERED WITH JESUS IN DEATH. HIS BLOOD HAS RESURRECTED YOU. NOW IT'S TIME FOR YOU TO REIGN WITH HIM!**

||||||||||||||||||||||||||||||||||||||||||||||||||||||||||||||||||||||||||||||||||||||||||||||||||||||

"She wore her battle scars like wings, looking at her you would never know that once upon a time she forgot how to fly."

— *Nikki Rowe*

||||||||||||||||||||||||||||||||||||||||||||||||||||||||||||||||||||||||||||||||||||||||||||||||||||||

**Heavenly Father,** I pray that you continue to enlighten me with your wisdom as I continue on this road called life. I now realize this road was only used to help grow my faith in you. Help me to continue to align myself with the will you have preordained for me. I know that you love me and are merciful towards me. For this reason, I trust your leadership and guidance. Thank you, Lord, for being everything that you are and everything that you have resurrected me to be.

In Jesus' name, Amen!

# PART EIGHT THE SOULUTION

# CHAPTER 26

# KEY TO LIFE

*They tried to clip your wings before you received them, but now that you have them fight to keep them.*

**1 Corinthians 13** NLT "If I could speak all the languages of earth and of angels, but didn't love others, I would only be a noisy gong or a clanging cymbal. If I had the gift of prophecy, and if I understood all of God's secret plans and possessed all knowledge, and if I had such faith that I could move mountains, but didn't love others, I would be nothing. If I gave everything I have to the poor and even sacrificed my body, I could boast about it; but if I didn't love others, I would have gained nothing. Love is patient and kind. Love is not jealous or boastful or proud or rude. It does not demand its own way. It is not irritable, and it keeps no record of being wronged. It does not rejoice about injustice but rejoices whenever the truth wins out. Love never gives up, never loses faith, is always hopeful, and endures through every circumstance. Prophecy and speaking in unknown languages and special knowledge will become useless. But love will last forever! Now our knowledge is partial and incomplete, and even the gift of prophecy reveals only part of the whole picture! But when the time of perfection comes, these partial things will become useless. When

I was a child, I spoke and thought and reasoned as a child. But when I grew up, I put away childish things. Now we see things imperfectly, like puzzling reflections in a mirror, but then we will see everything with perfect clarity. All that I know now is partial and incomplete, but then I will know everything completely, just as God now knows me completely. Three things will last forever—faith, hope, and love—and the greatest of these is love."

You've made it to the end, to the treasure that lies within. You've dug up all the agony, hurt, and pain. Hidden in your heart, you've found the greatest gift given to you by God. Love. It may have needed to be revived, given new breath and new life but still there. It may be a hard love, or a love you feel is unrealistic to obtain, but it's love, nonetheless.

Love is what carries you through tough times. It's what sets the captives free and breaks the chains of sin, oppression, pride, and hate. Love is all, and all is love. Love is not selfish and keeps no records of wrongs, meaning love forgives. Love gives mercy because mercy was given to you by God. Love is patient because God has been patient with you during your troubles, trials, and pain. True love is everything you could imagine, and when times get rough, it's the only thing you can dream of.

### LOVE IS *REAL*. LOVE IS *LIFE*. LOVE IS *YOU*!

You are the key to life, and your struggles are what's prepared you to transfigure and become love (just like Jesus).

Transfigure:

- Transform into something more beautiful or elevated.

Transfiguration:

- A complete change of form or appearance into a more beautiful or spiritual state.

It's been a long time coming; so many people have looked down on you or overlooked you altogether because they only saw you as broken. But it's time to rise up because many are called, yet you are the key that has been chosen; you are the future.

|||||||||||||||||||||||||||||||||||||||||||||||||||||||||||||||||||||||||||||||||||||||||||||||||||||||||||||||

"Christ is building His kingdom with earth's broken things. Men want only the strong, the successful, the victorious, the unbroken when building their kingdoms; but God is the God of the unsuccessful, of those who have failed. Heaven is filling with earth's broken lives, and there is no bruised reed that Christ cannot take and restore to glorious blessedness and beauty. He can take the life crushed by pain or sorrow and make it into a harp whose music shall be all praise. He can lift earth's saddest failure up to heaven's glory."

— *J.R. Miller*

|||||||||||||||||||||||||||||||||||||||||||||||||||||||||||||||||||||||||||||||||||||||||||||||||||||||||||||||

Now that you have the key that has set you free, the Lord wants you to use the same key to free others; bind it around your heart. This key will continue to help you for the rest of your journey, for the rest of your life.

> **Side Note:** *Your brokenness and past problems are a rite of passage to be used to unlock doors that lead to freedom, which no man can shut.*

## WAKE UP. YOU ARE THE SOLUTION YOU'VE BEEN LOOKING FOR!

The only true way to move through this life is to move in love. Jesus is life, and love is the key that opens the door to a life fulfilled. "Jesus answered, "I am the way and the truth and the life. No one comes to the Father except through me." (John 14:16) "I am the Door. Anyone who goes in through Me will be saved from the punishment of sin. He will go in and out and find food" (John 10:9)

> **Side Note:** *The door that leads to everlasting life is Jesus. But because people are being left at the door and not given any direction on how to pass through, they walk away from the only blessing that can save them. For this reason, you had to transfigure, convert, and change becoming love, to be an example of love to others.*

**YOU TEACH PEOPLE HOW TO LOVE BY THE WAY YOU LOVE THEM, ULTIMATELY SAVING THEIR LIVES.**

"Let no one look down on [you because of] your youth but be an example and set a pattern for the believers in speech, in conduct, in love, in faith, and in [moral] purity. Until I come, devote yourself to public reading [of Scripture], to preaching and to teaching [the sound doctrine of God's word]. Do not neglect the spiritual gift within you, [that special endowment] which was intentionally bestowed on you [by the Holy Spirit] through prophetic utterance when the elders laid their hands on you [at your ordination]. Practice and work hard on these things; be absorbed in them [completely occupied in your ministry], so that your progress will be evident to all. Pay close attention to yourself [concentrate on your personal development] and to your teaching; persevere in these things [hold to them], for as you do this you will ensure salvation both for yourself and for those who hear you." (1 Timothy 4:12-16)

In life, it's not always about what you know or say. It's equally about what you show through your actions. Showing others love during their hard times or trials allows them to feel loved and know personally what real love looks like. This helps them to become love themselves, and move through the door of life just like you.

**KEYS ARE BROKEN IN ALL THE RIGHT PLACES, SO THEY MAY BE ABLE TO UNLOCK AND OPEN DOORS THAT HELP ALL THE RIGHT PEOPLE.**

There are people in this world who only you can reach simply because you have been through and conquered what they are going through. For this reason, these people will trust you. Do not take their trust for granted, be to them what other people had not been to you when you were hurting. This means being that shoulder to cry on, that teacher who corrects, and the hands and feet that go about helping people who are hurting, just as Jesus did when he became the greatest example of love by giving himself for our sins.

"Thank God, the Father of our Lord Jesus Christ, that he is our Father and the source of all mercy and comfort. For he gives us comfort in our trials so that we in turn may be able to give the same sort of strong sympathy to others in theirs. Indeed, experience shows that the more we share Christ's suffering the more we are able to give of his encouragement. This means that if we experience trouble, we can pass on to you comfort and spiritual help; for if we ourselves have been comforted we know how to encourage you to endure patiently the same sort of troubles that we have ourselves endured. We are quite confident that if you have to suffer troubles as we have done, then, like us, you will find the comfort and encouragement of God." (2 Corinthians 1:3-7)

See it this way; your brokenness is not the problem. It's where you're anointing. Your crown comes from. "God blesses those who patiently endure testing and temptation. Afterward they will receive the crown of life that God has promised to those who love him." (James 1:12)

# THESE ARE THE TEST OF LOVE, WHETHER YOU'VE PASSED AND CAN WEAR THE CROWN. WELL, THE ANSWER IS IN YOUR HEART!

♥ **Discernment:**

- Discernment is tested because you still have freedom of choice (the ability to decide) whether you will do right and choose love.

- Discernment is tested to build better decision-making skills.

- To be a leader, you must be able to choose to do right and make the right decisions even when it's tough.

- **This test lets God see whether you will make good decisions.**

♥ **Faith:**

- Faith is tested because to trust is to love.

- Faith is tested to build your trust in God.

- God tests your ability to have faith in Him when you're going through tough times, which lets Him know if you trust and love Him.

- **This test lets God see whether you trust Him.**

♥ **Patience:**

- Patience is tested to measure how much you value or love what you desire to be blessed with.

- Patience is tested to build discipline.

- When you love or desire someone or something, you'll be patient and disciplined. Enduring pain and sticking things out through the most challenging times. Discipline is the second to last test that proves your love. It's also one of the toughest because it not only tests your love it also measures how much you love by testing your ability to be disciplined and patient while you wait and work for what you desire.

- **This test lets God see whether you are disciplined.**

♥ **Altruism:**

- Altruism is tested to determine the genuineness of your love.

- Altruism is tested to build loyalty.

- Some people who gain power tend to forget about God, using the blessings He gave to them to profit themselves, furthermore causing them to become numb. When a person is numb, they can't love because they have lost control of how they feel, which can lead to them being selfish and hurting others.

- **This test lets God see whether He can trust you to be loyal.**

God works like a businessman too. He tests, measures, and approves. Good decision-making skills test whether you love, trust tests whether you love, being disciplined measures your love, and loyalty tests approve or deny the genuineness of your love.

> **Side Note:** *These tests can be considered your struggles. They are what God has used to qualify you to become chosen, to become a leader, to wear the crown of life.*

## GOD WOULDN'T HAVE TESTED YOU IF HE DIDN'T PLAN ON BLESSING YOU!!!

My struggles in life (me losing my dad, my loved one being incarcerated, my family struggling) has become a crown I can now wear proudly on my head. How?

Well, it's simple. "I have fought the good fight, I have finished the race, I have kept the faith. Henceforth there is laid up for me the crown of righteousness, which the Lord, the righteous judge, will award to me on that Day, and not only to me but also to all who have loved his appearing." (2 Timothy 4:7-8)

Because I have conquered the trials and tribulations, the obstacles and roadblocks that have been thrown at me in life, I have now been qualified and anointed by God to become the blueprint and key to helping others overcome the same struggles I have faced.

The thought of this book would not have come about, nor would it possess the power that it possesses to heal others, if it hadn't been for my personal experience and struggles with the broken systems in society.

My pain is what has allowed me to better understand the people I am helping, as well as better help them.

## ISN'T IT FUNNY HOW LIFE CAN BE THE BEST TEACHER AND QUALIFIER?

As I said before, start looking deeper into the problems you face. You could very well be the solution to a problem, the roadmap someone else needs to follow, or a role model someone needs to look up to.

> **Side Note:** *The problems that are faced in society cannot be solved with money. Money alone doesn't solve problems; people solve problems. You possess the power to solve problems!*

What is your problem? My problem is the broken (oppressive) systems in society that are hurting people, and this book *Emancipation Freedom for the Incarcerated Soul* is meant to fix that problem.

**WHAT CAN YOU FIX JUST BECAUSE OF WHAT YOU'VE GONE THROUGH OR WHAT YOU'RE GOING THROUGH? CAN YOU BE THE CURE FOR PEOPLE WHO SUFFER FROM MENTAL ILLNESSES? ARE YOU THE CURE FOR PEOPLE WHO HAVE BROKEN HOMES? ARE YOU THE CURE FOR PEOPLE WHO STRUGGLE WITH SUBSTANCE ABUSE?**

God is looking for people to be healers in specific areas. Why do you think more and more people are showing up with the problems you're going through? It's because God is looking to use you as the answer to those problems. That's what purpose is; a set of problems you are meant to solve. A group of people you are meant to heal.

**YOUR DESTINY AND PURPOSE ARE HIDDEN IN YOUR PROBLEMS; THIS MEANS DESTINY IS REVEALED WHEN YOU LOOK AT YOUR PROBLEMS DIFFERENTLY.**

If you can change the way you see your problems, you can change the way you see yourself and your purpose. You are a blessing, but you'll only be able to be that blessing when you can see yourself as a blessing and not as that problem that tried to steal your blessing. You're greater than your last mistake than your last problem. And to be honest, if I didn't have these problems, I wouldn't have been able to embrace and take hold of my purpose.

> **Side Note:** *Whatever poison is in your past, you have been given the power to heal or fix that very problem. But you must stop viewing yourself as the problem. If you continue to do so, you cancel out the power you possess to be the solution.*

## THE POISON IN YOUR PAST IS THE SERUM SOLUTION FOR THE FUTURE.

Often to help someone who's on a road that leads to destruction, you must have been touched by what hurt them. To build them up, they need to see that you were once broken down and built up too. Everybody wants someone they can identify with, somebody they can trust. For this reason, God has called people from all walks of life, letting them know that no matter what you've been through, to stand tall and use the problems you have faced to be a part of freeing one another from a system that's built on your pain.

## YOU CAN STAND TALL NO MATTER WHAT YOU'VE BEEN THROUGH, NO MATTER WHERE YOU'VE COME FROM BECAUSE IT'S NOT WHERE YOU STAND; IT'S HOW YOU STAND!

Who better to reach out to a generation of people filled with hurt and pain than someone from that generation who's hurt the same?

> **Side Note:** *Nobody has more power to help change your situation and the struggles you've faced or are facing but you. If you've lived and conquered your pain and problems or are still conquering them, you could be the hope and light someone out in this dark world needs to see their way through. For me, I am now light in a world filled with darkness. Because my heart has suffered, I can end the suffering of the people who have experienced pain, just like me. Furthermore, leading to unity throughout the world.*

**Unity in the Body of Christ:** "I therefore, a prisoner for the Lord, urge you to walk in a manner worthy of the calling to which you have been called, with all humility and gentleness, with patience, bearing with one another in love, eager to maintain the unity of the Spirit in the bond of peace. There is one body and one Spirit—just as you were called to the one hope that belongs to your call—one Lord, one faith, one baptism, one God and Father of all, who is over all and through all and in all. But grace was given to each one of us according to the measure of Christ's gift. Therefore it says, "When he ascended on high he led a host of captives, and he gave gifts to men." (In saying, "He ascended," what does it mean but that he had also descended into the lower regions, the earth? He who descended is the one who also ascended far above all the heavens, that he might fill all things.) And he gave the apostles, the prophets, the evangelists, the shepherds and teachers, to equip the saints for the work of ministry, for building up the body of Christ, until we all attain to the unity of the faith and of the knowledge of the Son of God, to mature manhood, to the measure of the stature of the fullness of Christ, so that we may no longer be children, tossed to and fro by the waves and carried about by every wind of doctrine, by human cunning, by craftiness in deceitful schemes. Rather, speaking the truth in love, we are to grow up in every way into him who is the head, into Christ, from whom the whole body, joined and held together by every joint with which it is equipped, when each part is working properly, makes the body grow so that it builds itself up in love." (Ephesians 4:1-16)

As the hurricanes, fires, and viruses hit across not just the United States but the world, it may leave you to recognize that tragedy doesn't just strike people of specific statures. It hits all, and we all hurt. And because everyone's fighting for the same thing, it pushes us to take our eyes off what matters less so that we can see what matters more. Love and unity are what we've been neglecting, but it's trying to get our attention.

**WHEN ALL YOU SEE IS HURT AND PAIN, IT'S HARD TO RECOGNIZE ANYTHING BUT THE WOUNDS ON THE PERSON NEXT TO YOU. YOU CAN'T HELP BUT START TO JUDGE LESS AND LOVE MORE. TRAGEDY AND DISASTER HAVE A FUNNY WAY OF BRINGING PEOPLE TOGETHER WHILE ALSO REVEALING TRUTH.**

Now some of you may ask why God would allow us to go through all of this just to get us to love more. Well, it's simple, God knows there's only one thing that can set you free, but it's something you have yet to understand or see...

## LOVE TRUMPS LAW!

God wants you to be free from the broken systems that society has created to oppress you. But He knows the only way to do this is for Him to step back, allowing you to on your own open your eyes to see the truth: there's only one principle that trumps every law, and that is love.

If people loved more, there wouldn't be malice, there wouldn't be hate, and people wouldn't harm nor hurt others. If people loved one another, there would be no need for the law. See, love makes you want to do right without a doubt, so you're not double-minded because love is the only answer.

‖‖‖‖‖‖‖‖‖‖‖‖‖‖‖‖‖‖‖‖‖‖‖‖‖‖‖‖‖‖‖‖‖‖‖‖‖‖‖‖‖‖‖‖‖‖‖‖‖‖‖‖‖‖‖‖‖‖‖‖‖‖‖‖‖‖‖‖‖‖‖‖‖‖‖‖‖‖‖‖‖‖‖‖

"Hate cannot drive out hate; only love can do that."

— **Dr. Martin Luther King Jr.**

‖‖‖‖‖‖‖‖‖‖‖‖‖‖‖‖‖‖‖‖‖‖‖‖‖‖‖‖‖‖‖‖‖‖‖‖‖‖‖‖‖‖‖‖‖‖‖‖‖‖‖‖‖‖‖‖‖‖‖‖‖‖‖‖‖‖‖‖‖‖‖‖‖‖‖‖‖‖‖‖‖‖‖‖

"Let no debt remain outstanding, except the continuing debt to love one another, for whoever loves others has fulfilled the law. The commandments, "You shall not commit adultery," "You shall not murder," "You shall not steal," "You shall not covet," and whatever other command there may be, are summed up in this one command:

"Love your neighbor as yourself." Love does no harm to a neighbor. Therefore love is the fulfillment of the law." (Romans 8:8-10)

The only trap the devil needs to get you to fall into is hate because hate is the opposite of love. If you hate others, you live by the law, and not the only principle that cancels out the law.

||||||||||||||||||||||||||||||||||||||||||||||||||||||||||||||||||||||||||||||||||||||||||||||||||||||||||||||||

"Hate. It has caused a lot of problems in this world, but it has not solved one yet."

— *Maya Angelou*

||||||||||||||||||||||||||||||||||||||||||||||||||||||||||||||||||||||||||||||||||||||||||||||||||||||||||||||||

## LAW EXISTS BECAUSE OF HATE.

Most Government agencies can only employ people in certain fields because of fear and hatred. Take the United States Department of Homeland Security. DHS was founded in 2002 after the bombing of the World Trade Center on September 11th.

Now think, would DHS exist if the hatred of this world did not continue to persist? Would there be as much crime or a need for jails if people loved more? Would lawyers be needed to defend people, or judges be needed to judge?

"Therefore, just as sin came into the world through one man, and death through sin, and so death spread to all men because all sinned—for sin indeed was in the world before the law was given, but sin is not counted where there is no law." (Romans 5:12-13)

See, you can't govern nor patrol what isn't a problem. And let's face it, some people in this world like to cause chaos for this very reason. Chaos enables the government to paint pictures of people as animals. This helps the government how? Well, that imagery and those statistics of people being incarcerated at an alarming rate are what continue to prove why jails are needed. "Jails are needed because they are animals. They are animals because look at how many of them are in jail."

This world runs off stats, and without numbers, there is no funding. Businesses cannot get loans unless they prove how profitable they are or can be through their stats.

What does this mean for us? We are building prisons for ourselves and don't even realize it. Hating one another causes us to have more and more of what we despise to rise up each day. Now the stats don't lie, but the key that you have in your heart, love, doesn't lie either.

> **Side Note:** *You must do the opposite of what people expect you to do, meaning love when people expect you to hate if you want to become less predictable; confusing your enemy.*

You need to use new tools to fight new wars, not simply use only the old ones to do so.

It's great that you march that you have a dream, but if hatred is what fuels you when marching, it means nothing. You need to learn to march because you love the cause you're fighting for, not march simply because someone pushed you to fight for what you love.

See, I'd do anything for my loved ones, and that can be dangerous, but it can be powerful if perfected.

## CONTINUE TO LOVE THE PERSON, THING, OR CAUSE YOU ARE FIGHTING FOR—BECAUSE IT TAKES LOVE TO KEEP FIGHTING FOR WHAT YOU ARE FIGHTING FOR.

**Side Note:** *The power of love that lies within your heart is strong. It's fierce. It's a weapon. A force that can tear down any stronghold. That's why God used me; love is why He chose me to fight against the hatred in this world. God knows how strong and powerful my love is for my loved ones. God also knows that when love is strong, if fighting for something, someone, or a cause close to your heart, it's the key to keeping you going. It helps you to develop a passion and makes you persistent.*

"Love + Anger = Passion"

## — *Robert Kiyosaki*

If the love within your heart is not strong when you're fighting for something, you'd easily give up. That's why pain is used to steer you toward your destiny. When you are hurt, or someone you love is hurt, you'd do whatever it takes to set them free. I wrote to set my loved ones free. Now, this book will be the key that set's you free. "Take hold of my instructions; don't let them go. Guard them, for they are the key to life." (Proverbs 4:13)

To conclude, love can hurt and leave scars when you're hurt by someone you care about, but love can also heal those very same wounds. It's a weapon that can be used for good or bad depending upon the nature of the one using it. Therefore, use the love within your heart to the best of your ability. Be light in the midst of the darkness, be hope where there is no hope, be grace where people have been given no mercy, be love where there's nothing but hate.

"You, my brothers and sisters, were called to be free. But do not use your freedom to indulge the flesh; rather, serve one another humbly in love. For the entire law is fulfilled in keeping this one command: "Love your neighbor as yourself." If you bite and devour each other, watch out or you will be destroyed by each other. So I say, walk by the Spirit, and you will not gratify the desires of the flesh. For the flesh desires what is contrary to the Spirit, and the Spirit what is contrary to the flesh. They are in conflict with each other, so that you are not to do whatever you want. But if you are led by the Spirit, you are not under the law." (Galatians 5:13-18)

**New Life in Christ:** "So I tell you this, and insist on it in the Lord, that you must no longer walk as the Gentiles do, in the futility of their thinking. They are darkened in their understanding and alienated from the life of God because of the ignorance that is in them due to the hardness of their hearts. Having lost all sense of shame, they have given themselves over to sensuality for the practice of every kind of impurity, with a craving for more. But this is not the way you came to know Christ. Surely you heard of Him and were taught in Him, in keeping with the truth that is in Jesus, to put off your former way of life, your old self, which is being corrupted by its deceitful desires; to be renewed in the spirit of your minds; and to put on the new self, created to be like God in true righteousness and holiness. Therefore, each of you must put off falsehood and speak truthfully to his neighbor, for we are all members of one another. "Be angry, yet do not sin." Do not let the sun set upon your anger, and do not give the devil a foothold. He who has been stealing must steal no longer, but must work, doing good with his own hands, that he may have something to share with the one in need. Let no unwholesome talk come out of your mouths, but only what is helpful for building up the one in need and bringing grace to those who listen. And do not grieve the Holy Spirit of God, in whom you were sealed for the day of redemption. Get rid of all bitterness, rage and anger, outcry, and slander, along with every form of malice. Be kind and tender-hearted to one another, forgiving each other just as in Christ God forgave you." (Ephesians 4:17-32)

**WHAT'S LEFT IN YOUR HEART WILL BE THE KEY TO THE DOOR OF YOUR FUTURE. IS IT ENVY, HATE, OR PRIDE? OR IS IT LOVE WHICH WILL BE THE ONLY THING LEFT TO STAND AND LAST AT THE END OF TIME?**

|||||||||||||||||||||||||||||||||||||||||||||||||||||||||||||||||||||||||||||||||||||||||||||||||||||||||||||||||||||||||

"Love will not just heal your life or mine. Love will heal the world."

*— Marianne Williamson*

|||||||||||||||||||||||||||||||||||||||||||||||||||||||||||||||||||||||||||||||||||||||||||||||||||||||||||||||||||||||||

*Heavenly Father,* I pray that what I ask of you today brings peace along with heaven on earth now and forevermore.

Peace be still to those who are hurting and in pain right now. Peace be still to those who are struggling in the body of Christ, and peace be still to those who have not yet found the body of Christ. May love and unity abound through the earth, and may I continue to be an example of it.

In Jesus' Name, Amen!

# CHAPTER 27

# DESTINY REVEALED

*I have become vulnerable. I have been stripped down like Jesus. I have become naked just to show you the purpose and importance of having your destiny revealed to you by God and being awakened.*

**Hebrews 12:1** NLT "Therefore, since we are surrounded by such a huge crowd of witnesses to the life of faith, let us strip off every weight that slows us down, especially the sin that so easily trips us up. And let us run with endurance the race God has set before us."

I could have been hateful; I could have been vindictive after all I had been put through in life. But you know what I realized; if I became hateful, I would be just as bad as the people I despised, the people that hurt me. And heck, if I'm being honest, if it weren't for them, I wouldn't have learned how not to be.

So, to bring this book to a close, I would like to say thank you to the people who tried to rule me out or hurt me. You have helped make me a better you; by showing me how to be better than you!

I've learned a lot along this journey, and I hope you have too. By the time you start your own business, you will already know how to run it. You will already know what kind of boss to be because life and its circumstances have shown you how not to be.

> **Side Note:** *If you have been poor or down in life, you have been given and developed unique abilities that some people who have been rich all their lives may not have had the ability to, compassion & survival skills.*

Some people never learned how to triumph and push through tough situations, so if their business tanks, they wouldn't know how to live otherwise, but you do. Your position (where you came from) is not all that horrible. It's given you tools that you couldn't have developed if it had not been for those days you spent in the trenches. See, you'll fight for and to keep what you have because you fought for it to begin with. Now do you see why you had to go through what you went through? It was for you to learn how to persevere and appreciate the blessings that are about to be given to you. But the key is to remember to look at your circumstances differently; you must see them as steppingstones and not roadblocks.

> I've had many people in life try to hold me back, and if I only saw the pain, I wouldn't have recognized the lessons that God was teaching me.

God was teaching me to never give up while also showing me how it felt to be someone who was looked down upon and mistreated so that when He blessed me to have my own, I'd be humble and compassionate to others.

You see, I now know exactly what it feels like to be them; therefore, I wouldn't want to hurt them. I am them, and their pain is kin to me. Their flesh is wrapped around my body. We have become one (UNITED).

## UNITED WE STAND AND IF WE MUST, UNITED WE'LL FALL.

**One Body with Many Members:** "For just as the body is one and has many members, and all the members of the body, though many, are one body, so it is with Christ. For in one Spirit we were all baptized into one body—Jews or Greeks, slaves or free—and all were made to drink of one Spirit.

For the body does not consist of one member but of many. If the foot should say, "Because I am not a hand, I do not belong to the body," that would not make it any less a part of the body. And if the ear should say, "Because I am not an eye, I do not belong to the body," that would not make it any less a part of the body. If the whole body were an eye, where would be the sense of hearing? If the whole body were an ear, where would be the sense of smell? But as it is, God arranged the members in the body, each one of them, as he chose. If all were a single member, where would the body be? As it is, there are many parts, yet one body.

The eye cannot say to the hand, "I have no need of you," nor again the head to the feet, "I have no need of you." On the contrary, the parts of the body that seem to be weaker are indispensable, and on those parts of the body that we think less honorable we bestow the greater honor, and our unpresentable parts are treated with greater modesty, which our more presentable parts do not require. But God has so composed the body, giving greater honor to the part that lacked it, that there may be no division in the body, but that the members may have the same care for one another. If one member suffers, all suffer together; if one member is honored, all rejoice together.

Now you are the body of Christ and individually members of it." (1 Corinthians 12:12-27)

To conclude, that person who was once on a dark road is now one with God. Therefore you are filled with light. Yet, this is only true because you died to sin and were buried long enough to be changed and resurrected as the change this world needs. You are love, and now that you have enough light and love to give to others, you can be that walking billboard of God's truth and goodness that He always knew you were.

Kings and Queens, it's time to take and possess your rightful places on the throne. Stop being who everyone else was called to be and start to be who you were called to be.

**I AM A LOVER OF THE BROKEN, A FRIEND OF THE BROKEN, THE VOICE OF THE BROKEN. I AM THE *EYES OF THE BROKEN*, AND MY PURPOSE IN LIFE IS TO HELP PEOPLE WORLDWIDE BREAK FREE FROM THE BROKEN (OPPRESSIVE) SYSTEMS IN SOCIETY. WHAT'S YOURS?**

II

"You believe a man can change his destiny?" "I believe a man does what he can, until his destiny is revealed."

— *The Last Samurai (2003)*

IIIIIIIIIIIIIIIIIIIIIIIIIIIIIIIIIIIIIIIIIIIIIIIIIIIIIIIIIIIIIIIIIIIIIIIIIIIIIIIIIIIIIIIIIIIIIIIIIIIIIIIIIIIIIIIIIIIIIIIIII

*Heavenly Father,* I have learned so much from the lessons of blessings you've given me. Through the good times and trouble that I've encountered with others, I've learned how to be and how not to be as a person. Without these pleasant and unpleasant situations, I would not know right from wrong. But because of the way people in times have made me feel, I've learned not to treat others the same. So I acknowledge the things I may have to go through to learn, but I know that because of your grace, I am a conqueror just like David, just like Jesus. Thank you for the challenge and the people you have used to push me towards the mark of excellence, towards you. Your presence is a blessing to me.

"For you, God, tested us; you refined us like silver. You brought us into prison and laid burdens on our backs. You let people ride over our heads; we went through fire and water, but you brought us to a place of abundance." (Psalm 66:10-12) Thank you.

In Jesus' Name, Amen.

# CHAPTER 28

# FREE AT LAST

*Emancipation:*

- *The fact or process of being set free from legal, social, or political restrictions, liberation.*

- *The freeing of someone from slavery.*

*Freedom:*

- *The power or right to act, speak, or think as one wants without hindrance or restraint.*

- *The state of not being imprisoned or enslaved.*

**Acts 16:25-26** NIV "About midnight Paul and Silas were praying and singing hymns to God, and the other prisoners were listening to them. Suddenly there was such a violent earthquake that the foundations of the prison were shaken. At once all the prison doors flew open, and everyone's chains came loose."

# #FREE AT LAST (POEM)

Enslaved mentally but not physically.

God sees the hurt and the pain through your afflictions and iniquities.

But pleasure is pain my love.

Set your heart free and you can reign my love.

You were called to lose your life like wheat loses grain my love.

But a part of the harvest you will always be.

Because God picks us apart for a new start you see.

The love that God spreads through our hearts.

Bind us together as eternal counterparts.

Therefore, as you walk through the valley of the shadow of death that's before you.

Don't allow the tricks of the devil to detour you.

As you struggle through the pains and hard times of life.

## REMEMBER, YOU ARE BOUND WITH NAILS TO THE CROSS LIKE CHRIST.

This means don't continue to live for today while saving love for tomorrow.

Because life is something that you have borrowed.

You were bought at a price my friend.

So love for today and lose your life my friend.

Understand that we all must die in order to live.

Meaning in order to live you have to have something you'd be willing to give.

I know it sounds harsh, but it's truth be told.

Don't let the false promises of this world ruin your soul.

I am nothing like you and you are nothing like me.

But apart of one body we will always be.

Therefore, as you grasp with despair while sitting at the foot of His throne.

Remember, in the end, all praise will be to the Almighty our God alone.

As you step into the next dimension of your life, there is one last thing that I would like to leave you with. You need to remember this. It will help you remain humble, which helps you remain free.

"Moses said to the people, "Remember [solemnly observe and commemorate] this day on which you came out of Egypt, out of the house of bondage and slavery; for by a strong and powerful hand the Lord brought you out of this place." (Exodus 13:3)

## SPOILER ALERT: YOU DON'T RECEIVE PHYSICAL BLESSINGS OR WEALTH FROM GOD BECAUSE YOU DESERVE THEM.

"Once you were dead because of your disobedience and your many sins. You used to live in sin, just like the rest of the world, obeying

643

the devil—the commander of the powers in the unseen world. He is the spirit at work in the hearts of those who refuse to obey God. All of us used to live that way, following the passionate desires and inclinations of our sinful nature. By our very nature we were subject to God's anger, just like everyone else. But God is so rich in mercy, and he loved us so much, that even though we were dead because of our sins, he gave us life when he raised Christ from the dead. (It is only by God's grace that you have been saved!) For he raised us from the dead along with Christ and seated us with him in the heavenly realms because we are united with Christ Jesus. So, God can point to us in all future ages as examples of the incredible wealth of his grace and kindness toward us, as shown in all he has done for us who are united with Christ Jesus. God saved you by his grace when you believed. And you can't take credit for this; it is a gift from God. Salvation is not a reward for the good things we have done, so none of us can boast about it. For we are God's masterpiece. He has created us anew in Christ Jesus, so we can do the good things he planned for us long ago." (Ephesians 2:1-10)

"After the Lord your God has done this for you, don't say in your hearts, 'The Lord has given us this land because we are such good people!' No, it is because of the wickedness of the other nations that he is pushing them out of your way. It is not because you are so good or have such integrity that you are about to occupy their land. The Lord your God will drive these nations out ahead of you only because of their wickedness, and to fulfill the oath he swore to your ancestors Abraham, Isaac, and Jacob. You must recognize that the Lord your God is not giving you this good land because you are good, for you are not—you are a stubborn people." (Deuteronomy 9:4-6)

## WE'RE ALL SINNERS.

"But now the righteousness of God has been manifested apart from the law, although the Law and the Prophets bear witness to it— the righteousness of God through faith in Jesus Christ for all who believe. For there is no distinction: for all have sinned and fall short of the glory of God, and are justified by his grace as a gift, through the redemption that is in Christ Jesus, whom God put forward as a propitiation by his blood, to be received by faith. This was to show God's righteousness, because in his divine forbearance he had passed over former sins. It was to show his righteousness at the present time, so that he might be just and the justifier of the one who has faith in Jesus." (Roman 3:21-16)

You receive physical blessings and or wealth from God simply so that your life may be proof of His goodness to the people who are unbelievers, the people who "need to see it (blessings) to believe it".

"So Jesus said to him, "Unless you see signs and wonders you will not believe." (John 4:48)

**Side Note:** *God knows people are oftentimes shallow, and for them to believe the work that He has done within you (spiritual blessings), they need to see physical blessings, which are the result of spiritual blessings before their own eyes. So, if ever you decide you are going to brag, make sure it's about the Lord.*

"Brothers and sisters think of what you were when you were called. Not many of you were wise by human standards; not many were influential; not many were of noble birth. But God chose the foolish things of the world to shame the wise; God chose the weak things of the world to shame the strong. God chose the lowly things of this world and the despised things—and the things that are not—to nullify the things that are, so that no one may boast before him. It is because of him that you are in Christ Jesus, who has become for us wisdom from God—that is, our righteousness, holiness, and redemption. Therefore, as it is written: "Let the one who boasts boast in the Lord." (1 Corinthians 1:26-31)

We are all given the same opportunity: to have a second chance in life, to be emancipated and set free. So, before you allow that mustard seed of a thought to present itself within your mind telling you to become prideful again, remember this one thing. Your keyhole was dirty before God cleaned it, and your life was probably a mess before people had the chance to see it.

**Oneness and Peace in Christ:** "Don't forget that you Gentiles used to be outsiders. You were called "uncircumcised heathens" by the Jews, who were proud of their circumcision, even though it affected only their bodies and not their hearts. In those days you were living apart from Christ. You were excluded from citizenship among the people of Israel, and you did not know the covenant promises God had made to them. You lived in this world without God and without hope. But now you have been united with Christ Jesus. Once you were far away from God, but now you have been brought near to him through the blood of Christ. For Christ himself has brought peace to us. He united Jews and Gentiles into one people when, in his own body on the cross, he broke down the wall of hostility that separated us. He did this by ending the system of law with its commandments and regulations. He made peace between Jews and Gentiles by creating in himself one new people from the two groups. Together as one body, Christ reconciled both groups to God by means of his death on the cross, and our hostility toward each other was put to death. He brought this Good News of peace to you Gentiles who were far away from him, and peace to the Jews who were near. Now all of us can come to the Father through the same Holy Spirit because of what Christ has done for us." (Ephesians 2:11-18)

DON'T ALLOW HATE OR PRIDE TO PLACE YOU BACK INTO THE CHAINS THAT GOD HAS FREED YOU FROM. REMAIN UNITED, CONTINUE TO LOVE, AND FLY FREE AS THE BEAUTIFUL BUTTERFLY YOU WERE CREATED TO BE. "IT IS FOR FREEDOM THAT CHRIST HAS SET US FREE. STAND FIRM, THEN, AND DO NOT LET YOURSELVES BE BURDENED AGAIN BY A YOKE OF SLAVERY." (GALATIANS 5:1) "LIVE AS PEOPLE WHO ARE FREE, NOT USING YOUR FREEDOM AS A COVER-UP FOR EVIL, BUT LIVING AS SERVANTS OF GOD." (1 PETER 2:16)

"Free at last, Free at last, Thank God almighty we are free at last."

— *Dr. Martin Lurther King Jr.*

**Eyes of the Broken** is a Social Enterprise that provides minorities impacted by Incarceration, Unemployment, Homelessness, and Broken Homes with opportunities that have been taken away from them. That includes the opportunity to be free, whether it's Spiritual, Mental, Financial, or Physical Freedom—Eyes of the Broken provides a pathway that helps individuals journey towards it.

**Our Mission** is to help people incarcerated Spiritually, Mentally, Financially, and Physically break free from the broken systems in society by equipping them with the tools necessary to become the solution to their own personal problems and the problems in society.

**Our Vision** is to create a world where everyone can experience abundance and be free—a society where mass incarceration, unemployment, homelessness, and broken homes are no longer a persistent problem.

**The Problem:** Brokenness within families and communities which has been created by the broken systems (Government, Banking, Healthcare, Education etc.) in society. This includes:

- Mass Incarceration

- Unemployment

- Homelessness

- Broken Homes

**The Solution:** Eyes of the Broken comes at a time when the broken systems in society that lead to brokenness within families and communities have become unacceptable to people from all walks of life. Mass incarceration, homelessness, unemployment, and broken homes seem to be topics that weigh heavy on everyone's hearts and a list of items to be tackled or addressed on their agendas. But Eyes of the Broken has taken a different approach to resolve the problem.

Here at Eyes of the Broken, we believe the only way to create balance throughout the world and heal the brokenness created by the broken systems in society is to start with the people who have suffered because of its brokenness.

For this reason, we have developed a 3 PHASE master plan to promote social change, end mass incarceration, reduce unemployment, homelessness, and broken homes.

## EYES OF THE BROKEN SOLVES THE PROBLEM OF BROKENNESS WITHIN FAMILIES AND COMMUNITIES IN THREE WAYS:

## PHASE I

Written to free individuals incarcerated Spiritually, Mentally, Financially, and Physically—*Emancipation Freedom for the Incarcerated Soul* is a book that goes beyond teaching you how to break free from the broken systems in society. It also shines a light on the social and economic injustices minorities face because of its brokenness. *THE BOOK BUILDS HOPE.*

## PHASE II

**PRISONLIVESMATTERTOO THE COLLECTION** is a collection of clothing and other merchandise created for individuals impacted by Incarceration, Unemployment, Homelessness, and Broken Homes (individuals incarcerated Spiritually, Mentally, Financially, and Physically). This collection gives people who feel strongly about the problems in society (Mass Incarceration, Unemployment, Homelessness, and Broken Homes) the opportunity to not only voice their opinion about such matters but also promote hope by wearing the collection. *THE COLLECTION PROMOTES HOPE.*

## PHASE III

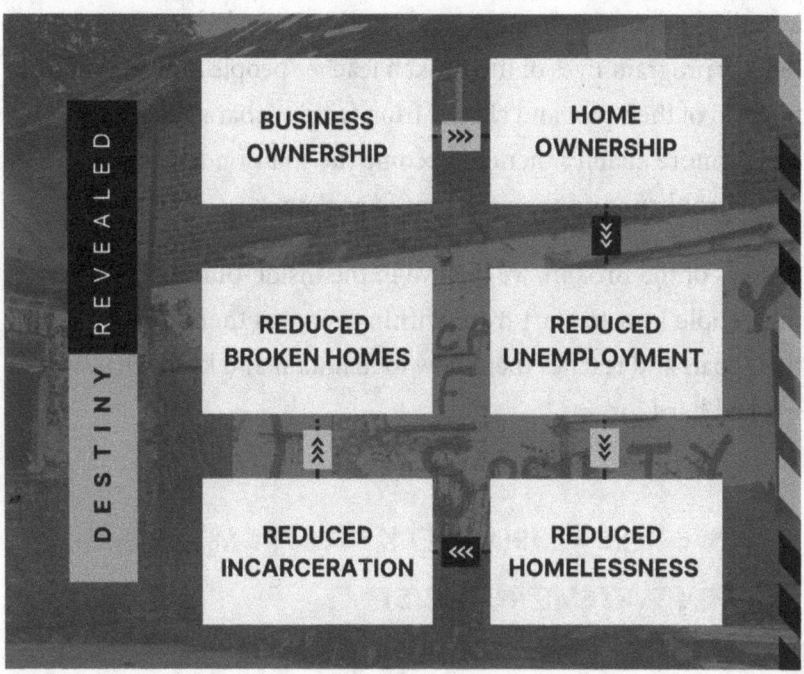

Destiny Revealed is a training and reentry program that focuses on mending the brokenness of the brokenhearted and creating a safe haven (recreational space) where individuals who have been impacted by Incarceration, Unemployment, Homelessness, and Broken Homes can receive love, help, hope, and support as they journey towards freedom. This program provides opportunities for participants to obtain and produce what's hoped for physically—such as business ownership and homeownership. *THE TRAINING AND RE-ENTRY PROGRAM TAKES WHAT'S HOPED FOR AND TURNS IT INTO REALITY.*

**Philosophy:** By utilizing *Emancipation Freedom for the Incarcerated Soul*—a book written by the business's founder Johnesha, PRISONLIVESMATTERTOO THE COLLECTION—a clothing line as well as other merchandise, and Destiny Revealed—a training and reentry program Eyes of the Broken teaches people how to heal from the pain of their past and change from within (character-wise), which furthermore enables them to become the solution to their own personal problems and the problems in society.

At Eyes of the Broken, we believe in the inside-out method. Teaching people how to start from within prepares them to accomplish their goals and teaches them how to maintain and keep what they've worked hard for.

**"WE HELP PEOPLE BREAK FREE FROM THE BROKEN SYSTEMS IN SOCIETY."**

# ACKNOWLEDGMENTS

**God:** *I would like to first and foremost thank you. Without you, this book wouldn't be possible. Without you, my story and my testimony wouldn't have meaning. You gave me a purpose, a reason to live, a reason to love, and a reason to dare to dream. Lord, there are not enough ways in the world to show you how grateful I am that you not only called me, but you chose me. All that I am and all that I have in life are because of you. Thank you for loving and protecting me.*

**Mom:** *The woman who brought me into this world. You inspire me to be better. You uplift me when I'm down. Whenever I felt like giving up, you would tell me that the pain would only be temporary. That God would help me get through. I've continued to hold those words close to my heart. They've helped me and continue to help me when I need it most. Thank you, mom, for loving me, nurturing me, and encouraging me to be the best version of myself. Without you, there would be no me.*

**AL:** *My best friend. You are my motivation, one of the reasons why I keep fighting. Every day you push me even when you are down, and for that, I am forever grateful. Without you, this book would not have come to fruition. I love you with all my heart. Thank you for motivating me!*

**Big Brother:** *My big brother whom I've fought and argued with but have never lost love for. The person who has always protected me.*

*Whenever in doubt, I knew and still know I can always count on you. You're a special person, and God knows it just as people do, which is why people have tried to count you out or tear you down. It's because you're special because you're strong. Because you are gifted, and as your sister, I want you to always remember that. Thank you for being the best big brother.*

**Little Brother:** *My little brother, I couldn't leave you out even though you can sometimes get on my nerves. You were one of the first people to believe in this book. I remember a commercial came on the TV mentioning something about self-publishing a book, and you wrote down the phone number. You made me a card, and, on my birthday, you gave me the card with the phone number inside. I laughed but secretly wanted to cry. Thank you for believing in me.*

**Granny Connie:** *You were always there for me throughout the years growing up. You practically helped my mom raise me. I remember after my dad passed, I'd always sleep in the bed with you. And whenever your boyfriend would come over, you'd tell him uh uh you can't spend the night my grandbaby is sleeping with me tonight. Those memories are ones I will never forget. They helped bring joy into my heart and even now put a smile on my face. Thank you, for the memories and the love.*

**Auntie Yanna:** *From the moment and even before I lost my dad, you were there for me. You loved me and made sure that I had everything I needed to succeed in life. From the educational books and computer games you'd buy me for Christmas, to you making sure my dad's love was always present through you. You were always there. Thank you for caring for and loving me.*

**Grandpa John:** *When my dad passed away, it was almost as if I was all that you had left of him. I could see that by the way you loved me* *and made sure I always had clothes or whatever was needed for school or otherwise throughout the years. Thank you, grandpa. Although I may struggle fully showing it, I want you to know that I love and appreciate you.*

**Great Grandmother AKA Aunt Doll:** *After my dad passed away, I remember you'd buy me these dresses for every holiday. Christmas, Valentine's Day, you name it, there was always a dress waiting for me to put on. The funny part is I never really liked dresses being that I dressed more like a tomboy. But being ladylike is what my dad wanted. He was so determined to make sure his little girl would grow up knowing what it meant to be a young lady. And after he passed, you made sure to continue his efforts. Thank you for encouraging me to be the "lady" my dad always wanted me to be.*

**Kathleen Holland-Roque:** *Someone who has become one of my closest friends, or should I say more like a second mother. Whenever I grew very ill, you made sure I was taken care of. You'd feed me and would never forget to check on me although I lived an hour away from you. While I was going through one of the most challenging battles in my life, you told me, "I GOT YOU," and you kept that promise. I am grateful for you and thank you for all that you do, not just for me but for all the people you touch positively on a daily. Thank you for being more than a friend to me.*

**Stephanie Wood-Pearsall:** *I have watched you grow; you have watched me grow. We've grown as friends. And through love and kind words, you've continued to be there for me. And although we hadn't been able to see each other as much, I do remember everything time we did you'd ask how I was doing and if everything was going okay. I just want you to know I notice that your heart is genuine, and I want to thank you for sharing the love within it with me.*

**Kesha Hughes:** *You are another one of my friends who I now consider family. Throughout my journey writing this book, you always encouraged me to keep pushing. Every time I would see you, no matter where or when you would always ask if I was almost done writing because you couldn't wait to read this very book. You simply being excited about my journey kept me motivated. For that, I want to thank you.*

**Bonnie McCreary (Career Counselor):** *You were my career counselor at work, but you were also the very first person to encourage me to turn my writings into a book. I remember it like it was yesterday. You told me to start a blog and develop the chapters of the book. After that, I took off. I created a website, started focusing on developing this book, and even created a crowdfunding campaign. I now look back and see how God truthfully placed you in my life when I needed you most. That guidance and advice (although not specifically about the college program you were helping me enter) were invaluable. You are a wise and gifted counselor. Thank you for leading and guiding me.*

**Ebony Smith (Business Coach):** *Not only were you the first person to buy my book through my crowdfunding campaign, but you also continued to reach out to encourage me and provide me with advice even after I'd exhausted all my appointments through our business coaching agreement. Thank you for believing in this mission.*

**Lisa Renee Johnson (Professional Coach):** *You have been such a godsend to me "literally". I remember telling myself I would take a break from writing because I was so confused about the process and had become so frustrated. And then you were sent to me by recommendation. When that opportunity presented itself although I hadn't been looking, it confirmed to me that God brought us together. I am grateful for you and would like to thank you for the work that you do.*

**Dad:** *Finally, to my dad John E. Robinson Jr. I lost you to gun violence on February 15, 1997, but I've never forgotten you. You have always been my reason for doing right and turning away from wrong. My mission in life has always been to make you proud, and I feel like I've finally accomplished that through this book. I can now be at peace because I know you are at peace with how I've made you proud. Thank you Dad, for being the best dad to me while you were here on this earth, as well as the best dad from heaven; thank you for being my Angel.*

*Until we meet again, your daughter,*

*Johnesha*

# NOTES

1. (n.d.). Retrieved from Wikipedia: https://en.wikipedia.org/wiki/Infection#:~:text=An%20infection%20is%20the%20invasion,and%20the%20toxins%20they%20produce.

2. (n.d.). Retrieved from Wikipedia: https://en.wikipedia.org/wiki/Forgiveness

3. (n.d.). Retrieved from Wikipedia: https://en.wikipedia.org/wiki/Courtship

4. (n.d.). Retrieved from Wikipedia: https://en.wikipedia.org/wiki/Survival_of_the_fittest

5. (n.d.). Retrieved from Bible Study Tools: https://www.biblestudytools.com/commentaries/gills-exposition-of-the-bible/ezekiel-36-26.html

6. (n.d.). Retrieved from BibleRef: https://www.bibleref.com/James/1/James-1-12.html

7. (n.d.). Retrieved from Wikipedia: https://en.wikipedia.org/wiki/Abundant_life

8. (n.d.). Retrieved from Wikipedia: https://en.wikipedia.org/wiki/Chronic_poverty

9. A Guide on How to Build a Relationship With God. (n.d.). Retrieved from Getting To Know Your Bible: https://www.gettingtoknowyourbible.com/a-guide-on-how-to-build-a-relationship-with-god/

10. Abrugar, V. Q. (n.d.). 12 Ways to Strengthen Your Relationship With God. Retrieved from Inspiring Tips: https://inspiringtips.com/ways-to-strengthen-your-relationship-with-god/

11. Andre, L. (2022, January 14). 45 Single Parent Statistics You Can't Ignore: 2022 Gender, Race & Challenges. Retrieved from Finances

Online: https://financesonline.com/single-parent-statistics/

12. Andrea Mathews LPC, N. (2016, March 12). What Does It Mean to Let Go? Retrieved from Psychology Today: https://www.psychologytoday.com/us/blog/traversing-the-inner-terrain/201603/what-does-it-mean-let-go

13. Aphinya. (2020, May 28). What it means to be vulnerable. Retrieved from Dechalert: https://dechalert.co/health-nutrition/vulnerable/

14. Ashley Nellis, P. (n.d.). The Color of Justice: Racial and Ethnic Disparity in State Prisons. Retrieved from The Sentencing Project: https://www.sentencingproject.org/publications/color-of-justice-racial-and-ethnic-disparity-in-state-prisons/

15. Babakhan, J. (2019, August 16). 7 Ways to Be More Accepting of Your Partner—and Build a Stronger Relationship. Retrieved from Readers Digest: https://www.rd.com/advice/relationships/build-a-stronger-relationship/

16. Baker, M. W. (2018, July 11). How Embracing Vulnerability Can Change Your Spiritual Life. Retrieved from Relevant Magazine: https://relevantmagazine.com/life5/why-the-bravest-people-are-vulnerable/

17. Beauchamp, Z. (2014, August 28). Have humans evolved to fight wars over territory? Retrieved from Vox: https://www.vox.com/2014/4/28/5661186/evolution-war-cause

18. Becker-Phelps, L. (2018, April 09). Healing the Pain Within. Retrieved from Psychology Today: https://www.psychologytoday.com/us/blog/making-change/201804/healing-the-pain-within

19. Bloom, J. (2016, January 29). How to Have Intimacy with God. Retrieved from Desiring God: https://www.desiringgod.org/articles/how-to-have-intimacy-with-god

20. Bloom, J. (2017, January 13). Lord, Fill Me with Your Spirit. Retrieved from Desiring God: https://www.desiringgod.org/articles/lord-fill-me-with-your-spirit

21. Breeden, T. (2013, April 06). Unpacking & Unpeeling: The Process of Healing Emotional Wounds – Part I. Retrieved from Ladies Loving God by Tonika Breeden: https://ladieslovinggod.wordpress.com/2013/04/06/unpacking-unpeeling-the-process-of-healing-emotional-wounds/

22. Brennen, B. H. (2002, November 07). To "Let Go" Takes Love. Retrieved from Soencouragement.org: http://www.

soencouragement.org/LET%20GO%20TAKES%20LOVES.pdf

23. Brenner, G. (2016, December 30). 10 Smart Choices to Heal the Pain of Your Past. Retrieved from Possibility Change: https://possibilitychange. com/heal-pain-past/

24. Buczynski, B. (2019, February 28). Build Your Down Payment With a Sweat Equity Mortgage. Retrieved from Nerd Wallet: https://www. nerdwallet.com/blog/mortgages/build-down-payment-with-sweat-equity-diy-mortgage/

25. Burns, P. (n.d.). Forgiveness Therapy. Retrieved from Christian Counseling Centers.

26. Carlton, G. (2018, September 27). How History's Most Famous Extroverts Changed History. Retrieved from Ranker: https://www. ranker.com/list/extroverts-who-changed-history/genevieve-carlton

27. Challies, T. (2005, January 16). Gain Discernment In Five Easy Steps. Retrieved from Challies: https://www.challies.com/articles/ gain-discernment-in-five-easy-steps/

28. Children and Stress. (2016, May 01). Retrieved from Child Savers: https://childsavers.org/children-and-stress/#:~:text=When%20 in%20constant%20survival%20mode,%2C%20weakened%2C%20 and%20worn%20out.

29. Cobb, W. J. (2003, September 29). Willie Lynch is Dead (1712?-2003). Retrieved from WayBack Machine: https://web.archive.org/ web/20031003153215/http://www.africana.com/articles/daily/ ht20030929lynch.asp

30. Cottrell, E. H. (2014). 6 Simple Steps To Building A Relationship With God. Retrieved from Heartspoken: https://www.heartspoken. com/6246/6-simple-steps-to-building-a-relationship-with-god/

31. Davenport, B. (2019, December 2). 20 Good Character Traits Essential For Happiness. Retrieved from Live Bold & Bloom: https:// liveboldandbloom.com/10/relationships/good-character-traits

32. Davis, R. (2016, August 18). Spiritual Healing - 3 Biblical Steps to Heal Your Wounds. Retrieved from iBelieve: https://www.ibelieve.com/ health-beauty/3-biblical-steps-to-healing-your-spiritual-wounds.html

33. Do You Have a Poverty Mentality? (n.d.). Retrieved from Business Blogs Hub: https://www.businessblogshub.com/2012/10/do-you-have-a-poverty-mentality/#:~:text=Poverty%20mentality%20is%20 a%20mindset,cause%20poor%20financial%20decision%2Dmaking.

34. Draper, D. (2016, December 5). Jesus the chief cornerstone of our faith. Retrieved from Chron: https://www.chron.com/ neighborhood/woodlands/news/article/Jesus-the-chief-cornerstone-of-our-faith-10695302.php

35. Durnell, L. (2012, September 19). How Do I Let Go? Retrieved from HuffPost: https://www.huffpost.com/entry/letting-go_b_1684141

36. Earth Science for Kids. (n.d.). Retrieved from Ducksters Educational Site: https://www.ducksters.com/science/earth_science/hurricanes. php#:~:text=Hurricanes%20form%20over%20the%20warm,huge%20 storm%20clouds%20to%20form.

37. Effects of Unemployment on Individuals, Society and the Economy. (2021, March 30). Retrieved from Indeed: https://www.indeed.com/ career-advice/career-development/effects-unemployment

38. Emotional and Psychological Trauma. (n.d.). Retrieved from Help Guide: https://www.helpguide.org/articles/ptsd-trauma/coping-with-emotional-and-psychological-trauma.htm

39. Eng, F. (n.d.). 20 Bible Verses About How and Why to Forgive. Retrieved from Cru.org: https://www.cru.org/us/en/train-and-grow/spiritual-growth/forgiveness-scriptures.html

40. Erving, M. (2019, June 30). 7 things about FLOW. Retrieved from Maria Erving | Transformational Teacher and Energy Healer: https://mariaerving.com/about-flow/

41. Everything you Need to Know About Water Damage Remediation. (n.d.). Retrieved from Triad Basement Waterproofing: https://www. triadbasementwaterproofing.com/blog/2014/08/everything-you-need-to-know-about-water-damage-remediation/

42. Fabrega, M. (2015, March 09). How to Get to The Root of Any Problem – The 5 Whys. Retrieved from Daring To Live Fully: https://daringtolivefully.com/the-5-whys

43. Fahkry, T. (2018, December 26). Let Go Of What No Longer Serves You, So You Can Attract What You Really Need. Retrieved from Rizzarr: https://rizzarr.com/let-go-of-what-no-longer-serves-you-so-you-can-attract-what-you-really-need/

44. Forgiveness. (n.d.). Retrieved from Psychology Today: https://www. psychologytoday.com/us/basics/forgiveness#:~:text=Forgiveness%20 is%20the%20release%20of,those%20who%20have%20been%20 victimized.

45. Gabriel, A. K. (2013, January 18). Does Sin Separate us from God? Retrieved from Andrew K. Gabriel: https://www.andrewkgabriel.com/2013/01/18/does-sin-separate-us-from-god/#:~:text=There%20is%20a%20sense%20in,12%20and%204%3A18).&text=Therefore%2C%20%E2%80%9Cseparation%E2%80%9D%20between%20God,only%20separated%20from%20God%20relationally.

46. Grace to the Humble. (n.d.). Retrieved from God.Net: https://god.net/god/articles/god-gives-grace-to-the-humble/

47. Gustafson, T. (2020, April 19). The Forecaster's Mistake. Retrieved from Our Daily Bread: https://odb.org/2020/04/19/the-forecasters-mistakethe-forecasters-mistake/

48. Hale, D. L. (2018 , October 13). How to Differentiate Between 3 Types of Forgiveness. Retrieved from Studio 5: https://studio5.ksl.com/how-to-differentiate-between-3-types-of-forgiveness/

49. Hariri-Kia, I. (2018, March 20). 7 Little Ways To Build Loyalty In Your Relationship. Retrieved from Bustle: https://www.bustle.com/p/7-little-ways-to-build-loyalty-in-your-relationship-8537670

50. Healing Past Wounds and Forgiving Present Scars. (2020, August 15). Retrieved from Experiencing God | First15 Daily Devotional: https://www.first15.org/08/15/healing-past-wounds-and-forgiving-present-scars/

51. Hewett, J. (2020, February 17). Forgiveness- a Key to Freedom. Retrieved from Jenny Hewett Coaching: http://www.jennyhewettcoaching.com/2019/05/11/forgiveness-a-key-to-freedom/

52. Hoekstra, B. (n.d.). Jesus Christ, Our Only Foundation. Retrieved from Blue Letter Bible: https://www.blueletterbible.org/devotionals/dbdbg/view.cfm?Date=0406

53. How are salvation and forgiveness related? (n.d.). Retrieved from Compelling Truth: https://www.compellingtruth.org/salvation-forgiveness.html

54. How can I come to really know God? (n.d.). Retrieved from Compelling Truth: https://www.compellingtruth.org/knowing-God.html

55. How Do Hurricanes Form? (2019, December 04). Retrieved from NASA Science Space Place: https://spaceplace.nasa.gov/hurricanes/en/

56. How does God restore the years that the locusts have eaten (Joel 2:25)?

(2012, September 11). Retrieved from Got Questions: https://www.gotquestions.org/restore-years-locusts-eaten.html

57.  How Good Is Your Decision Making? (n.d.). Retrieved from Mind Tools: https://www.mindtools.com/pages/article/newTED_79.htm

58.  How important is spiritual growth in Christian life? (n.d.). Retrieved from CompellingTruth: https://www.compellingtruth.org/spiritual-growth.html

59.  How is courtship different than dating? (n.d.). Retrieved from Institute in Basic Life Principles: https://iblp.org/questions/how-courtship-different-dating

60.  How Long Before I Can Drive On Fresh Concrete? (2014, June 05). Retrieved from A. Pietig Concrete & Brick Paving: https://apietigconcrete.com/how-long-before-i-can-drive-on-fresh-concrete/

61.  How to Be Patient; Staying Calm Under Pressure. (n.d.). Retrieved from Mind Tools: https://www.mindtools.com/pages/article/newTCS_78.htm

62.  How to Deal with Foundation Issues When Buying or Selling a House. (n.d.). Retrieved from Trulia: https://www.trulia.com/guides/foundation-repair-costs/

63.  How to Pour Concrete. (2020, October 8). Retrieved from WikiHow: https://www.wikihow.com/Pour-Concrete

64.  How to refine gold. (n.d.). Retrieved from Gold-Traders: https://www.gold-traders.co.uk/gold-information/how-to-refine-gold.asp

65.  Jesus, the Great Physician. (n.d.). Retrieved from Ligonier Ministries: https://www.ligonier.org/learn/devotionals/jesus-great-physician/

66.  Johnson, S. (2019, January 1). 7 Powerful Bible Verses About a New Beginning. Retrieved from Faith Ventures: https://www.faithventures.com/bible-verses-about-a-new-beginning/

67.  Jordan, R. B. (2018, September 13). A Beautiful Prayer for Repentance and Restoration. Retrieved from Crosswalk.com: https://www.crosswalk.com/faith/prayer/a-prayer-for-repentance-and-restoration.html

68.  Kelly, J. (2021, February 23). Does single parenting affect children? Retrieved from How Stuff Works: https://lifestyle.howstuffworks.com/family/parenting/parenting-tips/single-parenting-affect-children.htm

69. Kranz, J. (2020, June 19). Oppression and Social Justice in the Bible: A Beginner's Guide. Retrieved from Overview Bible: https://overviewbible.com/oppression/

70. Krejcir, D. R. (n.d.). Christian Character Traits. Retrieved from Discipleship Tools: http://www.discipleshiptools.org/apps/articles/?articleid=37084&columnid=

71. Leonard, J. (2019, April 25). Infected wound: Recognition, treatment, and when to see a doctor. Retrieved from Medical News Today: https://www.medicalnewstoday.com/articles/325040#how-to-recognize

72. Malcom, X. (2018, May 21). The Difference Between Preconception and Prenatal Care. Retrieved from Flushing Hospital: https://www.flushinghospital.org/newsletter/the-difference-between-preconception-and-prenatal-care/

73. Marie Hartwell-Walker, E. (2018, October 08). The What and How of True Intimacy. Retrieved from PsychCentral: https://psychcentral.com/lib/the-what-and-how-of-true-intimacy/

74. Meyer, J. (2016, June 20). The Healing Power of the Holy Spirit. Retrieved from Christian Post: https://www.christianpost.com/news/the-healing-power-of-the-holy-spirit-opinion.html

75. Meyer, J. (n.d.). The Poison of Unforgiveness. Retrieved from Joyce Meyer Ministries: https://joycemeyer.org/everydayanswers/ea-teachings/the-poison-of-unforgiveness

76. Meyer, J. (n.d.). Three Steps to Emotional Healing That Lasts. Retrieved from Joyce Meyer Ministries: https://joycemeyer.org/everydayanswers/ea-teachings/three-steps-to-emotional-healing-that-lasts

77. Morgan, R. (n.d.). What Happens to Us When We Love God. Retrieved from Robert J Morgan: https://www.robertjmorgan.com/devotional/what-happens-to-us-when-we-love-god/

78. Nierenberg, C. (2017, August 30). Having a Baby: Stages of Pregnancy. Retrieved from Live Science: https://www.livescience.com/44899-stages-of-pregnancy.html

79. No One Can Curse Your Blessing. (2016, November 20). Retrieved from Eric Dunbar: https://ericdunbar.com/no-one-can-curse-your-blessing/

80. Noyes, P. (2019, May 28). 10 Roles of the Holy Spirit in a Christian's Life. Retrieved from Christianity.com: https://www.christianity.com/wiki/holy-spirit/10-roles-of-the-holy-spirit-in-christian-life.html

81. Panait, A. (2017, December 20). The Key to Relationships. Retrieved from Medium: https://psiloveyou.xyz/the-key-to-relationships-27be37a0fe33

82. Patricia. (2019, June 14). Honesty Relationships Love. Retrieved from Hope For Children Foundation: https://hopeforchildrenfoundation. org/blog/honesty-relationships-love/

83. Piper, J. (1984, December 16). Satan Seeks a Gap Called Grudge. Retrieved from Desiring God: https://www.desiringgod.org/ messages/satan-seeks-a-gap-called-grudge

84. Planning for Pregnancy. (n.d.). Retrieved from Center for Disease Control and Prevention: https://www.cdc.gov/preconception/overview. html#PrconceptionHealthCare

85. Planning for Pregnancy. (2020, April 20). Retrieved from Center for Disease Control and Prevention: https://www.cdc.gov/preconception/ planning.html#:~:text=If%20you%20are%20trying%20to,of%20 having%20a%20healthy%20baby.

86. Ponio, J. (2021, July 18). Understanding Homelessness: Causes and Effects. Retrieved from Our Father's House Soup Kitchen: https:// ofhsoupkitchen.org/understanding-homelessness-causes-and-effects

87. Porter, D. (2016, April 18). 15 Real Life Examples of Famous Introverts With Extrovert Traits. Retrieved from Define Introvert: http://defineintrovert.com/examples-famous-introverts-extrovert/

88. Prenatal Care. (n.d.). Retrieved from Planned Parenthood: https:// www.plannedparenthood.org/learn/pregnancy/prenatal-care

89. Przybylski, D. (2018, July 06). A Prayer for Waiting on God's Timing. Retrieved from Crosswalk: https://www.crosswalk.com/faith/prayer/a-prayer-for-waiting-on-god-s-timing.html

90. Rampton, J. (2015, July 20). 23 of the Most Amazingly Successful Introverts in History. Retrieved from Inc.com: https://www.inc.com/ john-rampton/23-amazingly-successful-introverts-throughout-history. html

91. Ratliff, J. (2016, November 15). To Anyone Who Struggles With "Letting Go". Retrieved from Medium: https://medium.com/personal-growth/ to-anyone-who-struggles-with-letting-go-ed5bf12fb1e6

92. Repentance Bible Verses. (n.d.). Retrieved from Bible Study Tools: https://www.biblestudytools.com/topical-verses/repentance-bible-verses/

93. Ritenbaugh, J. (n.d.). Separation and At-One-Ment. Retrieved from Bible Tools: https://www.bibletools.org/index.cfm/fuseaction/Library.sr/CT/PERSONAL/k/576/Separation-AtOneMent.htm

94. Ritenbaugh, J. W. (2009, May 01). The Seventh Commandment. Retrieved from Bible Tools: https://www.bibletools.org/index.cfm/fuseaction/Library.sr/CT/PERSONAL/k/1449/Seventh-Commandment.htm

95. Ritter, M. (2017, September 08). How Do Hurricanes Form? Retrieved from VOA: https://learningenglish.voanews.com/a/how-do-hurricanes-form/4020889.html

96. Roes, D. (2018, April 26). On Forgiveness: The Three Types And When They Apply On Forgiveness. Retrieved from Full Life Reflections: https://fulllifereflections.com/2018/04/26/three-types-of-forgiveness/

97. Rogers, A. (n.d.). How God Develops Christian Character. Retrieved from OnePlace: https://www.oneplace.com/ministries/love-worth-finding/read/articles/how-god-develops-christian-character-8849.html

98. Ruggiero, A., & Debolt, D. (n.d.). Four deputies arrested for allegedly letting inmate throw feces in Santa Rita jail. Retrieved from East Bay Times: https://www.eastbaytimes.com/2017/08/31/four-sheriffs-deputies-arrested-on-suspicion-mistreating-inmates-at-santa-rita-jail/

99. Rust, B. (2018, April 02). What is the Holy Spirit & 10 Supernatural Ways He Empowers You. Retrieved from Crosswalk: https://www.crosswalk.com/faith/spiritual-life/10-supernatural-ways-the-holy-spirit-wants-to-empower-you.html

100. Sasson, R. (n.d.). What Is the Meaning of Letting Go of the Past. Retrieved from Success Consciousness: https://www.successconsciousness.com/blog/personal-development/letting-go-of-the-past/

101. Sawyer, W. (2020, 24 March). Mass Incarceration: The Whole Pie 2020. Retrieved from Prison Policy Initiative: https://www.prisonpolicy.org/reports/pie2020.html

102. Schocker, L. (2013, August 13). 16 Super Successful Introverts. Retrieved from HuffPost: https://www.huffpost.com/entry/famous-introverts_n_3733400#:~:text=Albert%20Einstein,he's%20widely%20quoted%20as%20saying.

103. Schumake, B. M. (2019). Reducing Mass Incarceration. Retrieved from Texas Southern University: https://urrc.tsu.edu/wp-content/

uploads/reducing-mass-incarceration.pdf

104. Schutte, S. (2009, January 01). Intimacy With God: The Way To True Fulfillment. Retrieved from Focus on the Family: https://www.focusonthefamily.com/faith/intimacy-with-god-the-way-to-true-fulfillment/

105. Scommeegna, P. (2012, August 10). U.S. Has World's Highest Incarceration Rate. Retrieved from PRB: https://www.prb.org/resources/u-s-has-worlds-highest-incarceration-rate/

106. Scott, S. (n.d.). Why Small Wins are a Powerful Way to Form Habits. Retrieved from Develop Good Habits: https://www.developgoodhabits.com/power-of-small-wins/

107. Sin and Our Relationship to God. (n.d.). Retrieved from Ligonier Ministries: https://www.ligonier.org/learn/devotionals/sin-and-our-relationship-god/

108. Spiritual blindness – What is it? (n.d.). Retrieved from Compelling Truth: https://www.easybib.com/mla8/website-citation/eval

109. Stanley, C. (2018, April 26). 8 Results of Disobeying God. Retrieved from In Touch: https://www.intouch.org/read/blog/8-results-of-disobeying-god

110. Stanley, C. F. (2014, December 31). Intimacy With God. Retrieved from In Touch Ministries: https://www.intouch.org/read/intimacy-with-god

111. State of Homelessness: 2021 Edition. (2021, August 16). Retrieved from National Alliance to End Homelessness: https://endhomelessness.org/homelessness-in-america/homelessness-statistics/state-of-homelessness-2021/

112. Stevenson, B. (2019, August 14). Why American Prisons Owe Their Cruelty to Slavery. Retrieved from The New York Times: https://www.nytimes.com/interactive/2019/08/14/magazine/prison-industrial-complex-slavery-racism.html

113. Strelnick, R. (2019, October 29). Developing Acceptance Skills in a Relationship. Retrieved from Marriage.com: https://www.marriage.com/advice/relationship/developing-acceptance-skills-in-a-relationship/

114. Struggle is Good! I Want to Fly! (n.d.). Retrieved from http://instructor.mstc.edu/instructor/swallerm/Struggle%20-%20Butterfly.htm

115. Summary of the Book of Exodus. (2008, October 17). Retrieved from

Got Questions: https://www.gotquestions.org/Book-of-Exodus.html

116. Sunshyne. (2019, February 21). Trust and Forgiveness in Relationships. Retrieved from Sunshyne Gray: https://sunshynegray.com/trust-forgiveness-relationships/

117. The Dos and Don'ts of Curing Concrete. (2019, November 18). Retrieved from Bob Vila: https://www.bobvila.com/articles/curing-concrete/#:~:text=Although%20concrete%20will%20harden%20soon,for%20at%20least%2010%20days.

118. The Employment Situation. (2020, 10 January). Retrieved from Bureau of Labor Statistics: https://www.bls.gov/news.release/archives/empsit_01102020.pdf

119. The Holy Spirit the Spirit of Healing. (n.d.). Retrieved from World Invisible: https://www.worldinvisible.com/library/murray/healing/healing14.htm

120. The Sin of Unforgiveness. (2018, October 29). Retrieved from Higher Aim: https://higheraim.org/2018/10/29/the-sin-of-unforgiveness/

121. Thomas, S. (n.d.). Getting to the Root of Our Problems. Retrieved from Bible Study Tools: https://www.biblestudytools.com/blogs/association-of-biblical-counselors/getting-to-the-root.html

122. Tidmore, D. (n.d.). Praise Builds Protection. Retrieved from Faithlife Sermons: https://sermons.faithlife.com/sermons/433708-praise-builds-protection

123. Trauma Types. (2018, May 25). Retrieved from The National Child Traumatic Stress Network: https://www.nctsn.org/what-is-child-trauma/trauma-types

124. Traumatic Stress Disorder Fact Sheet. (n.d.). Retrieved from Sidran: https://www.sidran.org/wp-content/uploads/2018/11/Post-Traumatic-Stress-Disorder-Fact-Sheet-.pdf

125. Trial and Error. (n.d.). Retrieved from Wikipedia: https://en.wikipedia.org/wiki/Trial_and_error#:~:text=Trial%20and%20error%20is%20a,until%20the%20practicer%20stops%20trying.&text=Lloyd%20Morgan%20(1852%E2%80%931936),and%20%22trial%20and%20practice%22.

126. Trusting God and Letting Go of Control. (2017, November 22). Retrieved from Deep Spirituality: https://deepspirituality.net/trusting-god-and-letting-go/

127. Types of Trauma. (n.d.). Retrieved from Your Experiences Matter: https://yourexperiencesmatter.com/learning/trauma-stress/types-of-trauma/

128. Types of Traumatic Experiences. (n.d.). Retrieved from Early Childhood Mental Health Consultation: https://www.ecmhc.org/tutorials/trauma/mod1_3.html

129. Unknown, A. (n.d.). To Let Go Takes.

130. UpChurch, J. (2019, August 15). 7 Daily Steps to Trust in the Lord with All Your Heart. Retrieved from Bible Study Tools: https://www.biblestudytools.com/bible-study/topical-studies/7-daily-steps-to-trust-in-the-lord-with-all-your-heart.html

131. Voices, B. (n.d.). Slavery Ended 148 Years Ago Today, But We Still Have A Long Way To Go. Retrieved from HuffPost: https://www.huffpost.com/entry/end-of-slavery-anniversary_n_4466330

132. Warren, R. (n.d.). God's Purpose Behind Your Problems. Retrieved from CBN.

133. Weather - Hurricanes Tropical Cyclones. (n.d.). Retrieved from Ducksters: https://www.ducksters.com/science/earth_science/hurricanes.php

134. What does the Bible say about grudges? (2014, March 12). Retrieved from GotQuestions.org: https://www.gotquestions.org/Bible-grudges.html

135. What does the Bible say about Grudges? (2014, March 12). Retrieved from Got Questions: https://www.gotquestions.org/Bible-grudges.html

136. What is Christian reconciliation? (2004, November 12). Retrieved from Got Questions: https://www.gotquestions.org/reconciliation.html

137. What is Intimacy? (n.d.). Retrieved from GoodTherapy.org: https://www.goodtherapy.org/blog/psychpedia/intimacy

138. What is spiritual maturity? (2011, July 31). Retrieved from GotQuestions.org: https://www.gotquestions.org/spiritual-maturity.html

139. Why are Christians encouraged to have daily devotions or quiet times? (n.d.). Retrieved from CompellingTruth: https://www.compellingtruth.org/daily-devotions.html

140. Wikipedia. (n.d.). Waiting Period. Retrieved from Wikipedia: https://en.wikipedia.org/wiki/Waiting_period

141. Will Joel Friedman, P. (n.d.). Acknowledgment Transcends Pride and Humility. Retrieved from MentalHelp: https://www. mentalhelp.net/blogs/acknowledgment-transcends-pride-and-humility/#:~:text=The%20flip%20side%20of%20pride,proud%20 and%20not%20self%2Dassertive.

142. Willie Lynch Letter: The Making of a Slave. (n.d.). Retrieved from The Final Call: http://www.finalcall.com/artman/publish/Perspectives_1/ Willie_Lynch_letter_The_Making_of_a_Slave.shtml

143. Wound Skin Infection. (n.d.). Retrieved from Summit Medical Group: https://www.summitmedicalgroup.com/library/pediatric_health/ hhg_wound_infection/#:~:text=Soak%20the%20wounded%20area%20 in,a%20weak%20germ%2Dkiller

144. Zuleger, D. (2016, December 1). Lord, Fill Me with Your Spirit. Retrieved from Desiring God: https://www.desiringgod.org/ articles/lord-fill-me-with-your-spirit

# ABOUT THE AUTHOR

**JOHNESHA ROBINSON** was born and raised in Oakland, California. Her childhood dream was to become a lawyer. But when the incarceration of a loved one opened her eyes to a broken system designed to keep people stuck, Johnesha instead started on a personal journey to help individuals worldwide break free from the broken systems in society.

*"I've grown to realize that all unfortunate situations are not unfortunate. To every unfortunate situation, there's a fortunate outcome. I am going to take my situation and make something good out of what seems to be bad. To let other people know that they too can do the same."*

# Eyes

## of the
## Broken

 WWW.EYESOFTHEBROKEN.COM

@EYESOFTHEBROK3N  INFO@EYESOFTHEBROKEN.COM

www.ingramcontent.com/pod-product-compliance
Lightning Source LLC
Chambersburg PA
CBHW011233120626
46549CB00009B/3250